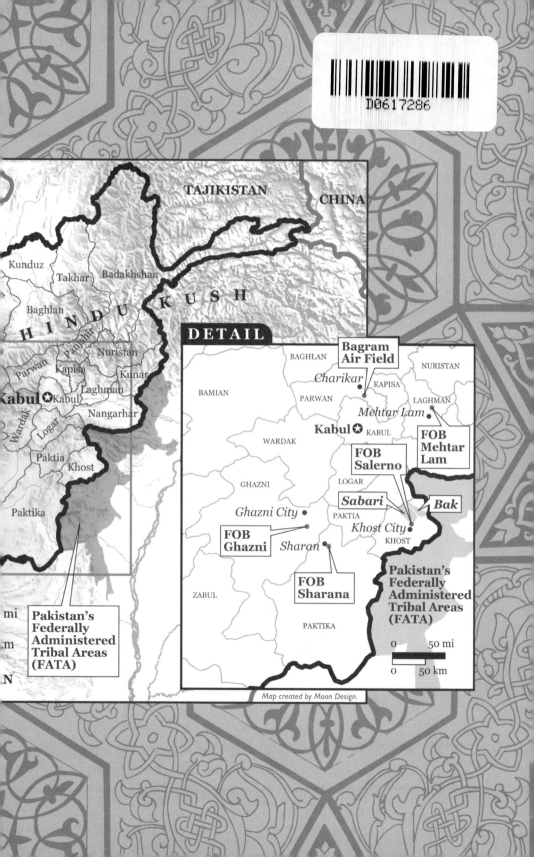

TAJIKISTAN

CHINA

Kunduz

Takhar   Badakhshan

Baghlan

H I N D U   K U S H

Parwan   Panjshir   Nuristan

Kapisa   Kunar

Kabul ✪ Kabul   Laghman

Wardak   Logar   Nangarhar

Paktia   Khost

Paktika

mi

m

N

**Pakistan's
Federally
Administered
Tribal Areas
(FATA)**

DETAIL

BAGHLAN

**Bagram
Air Field**

Charikar   KAPISA

NURISTAN

BAMIAN

PARWAN

LAGHMAN

Mehtar Lam

Kabul ✪ KABUL

**FOB
Mehtar
Lam**

WARDAK

**FOB
Salerno**

GHAZNI

LOGAR

Sabari   *Bak*

Ghazni City •

PAKTIA

Khost City •

**FOB
Ghazni**   *Sharan* •

KHOST

**FOB
Sharana**

ZABUL

**Pakistan's
Federally
Administered
Tribal Areas
(FATA)**

PAKTIKA

0   50 mi

0   50 km

Map created by Moon Design.

FUNDING THE ENEMY

How US Taxpayers
Bankroll the Taliban

FUNDING THE
ENEMY

Douglas A. Wissing

Prometheus Books

59 John Glenn Drive
Amherst, New York 14228–2119

Published 2012 by Prometheus Books

Top cover image © 2012 Corbis
Bottom cover image © Karl-Heinz Spremberg/123RF.com
Jacket design by Grace M. Conti-Zilsberger

Inquiries should be addressed to
Prometheus Books
59 John Glenn Drive
Amherst, New York 14228–2119
VOICE: 716–691–0133
FAX: 716–691–0137
WWW.PROMETHEUSBOOKS.COM

16 15 14 13 12   5 4 3 2 1

Library of Congress Cataloging-in-Publication Data

Wissing, Douglas A.
    Funding the enemy : how US taxpayers bankroll the Taliban / by Douglas A. Wissing.
        p. cm.
    Includes bibliographical references and index.
    ISBN 978–1–61614–603–0 (cloth : alk. paper)
    ISBN 978–1–61614–604–7 (ebook)
    1. Taliban—Finance. 2. Postwar reconstruction—Afghanistan. 3. Economic assistance, American—Afghanistan. 4. Economic development—Finance—Afghanistan. 5. United States—Foreign relations—Afghanistan. 6. Afghanistan—Foreign relations—United States. I. Title.

DS371.4.W57 2012
958.104′71—dc23

2011045844

Printed in the United States of America on acid-free paper

Here right and wrong are reversed: so many wars
in the world, so many faces of evil: the plough
not worthy of any honour, our lands neglected, robbed of farmers,
and the curved pruning-hooks beaten into solid blades.
Here Germany, there Euphrates wages war:
neighbouring cities take up arms, breaking the laws
that bound them: impious Mars rages through the world:
just as when the chariots stream from the starting gates,
add to their speed each lap, and the charioteer tugging vainly at the bridles,
is dragged on by the horses, the chariot not responding to the reins.

—Virgil, *Georgics*, Book 1

Contents

Contents

List of Abbreviations

ADT	Agribusiness Development Team
AID	Agency for International Development [USAID]
ANA	Afghan National Army
ANAP	Afghan National Auxiliary Police
ANP	Afghan National Police
AP3	Afghan Public Protection Program
ARG	Afghanistan Reconstruction Group
ATFC	Afghan Threat Finance Cell
A^3	Accountable Assistance for Afghanistan
AVIPA	Afghanistan Vouchers for Increased Production in Agriculture
AWK	Ahmed Wali Karzai
BAT-HIDE	Biometric Automated Toolkit and Handheld Interagency Detection Equipment
CA	Civil Affairs
CC	Contracting Company
CENTCOM	Central Command
CERP	Commander's Emergency Response Program
CHLC	Coalition Humanitarian Liaison Cell
CIA	Central Intelligence Agency
CJITF	Combined Joint Interagency Task Force
CJTF	Combined Joint Task Force
COIN	Counterinsurgency
COP	Combat Outpost
COPP	Compliance and Oversight Division for Partner Performance
COR	Contracting Officer Representative

CORDS	Civil Operations and Revolutionary Development Support
CPA	Coalition Provisional Authority
CT	Counterterrorism
DOD	Department of Defense
DST	District Support Team
EPLS	Excluded Parties Listing System
FATA	Federally Administered Tribal Areas
FOB	Forward Operation Base
4A	Assistance to Afghanistan's Anti-Corruption Authority
GAO	Government Accountability Office
GDP	Gross Domestic Product
GIAAC	General Independent Administration for Anti-Corruption
GIRoA	Government of the Islamic Republic of Afghanistan
HAM	Hearts-and-Minds (mission)
HoO	High Office of Oversight and Anti-Corruption
HTT	Human Terrain Team
IC	International Community
IED	Improvised Explosive Device
IMU	Islamic Movement of Uzbekistan
IRD	International Relief & Development
ISAF	International Security Assistance Force
ISI	Inter-Services Intelligence
JPEL	Joint Priorities Effects List
JSOC	Joint Special Operations Command
JSSP	Justice Sector Support Program
KLE	Key Leader Engagement
MAIL	Ministry of Agriculture, Irrigation, and Livestock
MAN	Malign Actors Networks
MCC	Millennium Challenge Corporation
MOI	Ministry of the Interior
MRAP	Mine-Resistant, Ambush-Protected
NATO	North Atlantic Treaty Organization
NDS	National Directorate of Security
NGO	Nongovernmental Organization
OCO	Office of Civil Operations
OGA	Other Government Agency
OIG	Office of Inspector General
PDPA	People's Democratic Party of Afghanistan

PLP	Bureau of Policy, Planning, and Learning
PRT	Provincial Reconstruction Team
PT	Physical Training
QA-QC	Quality Assurance-Quality Control
QIP	Quick Impact Projects
RAMP	Rebuilding Agricultural Markets Project
RC-East	Regional Command-East
SEALs	Sea, Air, and Land teams
SIGAR	Special Inspector General for Afghanistan Reconstruction
TF	Task Force
3Ds	Development, Diplomacy, and Defense
TIC	Troops in Combat
TNCC	Taranom National Construction Company
UN	United Nations
UNAMA	United Nations Assistance Mission to Afghanistan
UNODC	United Nations Office on Drugs and Crime
USAID	United States Agency for International Development
USDA	United States Department of Agriculture
USSR	Union of Soviet Socialist Republics
VSU	Vetting Support Unit
WHAM	Winning Hearts and Minds

Chronology

Timeline of Key Events in Afghanistan War

329 BCE: Alexander the Great's armies invade the region later known as Afghanistan, precipitating a native resistance that eventually ties up half of the Greeks' forces and 95 percent of his cavalry.

1221 CE: Genghis Khan's Mongol army invades Afghanistan, where his army suffers its only defeat outside of east Asia in eighty years.

1747–1773:   Ahmed Shah Abdali, founder of the Durrani dynasty, consolidates and expands Afghanistan, forming an empire that extends from central Asia to Delhi; from Kashmir to the Arabian Sea.

1773–1826:   Afghan rulers Zaman Shah, Mahmood, Shah Shuja, and the sons of Timur Shah rule over an Afghanistan rent with internal fighting and civil war.

1826–1863:   Dost Mohammad Khan takes power, beginning a rule that continues, with interruptions, until 1863.

1839–1842:   First Anglo-Afghan War ends with Britain suffering its worst colonial defeat. A withdrawing British force of over sixteen thousand soldiers and camp followers is reduced to a sole survivor.

1843:   Afghanistan is again independent under Dost Mohammad Khan, who returns from a three-year (1839–1842) British-mandated exile in India.

1878–1880:   Second Anglo-Afghan War concludes with negotiated settlement that cedes Afghan territories to British India. British forces withdraw from Afghanistan, though Britain retains control over Afghanistan's foreign relations.

1893:   The British-mandated Durand Line demarcates the Afghan border with British India, splitting the Pashtun tribal heartland in half.

1919:   Third Anglo-Afghan War ends in a second British defeat, allowing now-independent Afghanistan to oversee its own foreign affairs. Amanullah Khan assumes power after his father, Habibullah, is assassinated. Amanullah later initiates ambitious modernization efforts.

1929:   Conservative Afghans led by Tajik leader Habibullah Kalakani overthrows Amanullah Khan in reaction to his social reforms. Months later, the Pashtun Musahiban family led by Nadir Khan overthrows Kalikani, beginning a five-decade-long dynasty.

1933:   After Nadir Khan is assassinated, his son, Zahir, inherits the throne. Zahir Khan rules until 1973, a relatively peaceful period often referred to as the golden age of Afghanistan.

1934:   The United States officially recognizes Afghanistan.

1947:   Britain withdraws from India. Comprised of Indian and Pashtun lands, Pakistan is founded.

1949:   Afghan parliamentarians denounce Durand Line as legal boundary between Afghanistan and Pakistan. Pashtuns in Pakistan proclaim an independent Pashtunistan, but the world community fails to recognize it.

1959:   Zahir Shah begins reform and modernization efforts that continue into the 1960s. The Soviet Union increases military support.

1973:   While vacationing in Europe, Zahir Shah is overthrown in military coup led by Afghan Communist Party, the PDPA.

1975–1978: Communist-dictated modernization programs precipitate a conservative backlash. Armed resistance led by fundamentalist Islamic and tribal leaders erupts in the rural areas, beginning the Afghan *mujahideen* movement.

1979:   Faced with the near-collapse of their client Afghan government, the Soviet Union invades Afghanistan on Christmas Eve.

1979–1989: Soviet-Afghan War rages, with US, Saudi, and Pakistani governments arming and equipping the fundamentalist Islamic mujahideen to fight the Soviet military and their Afghan allies.

1986:   The United States begins supplying the mujahideen with Stinger® missiles, negating the Soviet air supremacy. The same year, Soviet Premier Mikhail Gorbachev announces a partial withdrawal of Soviet forces.

1989:   The last Red Army units withdraw from Afghanistan.

	Fighting continues between the mujahideen and the Afghan communist government led by Najibullah.

1992: The mujahideen close in on Kabul, and Najibullah falls from power. An anarchic civil war between ethnic-based warlord armies breaks out, eventually destroying much of Kabul.

1994: The Taliban rise in southern Afghanistan, beginning a campaign that leads to control over most of Afghanistan by 2000.

1998: The United States fires cruise missiles on al Qaeda training camps in Khost Province, where jihadis led by Osama bin Laden planned attacks on American embassies in Tanzania and Kenya.

1999–2001: International pressure mounts against the Taliban to force it to hand over bin Laden, whom it is harboring.

2001: On September 9, al Qaeda suicide bombers assassinate Ahmed Shah Massoud, the Tajik leader who fought both the Soviets and the Taliban. Two days later, on 9/11, al Qaeda operatives hijack four commercial jets and crash three of them into the World Trade Center towers and the Pentagon. Fifteen days later, a CIA team code-named Jawbreaker lands in Afghanistan to begin the campaign against the Taliban. By the end of the year, Taliban leaders and fighters disperse as the United States begins to plan the war in Iraq. Pressured by US diplomats, anti-Taliban Afghan groups choose Hamid Karzai as leader of the interim government and sign the Bonn Agreement, which laid out plans for a representative government.

2002: Led by the United States, international militaries arrive in January to stabilize Afghanistan and hunt the remnants of al Qaeda and Taliban forces. In August, insurgents launch operations in Kandahar and Khost Provinces, signaling the start of the rebellion against the Karzai government. Civilian casualties caused by errant US air strikes and raids prompt Afghan protests. In April, President George Bush announces a "Marshall Plan" for Afghanistan, linking an ambitious development plan with security goals.

2003: The United States invades Iraq, shifting focus and resources away from Afghanistan. Clashes in the south and the east between Taliban fighters and US-led coalition forces increase. NATO takes over security in Kabul, the organization's first operational commitment outside of Europe.

2004:   The *loya jirga* grand assembly approves a new unitary constitution that institutes a strong presidency. Afghans elect Karzai
president with 55 percent of the vote. As international aid
money pours into Afghanistan, the insurgency increases. Corruption from the booming opium industry and skimmed
international development and logistics funds begins to wrack
the country.

2005:   The insurgency continues to grow, with an increasing use of
Improvised Explosive Devices (IEDs) and suicide bombers.
Well-armed Taliban begin to attack the cities and challenge
US-led coalition forces. The rampant opium industry run by
US-allied warlords and the Taliban effectively turns
Afghanistan into a narco-economy. As insurgents reestablish
training camps in the Afghan–Pakistan borderlands, Afghans
vote in their first parliamentary election.

2006:   Fueled by frustrations over corruption and failed development, anti-US riots erupt in Kabul in May. Beginning in the
spring and continuing through the warm-weather "fighting
season," the US-led coalition launches major offensives in
southern and eastern Afghanistan to try to counter the
growing insurgency. NATO takes over southern Afghanistan
security in July and the entire country in October. In August, a
suicide car bomb attack against a NATO convoy in Kandahar
kills twenty-one. In November, disagreements over NATO
national caveats that restrict individual countries' contributions in Afghanistan disrupt the NATO annual meeting in
Riga, Latvia.

2007:   Afghan opium-poppy production sets new record, continuing Afghanistan's infamy as the world's largest opium producer. Afghan
government corruption is endemic. Insurgent attacks grow.

2008:   With the Taliban and other jihadi groups resurgent, the
United States, Britain, and Germany all boost their troop
levels. President Bush terms it a "quiet surge." After Afghan
insurgents bomb the Indian embassy in Kabul and kill fifty in
July, US intelligence sources report that Pakistan's intelligence
services, the ISI, is involved, continuing its longtime support
of the Afghan militants.

2009:   As insurgent attacks continue to set new records for violence each year, President Barack Obama announces a nearly 50 percent surge in US forces in Afghanistan and increases aid and development funds. Transparency International ranks Afghanistan as the second most corrupt country in the world. Hamid Karzai is declared the winner of the presidential election, reportedly rife with fraud. The *Nation* reveals US military contracts help fund the Taliban.

2010:   General Stanley McChrystal resigns under pressure after a *Rolling Stone* article reveals his criticism of the US civilian leadership. Wikileaks releases 90,000 government documents relating to the war in Afghanistan. The *Wall Street Journal* reports that corrupt Afghans fly billions of dollars skimmed from US-funded aid and logistics programs out of Kabul. US intelligence documents indicate that the insurgents have shadow governments in thirty-one of Afghanistan's thirty-four provinces. A congressional investigative report, *Warlord, Inc.*, confirms US military logistics contracts systematically fund the Afghan insurgency.

2011:   US Navy SEALs kill Osama bin Laden in Abbottabad, about a mile from Pakistan's West Point. President Obama announces a rapid withdrawal of ten thousand US troops from Afghanistan, with thirty-three thousand to follow in the summer. The bipartisan congressional Commission on Wartime Contracting in Iraq and Afghanistan reports that at least $31 billion of US taxpayer money has been lost to fraud and waste.

Outsourcing and Incoming, 2001

DEEP IN THE FASTNESS of eastern Afghanistan's White Mountains, the American commandos called down massive bombs on Tora Bora, the fortified cave complex where al Qaeda and Osama bin Laden were making their last stand in December 2001. Apocalyptic blasts shook the jagged peaks and echoed down the steep Wazir and Agam valleys. Almost one hundred American air strikes a day pounded the six-mile-square al Qaeda redoubt with precision-guided explosives—over seven hundred thousand pounds of explosives in three days alone.[1]

Emboldened by the strikes, the ragtag Afghan tribesmen the Americans recruited to storm Tora Bora were finally giving some serious fight. By December 11, as Afghan leader Hamid Karzai was being sworn in as the interim government's prime minister, the surviving al Qaeda fighters huddled in trenches and caves at heights above eleven thousand feet. It was below zero at night; snow fell along with the bombs. Even Osama bin Laden seemed to lose his taste for the fight. The US Delta Force commander leading the assault, pen-named Dalton Fury, reported signals-intelligence operators had snagged an al Qaeda radio message the day before: "Father [meaning bin Laden] is trying to break through the siege lines."[2] When Fury received intelligence on bin Laden's location, the elite special ops team headed up the mountain, intent on killing or capturing the world's most wanted man. Barely three months after 9/11, revenge for al Qaeda's murderous assault on America seemed near.

But it was not to be. Through American arrogance and Afghan treachery, Osama bin Laden and his al Qaeda fighters escaped Tora Bora. And the hubris and duplicity in the war's earliest days have set the tone for the American experience in Afghanistan since.

*　　*　　*

Only a few weeks before, a small team of CIA agents and special operations troops arrived in Tora Bora with a few thousand haphazard Afghan tribal militiamen commanded by two squabbling warlords, Hazrat Ali and Hajji Zaman Ghamsharik.[3] Intending to win the war on the cheap—in dollars, diplomatic effort, and American lives—the Bush administration had outsourced much of the Tora Bora ground fighting to Afghan militia. The Washington-mandated "light footprint" was so faint, there were more Western journalists in Tora Bora than American troops.[4]

Ostensibly fielded by the Eastern Shura (the ad hoc government the United States cobbled together after the Taliban fled in mid-November), the militiamen were as conflicted as their leaders, who supported the Taliban and al Qaeda. The al Qaeda sympathizers included the powerful Nangarhar Province leader, Maulvi Younus Khalis, a wizened *mujahideen* who had fought the Soviets. In 1996, Khalis welcomed both the Taliban and Osama bin Laden to Jalalabad. Khalis later helped bin Laden fortify Tora Bora, about six miles from the Taliban-friendly haven of the Federally Administered Tribal Areas (FATA) of Pakistan.[5] After the US-supported Northern Alliance forced the Taliban to withdraw from Jalalabad, bin Laden facilitated transfer of the city authority to Khalis.[6] In late November, Khalis—now purportedly a member of the US-rented Eastern Shura—announced, "The Americans can bomb all they want, they'll never catch Osama."[7]

The Afghan militia commanded by Ali and Ghamsharik were remarkably poor soldiers, perhaps reflecting their regard for both the al Qaeda fighters and their own leadership. General Ali was the Eastern Shura security chief. Long on the CIA payroll, Ali was a short, blue-eyed Pashai tribal warlord with a fourth-grade education and a wry smile—the "laughing warlord," the Western press called him. Since Ali came from a remote northeastern Afghanistan Pashai village, the Pashtun tribesmen of eastern Afghanistan called him *Shurrhi*—the Pashto word for "hillbilly."[8] Ali had fought as a US-funded mujahideen field commander against the Soviets and then joined the Taliban before defecting to join the Northern Alliance.[9] Delta Commander Dalton Fury wrote that General Ali would follow anyone as long as he "didn't impede the cash and arms flowing in from the good ole United States of America."[10] Or from al Qaeda, as it turned out. While General Ali's men were attacking Tora Bora on December 3, the wily warlord was thirty miles away, in the tatty Spin Ghar Hotel lobby in Jalalabad, negotiating safe passage for three al Qaeda fighters.[11]

Ali's rival, Hajji Zaman Ghamsharik, was a wealthy, CIA-connected opium lord. The United States arranged for Zaman to serve as the Eastern

Shura Jalalabad commander to balance Ali's power. Natty, well-educated Zaman had visited Alexandria, Virginia, numerous times. During the Soviet war, Zaman commanded mujahideen before fighting for and against the Taliban. After Zaman fell out with the then-ruling Taliban over their campaign against opium poppies, he lived a well-cushioned life in Dijon, France. Just after 9/11, the United States lured him back to Afghanistan—probably with a promise to allow his opium empire to again flourish.[12] Ali and Zaman wrangled from the beginning, though they shared a hunger for money and armaments—no matter who was doling them out. Ali accused Zaman of letting forty Arab al Qaeda escape into Pakistan.[13] By that time, Zaman had already sent emissaries to al Qaeda to "give them some options."[14]

On December 12, with al Qaeda on the ropes from the bombing, Zaman made a startling announcement: al Qaeda was surrendering. "This is the greatest day in the history of Afghanistan," he crowed to Fury.[15] When Zaman demanded a cease-fire for negotiations, the special ops commanders were suspicious, particularly when the Afghan commander radioed, "Under no circumstances are the Americans allowed to attack al Qaeda."[16] When twenty-five American commandos started up the mountain to engage the enemy, eighty of Zaman's fighters leveled their AK-47s at the team. The fix was on.

In the ensuing two-day cease-fire, as many as eight hundred of the al Qaeda fighters at Tora Bora paid local Afghans $500 to $5,000 to guide them to safety—"a golden opportunity," one tribal leader termed it.[17] Only a diversionary force of a few hundred jihadis remained.[18] "There was no doubt that the whole surrender gesture was a hoax," Fury wrote.[19] The largest concentration of al Qaeda fighters in Afghanistan had escaped.[20]

When not a single al Qaeda fighter surrendered, the bombing resumed on December 13. The same day bin Laden radioed his men, "Our prayers have not been answered. Times are dire," and gave them permission to surrender.[21] On December 14, the dispirited bin Laden wrote his last will and testament. He wrote, "Allah bears witness that the love of jihad and death in the cause of Allah has dominated my life and verses of the sword has [sic] permeated every cell in my heart," and quoted the Koran to his followers: "'and fight the pagans all together as they fight you all together.'"[22] By December 16, Osama bin Laden was long gone from Tora Bora, helped by double-dealing Afghan warlords and a US command distracted with already planning the next war—in Iraq.[23]

Aided by America's erstwhile Afghan allies, Osama bin Laden simply walked into Parachinar, a Pashtun tribal region of Pakistan that juts into Afghanistan.[24] In late December, a videotape of a wounded, dispirited bin

Laden surfaced. He said, "I am just a poor slave of God. If I live or die, the war will continue."[25] Bin Laden escaped because the Afghan commanders failed to guard the exit routes—some journalists say because of al Qaeda payoffs ranging up to $6 million, though the figure was probably much less.[26] General Ali paid Ilyas Khel, a particularly untrustworthy lieutenant, $5,000 to block the main routes, but as CIA Field Commander Gary Berntsen wrote, "Our problem was the Arabs paid him more."[27] Ilyas Khel scampered off to Pakistan with both the American and the al Qaeda money. Ali, Zaman, and Khalis were all implicated in the al Qaeda escape.[28] Gulbuddin Hekmatyar and Jalaluddin Haqqani, US-supported mujahideen leaders in the Soviet era who later become anti-American insurgents, both took credit for bin Laden's disappearing act. Haqqani told a Pakistani newspaper, "We will retreat to the mountains and begin a long guerrilla war to claim our pure land from the infidels and free our country again like we did against the Soviets. We are eagerly awaiting the American troops to land on our soil. They are creatures of comfort."[29] Washington failed to comprehend that American largesse couldn't trump culture and religion. In spite of the $70 million the CIA had paid Afghan warlords, the United States was learning a lesson that the British, with their long, painful experience in Afghanistan, had ruefully summarized: "You can't buy an Afghan's loyalty, but you can certainly rent it."

Pakistan, America's richly rewarded coconspirator in the 1980s anti-Soviet war, was not much help at Tora Bora either. Though the United States had given Pakistani authorities almost $1 billion to seal the borders, there were few troops on the Pakistan–Afghan frontier.[30] The Pakistan Frontier Corps guarding the passes were lightly armed tribesmen beholden to their local leaders, who were sympathetic to al Qaeda. The Pakistani military certainly wasn't going to make a stand, given its preoccupation with India and Pakistan's decades-long support of fundamentalist Islamic jihadists. After al Qaeda escaped, special ops teams discovered the jihadi ammunition came from the Pakistanis, who used American dollars to buy American bullets for the terrorists.[31]

Though the CIA and special ops teams pleaded for more American troops to bottle up the al Qaeda fighters, the Bush administration refused to put more American soldiers on the ground.[32] By then, the Bush administration was already focused on Iraq. As early as November 21, 2001, while the American-supported Northern Alliance was still fighting thousands of Taliban and al Qaeda fighters massed in the north, and Osama bin Laden was retreating to Tora Bora, President Bush and Secretary of Defense Donald Rumsfeld ordered General Tommy Franks to immediately update war plans for Iraq. "Son of a bitch," Franks remembered thinking. "No rest for the weary."[33] Military intelligence and planning immediately shifted focus from Tora Bora to Baghdad.

Even as the Ali and Zaman militias dragged the last bedraggled al Qaeda out of their Tora Bora caves on December 16, Americans and Afghans were already in their torturous relationship. It was a troubled couple: the arrogant Americans, infatuated with free-market ideology and high-tech warfare and morally enraged by attacks on the very symbols of the imperium; the Afghans, cynical after generations of war waged by reborn Great Gamers and home-grown thugs who'd perfected their treachery on fields of opium and battle.

Within scant months of Tora Bora, the seeds of American failure in Afghanistan were sown: the US consort with deceitful Afghan warlords and leaders; the American complicity in the revived Afghan opium trade; and the flawed US logistics-and-development schemes that fueled corruption and helped finance the Taliban. A gallery of rogues soon arrived: Iraq-distracted careerist US military and development officials; neoconservative ideologues; high-priced nongovernmental organization (NGO) consultants; and venal Afghan leaders, including Hazrat Ali.

In spite of his duplicity, Ali went on to become a powerful figure in President Hamid Karzai's US-backed government of Afghanistan—almost serving as a poster boy for subsequent United States–Afghan relations. Though the CIA internally debated having the Afghan government arrest Ali after Tora Bora, President Karzai instead made him a three-star general. Ali became the strongman of eastern Afghanistan, as well as a member of the Afghan parliament for Nangarhar Province, where he skimmed staggering amounts of US aid.[34] Though he was fingered for corruption by an earnest Afghan attorney general in 2006, Hazrat Ali dodged that too.[35]

Introduction

I WENT TO AFGHANISTAN to cover a team of Midwestern farmer-soldiers who were on a mission to improve Afghan agriculture. They'd picked their destination, a province along the Pakistani border called Khost, because it was green on a map—indicating water in an arid land. "We can work with that," they said. Only later did they learn Khost was the most violent province in Afghanistan.

Trundling around mountainous eastern Afghanistan in the team's armored vehicles, dodging ambushes and hitting IEDs, I began to hear grotesque tales of corruption and failed development. Soldiers, diplomats, and development officials told me of a vast collusion between American and Afghan officials that resulted in US taxpayers funding the Taliban. "We're funding both sides of this war," one sergeant blithely told me. At first, it seemed preposterous. But as I encountered story after story, I began to realize the soldiers and aid people were telling the truth. There was a toxic system that connected distracted American careerists, private military and development contractors, Afghan kleptocrats, and wily jihadists. "It's the perfect war," one US intelligence officer sardonically told me. "Everyone is making money."

Trained as a historian, I wanted to know the origins of this pernicious system. As a journalist, I wanted to see how the patterns played out on a day-to-day level.

My questions started me on a journey back to the Afghanistan front lines and into the long corridors of power in Washington. I talked to generals and grunts in the field; ambassadors and everyday Afghans; aid workers and dissidents; congressmen, government staffers at a dozen levels, academics, wartime contractors, and journalists; apologists for the status quo and people fervently opposed to the current war and development cultures. While I found most to be hardworking, dedicated people—patriots in the best sense of the word—they were operating in a dysfunctional, self-aggrandizing system that demanded short-term results in a war with generational timelines. The perfect war might have worked for the beneficiaries of the system, but it was for the most part catastrophic for the Afghan people and the American taxpayers.

*   *   *

My subsequent coverage of a number of development teams operating in eastern Afghanistan provided a great window into the whole spectacle of counterinsurgency, from combat and conflict-zone development to interagency initiatives and cross-cultural interactions. I discovered that war and development policies that sounded so foolproof from the podiums of Washington played out much differently on the front lines of Afghanistan. I observed the voraciousness of a corrupt Afghan government manipulating an arrogant, ADD-afflicted American bureaucracy. I learned that the linkage between third-world development and US national security that foreign-aid lobbyists peddled to American policymakers was a faith-based doctrine with almost no foundation in research. Development experts told me that foreign aid might be the right thing to do for humanitarian purposes, but there was little data to indicate it made America safer. Indeed, some research indicated poorly administered foreign aid actually destabilized countries. Like Afghanistan.

So *Funding the Enemy: How US Taxpayers Bankroll the Taliban* depicts what I experienced and what I learned. Following a generally chronological order, the book explores the roots of the problem in the post-9/11 US government decision to ally with Afghan warlords who were tied to their centuries-old tribal culture and the international opium trade. The decision provided a cheap way to subdue Afghanistan as the Bush administration raced toward the ill-starred Iraq invasion. But the devil's bargain in Afghanistan fostered a culture of corruption, fueled by a rampant opium industry and massive sums extorted from US development and military logistics contracts.

With the United States focused on Iraq, the strategy in Afghanistan shifted repeatedly—almost a strategy *du jour* as commanders and mission directors rotated in and out on absurdly short tours of duty. As the Afghan insurgency flared, Washington executed the typical bureaucratic response to a problem: throw money at it. But it just made it worse. More money, more corruption, more insecurity. Attracted to the increased appropriations, the guns-and-aid crowd flocked to Afghanistan, engendering the "Kabubble," wartime Kabul awash with international aid money and the private military and development contractors who fed on it.

As the Bush administration departed, the US government belatedly and reluctantly recognized the mess in Afghanistan. Consequently attempting to roll out a dandied-up counterinsurgency strategy and reformed development policies, the Obama administration encountered a now–deeply entrenched system with a host of beneficiaries. The result was the perfect war.

Chapter 1

True Peace, 2002

FOUR MONTHS AFTER TORA BORA, President George W. Bush was at the crenellated Virginia Military Institute calling for a new "Marshall Plan" for Afghanistan. Speaking at the venerable alma mater of General George C. Marshall, architect of the post–World War II plan that revived Europe and Japan, President Bush said, "We know that true peace will only be achieved when we give the Afghan people the means to achieve their own aspirations."

Bush promised support for a stable Afghan government, a strong national army, and education for both sexes, as well as roads, healthcare, and business expansion. Development—very expensive development—was going to be the key to transforming the impoverished, war-ravaged Afghanistan into a peaceful country that would no longer harbor Islamic terrorists. "As the spring thaw comes," Bush said, "we expect cells of trained killers to try to regroup, to murder, create mayhem, and try to undermine Afghanistan's efforts to build a lasting peace. We know this from not only intelligence, but from the history of military conflict in Afghanistan. It's been one of initial success, followed by long years of floundering and ultimate failure. We're not going to make that mistake." Reversing his earlier disdain of "nation building," Bush promised a broad-based, long-term US commitment to Afghanistan: "We will stay until the mission is done."[1]

*　　*　　*

Bush was right about the history of Afghanistan. Afghans have successfully resisted imperial ambitions for centuries. Time and again, powerful invaders have prevailed on the battlefield and still lost the war. Alexander the Great marched into Bactria, the region that includes today's northern Afghanistan, in 329 BCE. It was initially an easy campaign, though marked by Bactrian warlords' serial

betrayals. Bactria seemed pacified. But a resistance movement led by local commanders soon emerged to challenge Alexander's army. In the battle at Poly-
timetus River, Alexander's army suffered its greatest defeat, losing every officer
and most of the soldiers to a wily warlord, Spitamenes, who used protoguerrilla
tactics.[2] Alexander called the natives "lawless savages," "enemies of civilization."
He told his men they were saving Greece itself: "This is a noble cause, and you
will always be honored for seeing it through to the end."[3] Though Alexander's
army conquered Bactria, it was never a quiescent province. Rebellions and revolts
raged against the outlander Greeks, forcing Alexander to garrison half his
infantry and 95 percent of his cavalry in this one small corner of his vast empire.
Mountainous eastern Afghanistan created particular problems for Alexander's
soldiers. The native fighters attacked and then retreated into the remote upper
valleys. In spite of Alexander's total war policies (which included both scorched-
earth campaigns and "hearts-and-minds" programs that included Greek colo-
nization), more Greeks and Macedonians died in Bactria than in any earlier campaigns.[4] After his painful experiences, Alexander is said to have lamented that
Afghanistan is "easy to march into, hard to march out of."[5]

In 1221, Genghis Khan's Mongol army invaded today's Afghanistan with
the Mongols' typical duplicity and wholesale butchery. But at Parwan, where
today's Bagram Airfield (the US-led Coalition's headquarters) is located, the
Afghans and their Turkic allies confronted thirty thousand Mongol warriors in
a steep defile. When the day was done, half the Mongol army lay in piles
through the valley. It was the only defeat the Mongols suffered outside of east
Asia in eighty years. The Afghans' victory at Parwan inspired uprisings across
Afghanistan, but Khan retaliated with legendary slaughters at Bamiyan, Herat,
Ghazni, and Balkh, where sedentary Afghans bore the brunt of the Mongol
rage while the nomadic mountain people remained relatively unscathed. Soon
after Khan's death in 1227, his quarrelsome Afghan empire devolved into independent satrapies.[6] In the subsequent centuries, Afghans continued to challenge the might of the Mongol Empire—both the famous fourteenth-century
Mongol Tamerlane and the founder of India's Mughul Dynasty, Babur, fought
some of their fiercest battles in Afghanistan.[7]

Full of imperial vigor, the British marched into Afghanistan in 1839,
intent on countering the Russian Czarist advances into central Asia. The invasion was an early gambit in the Great Game, the rivalry between the Russian
and British empires for the wild lands between the Caucasus Mountains and
the Khyber Pass.[8] After an easy victory against their mismatched Afghan oppo-
nents, the British force, many with their families, ensconced themselves in a

comfortable cantonment in Kabul. But it was a hollow victory. In November 1841, thousands of Afghans declared a holy war on the British, forcing the entire British retinue of more than fifteen thousand soldiers and camp followers to flee toward the safety of India. The Afghans attacked the beleaguered column until it was a bare remnant, killing in one winding, four-mile-long pass three thousand men, women, and children. Britain's inglorious defeat culminated in January 1842 at Gandamak, where sixty-five soldiers made their last stand on a hilltop before the Afghans slaughtered them. Printed copies of William Barnes Wollen's vivid painting, *The Last Stand of the 44th Regiment at Gundamuck*, were widely distributed in Britain. Akin to the depictions of Custer's last stand that decorated countless saloons across America, the prints seared Afghanistan into the minds of the British public. In 1843, an Afghan War survivor, army chaplain reverend G. R. Gleig, summarized the conflict in his memoir: "A war begun for no wise purpose, carried on with a strange mixture of rashness and timidity, brought to a close after suffering and disaster, without much glory attached either to the government, which directed, or the great body of troops, which waged it. Not one benefit, political or military, has Britain acquired with this war. Our eventual evacuation of the country resembled the retreat of an army defeated."9

A generation later, the British were still playing the Great Game. Fearing the Afghans were about to favor Russia, the British launched their second invasion in 1878 with thirty-five thousand British troops. As with the first war, it was a quick, easy conquest. On May 26, 1879, the British imposed a punitive peace with a treaty signed at Gandamak, the village where the ignominious defeat had taken place forty years before. But as with the first Anglo-Afghan War, the easy conquest soon turned hard. By early September, the British delegation in Kabul was surrounded by thousands of angry Afghan tribesmen. As before, there was butchery in Kabul. Though the British soldiers at Kabul killed six hundred Afghans, over seventy of the British also died. A British retribution force was soon on its way to Kabul, where it exacted a harsh justice, hanging one hundred of the alleged perpetrators—including some who were reportedly innocent. English-language newspapers in Britain and British India fretted the British force was, in the words of one paper, "sowing a harvest of hate."10

And the harvest soon came. By December, tens of thousands of tribesmen were streaming to Kabul to confront the 6,500 infidels quartered there. In the early hours of December 23, 1879, fanatic *ghazis* attacked, leading sixty thousand howling tribesmen against the cantonment. The detachment's artillery and Gatling guns carried the field that day. The Afghans lost over three thousand men; the British only five. But at the village of Maiwand in southern Afghanistan, the British suffered one of the worst defeats the empire ever suffered in Asia, losing one thousand men. Among the Afghan heroes that day was a shepherd's daughter named Malalai, who is still invoked as a symbol of the indomitable Pashtun fighting spirit. According to legend, Malalai snatched a falling flag and rallied the fighters, who included her new husband, with a call: "Young love! If you do not fall in the battle of Maiwand, by God, someone is saving you as a symbol of shame!"[11] In the battle, the British won the war and some oversight in Afghanistan, but it only garnered them a momentary advantage in the Great Game.[12] In the war's aftermath, the British commander Major General Frederick Roberts, the diminutive craggy-faced frontier veteran his soldiers called "Bobs," summarized his experience: "It may not be very flattering to our *amour propre*, but I feel sure I am right when I say that the less the Afghans see of us, the less they will dislike us."[13]

And sure enough, even Britain's "light footprint"—control of Afghanistan's foreign policy and a few military posts—chafed the Afghans.[14] This was despite the large British subsidies to Afghan strongman Abdur Rahman, whom the English press dubbed the "Iron Emir" for his ruthless campaigns against the mullahs and tribal powers. During World War I, the British stipends continued to his heir, Habibullah, though the new emir also plotted with Turkish and German agents about an invasion of India. When assassins felled Habibullah in February 1919, his brother Amanullah inherited the emir's throne. With Britain distracted by the war in Europe, Amanullah unleashed the third Anglo-Afghan War in May 1919. When the Afghan Army attacked across the specious Durand Line that the British had drawn in 1893 to divide the Pashtun heartland—Pashtunistan, as it is known—between Afghanistan and British-controlled India (today's Pakistani tribal territories), the mullahs roused the Afghan tribes with calls for a jihad, a holy war against the infidels. The Afghans sacked British frontier posts before the British counterattacked. The balance shifted when British aircraft bombed Kabul and Jalalabad, forcing Amanullah to seek peace. While Amanullah lost his generous stipends and had to accept the Durand Line, he regained control of his country's foreign affairs, ending a long chapter of the Great Game.[15]

*   *   *

Then there were the Soviets, determined to help the Afghans join the community of modern Socialist countries, and the United States, equally eager to draw

Afghanistan into the capitalist sphere. And the Afghans, who were happy to let the two superpowers fight their Cold War chapter of the Great Game with competing foreign-aid incentives. The initial Soviet aid followed the Afghan–Soviet Treaty of 1921—the first international agreement signed by the infant Soviet government. Through the 1950s and 1960s, the Soviet Union provided enormous amounts of development aid in northern Afghanistan, building roads, schools, dams, river ports, and irrigation systems. The United States contributed competing aid projects south of the Hindu Kush range, which bisects Afghanistan. The projects included a gargantuan Helmand Valley hydrology project and a major airport in Kandahar. By the end of the 1970s, the Soviet Union had contributed about $1.25 billion in development funds; the Americans, about $0.5 billion.

But it was ultimately military aid that drew Afghanistan toward the Soviets. When the United States refused Afghan requests for arms and training in the 1950s, the Soviet Union began military aid, which eventually topped $1 billion. Thousands of Afghan soldiers, students, and technicians studied in the USSR, and the Afghan Army bought Soviet and Czech armaments on easy credit terms. Inculcated with the same Soviet ideology that had transformed the Muslim "-istans" along the USSR's southern flank, the Afghan government officials initiated some modest modernization programs, including female education and job opportunities, which alienated fundamentalist Afghans— especially the conservative Pashtun tribes. In 1978, backed by rebellious Soviet-trained and Soviet-advised army units, the leftist People's Democratic Party of Afghanistan took over the government.

Peace didn't last long. Soon after the Afghan Communists announced a compulsory female literacy campaign, credit reform, land redistribution, and minority-group empowerment in March 1979, Herat erupted in rioting. Across Afghanistan, Pashtun tribesmen once again brandished their rifles. The Hindu Kush became a stronghold of anti-Communist insurrection. Afghan soldiers defected in droves; units mutinied. Responding to their client state's alarming deterioration, the Soviet Union dispatched thousands of military advisers, hundreds of tanks, helicopters, and other armaments. But in midsummer 1979, the opportunist United States began to surreptitiously supply the fundamentalist Islamic insurgents. Hoping to fuel an intractable Vietnam-style insurgency in the Soviet sphere of influence, the CIA initially provided the Islamic fighters $500,000 of propaganda, radios, medical equipment, and cash. It was the first tiny rivulet of what came to be a raging river of money. As the superpowers began parrying with their Afghan proxies, the Great Game got hot again.

By late 1979, the isolated Afghan Communist government was foundering. Despite the Afghans' history of resistance and the Islamic clerics' overweening influence, the Politburo made a fateful decision to invade Afghanistan. On December 24, 1979, Soviet airborne troops landed at the Kabul International Airport and Bagram Airfield. The next morning, the Soviet Fortieth Army crossed the Amu Darya River as Soviet tanks began clanking across the border.[16] "It'll be over in three to four weeks," Communist Party general secretary Leonid Brezhnev predicted to Anatoly Dobrynin, the Soviet ambassador to the United States.[17] But it was another story of easy to get in, hard to get out.[18]

There were soon almost one hundred thousand Soviet troops stationed in Afghanistan. The Soviet soldiers called the Afghan fighters *dukhi* (ghosts), who could emerge like wraiths from the mountainsides and disappear as quickly. It was a will-o'-the-wisp war waged by a hydra-headed resistance that sprang up in Afghanistan's hinterlands. Though the Soviets had clear superiority in armaments and technology, the Afghans called on their age-old tactics: surprise, flexibility, and terror, inventively using simple materials to wreak unexpected mayhem. And with Pakistan's ardent *mujahideen* support that was financed by over $3 billion of US covert aid (which Saudi Arabia matched dollar for dollar), the Islamic fundamentalist fighters had a sanctuary, suppliers, and two powerful bankers.[19] The CIA turned the Afghan irregulars into a new breed of techno-guerrilla, ready to do age-old battle with burst-transmit radios, GPS systems, and modern weaponry, including Stinger® antiaircraft missiles that the United States began providing in 1986. USAID, the US agency responsible for development and humanitarian aid, also supported the mujahideen war through a cross-border program that delivered tons of food and medicine to Pashtun villages in the Afghan–Pakistan borderlands. The program, which soared from $6 million in 1985 to $90 million in 1989, was designed to keep functioning Pashtun villages to support the mujahideen.[20]

While mujahideen leaders, such as Younus Khalis, Gulbuddin Hekmatyar, and Jalaluddin Haqqani, were happy to take the US money and material, they had nothing but contempt for the American infidels. The mujahideen exhibited early on the double-dealing that characterized their subsequent interactions with the Americans. CIA operative Howard Hart, who ran the mujahideen assistance program in the 1980s, said about the Afghan fighters, "They're so crooked that when they die you don't bury them, you just screw them into the ground."[21] The mujahideen knew their power. When the Soviets sent twenty thousand troops to overrun a guerrilla base in Khost Province, *Time* magazine quoted Haqqani: "We stood alone at first against the Soviet invader with bare hands. It is the bravery of the Afghan people that has attracted the foreigner to help."[22]

*   *   *

The Afghans' true advantage was culture—a deeply rooted, xenophobic culture that saw time, weather, and terrain as part of their weaponry and their tribes, clans, and mullahs as allies against the infidels. While many of Afghanistan's numerous ethnic groups, including the Tajik, Uzbek, and Hazara communities, have fearsome reputations, it was the conservative Pashtun tribe that formed the bulwark of the mujahideen. Approximately twenty-five million Pashtuns are centered in eastern and southern Afghanistan and northern Pakistan, forming the world's largest ethnic group without a nation-state. The Pashtuns are a highly segmentary society, delineated into approximately three hundred fifty tribes, further divided into a multitude of clans—or *khels*—subkhels, and extended family groups called *kahols*.

The thousand-year-old Pashtun society has an obdurate warrior culture embedded in the tribal code of *Pashtunwali*, which emphasizes personal freedom, honor, revenge, and chivalry.[23] Among the code's many tenets, *nang* is the word for honor, associated with the egalitarian mountain Pashtuns who fiercely defend their independence from outside authority. In the Pashtun mountain heartland, the central government has seldom been anything other than a vague distant entity. Nang extends to the defense of the Pashtun tribesman's personal honor, property, and women. *Tora* means sword, the concept for courage. *Badal* is the word for revenge, an important aspect of this endlessly warring society. A warrior must avenge his loss, however long it takes. One Pashtun proverb states, "I took my revenge after a hundred years, and I only regret that I acted in haste."[24] The celebrated seventeenth-century Pashtun warrior-poet Khushal Khan defended his tribe's mountain home against both the Moghuls and other Pashtun tribes. He wrote:

> Now blooms the rose, now sharply pricks the thorn,
> Glory's the hazard, O man of woman born!
> The very name Pashtun spells honor and glory,
> Lacking that honor what is the Afghan story?
> In the sword alone lies our deliverance.[25]

The Pashtuns' embrace of *melmastia* (hospitality to guests) and *nanawati* (sanctuary to a defeated foe) are cultural cornerstones as important as courage and revenge. Pashtun lore resounds with tales of a defeated foe asking his enemy for nanawati, and the victor being forced to offer haven rather than face dishonor. Nanawati requires the tribesman to provide food, shelter, and protection, even at the risk of his own life. When the US government demanded the Taliban surrender Osama bin Laden, the American officials failed to understand the power of nanawati, which required the Taliban to refuse. Taliban leader Mullah Omar told a Pakistani journalist, Rahimullah Yusufzai, "I know I can't fight the Americans, but if God helps me, I will survive. I don't want to go down in history as someone who betrayed his guest. I am willing to give my life, my regime, since we have given him refuge. I cannot throw him out now."[26] Later at Tora Bora, nanawati informed Younus Khalis's insider assertion that the Americans would "never catch" his guest, Osama bin Laden.

A conservative branch of Sunni Islam, Deobandism, also fired the mountain Pashtuns. Emerging from nineteenth-century Muslim theologians based in Deoband, India, the strict creed echoed many of the austere beliefs of Saudi Arabian Wahhabis, who harkened back to early Islam's pure desert ways. As Victorian-era Deobandism developed in the Pashtun tribal regions, the creed became increasingly anticolonial and antimodern, fueling the Pashtun zealotry that the British encountered. In the Soviet war era, financial support from Pakistan, Saudi Arabia, and the United States helped nurture thousands of Deobandist *madrassas* (schools) in the Pashtun border regions.[27] These strict religious schools shaped a generation of mujahideen.[28]

*   *   *

The mujahideen won. The last Soviet troops crossed the Amu Darya River back to Soviet Uzbekistan on February 15, 1989. Before their final withdrawal, more than 620,000 Soviet troops served in Afghanistan. Though the Soviets kept between 90,000 to over 104,000 troops in Afghanistan for almost a decade, they were spread very thin over a country five times the size of Vietnam, where the United States had over 500,000 troops. Experts concluded the USSR never had enough troops in Afghanistan to win.[29] The long conflict bled the Soviet Union. During nearly ten years of war in Afghanistan, the Soviets suffered almost 15,000 deaths and 469,685 wounded or seriously ill.[30] The war that was ultimately judged a defeat left a generation of ravaged Soviet veterans.

The war also wracked the Afghan population, with millions killed and wounded. More than five million Afghan refugees fled the country, with additional millions internally displaced. In the 1980s, half of all the refugees in the world were Afghans.[31] Though the Afghan fighters persevered against the Soviets, they suffered grievous casualties to do so. Roused by their mullahs and tribal leaders, the Afghan warriors continued to emerge from the hills, mountains, cities, and refugee camps to wage a war for national honor and Islam that finally brought down a modern superpower.

In the years following the defeat of the Soviets, US interest in the mujahideen waned.[32] They'd served their purpose. By the end of 1991, both superpowers had dramatically reduced their spending in Afghanistan. With the brief Gulf War over, the United States focused on Iraq and Saddam Hussein, though under President George H. W. Bush the CIA continued reduced covert aid to the mujahideen, with an inordinate amount going to Gulbuddin Hekmatyar, the radical anti-American warlord.[33] And as for the Soviets, soon they were simply no more. Gorbachev's resignation on Christmas Day 1991 signaled the dissolution of the Soviet Union, with each of its constituent republics becoming independent nations. So Afghanistan's communist government was left to its own devices.

Bribed with Saudi money and cajoled by Pakistan's Inter-Services Intelligence (the ISI was the primary Pakistani agency that funneled US aid to the mujahideen), seven mujahideen leaders formed the Afghan Interim Government in February 1989, anticipating taking control after the Soviet withdrawal. But the alliance fractured into warring factions, primarily along tribal lines. Gulbuddin Hekmatyar was soon out assassinating Afghan rivals. Hundreds of millions of US taxpayer dollars funded Hekmatyar's radical Islamic agenda.[34] But rival Tajik and Uzbek forces thwarted Hekmatyar when they took Kabul from the Communists in the spring of 1992. It was a watershed event: for the first time in three hundred years, the Pashtuns lost control of the capital. A vicious civil war ensued as heavily armed Pashtun, Tajik, Uzbek, and Hazara militias battled for control of the country. Afghanistan had plenty of guns. After the 1980s arms race between the Soviets, the United States, and China in Afghanistan, thirty million Afghans had more personal weapons than over one billion Indians and Pakistanis combined.[35] As the war raged, interminable rocket and artillery attacks reduced Kabul to rubble. Historians estimate thirty thousand Kabulis lost their lives, with over one hundred thousand wounded.[36] With the country in chaos and foreign aid scarce, Afghanistan became a center of the world's opium trade. Warlords, with their militias and logistics, allied with rural farmers in desperate need of a cash crop.

Once the warlords connected with heroin labs in Pakistan and the former Soviet republics, an industry was born. Afghanistan was soon supplying 70 percent of the world's heroin supply.[37]

By mid-1994, competing warlords had divided the country into fiefdoms, some ruled by *lex talionis*, or "the law of retaliation." Many Afghans, especially in southern Afghanistan, were living a brutish reality. Espousing a passionate belief in an austere, messianic Islam, the Taliban emerged out of the anarchy. The movement began in southern Afghanistan near Kandahar, where local tribesmen approached a mullah named Mohammed Omar about a warlord who had raped several girls. Omar called on his religious students to help him. After they killed the warlord, they went on to confront armed brigands. The Taliban quickly became a force in southern Afghanistan. Seizing the opportunity to quell the anarchic border regions and extend their power over Afghanistan, Pakistani officials supported the Taliban with arms, training, and advisers. Swelled with thousands of recruits from the borderland madrassas, the Taliban army swept across southern Afghanistan over the next months. In early 1995, the Taliban turned north through the mountain provinces along the Pakistan–Afghan boundary, with bands of mujahideen either surrendering or joining them. The growing Taliban army even forced powerful Gulbuddin Hekmatyar to flee to Pakistan. In September 1995, the ancient city of Herat, on the western border with Iran, fell to the Taliban. The western warlord, Ismail Khan, scurried to safety in Iran. By that point, the Taliban had over fifty MiG-21 attack jets, helicopters, tanks, and sixty artillery pieces.

The Taliban turned its attention toward Kabul, momentarily controlled by the forces of the Tajik leader, Ahmed Shah Massoud. As rockets rained down in the winter of 1995–1996, the United Nations had to organize emergency airlifts of food. In the summer, not long after the Taliban gave sanctuary to Osama bin Laden in Jalalabad, Gulbuddin Hekmatyar returned to Kabul to take the post of prime minister. The Uzbek warlord Abdul Rashid Dostum joined the government, as did Hazara leader Karim Khalili. But the Taliban had the momentum, continuing its siege of Kabul. Led by Mullah Omar, the Taliban unleashed an offensive east of Kabul, where it took Jalalabad and its critical supply line to the capital. With the Taliban threatening the remaining supply line to Kabul from the north, Massoud's Tajiks withdrew from Kabul on September 26, 1996. The next day, the Taliban warriors rolled into the city with their trademark machine-gun-mounted pickups. They broke into the United Nations compound, where they found Dr. Mohammed Najibullah, the former Communist leader. After torturing, castrating, and killing him, they strung up his body near the UN headquarters. Within twenty-four hours, the Taliban was enforcing its strict Islamic law: girls' schools were closed, affecting seventy thousand female students. Women were sequestered without education. Criminal punishment included lopping off of hands, ears, and heads.[38] Public stoning was the penalty for adultery. Kite-flying, cameras, and music were banned. Strung-up radios and televisions hanging from Kabul utility wires evidenced the Taliban's Department for the Propagation of Virtue and Suppression of Vice's summary justice.

*   *   *

In spite of a torrent of negative stories in the American press about the Taliban takeover, there was a studied nonchalance in the upper tiers of US policymakers. Indeed, there was even some mild enthusiasm in the Clinton administration for the perceived stability the Taliban was bringing to the chaotic country. While the State Department issued weak statements protesting Taliban human-rights policies, the US government's default policy condoned the support Pakistan and Saudi Arabia gave the Taliban.[39] There was also tacit US government support for the American company Unocal and its proposal for a gas pipeline project across Afghanistan to link Turkmenistan gas fields with south Asian markets. Unocal was prepared to do business with any Afghan faction in power, irrespective of human rights or political correctness.

But by late 1997, US officials were voicing a changed view of the Taliban. The deteriorating political and economic situation in Pakistan concerned Washington, as did Pakistan's refusal to confront the Taliban about its gender policies. The plight of Afghan women had become a *cause célèbre* in the United States, and feminist activists forced the Clinton administration to take a stronger stand against the Taliban.[40] The administration had a perfect spokesperson in Secretary of State Madeleine Albright, who traveled to Pakistan in November 1997 to condemn the Taliban. Standing on the steps of the Pakistan Foreign Ministry that supported the Taliban, she said, "It's very clear why we're opposed to the Taliban. We're opposed to their approach to human rights, to their despicable treatment of women and children, and their lack of respect for human dignity, in a way more reminiscent of the past than the future."[41] But over the next couple years, the Washington policy toward Afghanistan was muddled at best. While publicly hammering the Taliban over human rights, the United States also continued diplomatic contact, particularly regarding the Unocal deal.[42]

When the Taliban gave Osama bin Laden sanctuary in Jalalabad in September 1996, one arm of the diplomatic corps demanded the Taliban give him up. But nine days later, Secretary of State Warren Christopher negated that message by telling the Taliban, now in possession of Kabul, "we wish to engage the new 'interim government' at an early stage." A May 10, 1997, State Department memo stated that US policy "will inevitably be messy and the policy we follow will be ridden with inner tensions, as we simultaneously engage with the Taliban and criticize their abuses."[43] The Taliban proved to be the more facile party at double-dealing; the diplomatic green-tea drinking yielded few positive outcomes, except for the Taliban's acceptance of US funds for alternative crops to replace opium-poppy cultivation. The Taliban dodged the US diplomats' requests for inspections of the al Qaeda training camps long enough for al Qaeda to plan the August 7, 1998, attacks on the US embassies in Kenya and Tanzania, where 212 were killed and over two thousand wounded. Though the US retaliated thirteen days later with seventy-five cruise missiles launched at the al Qaeda training camps in eastern Afghanistan, bin Laden and his al Qaeda leaders left the camps before the missiles landed.[44]

Despite the bombings, the contradictory US policy toward the Taliban continued. While al Qaeda's embassy attacks prompted President Clinton to attack, it was the feminists, a powerful interest group for the Democrats, who ultimately forced the US government to harden its position toward the Taliban with legislation and aid programs targeted toward Afghan women.[45] President Clinton's July 1999 executive order began sanctions against the Taliban after the discovery of bin Laden's banking links to the regime. Secretary of State Albright told a women's conference on October 3, 1999, "the Taliban seems determined to drag Afghan women back from the dawn of the [twenty-first] century to somewhere closer to the [thirteenth]."[46] Despite the critical public rhetoric and legislation, the Clinton administration continued its conflicted Taliban policies, as US State Department representatives squired Taliban delegations around the country to build support for the pipeline project.[47]

But after the Taliban destroyed the giant seventh-century stone Buddhas in Bamiyan Province in March 2001, the global condemnation made Mullah Omar and Osama bin Laden international pariahs.[48] In the face of increasing international pressure, the two radical Islamic leaders solidified an alliance of convenience that served their differing visions of jihad. The uneasy partnership climaxed on the morning of September 11, 2001, when two passenger jets wheeled out of a clear, blue New York sky, and crashed into the World Trade Center towers.

The United States rapidly moved from demands for the al Qaeda perpetrators to war in a matter of weeks. But even as the US bombs began dropping on October 7, 2001, so did aid. Hoping to mollify international criticism, the United States dropped tons of packaged meals into Afghanistan. Like much of the subsequent American aid to Afghanistan, the meals did little. Noting that a million Afghans were fleeing the US attack, Doctors Without Borders said the US combined bombs and aid drop was counterproductive. "Such action does not answer the needs of the Afghan people and is likely to undermine attempts to deliver substantial aid to the most vulnerable," said Doctors Without Borders spokesman Dr. Jean-Hervé Bradol. The mullahs were likewise not impressed, calling for jihad "if infidels invade an Islamic country."[49]

Though the United States had vastly superior firepower, a former Clinton administration official noted the problem of asymmetrical warfare: "When we looked at Afghanistan before, the sense was we were going to bomb them *up* to the Stone Age. There is just so little to attack."[50] Ever-confident president George W. Bush told a group of senators, "When I take action, I'm not going to fire a two-million-dollar missile at a ten-dollar empty tent and hit a camel in the butt. It's going to be decisive."[51] But like the other invaders of Afghanistan, Bush found his decisive moment to be elusive.

The Taliban fighters quickly melted away. Accompanied by his bodyguards, Mullah Omar puttered over the Pakistani border on a motorbike. The warlords began retaking their old territories: Abdul Rashid Dostum in Mazar-e-Sharif; Massoud's Tajik successors in the north and Kabul; Ismail Khan to the west. Gulbuddin Hekmatyar returned to grab his old power center to the east of Kabul. In Jalalabad, the aged mujahideen and bin Laden patron Younus Khalis took control. The major mujahideen commanders who had fought the Soviets and each other during the civil war were back in power—ready to confront a new set of infidels.

*　　*　　*

Far from the central Asian battlefield, a coterie of international powers and four factions of anti-Taliban Afghans convened in Petersburg Castle, a luxury hotel outside of Bonn, Germany, to organize an interim government for Afghanistan. The delegates were also choosing the leader of the new Afghan government, a critical issue for US officials.[52] The four Afghan factions included the US-aided Northern Alliance, primarily comprised of Tajiks, Uzbeks, and Hazaras. The Rome Group was comprised of representatives of the eighty-seven-year-old former king, Zahir Shah, exiled in Italy since 1973. Long before 9/11, Washington had been wooing the royalists, with Congress even allocating funds to the king to convene a *loya jirga*, a grand assembly of tribal leaders.[53] The two other delegations in Bonn included the Cyprus Group of Iran-backed exiles and the Peshawar Group, which the Pakistani ISI had hastily organized a month before with a convention of seven hundred mullahs, tribal leaders, and mujahideen. The four groups shared little but mutual distrust. Adding to the intrigue, diplomats from more than two dozen countries jostled to advance their agendas.

The US officials lobbied hard for Hamid Karzai to be the interim government's president. The Americans perceived Karzai to be a moderate, anti-Taliban, aristocratic Pashtun with a pro-Western cant. Hamid Karzai was the scion to an important family of the powerful Pashtun Popalzai tribe, whose power base was in Kandahar. During the Soviet invasion, Karzai and his wealthy extended family fled to Quetta, Pakistan. During the anti-Soviet resistance, he served as a press and humanitarian-aid coordinator for the royalist mujahideen faction. Karzai's fluent English, noble heritage, and diplomatic ways caught the attention of the international crowd.

After the defeat of the communist government, Karzai served as the deputy foreign minister in the embattled Kabul government until he was imprisoned on suspicion of colluding with Pakistan's ISI. Though severely beaten, Karzai used a serendipitous rocket attack to escape back into exile in Pakistan. Not long after his return to Pakistan, a group of religious warriors calling themselves the Taliban began to impose order on Karzai's anarchic Kandahar homeland. Karzai knew the Taliban from Kandahar: "They were my buddies," he told journalist Steve Coll, "They were good people."[54]

Karzai gave the Taliban $50,000, a large cache of weapons, and introductions to other Pashtun leaders. Using Pashtun connections and the support of Pakistan's ISI, Taliban leader Mullah Omar was able to broaden his campaign to take Afghanistan. "The Taliban will fight until there is no blood in Afghanistan left to be shed and Islam becomes a way of life for our people," Omar said.[55] Alienated by the Taliban's reliance on the ISI and bin Laden's al Qaeda, Karzai began to organize political resistance. When the jihadists retaliated by killing his elderly father, Hamid Karzai leapt into a campaign of revenge. He allied himself with the Americans, Massoud, and other groups fighting the Taliban. Karzai was soon part of America's invasion of Afghanistan, helping to rally Pashtuns against the Taliban. It was a dangerous mission. In October, Taliban fighters surrounded Karzai, forcing him to call in the Americans, who reportedly helicoptered him to safety.[56] Until Karzai began his quixotic campaign to sway Pashtuns, US diplomats hadn't taken him too seriously. The Americans decided that since he was the only qualified Pashtun leader fighting the Taliban, they would support him to lead the interim Afghan government.[57]

As the diplomats began gathering at the Bonn castle, Karzai was in Afghanistan negotiating with Mullah Omar. When the Taliban sent one thousand fighters to assassinate Karzai, American special operations forces assigned to protect him called down precision bombs on the convoy, sending the survivors skittering back to Kandahar.[58] His combat credentials burnished, Karzai awaited developments in Bonn.

In an attempt to increase Karzai's prominence, the United States arranged for him to address the opening conference event in Bonn with a dramatic speech from the Kandahar front lines—delivered via a CIA-rigged satellite phone link. In his address, Karzai urged the factions to make a decision that would benefit the entire nation, not just each one's ethnic group. "This meeting is the path towards salvation," Karzai said.[59] Goaded by the international powers, the Bonn Conference delegates swiftly hammered out an agreement on an interim government that would run the country for some months until a loya jirga could be held. But the conference lost whatever amity it had when the delegates began debating about peacekeeping forces and the choice of interim leader. Wanting to maintain its newly won military advantage, the Northern Alliance called for all-Afghan peacekeepers. The other three delegations feared that a Northern Alliance–dominated force would trigger another civil war and demanded the UN organize a multinational force, which became the International Security Assistance Force, or ISAF. As the conference wound down in Bonn, two candidates vied for interim leader: Abdul Sattar Sirat, an Uzbek royalist backed by the Rome Group, and Hamid Karzai, the US favorite.[60]

On December 3 the United Nations posted a web story citing Reuters, CNN, and Agence France-Presse reports saying, "Following presentation this weekend of a UN proposal for governing Afghanistan in the months ahead, Afghan delegates meeting in Koenigswinter, near Bonn, are reportedly ready to name Abdul Sittar [*sic*] Sirat, a top aide to exiled former King Zahir Shah, to serve as interim prime minister until a traditional grand council is convened to set up a longer-term administration."[61] But although the Northern Alliance and the Rome Group agreed on the royalist Sirat, the story wasn't over.

In his opening address, UN secretary-general Kofi Annan warned the Afghan delegates that $6–10 billion of reconstruction aid was contingent on approval of the US- and UN-concocted plan. In numerous sidebar meetings, US special envoy on Afghanistan James Dobbins seconded the point. Earlier in the week, a *Washington Post* editorial laid down the Bush administration position: "The prospect of international reconstruction aid can be used as leverage; so can eventual Western and UN recognition for an Afghan government, which is something the Taliban never achieved." The editorial said further, "a stable Afghan solution will require the Northern Alliance to accept the political primacy of the southern Pashtuns." The editorial ominously concluded, "For now, with crucial battles still to be fought against al Qaeda, it's worth giving our Afghan allies that chance to be reasonable. Yet, over time, if reason fails, stronger steps should not be ruled out."[62] Stronger steps were already being taken. Back in southern Afghanistan, one thousand US Marines were seizing the Kandahar airport.[63]

As the United States and other international players pressured the delegates to choose Karzai, the Northern Alliance delegates prepared to return to Kabul for "further discussion." Worried the Northern Alliance was bolting, Dobbins called Secretary of State Colin Powell for direction. Powell told *Frontline* that he told Dobbins, "'Do not let them break up. Keep them there. Lock them up if you have to. We do not want this to go anywhere else. We're almost there, and this is the time to grind it out on this line. If they go off, I don't know when I'll get them all back together.' Rich Armitage [deputy secretary of state] loves the little idea that once you get frogs in a wheelbarrow, you don't let them get out. That was a good analogy. So we kept them in. . . ." Powell also called his Russian counterpart, Russian foreign minister Igor Ivanov: "Well, I called Igor and let him know that this was starting to slip away from us, and to make sure that he emboldened his representatives there to keep them there." Worried about Islamic radicalism in their former Muslim republics, the Russians likewise pressured the Northern Alliance, warning it that aid would not be forthcoming if it didn't accept Karzai as the interim president.

After a US rocket "accidentally" landed near the home of Northern Alliance leader Burhanuddin Rabbini, the group fell into step for Karzai.[64]

On December 5, 2001, the Bonn Conference delegates announced that Hamid Karzai had been selected as the interim president. (According to Afghan insiders, even the first election of the new Afghan government was tainted. The insiders intimated that while Sirat received the overwhelming majority of the votes in the election, the international powers ensured Karzai, who garnered only a small number of votes, became the president.)[65] But at that moment back in Afghanistan, a misdirected American bomber was dropping a two-thousand-pound bomb on the very spot where Karzai was standing. Ten people died and scores were wounded, including Karzai, who took the blast in his face. Scarce moments later, Karzai's cell phone rang. It was a BBC journalist calling to tell him he had been chosen as the interim president of Afghanistan.

A half hour later, the Taliban surrendered Kandahar to Karzai after days of negotiation—but it was too late. Using the same strategy that al Qaeda employed in Tora Bora, the Taliban engaged indecisive Karzai in a duplicitous negotiation that bought time for Mullah Omar and his fighters to escape. When Karzai finally entered Kandahar four days later, a CIA-recruited former mujahideen warlord, Gul Agha Sherzai, had already grabbed power. Compelled to appoint Sherzai as governor, Karzai began his deference to powerful Afghan warlords.[66] In the post-Bonn interim government cabinet, Karzai was the only southern Pashtun. The Northern Alliance held seventeen cabinet seats, including the critical posts of ministers of defense, interior, intelligence, and foreign affairs. With the Taliban on the run, the United States continued to empower the warlords who had emerged to retake their regions. Though he was pilloried as a mass murderer for the deaths of Taliban prisoners, the United States considered Abdul Rashid Dostum in the north to be an ally. Eastern warlord Abdul Qadir was likewise the beneficiary of extensive CIA support. Karzai's nemesis in Kandahar, Gul Agha Sherzai, gained control of four important southern provinces with US support. The US authorities curried Ismail Khan's attention in the west and pumped up support of Hazara warlords, such as Karim Khalili. The Tajik warlord Mohammad Fahim held the powerful position of defense minister, allowing him to channel government funds to other warlords in exchange for support for himself and his Tajiks.

The Bonn Agreement that facilitated the rise of Hamid Karzai greased his selection in the June 2002 loya jirga as head of the transitional government. But with the US decision to empower the warlords, President Karzai was fatally compromised, forcing him to constantly cut deals with warlords more interested in financial gain than in statesmanship. As he faced the problems of a weak central government trying to administer a ravaged, warlord-plagued nation, Karzai warned the international powers against withdrawing financial support as they had after the Soviet retreat. "The international community saw the consequences of neglecting Afghanistan," he said. "It should be wise enough not to do it again."[67]

Karzai was heartened by Bush's April 2002 "Marshall Plan" speech at the Virginia Military Institute. But Bush's lofty rhetoric, which Colin Powell's

State Department orchestrated to gain some influence over Afghan policy, ultimately came to little. With Secretary of Defense Donald Rumsfeld decrying nation building, the National Security Council under Condoleezza Rice never organized a plan or allocated resources. President George Bush never mentioned a Marshall Plan for Afghanistan again.

Glorying in tough-guy solutions, the Bush administration neoconservatives turned over many of the postwar issues to the CIA and the Pentagon, sidelining State Department diplomats and development officers. Even USAID humanitarian food deliveries were taken over by military teams. It took a year for the State Department to appoint a full-time coordinator for Afghanistan reconstruction. William Taylor arrived at the Kabul embassy in October 2002, where he discovered that the CIA still had most of the money and the other American development players were uncoordinated and often at odds.[68]

In January 2002, the war in Afghanistan was very cheap: $3.8 billion for a quick and easy war with seventeen special ops teams directing laser bombs, Hellfire®-laden drones, and a host of inexpensive Afghan proxies. On the eve of the loya jirga in May 2002, it was still an extremely affordable war, costing only $17 billion, a pittance compared to the hundreds of billions later squandered.[69] America had her moment of victory. But it was soon to get much more expensive. As the United States became increasingly preoccupied with Iraq, Karzai's corrupt cohorts were in cahoots with neoconservative free-market ideologues, high-priced international NGO consultants, ambitious US military officers and development officials, and their incestuous multinational corporate partners. US taxpayer money began to lubricate an entire system of corruption that eventually extended even to the Taliban.

*　　*　　*

Scene: Jalalabad, Afghanistan, February 23, 2010. A suicide bomber killed Afghan warlord Hajji Zaman Ghamsharik during a government-sponsored ceremony for returning refugees at the village of Dasht-e-Chamtala. Infamous for drug smuggling and his role in Osama bin Laden's Tora Bora escape, Hajji Zaman Ghamsharik had lately been trumpeted as a political supporter of President Hamid Karzai.

In the uproar following Tora Bora, Hajji Zaman Ghamsharik fled, bolting to eight years of exile in France and Pakistan, where he continued to spin his webs. Ghamsharik was implicated in the 2002 assassination of Hajji Abdul Qadir, a Karzai administration vice president from eastern Afghanistan who had thrown

Ghamsharik out of power. Qadir was a Bonn Conference delegate who had voted for Karzai and one of the few ethnic Pashtuns in Karzai's Tajik-dominated government. Hajji Abdul Qadir's murder launched a blood feud between the Ghamsharik and Qadir families. Besides his other tribal and opium-trade rivals, the CIA and special forces burned at Tora Bora also had it in for Ghamsharik. "He was bitterly disliked by very many people. And then there were business interests, too," Mirwais Yasini, *a Parliament member from Nangarhar Province, told the* New York Times.

But during his 2009 presidential campaign, Hamid Karzai called Ghamsharik back from exile to bolster Pashtun political support, a reprise of Karzai's penchant for making deals with unsavory characters. Ghamsharik returned to Afghanistan a tribal hero, traveling from the Khyber Pass in a huge motorcade with thousands of supporters cheering him, a replay of his return from exile in 2001, when his tribesmen welcomed him with a thousand-gun salute. But within a few months of his 2009 return, Hajji Zaman Ghamsharik was assassinated in the contract suicide attack that illustrated Afghanistan's ceaseless tribal and governmental machinations. Though the Taliban normally took responsibility for successful suicide attacks, their spokesman, Zabiullah Mujahid, said he didn't know who did it. There were so many suspects, investigators hardly knew where to start.[70]

Chapter 2

The Creeping Mission
Development and the Military

OPERATION ANACONDA WAS A DO-OVER for the US military. Attempting to make up for the Tora Bora failure, the Pentagon replaced its light-footprint tactics with a heavy boots-on-the-ground presence in the Shah-i-Kot Valley, where hundreds of al Qaeda and Taliban fighters were entrenched in March 2002.[1] One hundred miles southeast of Tora Bora, in mountainous Paktia Province, Shah-i-Kot was another *mujahideen* sanctuary where Islamic fighters had twice defeated the Soviet army. Located about twenty miles from the scruffy provincial capital of Gardez, the highly defensible valley lay in the cleft of two-mile-high mountains with passes to the adjoining Pakistani tribal regions. The CIA and special ops team established their command post, Fire Base Gardez, at the eastern edge of Paktia's provincial capital, where they rented an Afghan *qalat*, a wealthy landowner's traditional compound of adobe structures surrounded by twenty-five-foot-high mud-brick walls that stretched one hundred meters on each side. As much a bastion as a farm compound, Fire Base Gardez was Fort Apache in eastern Afghanistan's "Indian Country"—the soldiers' term for insurgent territory. Inside the six-foot-thick walls, the sprawling courtyard was chockablock with the Americans' tents, trash, equipment, and vehicles that could slip through the compound's steel gate. A satellite dish perched on the medieval walls. In the evenings, dozens of coalition soldiers and operatives clustered around the adobe farmhouse's pot-bellied stoves, reading fresh intelligence and the history of Afghan warfare, particularly the Soviet–Afghan War.[2]

As at Tora Bora, the Americans planned to use special operations forces and Afghan fighters, led this time by a tall, young warlord with CIA approval from Logar Province, Zia Lodin. The ostensibly "friendly" Afghan force that the Eastern Shura had cobbled together included many former Taliban.[3] It was another cash-for-allies operation. Every few days, a CIA helicopter landed beside Fire Base Gardez and the CIA moneyman hopped out with carryalls stuffed with US cash for Zia and other Eastern Shura warlords.[4] But the American military planners were conflicted about their Afghan proxies. While they still wanted to put an "Afghan face" on the war, they feared Afghan betrayals. To avoid another Tora Bora fiasco, the Pentagon overcame its aversion to US casualties and deployed substantial American ground troops to Anaconda.[5]

Spring 2002 was a heady time for American officials. The US military and CIA were crowing about their quick air- and proxy-powered victory over the Taliban. The commander of the British forces, Brigadier Roger Lane, announced that the war in Afghanistan was "all but won," and thought the mopping-up work would be "completed in a matter of weeks rather than months."[6] In late March 2002, there were only 5,300 American troops in Afghanistan. The US warlord strategy let them administer the country through alliances of convenience with local power brokers. Though the coalition partners were already planning their withdrawals, they first wanted to make up for Tora Bora with a big win at Shah-i-Kot.

According to the US plan for Operation Anaconda, the force of friendly Afghan fighters and special ops soldiers would drive the jihadi fighters from the valley into the upper slopes, where a brigade-sized US infantry force that had been helicoptered in would kill or capture them. In military parlance, the friendly Afghans and special ops were the hammer, and the US infantrymen were the anvil.

But the operation was deeply flawed. In violation of the military's cardinal rule of unity of command, the air and infantry were under bifurcated commands—and special ops teams were under yet another.[7] The infantrymen were woefully undersupported: no artillery and scant air assets. With Iraq already dominating the agenda, the Anaconda operational planning was uncoordinated and understaffed, in part because Central Command (CENTCOM) contended that the Afghanistan war was over, so they could focus on the juicy *new* war. Though the al Qaeda leadership was still virtually intact and the Taliban had merely removed itself from the battlefield without surrender, much of the senior US military staff had moved on to Iraq matters.[8] Intelligence missed something big. Though a Taliban informant provided accurate numbers, US military intelligence mistakenly thought there were 150–200 al Qaeda fighters in the valley, rather than the 700–1,000 seasoned Arab and Afghan fighters who were dug in there. And, also as at Tora Bora, the US military and CIA wholly overestimated their Afghan proxies' capacities.

The attack went badly from the start. The convoy of thirty-five trucks carrying two special forces A-teams and the four hundred Afghan proxies over-turned on the mountain roads, and then was attacked by a huge AC-130 Spectre gunship, which began to strafe the unit with its fearsome cannons and machine guns, destroying trucks and killing several Afghans and Chief Warrant Officer Stanley Harriman.[9] The soldiers reported the last words Harriman whispered: "I hope that this has not been in vain."[10]

When the survivors arrived at Shah-i-Kot, they anticipated an immense aerial barrage to devastate the jihadi positions. Instead, a paltry six bombs landed. When the frustrated Afghan fighters began to take intense mortar and small-arms fire, Zia's men gave up the fight, heading back to Fire Base Gardez, where Zia's fighters railed about American mistakes to anyone who would listen.[11]

In the meantime, Chinook[*] helicopters ferried the US conventional forces to their first battle in Afghanistan—and landed them in a kill zone. Almost as soon as the soldiers hit the ground, they were pinned down by heavy mortar fire. The jihadi fighters already held the high ground and had the landing zones zeroed in. Intense ground fire held off the Apache[*] helicopters sent to provide cover, and the US soldiers were unequipped to respond to the al Qaeda mortars. The military planners didn't anticipate that al Qaeda might have mortars or artillery, nor did the planners take note of the propensity the mujahideen had demonstrated during the Soviet war to take the high ground.

With the battle still raging days later, an ill-advised helicopter landing on a Shah-i-Kot mountaintop swarming with al Qaeda allowed the enemy fighters to hit a Chinook with rocket-propelled grenades (RPGs), causing a Navy SEAL, Petty Officer First Class Neil C. Roberts, to fall out the back ramp. The subsequent wildly uncoordinated rescue mission precipitated a vicious fire-fight that downed the Chinook carrying the would-be rescuers. Lightly armed guerrillas firing bullets costing a few cents were downing multimillion-dollar, high-tech war machines. Infighting erupted between US commanders in Bagram and those on the ground.[12]

Once the military sorted out the snafus, the air force had heavy bombers, fighter jets, and gunships stacked eight miles high over the valley loosing their munitions, including almost 3,500 bombs.[13] The CIA and special forces oper-atives managed to coax Zia back into the fight.[14] Though the US forces clearly did the heavy lifting, the Bush administration presented their Afghan proxies as the Shah-i-Kot victors. When the major carnage was over, over eighty US sol-diers were casualties, including eight dead. Helicopters were downed and dam-aged by rockets and shells. Though the US military claimed between six hun-dred and one thousand enemy fighters were killed, Green Berets and Afghan commanders on the ground questioned the figures.[15] An indeterminate number of mujahideen may have escaped, perhaps including some important leaders, such as Jalaluddin Haqqani and Osama bin Laden's second-in-command, Ayman al-Zawahiri. Some news reports even placed bin Laden at Shah-i-Kot in the weeks prior to Anaconda and blamed his escape on slow US planning.[16]

CENTCOM Commander General Tommy Franks declared Operation Anaconda "an unqualified and complete success," though journalist Seymour Hersh later called it "a debacle." At a press conference after the battle, an American sergeant raged about Zia Lodin: "He punked out on us. I don't know how much we paid him, but I'll shoot him myself."[17] In spite of American infantry boots on the ground, Operation Anaconda failed to break the will of the al Qaeda fighters—the American snafus and Afghan turnabouts may have even given them a sense of the possible. Not long after Anaconda, an al Qaeda spokesman, Abu-Ubayd al-Qurashi, wrote, "Anyone who follows the news from Afghanistan will see how the different factions are playing with the Americans in order to prolong the flow of dollars as much as possible and are trying to strengthen their own interests without participating seriously in the American crusade."[18] Some Americans agreed, saying the cash the CIA passed out to the unreliable Afghan proxies helped nurture the culture of duplicity. A senior CIA officer who led and advised the bin Laden desk, Michael Scheuer, concluded, "the conduct of this war approaches perfection—in the sense of perfectly inept."[19]

*   *   *

In an influential summer 2002 *Foreign Affairs* article, the Brookings Institution's Michael O'Hanlon trumpeted the American invasion of Afghanistan as "one of the greater military successes of the twenty-first century." But he warned that the United States needed to both increase troops to between twenty and thirty thousand, and to "work hard with other donors to make reconstruction and aid programs work in Afghanistan" to avoid a resurgence of the Taliban and al Qaeda.[20] US officials were thinking the same thing as they formulated a type of military aid-and-development unit that could deal with the challenges posed by a failed state still in active conflict.

The US-led coalition had essentially conquered a catastrophe, one of the world's least developed countries in the midst of a humanitarian emergency. In 2001, the United Nations Development Programme ranked Afghanistan 173 out of 177 countries on the Human Development Index.[21] Over one million Afghans had died in the previous decades of war; many millions had fled the country, including most of the educated professionals, bureaucrats, and businesspeople. The few paved roads that existed hadn't been maintained since they were built in the 1960s. There was virtually no power-generation capacity. No fiscal or regulatory agencies; no centralized capacity to raise government revenues. After a generation of war, the agrarian sector was in total disarray. Once food exporters, Afghans were now at a subsistence level, ranking near the bottom of the international index of calories per person. According to UN figures, the average Afghan consumed 1,523 calories a day, less than half the 3,108 calories consumed in industrialized countries, and even far below the South Asian average of 2,356. In this calorie-deficient society where people lived an average of forty-four years, Afghans often slowly starved in the winter.[22]

Fire Base Gardez, the Operation Anaconda special ops post, was also a genesis point for development units that came to be called Provincial Reconstruction Teams or PRTs. Hybrid military–civilian development teams designed to operate in active war zones, PRTs quickly became a key aid and counterinsurgency element in Afghanistan. Fire Base Gardez was a good spot to break in a combat-and-development team. Even after Anaconda, Fire Base Gardez remained a lively place as insurgents continued to regularly attack the compound with 105 mm rockets and RPGs. "It was Beau Geste—a mud fort outside of town," USAID official and PRT veteran Nick Marinacci said. "The living conditions were Spartan."[23]

The PRTs emerged from ad hoc CIA and special operations teams focused on intelligence and combat support. When US Army Civil Affairs joined the teams, the work broadened to include small nation-building projects, or "hearts-and-minds" work, a term the military persisted in using despite its uncomfortable association with Vietnam. WHAM—Winning Hearts And Minds—was the inevitable military acronym. Thus began the PRTs' commingled intelligence, combat, and development mission that has complicated US efforts ever since.

The proto-PRTs were initially called Joint Regional Teams, a name that was soon changed to Coalition Humanitarian Liaison Cell, CHLC— "Chicklets" to the coalition forces. "I was part of a Chicklet, but didn't know it until later," says Lieutenant Colonel Simon Gardner, a senior civil-affairs officer who arrived in Afghanistan in December 2001.[24] He and his four-man team worked on humanitarian aid at Bagram while they did assessments and reconnaissance. "We went up to the Salang Tunnel, got to schools, refugee camps, administrative centers. We had weapons and transport, so we could get around. It was very hard to focus on civil affairs because the theater was still very fresh, immature. We still hadn't figured out the funding stuff." Gardner was the man for the Afghan job. Jockey-taut, English-born Gardner was an accomplished horseman who competed in the Afghan national sport, *buzkashi*, a wild pololike game played with a headless goat. He had a deep sense of central Asian culture from his academic research for his Naval Postgraduate School master's thesis on the causes of radical Islamic violence.

In the days leading up to Anaconda, Gardner led his team into insurgency-plagued Khost Province, which abuts the Pakistani tribal territories. The team arrived in a special forces helicopter, landing near Khost City—the closest airfield to Shah-i-Kot. Logistics were still pretty basic, so Gardner arrived with a heavy rucksack filled with $50,000 in cash, keeping his accounting in a little green book. To get around the restive region, the team bought a battered Land Cruiser® off a car lot with a stack of cash. Gardner says, "We were four bearded dudes in a Toyota®. We were sort of like the scouts. Living the dream."

Gardner's unit, the Ninety-Sixth Civil Affairs Battalion, is the only active-duty civil-affairs (CA) battalion, and its Charlie Company works directly with the special forces on the battlefield to perform missions with the local populations. "We were helping special forces guys to help stand up local forces; stabilize local communities. Khost was so immature, so insecure, there were no NGOs, no USAID. It was dangerous at that time. There was no one to do what CA does, leveraging people." Once on the ground, the CA soldiers organized delivery of six hundred metric tons of humanitarian aid to sixteen different local tribes and Kuchi nomads. Distributed through local strongmen the United States had tapped for leadership, the US largesse was intended to slow down support of the Taliban, lure the tribesmen into joining the other Afghan proxies, and, importantly, to extract intelligence for the special forces. The CA team paid Afghans top dollar to drive, translate, dig wells, clean out irrigation canals, and fill sandbags in order to pump money into the impoverished region. In hopes of reducing sniper fire at the airbase, Gardner's team handed out food to every Afghan within rifle range of the runway. "The paperwork was very, very easy," says Gardner. "It's nice for operators when it's an immature theater. When the brass comes in, you get more bean-counters, architects—it's more regimented."

In early 2002, the first US State Department and USAID officials began to rotate through the Chicklets.[25] Both the civilian departments were anxious to place their staff in the emerging development units lest the military take control of a growing aid program. In August 2002, the State Department and the military signed an interagency agreement, and in December 2002 USAID signed a similar memorandum of understanding. The agreements allowed civilians to work alongside the military with the ten- to twelve-man teams doing small humanitarian projects. As the drumbeat of the Iraq War began to boom in early 2003, the combined civilian–military units became known as Provincial Reconstruction Teams (PRTs). The PRT construct resulted in a series of working groups convened in mid-2002 at Bagram Airfield, where various international NGOs, including the United Nations Assistance Mission to Afghanistan (UNAMA), contributed their thoughts on a military–civilian development-team model. Following President Bush's National Security Strategy, promulgated in September 2002, the PRTs were to use an integrated military–civilian approach to combine the "3Ds"—the Bush moniker for the critical US foreign-policy elements: development, diplomacy, and defense.[26]

State Department diplomat Thomas Praster was the first PRT civilian at Fire Base Gardez, where he was joined by a contract USAID officer, retired US Army lieutenant colonel Randolph Hampton. Beyond co-opting local power brokers, the early Fire Base Gardez PRT projects included constructing schools and medical clinics in Paktia, Khost, and Ghazni Provinces. As envisioned in the Bagram talks, the pilot PRTs posted across Afghanistan included international partners: the United Kingdom in Mazar-e-Sharif, New Zealand in Bamiyan Province, and Germany in Kunduz, along with US teams at Kandahar, Parwan, and Herat. With rosters of about one hundred military and civilian personnel and substantial logistical requirements, the PRTs were never cheap. As the later ISAF PRT handbook noted, "PRTs are extremely expensive in terms of personnel, maintenance, and activity costs."[27] The Government Accountability Office, or GAO, estimated that each PRT cost about $20 million to stand up. Much of the cost related to security, particularly among the US PRTs located in unstable eastern and southern Afghanistan. While the initial discussions envisioned the PRTs working in relatively pacified areas, the United States morphed the concept and stationed the teams in active war zones, causing NGOs to snort that they had made the term "reconstruction team" absurd.[28] It was not unusual for PRT soldiers to be involved in kinetics (the military term for things exploding). PRT Captain Dan Still was one of those. A Las Vegas prosecuting attorney, Still told me of standing ankle-deep in spent machine-gun cartridges as he helped repel a complex insurgent attack in Khost City. "It was a gun battle from hell," the civil-affairs officer assigned to reconstruction says.[29]

The PRTs were the first attempt to integrate multiagency civilian staffers and the military since the Vietnam War's ill-fated pacification program known as CORDS, short for Civil Operations and Revolutionary Development Support. CORDS included the Phoenix Program, the US-funded anti–Viet Cong campaign that became one of the war's most criticized initiatives. CIA veteran and head of CORDS William Colby later admitted, "The word 'Phoenix' became a shorthand for all of the negative aspects of the war."[30] Like its PRT descendent, CORDS was part of a pacification program designed to bind a hostile local population to the central government. It was the first US attempt at WHAM, which included President Johnson's economic development offer to North Vietnam to build a multibillion-dollar Mekong River valley version of the Tennessee Valley Authority, mistakenly thinking that if he built it, the North Vietnamese would come along. USAID made Vietnam a showcase of development, sending thousands of American civilian experts to work there. In 1967 alone, USAID spent $550 million in aid to Vietnam out of the agency's global budget of $2 billion. Unlike the State Department officers who were assigned to PRTs in Afghanistan with little preparation, CORDS officers signed on for eighteen-month to two-year tours preceded by four to six months of intensive language and culture training.[31]

Presaging the US development efforts in Afghanistan, CORDS suffered from uncoordinated and fragmented American leadership, as well as the South Vietnamese officials' reluctance to defer to American administrators. Dealing with corrupt South Vietnamese officials created enormous challenges for the CORDS officials trying to bond the locals to their dysfunctional government.[32] With the majority of the resources, the military had an outsized role in the civilian–military program. As the program devolved along with troop levels, various civilian agencies tried to wrest control of their programs back from CORDS. Richard Holbrooke, who later helped broker the Balkan peace accords and became the viceregal special envoy to Afghanistan and Pakistan, served for six years as a USAID officer in Vietnam, where he was an architect of the Office of Civil Operations (OCO), which was responsible for integrating the US civil support for pacification. The precursor of CORDS, the OCO came about in a period when President Johnson had flirted with giving the military responsibility for pacification. In an oral history of the Vietnam War, Holbrooke recalled being enraged by the misreporting of the on-the-ground reality. He thought the only problem was reporting and the need "to seek truth from facts." Holbrooke said, "It never occurred to me in the year 1963 that the United States could lose a war. How could it?"[33] However checkered the program, the work CORDS did in civil affairs, force protection, and mentoring of Vietnamese authorities did give the US military experience with nation building. But with the defeat in Vietnam, the military wanted to forget its failed pacification experiment. By the time the next generation of American soldiers dealt with hearts-and-minds projects in the Balkans during the ethnic wars of the 1990s, they were basically starting over.[34]

Despite the earlier integrated US civilian–military pacification programs, the PRTs in Afghanistan initially had virtually no structure to define the relationship between each agency. The first directional document, "PRT Policy Guidance," didn't come out until June 2003, and even then it was no more than a three-page outline. For a year and a half, the outline served as the only inter-agency document of guidance for development teams in a shattered country where an unvanquished foe was regrouping. In lieu of organization and direction, each PRT cobbled together working groups, which operated on a catch-as-catch-can basis. In the early years, the PRT civilian staffers (particularly the USAID officials) were older males (some veterans of the Vietnam-era military or CORDS), and twenty-something females with master's degrees—"Aid Chicks," as one USAID staffer who served on a PRT termed them. While only about 10 percent of the USAID applicants were female, about one-third of the civilians on PRTs were women. "Back then, there were a lot of people on PRTs who were running from something, or running to something," the staffer recalled.[35] For ambitious foreign-service careerists on their way up, an Afghanistan rotation was a way to gain street cred. One PRT civilian official ironically mocked his colleagues, "Why are we here? 'Because I've got a resume.' Even if an Afghan can do it, we need to do it. Why? 'I need the credit.'"[36] Another PRT veteran confirmed: "It was spend, spend, spend. You've got a six-month tour to prove what you can do."[37]

The PRT civilian–military integration in Afghanistan was erratic. In some instances, the military command had scant use for civilians and relegated them to the backbench. In others, the commanders understood the value of intera-gency cooperation and included them in decision making. Other factors impacted the teams' effectiveness. The teams didn't train together, so they had to form relationships out in the field. In the early years of the war, USAID project leaders had rotations of six months, an absurdly short period of time to try to comprehend an opaque tribal culture, organize a project, obtain community buy-in, and manage it correctly. There were USAID projects with seven project leaders in two years.[38] The US Department of Agriculture (USDA) foreign-assistance officers who flew in to help with agricultural development were initially on even shorter rotations: three months. Promises made and promises broken became the norm as one development leader replaced another. The different lengths of rotation created havoc: as the war went on, USAID and the

State Department had one-year rotations, but USDA had six-month rotations. All the civilians and military were on merry-go-rounds of leaves and furloughs. So in the absence of integration-enhancing policy and procedure, the multi-million-dollar reconstruction and aid programs were almost completely personality-driven. Simon Gardner says, "It's amazing how much the PRTs were dependent on personalities."[39]

With the army providing the PRT support functions, including food, shelter, transportation, medical, and all-important security, the perception was that the military was in charge. In the early years, this often meant civilian officers had to constantly justify their mission to get resources to do their work— sometimes to even get a seat at the table. In one case in 2004, the Jalalabad PRT military commander informed the team's USAID representative, Michelle Parker, she did not need to attend a PRT briefing for Secretary of Defense Donald Rumsfeld, Joint Chiefs of Staff Chairman Richard Myers, and US Ambassador Zalmay Khalilzad; the commander "determined that civilians did not need to participate in the briefing because it was a DOD visit." He accordingly instructed his staff to not put out a seat for USAID. Nonplussed, Parker waited until the commander was at the landing zone greeting the VIPs to place her own chair and name card at the table. When Rumsfeld arrived, he spent much of the time quizzing the civilians on their programs and lamenting how few civilians there were in the PRTs. According to Parker, in subsequent Jalalabad meetings USAID had a seat at the table.[40] Ambassador Khalilzad and Lieutenant General David Barno, the head of the combined forces in Afghanistan, decided they wanted another sixteen PRTs spun up across the insurgent south and east. "It was a growth spurt," says USAID's Nick Marinacci, who had arrived in Kandahar in December 2003.[41] A veteran of conflict-zone NGO aid projects, Marinacci had "answered the ad— Afghanistan seemed interesting." He went on to head up the enormous PRT expansion. "We were slapping up plywood huts and taking over old madrassas all over the south and east."

While the PRT policy–guidance document called for the PRTs to coordinate with the Afghan government and UNAMA, the UN relief agency in Afghanistan, the actual working relationship was haphazard and sometime contentious. Lack of coordination with the Afghan government ministries meant US taxpayer dollars were used to build schools without teachers or books, medical clinics without doctors or medicine. Often the structures were so shoddily built, they started falling apart almost as soon as the Afghan and US dignitaries sped away from the ribbon cutting. "A lot of projects weren't that good," says Marinacci. Seldom was there any concern about the capacity of an impoverished provincial ministry to sustain a project. As international development organizations flocked to Afghanistan, even seemingly benign projects, such as drilling wells, became problematic when uncoordinated. One US Department of Agriculture official with long experience in Afghanistan, Gary Domian, says about the 2002–2004 era, "Projects had adverse effects. We punched in a lot of wells—may have impacted the shallow water table."[42] Every development group—NGOs, the military, UNAMA, everybody—drilled wells, thinking, what could be more benign? Give the poor Afghans a well, "bet it will make them love us." But without planning, suddenly good farming areas couldn't be used because the water table dropped. Villagers and neighboring farmers were at one another's throats about the new wells. "I had farmers coming up to me—'Please don't drill any wells. Please don't drill another one,'" says a PRT civilian who served in eastern Afghanistan.[43] "The only ones who benefit are the contractors who drill the wells. They get paid Lord-knows-how-much to drill those things."

Critics, especially in NGOs, began assailing the military–civilian model, slinging charges of military mission creep, self-defeating organizational tactics, and unsound development strategies. Though also accustomed to paying local power brokers, including warlords and the Taliban, to carry out their missions, the NGOs claimed the PRTs' flawed development fueled corruption and popular discontent.[44] The conflict between PRTs and NGOs often flared into public fights. In spring 2003, international NGOs vociferously protested the military's plan to use PRTs as the primary coordinators for provincial reconstruction, forcing the US armed forces to abandon the idea.[45]

As with the Chicklets, the PRTs commingled their development mission with intelligence work—sometimes done in conjunction with CIA agents. "In a sense, it's a bad deal," says one civilian PRT official. "Do you want to do development or military?"[46] While the PRTs had a functional need for field information so they could mediate between the local power brokers, intelligence-gathering sometimes took an outsized role in their work. Even the State Department came to criticize Washington's incessant calls for more intelligence reporting from the redevelopment teams.[47]

Funding in the early PRT days came from a variety of sources, including Department of Defense and USAID pots. Again, it was uncoordinated and idiosyncratic, depending on the personalities and the level of military–civilian cooperation and integration. One PRT civilian official who served in Afghanistan between 2004 and 2006 says spending was particularly loose in the first few years of the PRTs: "When I arrived in 2004, my boss said, 'Here's $3 million. Go do some good.' I said, 'What if I screw up?' He said, 'You can't—there's no rules.'"[48] The official went on to manage about $70 million in reconstruction funds over the next few years. "It was Aid 101—wells, schools, clinics," the official says. The funds were part of the $800 million a year USAID spent, on average, in Afghanistan from 2004 to 2006.[49] When President Karzai made opium-poppy reduction a priority, the PRTs began to focus on counternarcotic projects, which later came under the much-criticized Alternative Livelihoods program. Depending on the level of integration between the agencies and the military, the projects could reflect a coordinated approach to solving larger problems—or be pet projects that withered on the vine once the sponsoring staffer rotated out of the country.

Often the military would use DOD funds for smaller projects with short completion cycles (sometimes known as Quick Impact Projects or QIPs), while civilians would tap USAID for complex, long-term projects. In 2004, the Commander's Emergency Response Program, or CERP, began to be used in Afghanistan for projects big and small. CERP started in Iraq with seized Ba'athist Party cash. Devised to be a rapid-response funding mechanism for combat commanders and frontline development officials to do "small-scale, urgent humanitarian relief and reconstruction," CERP operated with little review or oversight above the brigade level. "The problem began in Iraq," says one congressional staffer who worked for the late representative John P. Murtha, chair of the powerful Defense Appropriations Subcommittee, who was critical of CERP.[50] "The money was from Saddam, and there really was a lot of cash in commanders' pockets. CERP started off as money for small projects—a few thousand dollars. But soon they [were] building hotels and doing million-dollar murals."

The pattern continued in Afghanistan, where CERP funds began to be tapped for mammoth projects, including roads and other large construction contracts. Hundreds of ill-conceived and poorly executed development projects were pushed through the now–congressionally funded CERP program with little thought about their cost or sustainability. In the larger scheme of things, the PRTs were spending pocket change in Afghanistan. The GAO found that out of the $4.39 billion in reconstruction aid spent by the United States in the 2002–2006 period, only $172 million (3.9 percent) was allocated to PRTs.[51] There were far bigger fish in the reconstruction sea.

Toward the end of every fiscal cycle, there was a land-rush of proposals for expensive, hurriedly organized projects designed to do little more than ensure that all the allocated funds were spent. The kudos and career advancement went to the development officers who spent their money—period. Oversight, continuity, and effectiveness were prioritized distinctly low. What few metrics were used to monitor the development projects enumerated input, with virtually no measure taken of the impact on the insurgency.[52] While the PRT civilian officials looked at metrics differently, they agreed on one thing: no one wanted to get into measuring the effect of development projects on security in Afghanistan. In spite of a dearth of evidence that aid helped quell insurgency, development careerists in Afghanistan considered the link between development and counterinsurgency to be a given.[53] But among that crowd, questions about metrics were often uncomfortable. "Metrics are hard," says the USAID staffer.[54] "AID measures outputs: 'twenty teachers trained; kilometers of roads built,' whatever. State measures outcomes, like 'education.' It's just hard to do linkages for counterinsurgency." So the agencies and the military bumbled on, merrily dispensing hundreds of millions of dollars of development money with little oversight and even less understanding of its effectiveness in quelling a simmering insurgency.

The result of massive piles of uncoordinated, poorly supervised development and logistics dollars dropped into a broken, war-ravaged system was corruption—endemic, omnipresent corruption. "The indiscriminate use of CERP creates corruption—I've read all the academic papers," says Simon Gardner. "There's a governor, subgovernor, police chiefs—everyone gets their share of the *baksheesh*. People think we're just propping up the sons of bitches whom the Taliban kicked out."[55]

*   *   *

Scene: Khost Province, Afghanistan, 2002. Simon Gardner and his civil-affairs team were indeed dealing with an immature theater of war. "We would just push money around," Gardner says, "build things, rent tractors, deliver humanitarian aid." And unload stuff. Perhaps thinking Khost Province was an emerging DIY market, The Home Depot® donated planeloads of lumber, hammers, and wheelbarrows. But the lumber arrived loose in the plane, so in the middle of the night in the middle of a war zone, soldiers using night-vision goggles unloaded stacks of lumber by hand. Later they found a lumberyard two miles down the road that could provide the lumber, and an enterprising Pakistani company to package up "village kits" for distribution. The kits included a variety of tools, construction materials, cooking oil, and tons of grain, including bagged wheat that US planes had airdropped onto the Khost airfield, a long, dirt, Soviet-built runway. Like generals fighting the previous war, the military planners had organized for the last major humanitarian airdrop, which was in the Balkans, where the dropped bags were designed to split open on impact to prevent hoarding. But when the bags began to split open on the Afghan runway, Simon Gardner knew they had a problem: "We had thirty-two tons of wheat in piles on a dirt runway. The air force guys were not happy. We had to hire a hundred locals and a dump truck to shovel it up. When spring came, the runway was green from the sprouting wheat."[56]

Chapter 3

Making Some Arrangements
The United States, Opium, and the Afghans

AN INTERNATIONAL NARCOTICS EXPERT, Rensselaer Lee, told the Senate Judiciary Committee in May 2003 that the Bush administration was using opium to recruit allies against the Taliban and al Qaeda. As Lee delicately put it, "To build these alliances, unfortunately, we've had to make some arrangements, compromises with people who frankly may have some history of involvement with the drug trade and may be even currently protecting the drug trade."[1] Lee was referring to the cynical agreements the CIA and special ops teams made with Afghan warlords and drug barons during the invasion in 2001, when the Americans agreed to let the warlords restart the opium trade the Taliban had banned the prior year.[2] These were decisions made by high-level Bush administration officials who wanted to wage war on the cheap. Though Defense Secretary Donald Rumsfeld often responded to questions about counternarcotics policies with a snippy, "We don't do drugs" response, he and other American officials were happy to deal with those who did.[3] Afghan expert Barnett Rubin wrote, "When he visits Afghanistan, Defense Secretary Donald Rumsfeld meets military commanders whom Afghans know as the godfathers of drug trafficking. The message has been clear: help fight the Taliban and no one will interfere with your trafficking."[4]

From the beginning of the post-9/11 invasion, US officials colluded with the Afghan drug trade. Though almost two dozen major Afghan heroin labs—some the size of small towns—were on the US list of potential Afghan bombing targets, the Pentagon and the White House refused to order them attacked. The Pentagon's rules of engagement tacitly encouraged American commanders to ignore drug shipments, particularly if they belonged to a powerful warlord the United States wanted to keep happy.[5] American troops were ordered to ignore heroin and opium even if they stumbled onto them. Rensselaer Lee, now senior fellow of the Foreign Policy Institute, told me of marines on patrol delicately stepping through an opium-poppy field to avoid damaging even one of the flowers.[6]

US counternarcotics officials, concerned about the immense postinvasion increase in poppy cultivation, frantically tried to convince the White House and the Pentagon to curb the burgeoning poppy crop with aerial spraying.[7] But their entreaties went nowhere. Instead of aerial spraying, haphazard (and extremely expensive) USAID-financed programs to eradicate poppies with old tractors and Afghan laborers wielding mulberry switches barely made a dent in the record crops. The opium-trading warlords quickly figured out how to use the US-backed Afghan government to their advantage. Trading on their American connections, the warlords took positions of power in the new Karzai government, laying the foundation for the corrupt nexus between drugs and political power that soon pervaded Afghanistan.[8]

Using opium and heroin as a political tool was certainly not a new tactic for the US government.[9] "We've consistently made alliances for larger strategic reasons with warlords who grow opium," Lee says. *Parapolitics* is the term political scientists now call the naughty things governments do in the shadows.[10] In World War II, federal officials released mobster Lucky Luciano in exchange for his southern Italian Mafia brethren's help with the allied invasion of Sicily. "The US policy since the beginning of the Cold War has been to make agreements with criminals all over the world," Lee says. "These are not people you'd invite home to dinner." The CIA's alliances with Golden Triangle drug lords helped make southeast Asia the illicit drug capital of the world—until the US moved on to Afghanistan, where American officials began doing deals with Afghan opium lords in the 1970s. "Agreements with drug traffickers: that's the name of the game in Afghanistan since the Russians were there," Lee says.

While Afghan farmers have cultivated opium poppies for millennia, the Soviet war transformed the devastated agricultural areas into a global powerhouse of opium production. Opium poppy was a perfect crop for impoverished, drought-stricken Afghanistan. Like the Afghans, poppy is tough and resilient. When the farmer scrapes the opium resin from the poppy bulb and processes it into gum, the product brings in anywhere from five to twenty-five times as much as wheat. The gum stores for years without refrigeration or much fuss. And there is a ready market for the product, run by traders who offer generous credit terms. Throughout the Soviet war, the US government tolerated the *mujahideen* opium dealers.[11] To name just one example, Younus Khalis, the Tora Bora double-dealer, was a major heroin dealer in Nangarhar Province. Reflecting the American government's acceptance of useful drug lords, a former US official said, "Khalis was a drug dealer and a thief. He was also an effective fighter."[12]

It wasn't until the Soviets were withdrawing in 1987 that USAID in Pakistan finally initiated some counternarcotics projects. The agency's Alternative Livelihoods programs included new crops, tools, loans, and cash-for-work subsidies. But when the Soviets left in 1989, political support in Washington for Afghanistan evaporated. As US military and aid funds plummeted, the Afghan opium trade took off. There weren't many alternatives. In 1989 and 1990, Younus Khalis's stomping ground of Nangarhar Province alone produced 355 tons of opium.[13] Nangarhar Province continued to be a major poppy-growing area—indirectly helped by US aid. Barnett Rubin quoted a reporter who wrote in 1992, "For miles around Jalalabhad, 80 percent of the arable land produces nothing but poppies, UN officials say. And the farmers like it that way. Today opium brings the farmer ten times more money than wheat—and there is plenty of cheap bread for sale in town, thanks to the flow of free flour [from USAID]."[14] Both the Bush and Clinton administrations continued to cut funding through the 1990s—with Clinton reportedly zeroing the USAID budget for Afghanistan in 1993.[15] As the Afghan civil war combusted in the nineties, poppy was the go-to crop; opium, Afghanistan's main industry. In 1997, Afghanistan passed Burma as the world's top opium producer with 2,804 metric tons. Production soared in 1999 to 4,581 metric tons—75 percent of the world's total. The Taliban controlled 97 percent of the 90,983 hectares planted in opium poppy.[16]

In the late 1990s the Taliban began discussions with the international community, offering to eradicate opium poppy in exchange for aid, official recognition, and the lifting of UN sanctions. The Taliban had also reportedly warehoused enormous stockpiles of opium, so stood to incrementally increase their stash's value. For whatever reasons, Mullah Omar in July 2000 banned poppy production, and the following year, Afghanistan's opium production plunged 98 percent to seventy-four metric tons.[17] Deprived of their only cash crop, Afghan poppy farmers in the Pashtun opium belt of the south and east faced widespread hunger and economic hardship. Farmers began grumbling against the Taliban. With their great money machine stopped, the Afghan drug kings were livid—an anger that the CIA and US Special Forces exploited after 9/11 to make their diabolical deals. Soon after the United States invaded, the Taliban reversed its poppy ban, saying cultivation was permitted "for medicinal reasons."[18] Lee says, "Then the Taliban turned to the [United States] for aid to keep the lid on opium, but that didn't work out. We're still doing deals with drug traffickers. It's just the way the politics and resources are configured in that country. It's just been a history of failure so far—one of the great tragedies of modern times."

Looking for a quick solution, US policymakers ended up creating a grotesque long-term problem. "What happened is we always took a short-sighted strategic view of this," Lee says. "You end up with a country awash in opium and heroin. When you have a country awash in opium and heroin, it gives the satraps, chieftains, warlords, whatever, all the power. In the short run, you can form alliances with the drug lords to defeat your enemy—the Russians, the Taliban—but in the long run, you are going to finance the Taliban. That's an invitation to political suicide. You can't build a country on opium."

From its 2001 nadir of 185 tons after the Taliban banned poppy planting, opium production soared to 3,400 tons the year after the US invasion. By 2003, opium production was a $2.3 billion industry, roughly half of Afghanistan's gross domestic product.[19] Opium production doubled again each of the following two years. US officials were afraid of alienating the ostensibly Taliban-fighting drug lords, who might turn on the United States if their fiefdoms were disturbed. With Iraq preeminent, the United States simply didn't have the troops to deal with messy counternarcotics problems. By 2004, more than a third of one million acres in every one of Afghanistan's provinces were planted in poppies, generating 87 percent of the world's opium.[20] In 2006, Afghanistan's opium harvest was the largest any country has ever produced, and the harvest increased another 17 percent the next year.[21] Referencing the gargantuan harvests of 2007–2009 that totaled between 6,900 and 8,200 metric tons, Rensselaer Lee says, "Now it's almost too big; how do you tackle a monster this size?"

*   *   *

As the corrupt US-supported drug lords (*née* government officials) began wrapping themselves in a cloak of government legitimacy, narcotics production accelerated. Afghanistan was sucked into a vortex of criminality, government corruption, failed international aid efforts, and insurgency.[22] The endemic corruption extended to the top of the government, with the *Times* reporting that "narco-kleptocracy has extended its grip around President Karzai, a figure regarded by some as increasingly isolated by a cadre of corrupt officials."[23] Thomas Schweich, Washington's principal deputy assistant secretary for international narcotics, stated that the Afghan "drug trade is causing tremendous amounts of political corruption."[24] Schweich wrote of an entire panoply of Afghan government officials being in on the narco-take: hundreds of police chiefs, judges, and senior government officials, including twenty particularly dirty high government officials protected by President Hamid Karzai, who instructed his attorney general to not prosecute any of them "for political reasons."[25] Journalist Eric Margolis plainly stated in Pakistan's *Dawn* newspaper, "Drug money has become the fuel on which Afghanistan now runs. America's Drug Enforcement Agency has been ordered to shut its eyes and freeze activities in Afghanistan and Pakistan so as not to interfere with the drug business of Washington's local allies."[26]

At the top of the heap was Ahmed Wali Karzai, President Hamid Karzai's half brother and head of the Kandahar Provincial Council; he reported to drug traffickers, who allegedly bribed him to grease the skids for them.[27] A long list of Afghan government officials were implicated in the drug industry, including General Azzam, chief of staff to the minister of the interior, who was responsible for national security and, according to the *Times*, "remains the worst offender" for drug-related corruption. "Everyone in the Ministry of Interior is corrupt," one disgruntled Afghan general told the *Times*. "They wouldn't sleep with their wives without wanting a backhander first."[28]

One long-time opium kingpin, Sher Muhammad Akhundzada, served as governor of Helmand Province in 2004–2005, when poppy production was at intoxicating levels—despite the $18 million USAID cash-for-work counternarcotics program run by Chemonics International, USAID's largest "implementing partner."[29] In his book *Opium Season*, the Chemonics cash-for-work deputy director, Joel Hafvenstein, called Sher Muhammad Akhundzada "the indispensible warlord," one of many drug kings whom the United States allowed to keep their rackets as long as long as they maintained a semblance of order.[30] Helmand's high government officials and police commanders, primarily drug traffickers, were self-protected from the poppy eradication—their fields left unscathed as the government counternarcotics teams plowed under their neighbors' poppy.

In June 2004, Afghan and US counternarcotics agents raided Governor Sher Muhammad Akhundzada's mansion. Inside they bagged the largest cache of opium ever found in Afghanistan: nine metric tons. The governor blithely explained he had seized the opium from drug traffickers and was just storing it until he could dispose of it properly.[31] After a profitable turn as governor, harvesting both opium and US counternarcotics money, Akhundzada went on to serve in parliament.[32]

Drug smuggling was another profitable business. One border police commander in eastern Afghanistan was reportedly clearing $400,000 a month from heroin smuggling. Police near Kabul stopped a border police car that was found to be carrying almost 125 kilos of heroin worth nearly $300,000. The five men inside were four policemen and the secretary of the Nangarhar Province border police commander, Hajji Zahir, who was questioned and released—though he did lose his job.[33] All the potential dough made government positions expensive: Within a few years of the US invasion, it cost $300,000 in bribes to buy a powerful position in an opium province. Even a detective needed to pay $10,000.[34]

The warlords also learned there were alternative ways to make money from opium: counternarcotics and development funds. The druglord Akhundzada family had already figured out how to milk the international counternarcotics teat. In 1989, the US embassy in Islamabad offered Sher Muhammad's uncle, Nasim Akhundzada, $2 million to reduce poppy production, which, surprisingly, he did. The following year, another of the US-supported mujahideen, Gulbuddin Hekmatyar, allegedly ordered Akhundzada's assassination so the drug trade could proceed unimpeded. When Sher Muhammad Akhundzada was governor in 2002, he slashed poppy production in half, anticipating the money to be had from a British program that paid farmers to destroy poppy in the field (which, naturally, created a perverse incentive to plant poppy). When fraud and underfunding closed the British program, Akhundzada once again encouraged unfettered poppy production. The result was the record 2004 harvest that precipitated the US-funded Chemonics cash-for-work project.[35]

*　　*　　*

The bumper poppy crops allowed the Taliban and the US-allied drug lords to profit from sky-high opium prices, which attracted heroin labs from Pakistan to the poppy-growing regions, resulting in even higher profits.[36] An avalanche of Afghan heroin descended on Europe and the United States, the profits helping to finance the reviving insurgency.[37] By the summer of 2004, Foreign Minister Abdullah Abdullah warned journalist Peter Bergen that Afghan drug cartels and vicious opium lords were "the biggest danger and threat to stability."[38]

"Around 2004 and 2005, we began to tell the military, 'Hey, the Taliban is coming back,'" says USAID official Michelle Parker, who was part of the Nangarhar Provincial Reconstruction Team.[39] "We'd brief the general, but the military didn't want to hear it." Part of the US response was to throw money at problems, which often only exacerbated them. The Nangarhar counternar-cotics program was a case in point. After taking power, President Hamid Karzai had appointed Hazrat Ali, the duplicitous warlord of Tora Bora infamy, as the police chief of Nangarhar Province, which had one of country's highest rates of poppy production. Ali had used his opium profits to arm six thousand militia and install himself as security chief. In the early 1990s, Ali used his position as head of the Jalalabad airport to grift the weekly flights of opium to the Gulf States.[40] When USAID began implementing a $70.1 million Alternative Livelihoods plan in 2004, Hazrat Ali saw a pile of development money. Ali ordered his policemen to jail poppy farmers until they agreed to allow their fields to be plowed under. When the tines stopped turning, there was a 96 percent drop in poppy cultivation.[41] "Hazrat Ali is not a good guy—no one is," says Michelle Parker, who ran the USAID program. "They've been at war for thirty years. There are no angels."[42]

The following year, analysts reported precipitous drops in Nangarhar household incomes. In spite of a cash-for-work project run by the USAID-contracted Development Alternatives, impoverished Nangarhari farmers were forced to sell their cattle, mortgage their farms, and migrate for work. In onerous situations, they had to surrender their daughters as wives to opium lords to settle debts. With narcotics forming such a large part of the economy, even licit businesses suffered from eradication.[43] Reports of corruption related to the Nangarhar counternarcotics program soon followed, along with an accompanying increase in insurgent attacks. Financed with drug profits and fired by widespread hostility toward corrupt governance and failed development, the Afghan insurgency erupted in 2005 to its most dangerous levels since the invasion.[44] In embattled Khost Province, a US officer told me that many in the intelligence community thought the insurgency exploded precisely because the United States reneged on its promise to the Afghan drug lords that they could deal narcotics.[45]

As opium production climbed another 15 percent in 2007, Washington began to rattle about counternarcotics misadministration in Afghanistan. In a joint statement following the release of the Afghan strategy document, the senior-ranking Democrat and Republican members of the House Committee on Foreign Affairs, Representatives Tom Lantos and Ileana Ros-Lehtinen, complained that "Afghanistan is approaching a crisis point, and that immediate action is required to eliminate the threat of drug kingpins and cartels allied with terrorists so we can reverse the country's steady slide into a potential failed narco-state."[46] When presidents George Bush and Hamid Karzai met at Camp

David in August 2007, they spent "more than a fair amount of time" talking about narcotics. During the press conference, Karzai acknowledged "the problem of poppies and narcotics in Afghanistan" but emphasized the need for "time" and foreign assistance. Lots of time and lots of foreign assistance.

In 2007, the United States revised its counternarcotics strategy to target Helmand Province, where approximately half of Afghanistan's narcotics production occurred. Sources estimated half of Helmand farmers began cultivating poppy after the failed Chemonics cash-for-work program began in 2004. Ever hopeful that more money would turn the battle, the Bush administration announced plans to allocate about $270 million in aid to the province—making Helmand (if it were a country) the fifth-largest recipient of US development aid in the world.[47] It was totally counterproductive. There was no reduction in the insurgency. There was no relationship of development funding and stability. As the poorly conceived and badly managed counternarcotics programs pulsed billions into the southern opium-producing heartland, the resurgent Taliban took over governance in major parts of the region. In some places, poppy flowers bloomed to the horizon.[48]

There was a grand collusion between the insurgents and Afghan government authorities. Journalist Gretchen Peters wrote, "But it's a pattern repeated over and over. Across Afghanistan, traditional enemies are working together wherever there's a chance to make money. And instability is vital for the drug business, creating a powerful disincentive for Afghan government officials to build a more peaceful country."[49] Reflecting the convoluted logic of Afghan politics, Peters contended that Karzai was protecting his drug-dealing cronies' partnerships with insurgents to counterbalance Pakistan's relationship with the opium-financed Taliban.

With US and Afghan government facilitation, the opium trade became a major source of insurgent funding through *ushr* taxes on farmers, partnerships with morphine and heroin labs, and running protection for smuggling convoys. There were wild variations in the estimates of the drug money going to the insurgents—anywhere from $70 million to $500 million annually.[50] To add to the problem, the Taliban also discovered development and counternarcotics money as a source of funding. When Joel Hafvenstein rolled away from one cash-for-work payday dispensing tens of thousands of dollars in a Helmand village, his Afghan colleague remarked, "You know, I think half of the people we paid today were Taliban."[51] By the summer of 2005, the now–plentifully financed insurgency had flared to its most dangerous levels since the invasion.[52]

Faced with the hot insurgency, the commander of the eastern front, General Benjamin Freakley, did an about-face on counternarcotics, shutting down all of the Nangarhar antidrug operations, as "they were an unnecessary obstacle to his military operations."[53] With the United States still embracing its warlord strategy, the military commanders couldn't afford to alienate their drug lord allies.[54] Thomas Schweich wrote of meeting President Karzai, who brightened when the US official laid out the new counternarcotics incentives but became "sullen and unresponsive" when the discussion turned to eradication and arresting high-level traffickers.[55]

The US counternarcotics development projects commonly had unintended results. Afghanistan's first vice president, Ahmad Zia Massoud, railed about counterproductive development in a 2007 editorial in London's *Sunday Telegraph*: "Millions of pounds have been committed in provinces including Helmand Province for irrigation projects and road building to help farmers get their produce to market. But for now this has simply made it easier for them to get their opium to market."[56]

The international development players often dictated the projects to the Afghans with little consultation or understanding of the situation on the ground. Chemonics's cash-for-work project in Helmand was typical: the goal of paying for 2.5 million work days was a number plucked out of the blue in Washington, yet became the unattainable metric out in unstable Helmand, where the torrent of undersupervised money ultimately helped inflame the insurgency.[57]

With short rotations, ill-considered plans, and woefully lacking oversight, it was inevitable that corruption and development would become conjoined. Afghan government officials were facile at directing the subcontracts to unscrupulous cohorts, who were sometimes in cahoots with the insurgents. In one case, an innovative Afghan official figured out how to better use the cash-for-work program: he used it to pay for a dozen laborers to work in his poppy fields.[58] Even when the money wasn't being abused, Chemonics's cash-for-work was often just stopgap employment until it was time for the opium harvest, negating the purpose of hiring farmers who had stopped poppy cultivation. Come harvest time, even the Afghan police abandoned the Chemonics project to help gather opium resin.[59]

Tales of wildly conceived and poorly administered projects were rife. In some cases, the projects destabilized Afghan society. As the international development machine rolled into Afghanistan, the agencies vacuumed up the best and the brightest Afghans to work as factotums. Ministries and institutions were drained of their best people as Afghan doctors and educated government officials left to earn ten times their Afghan salaries as drivers and interpreters for international aid organizations. Senior Afghan government officials made $150 per month; NGO drivers, $1,000 a month.[60] For many educated Afghans, the choice was easy.

In the rural areas, development money could devastate traditional culture. The Helmand project paid farmers to clean silt and muck out of the canals, a task the Afghans had traditionally done with *hashar*, the volunteer labor system farmers used to maintain infrastructure such as canals and roads with communal work parties a few days a year—often accompanied by festivities as the region's people gathered together for shared work.[61] But foreign aid undermined those patterns. One USDA official on an eastern Afghanistan Provincial Reconstruction Team fumed to me, "The Afghans have been keeping their canals open for centuries. Now they won't do it unless we pay them."[62]

None of the problems fazed the seasoned development advisers. One veteran development official said, "Guys, I've worked in international development for forty long years, and I tell you: This business is one failure after another. You get an idea, you take a swing at it, you hope it'll work . . . and it almost never does."[63] And that was the case with the $18 million Chemonics cash-for-work Helmand Province project, which was canceled after the Taliban killed eleven Afghans associated with the project. Soon after the cancellation of the Helmand project, Chemonics inked a USAID contract for a four-year, $119 million Alternative Livelihoods project in southern Afghanistan, where the international development professionals dispensed an array of aid goodies, including new high-value crops, loans, village electricity, and cash-for-work gigs.[64] It was a cynical triumph of business-as-usual over experience.

Helmand wasn't a unique example of throwing good money after bad. With the United States coddling corrupt Afghan drug lords with an ineffective eradication policy, a cornucopia of counternarcotics money and toothless enforcement of corruption and narcotics laws, the US policy was all carrot and no stick.[65] As the Afghans tracked the stupendous sums the international community trumpeted about investing in Afghanistan against the actual impacts in their villages, they found all too often there was little to show for the money. As the Afghans' hopes curdled into bitterness, frustrations over corruption, rising violence, and flawed programs contributed to the rising insurgency.[66]

The US strategy in Afghanistan relied on cozy connections with Afghan drug lords. The policies continued the Quiet American–style blend of ruthlessness and naïveté that has characterized so many of America's post–World War II forays into the world. Focused on short-term outcomes, arrogant US officials trusted the power of American dollars and expertise to magically fix security issues. Instead of a cheap, expeditious remedy, the American government's confused Afghan drug trade policy contributed to the intertwined, codependent culture of corruption, aid, and militarism that fueled the enduring war.

*   *   *

Scene: Helmand Province, southern Afghanistan. The massive Kajaki Dam was the centerpiece of the 1950s US development assistance to Afghanistan, part of President Harry Truman's Point IV program to battle Communism with international development. Echoing the ongoing American belief that economic aid would eventually engender docile capitalists, Cold Warrior Walt W. Rostow promised the CIA in 1954 that development would nurture "an environment in which societies which directly or indirectly menace ours will not evolve."[67] *Built by Morrison Knudsen, the American firm that engineered the Hoover Dam, the Kajaki Dam stood 320 feet high and extended almost 900 feet long, holding back almost one million acre-feet of water to irrigate about 650,000 acres of otherwise arid desert. A vast concrete symbol of technological power wedged into the hills about one hundred miles from Kandahar, the dam was designed to make the Helmand Valley the breadbasket and cotton bowl of Afghanistan. The Kajaki was also the lodestone of the Helmand–Arghandab Valley Authority (HAVA), a US scheme to implant a comprehensive version of the Tennessee Valley Authority into central Asia. Headquartered in the brand-new planned city of Lashgar Gah, which the American engineers and their families dubbed "Little America," HAVA oversaw an immense complex of dams, drainage works, and three hundred miles of canals designed to bring irrigation and electricity to southern Afghanistan. Canals pulsed water across the desert to two islands of reclaimed land, called Marja and Nad-i-Ali, where the Afghan monarchy resettled colonies of Pashtuns displaced by the construction. Green began to tint the brown desert.*

But Afghanistan wasn't America. Over the next fifteen years, the HAVA project devoured more than $80 million of US Export-Import Bank loans, consuming a fifth of Afghanistan's total governmental expenditures through the 1950s and into the 1960s. The salaries of the Morrison Knudsen technicians and consultants alone cost the equivalent of Afghanistan's total yearly exports. The monarchy and Morrison Knudsen failed to address the issue of land titles in most of the irrigated areas, forcing most Afghan farmers to work as tenants. Ecological problems quickly became apparent. As the waterways rapidly clogged, the HAVA engineers learned *that dam-caused siltation was more pronounced outside of the temperate zone. Never adequately studied prior to construction, soils became waterlogged and weed-choked as the reservoirs raised the water tables. After a few years of irrigation-spiked bumper crops, soluble salts and alkalis leached to the topsoil, creating deserts. Long-distance canals carried the salt and gypsum downstream, destroying vineyards and orchards. British adventurer Eric Newby drove through Afghanistan in 1956, when he wrote of an elderly Afghan's lament about the Kajaki Dam, "We asked him about the dam, that vast scheme of which so much vague ill had been spoken along the way. 'It is all salt,' he moaned, 'the land below the American dam. They did not trouble to find out and now the people will eat* namak *(salt) forever.'"*[68]

Despite the problems, the United States and Afghanistan kept Kajaki and its sister dams and canals going through the 1960s and 1970s, making Helmand Afghanistan's most productive region. In 1975, USAID commissioned two 16.5-megawatt generators to bring hydroelectric power to Kandahar city. But when the Soviets invaded in 1979, the United States pulled out of Helmand. As anarchy raged through the region in the 1980s and 1990s, poppies began to replace grains and cotton. The grandiose American plan to green the desert instead watered an opium economy. The wheat-green and cotton-white island of Marja became multicolored with pink, crimson, and white poppy flowers.

When the United States began to bomb after 9/11, the Kajaki generating plant was one of the first targets, despite UN concerns that bombing could cause "a disaster of tremendous proportions."[69] *The United States began rebuilding the structure almost immediately. It was the eternal logic of Washington: build it, blow it up, and then pay to rebuild it again. The USAID-contracted company, the Louis Berger Group, got one unit sporadically going and began an expensive rehab project on a second generator, with plans for a new Chinese turbine to be installed in 2007. But the enemy had a vote. By the fall of 2006, the resurgent Taliban targeted the Kajaki Dam, preventing repairs, installation of the new turbine, and even resupply of the besieged work crews. NATO eventually launched Operation Kryptonite in February 2008 to drive the Taliban away, but sustained attacks continued to isolate the facility.*[70] *It took four thousand Coalition troops with full air support to escort the new turbine to the plant in August 2008, but six months later the turbine was not yet unpacked. To install the turbine, the engineers needed nine hundred tons of cement, which couldn't be delivered because of the insecurity.*[71]

Watered by Kajaki irrigation, Marja became a thriving center of Taliban-controlled poppy cultivation. Its dusty little bazaar was awash with opium, making Marja a regional drug-smuggling center.[72] *Marja and Nad-i-Ali, the two*

oases the Americans had created in the 1950s, had become global opium centers.[73]
*One report indicated 10 percent of the world's illegal opium came from these two
small districts, which produced more opium than Laos, Colombia, and Mexico
combined.*[74] *In March 2009, seven hundred NATO and Afghan army troops
attacked Marja, but after the Coalition troops withdrew, the Taliban returned in
force almost immediately. On May 19, 2009, US and Afghan forces launched
another attack on Marja, seizing one hundred tons of drugs and chemicals, along
with a large cache of weapons, but left a portion of the Marja bazaar untouched.
After the withdrawal, the Taliban were soon back in force. By early 2010, the US
command announced plans to take Marja with a giant offensive of marines and
Afghan government officials. This time for sure.*

*When the offensive launched on February 13, 2010, the Coalition forces met
stiff resistance.*[75] *The Taliban used the American-engineered canals for cover to
fire on the troops, a kinetic rebuttal to Walt Rostow's unproved thesis that development yielded long-term stability.*[76] *After a five-day firefight, the Taliban fighters
put down their weapons to harvest the poppy crop. With about two-thirds of
Marja's population dependent on the opium trade for their livelihoods, US commanders ordered the Coalition troops to turn a blind eye on the poppy fields to
avoid a humanitarian and public-relations crisis. Not long after the harvest, the
Taliban returned to the battle. The US command's vaunted "government in a box"
tactic, which involved helicoptering in reluctant Afghan government officials to
administrate the Taliban stronghold, came to little, as most of the Afghan officials
hunkered down twenty miles away in the relative safety of Lashkar Gah. The Taliban soon reestablished their control. In late May, General Stanley McChrystal,
the US and NATO commander in Afghanistan, told officers and officials of a
growing perception that Marja was "a bleeding ulcer."*[77]

Chapter 4

Loss of Focus

PRESIDENT GEORGE W. BUSH PLUMMETED toward the aircraft carrier USS *Abraham Lincoln*, which sported a giant "Mission Accomplished" banner as it sailed in circles near San Diego on May 1, 2003. A few hours after the Lockheed S-3 Viking jet hauling the president had jerked to an arrested landing, Bush stood in front of the stage-managed banner to proclaim to the assembled sailors and press: "Major combat operations in Iraq have ended. In the battle of Iraq, the United States and our allies have prevailed. And now our coalition is engaged in securing and reconstructing that country."[1] The story dominated the airwaves and press the next day.

A few hours earlier in Kabul, at the scruffy presidential palace, Secretary of Defense Donald Rumsfeld had stepped to a podium to likewise proclaim that major combat in Afghanistan had ended. With President Karzai at his side, Rumsfeld told reporters that Bush, Karzai, and US Central Command Chief Tommy Franks had "concluded we're at a point where we clearly have moved from major combat activity to a period of stability and stabilization and reconstruction activities. The bulk of this country today is permissive, it's secure." But instead of front-page news, the Afghanistan story was buried on page 16 of the *Washington Post*, barely rating a mention on CNN.[2] Like so much of the war in Afghanistan, it was the side story, the second theater.

And of course, Bush and Rumsfeld were both wrong. Soon after Bush's tailhook landing, a vicious guerrilla war broke out in Iraq that stymied the United States for years. The vast majority of military and civilian casualties in Iraq occurred after Bush's "Mission Accomplished" moment.[3] In Afghanistan, Rumsfeld was downplaying the coordinated jihadi attacks that erupted across the east and south beginning in the summer of 2002.[4] Instead of the small-scale mop-up combat operations that Rumsfeld envisioned, the US commanders were seeing the start of the Taliban-led insurgency. The commanders should have known.

Afghan interior minister Ali Jalali had warned the Americans about the latent threat the Taliban presented, quoting a seventeenth-century Pashtun warrior: "When you encounter a stronger enemy force, avoid decisive engagement and swiftly withdraw only to hit back where the enemy is vulnerable. By this you gain sustainability and the ability to fight a long war of attrition."[5]

The Americans were well aware of the Afghans' strategy of exhaustion. During the Soviet war, CIA analysts had provided intelligence about Soviet stress points to the *mujahideen*, who used it to attack convoys and other vulnerable points. The relentless attacks caused the Soviets to withdraw into fortified cantonments, increase the armor on their vehicles, and rely on air power, all serving to isolate and alienate them from the Afghan population. Al Qaeda likewise fought the West with four tactics: provocation, intimidation, protraction, and exhaustion.[6] Osama bin Laden himself stated in 2004: "All that we have mentioned has made it easy to provoke and bait this [US] administration. All we have to do is send two [mujahideen] to the furthest point east to raise a cloth on which is written al-Qaeda, in order to make the [US] generals race there to cause America to suffer human, economic, and political losses without achieving for it anything of note . . . so we are continuing this policy of bleeding America to the point of bankruptcy."[7] Like rebels waging asymmetrical war from time immemorial, the Islamic radical fighters counted on the imperialists' flailing (and expensive) military reactions to estrange the local population and bond them to their cause. It's Insurgency 101, a subject the West has been failing for decades.

When the Afghanistan insurgency began to take off in mid-2002, the Western forces were ill-prepared.[8] There weren't enough US and ISAF soldiers to prevail over a determined adversary that was reorganizing for a long fight. Nor were the US forces in Afghanistan going to get much help—Iraq was dominating the resources.[9] Even without Iraq sucking up soldiers and resources, US planning and execution were problematic. There was no off-the-shelf battle plan for Afghanistan. Intelligence was woefully weak. Few in the US military, including those soon to be deployed in the country, knew anything about the complex central Asian land. Bush's cabinet may not have been much better. Journalist Bob Woodward described one pre–Iraq invasion cabinet-level meeting with then national security adviser Condoleezza Rice: "At some point, someone said this was not likely to be like the Balkans, where ethnic hatreds had occupied the Clinton administration for almost eight years. 'We're going to wish this was the Balkans,' Rice said, the problems of Afghanistan and the surrounding regions were so complicated."[10]

The Bush administration's failure to focus on Afghanistan was a tragic shortfall, as many analysts thought the US-led Coalition had a moment of reprise after the Taliban was routed—the "golden hour of opportunity," in the phrase of policymakers and pundits. The "golden hour" advocates contended that the Afghan population—even in the Pashtun south and east—might have been persuaded to come over to the side of the Coalition's client Afghan government after the shooting stopped.[11] Major General Franklin Hagenbeck, a top Coalition commander, said that his early intelligence work among the Afghans in spring 2002 indicated they might turn against the surviving al Qaeda fighters who were hiding amongst them. He said, "there was an opportunity, a fleeting opportunity, where we could have killed them all."[12] According to Hagenbeck, their own culture of vengeance led the Afghans to understand the Americans' desire for blood retribution. "Their response to-a-person, basically was, OK. You can do that. You can stay here. We will be neutral until you dishonor us, our families, or our tribes. Then we will be your enemies."[13] But soon after the invasion, culturally insensitive international military door-kicking policies soon began to turn the Pashtuns against the American-led Coalition forces and their client government.[14] One disillusioned Afghan deputy minister said, "We had such hopes in 2001 and 2002; we believed the Americans when they said we were going to have human rights and democracy. Now the people are hopeless."[15]

In an effort to stabilize the devastated country at least until the June 2002 *loya jirga* could decide a new Afghan government, the interim Coalition planning staff organized a military campaign in mid-2002 designed to pursue the enemy fighters while retaining the Afghans' support. The planners called the strategy *full spectrum operations*, which included offensive and defensive military actions as well as stabilization and development operations with units such as the Provincial Reconstruction Teams. The full-spectrum-operations concept was the first articulated plan since the US Central Command (CENTCOM) promulgated the seat-of-the-pants Operation Enduring Freedom invasion plan in November 2001. The full-spectrum plan was ambitious, organized by a drastically shorthanded Coalition command.[16]

In spring 2002, the distracted CENTCOM realized the Coalition needed a more robust command structure in Afghanistan to handle both military and political issues. The result was the Combined Joint Task Force (CJTF-180) that the Department of Defense formed in June 2002.[17] From Washington's perspective, Afghanistan was still a wham-bam war that was soon to be over. CJTF-180 commander Lieutenant General Dan K. "Bomber" McNeill said

Army Vice Chief of Staff General John Keane told him, "Don't you do anything that looks like permanence. We are in and out of there in a hurry."[18] Secretary of Defense Donald Rumsfeld continued to disparage nation building, the anathema of his "quickie war" concept.[19] As the golden hour dimmed, the senior US military and civilian officials still just wanted two things: kill or capture al Qaeda and Taliban personnel, and stand up the Afghan security forces. And the officials wanted it done with an informal force cap of only seven thousand US military personnel. As demands for Iraq grew, competing needs hobbled efforts in Afghanistan. It was the same across the board: US commanders and diplomats working to prevent an Afghan narco-state or civil war or Taliban takeover would request more forces, more resources, more development funds, whatever—and senior US officials with Baghdad on their minds would shoot down the requests.[20] With a constant shortage of combat arms soldiers in 2002, the US Army units could temporarily suppress the Afghan insurgents, but then would have to withdraw to their bases, allowing the jihadis to quickly return to their havens. "Mowing the grass," soldiers called it.

Even the headquarters staff was pared down and down. Then brigadier general Stanley McChrystal, the XVIII Airborne Corps chief of staff, recalled the pressure from the Pentagon to reduce the headquarters staff from the 800 called for by standard operating procedure down to 368—and few of those had any firsthand knowledge of Afghanistan, so planning was often conjectural. And the planners and other officers didn't know how long they'd be engaged with Afghanistan—Iraq was clearly imminent.[21]

The military leadership of the newly established CJTF-180 recognized the need to stand up an Afghan National Army (ANA) as well as the importance of nation-building operations. But the hearts-and-minds work was far more than mission creep—it was more like mission leap. With the new responsibilities, the military needed to jump from deposing a rogue regime that harbored international terrorists to undergirding the entire structure and acceptance of a yet-unformed Afghan government. And all this had to be done with a bare-bones staff.

On the civilian side, reconstruction and development efforts were likewise hampered by lack of qualified staff, inadequate resources, and competition with Iraq. In fiscal years 2002 and 2003, the United States obligated $1.4 billion and spent $900 million for nonsecurity assistance to Afghanistan. Of the $900 million that the US government spent, over 75 percent went to short-term humanitarian assistance, such as emergency food and shelter. Only about 20 percent went to long-term projects. USAID, as the primary providing agency for nonsecurity assistance, spent a total of $508 million. The Department of State spent $254 million, primarily on refugee and humanitarian assistance, and the Department of Defense spent $64 million, mainly on food assistance and quick-impact projects such as wells and school repairs.[22]

During fiscal years 2002 and 2003, funding for Afghanistan reconstruction projects was parsimonious compared to Iraq reconstruction support. The paltry $92 million that was allocated to USAID for Afghanistan reconstruction came in stutter steps, and a large chunk of these funds had to be used for emergency humanitarian aid. As a result, USAID was only able to initiate two major reconstruction projects by late 2002. A GAO report on Afghanistan reconstruction stated that the agency was able to implement programs much faster in Iraq. Within a month of Bush's victory flight, USAID had obligated $118 million for reconstruction activities in Iraq, and seven months later, USAID had already contracted $1.5 billion for Iraq reconstruction.[23]

Though Afghanistan aid was momentarily circumscribed, it didn't slow the development contractors down. Afghanistan scholar Barnett Rubin wrote, "Rather than delivering a coherent aid package to the new government, the aid bazaar opened with a rush of contractors and NGOs."[24] There was virtually no coordination among the Western donor countries or with the Afghan government—just a drive to spend money, fast.

One international development staffer recalled a Kabul meeting of USAID officials. The lead USAID official lauded one team that had managed to complete some particularly expensive, ineffective projects. "He shouted, 'Yeah! That's the way to do it! They spent all their funding! Yeah!'"[25] The "burn rate," they called it. It was all about gaming the budgeting process—spend the money to get more in the next budget cycle. There were virtually no metrics to measure the impact of the millions spent on stabilizing Afghanistan. The few measurements that were kept tracked input—number of trees planted, schools built, roads paved, wells dug, chickens distributed—but virtually no inquiry into the effect of the aid on quelling the growing insurgency. Indeed, development officials often got nervous when questions arose about oversight and sustainability. For instance, a follow-up question about how many of the thousands of seedling trees had survived brought blank stares. Or how many new schools had teachers? Or did the wells lower the water table? Or were the slapdash roads already impassable? It was all about input—spend the money. Do some good. Yeah!

National security pundit Anthony Cordesman wrote critically about development metrics: "This raises a critical failing in both Afghanistan and

Iraq: the almost total lack of honest and meaningful metrics and reporting by USAID, the Corps of Engineers, and similar actions by allied countries. Spending has never been a meaningful metric."[26] He lambasted the showpiece development projects—the Potemkin villages of the media age—that credulous press and VIPs were trotted out to view: "Competing showpiece and demonstration projects and aid efforts do not win hearts and minds; they lose them by telling those who are excluded that they lost something and someone else won." Cordesman railed at "the profiteering impact of wartime spending" and the lack of sustainability. He wrote, "the key test of both wartime aid and development is whether aid and development activity is actually funded, actually in progress, and actually succeeding in meeting key needs in ways that help a given area."

The dearth of central command and control, or even coordination, meant the thousands of military, civilian government, and NGO staffers were racing around doing sometimes-conflicting projects. It was personality-driven chaos. Neocon free-market doctrinaires with little understanding of the Afghan reality—"heroic amateurs" in diplomat James Dobbins's phrase—began to proffer grandiose ideas with a tropism toward expensive megadevelopment projects, such as cell service, national banking, international trade centers, and airports for virtually undeveloped Afghanistan, where subsistence farmers earned less than $400 a year.[27] Though 85 percent of the Afghan people were dependent on agriculture for their livelihoods, only about 5 percent of the annual reconstruction budget went to farming projects—and most of those were Alternative Livelihood projects designed to wean farmers in southern Afghanistan off poppy cultivation. There was a scandalous dearth of oversight. The few development metrics that did exist rewarded ill-considered, expensive projects over small, sustainable, Afghan-appropriate ones. Soon Afghanistan was rife with tales of waste and defective projects.

*   *   *

The launch of the Iraq War in March 2003 solidified Afghanistan's second-theater status. Within weeks of Rumsfeld's orchestrated May 1, 2003, announcement in Kabul that major combat activity was over, the bulk of CJTF-180's XVII Airborne Corps left Afghanistan. In replacement, a significantly smaller senior command under Major General John R. Vines took over the eleven thousand Coalition troops. Almost immediately, attacks against Coalition forces across the south and east spiked as the well-organized insurgent groups began to prove with lead and explosives that the war in Afghanistan was far from over. The US forces were handicapped. Vines told US Army historians that beginning in late 2002, CENTCOM was "under enormous pressure not to overcommit resources to Afghanistan, to make sure everything was available for Iraq."[28] Throughout the 2003 to 2005 period, troop levels in Afghanistan were about 15 to 20 percent of those in Iraq—not enough resources to suppress the growing insurgency.[29] When the Bush administration invaded Iraq in 2003, the US government slashed spending for Afghanistan, dropping it from $20 billion in 2002 to $14.7 billion in 2003, just as the insurgency was gathering momentum. In contrast, the government spent $53 billion in Iraq in 2003. From 2004 to 2006, the US government spent four times as much money in Iraq as in Afghanistan.[30] The Afghan insurgents were quick to note the lack of focus. "The Taliban were always in Afghanistan," Khalid Pushtun, an Afghan government spokesperson in President Hamid Karzai's Kandahar office, stated.[31] "They stayed in their houses, in their villages. They were just waiting for some kind of green light to start fighting the American and Afghan authorities." Attacks dramatically increased through the 2003 summer fighting season as the insurgents began to target Afghan civilians and military, as well as representatives of international agencies and NGOs.[32] Joanna Nathan of the International Crisis Group concluded, "The desire for a quick, cheap war followed by a quick, cheap peace has brought Afghanistan to the present, increasingly dangerous situation."[33]

With Iraq sucking up all the troops, there was little the undermanned US-led military could do in Afghanistan.[34] All told, there were only about thirty thousand total Coalition, ISAF, and half-baked Afghan troops available to fight the insurgency in 2003. It was a smattering of soldiers in a rugged, underdeveloped country the size of Texas. US battalions of eight hundred soldiers were trying to pacify regions of over twenty thousand square miles. By historic counterinsurgency standards, the thirty thousand soldiers trying to provide security to the approximately twenty-eight million Afghans yielded a laughably low troop density ratio—less than one soldier per thousand Afghans. Even drilling down to the population density subset of 6.5 million Afghans in the insurgency-plagued south and east, there were still only about two to three soldiers per thousand Afghans. In successful COIN operations such as British Malaya in the 1950s or the 1990s NATO campaign in Kosovo, the troop density ratio was over twenty soldiers per thousand inhabitants. In Iraq, the 150,000 Coalition troops constituted a troop density of six soldiers per thousand Iraqis—a tight-fisted ratio that was also to have an unfortunate outcome.[35] And with the Iraq War hogging the spotlight, there was another pernicious effect on the war in Afghanistan: now ambitious US civilian officials and military officers were anxious to quickly punch their tickets in backwater Afghanistan and move on to the bright lights of Baghdad, where their careers could really take off. By the fall of 2003, the under-resourced international forces were back on their heels, forcing the command under Lieutenant General David W. Barno to institute a counterinsurgency (COIN) strategy in Afghanistan.[36] The long war was on.

*   *   *

Scene: Tani District, Khost Province, 2009. Even the governor of Khost Province had traveled out to the inauguration of a US-funded dam project in Tani District, a volatile eastern Afghanistan region swarming with insurgents. The governor joined a slew of Afghan government dignitaries and American military officials to celebrate the completion of the dam. The Tani Dam was a big development deal, designed to improve irrigation and bond the local population to the Karzai government. Tight security surrounded the knot of Afghan government officials and high Coalition military officers standing on the new dam for the ribbon cutting. Directly behind the governor, an Afghan National Army (ANA) soldier stood guard, his automatic rifle at the ready as he scanned the nearby hills for insurgents.

Over on the bank, a crowd of US development officials and soldiers nervously watched the event. A civilian PRT development specialist remembers: "We were up on the bank, all the dignitaries were down on the dam, surrounded by ANA security. We were standing there, and bam! *We all started looking around, thinking it was an attack. Then we figured out it was an ANA guy who'd negligently discharged his rifle." The governor's guard had accidentally pulled his trigger, shooting himself in the foot.*

The ANA's lack of training and discipline was notorious among Americans out in the field. The ANA's propensity to accidentally discharge their weapons was cause for major concern. One day I was with a team of American soldiers out in a fortified district center, where a platoon of ANA were milling about with their weapons. "Waiting for night so they can start smoking hash," an American sergeant snorted. I was watching one ANA soldier twirl his handgun like a Western gunslinger. "Best keep something solid between you and them," the sergeant counseled.

After the accidental discharge at the dam ceremony, the hubbub died down as the dignitaries and their guards realized the shot wasn't the start of an attack.

"They started checking people out, seeing if there were ricochet wounds," the PRT specialist says. "They looked down and realized the bullet penetrated three inches into the concrete. Wow, that concrete was no good. If that concrete had been any good, someone would be dead."

Poor construction and oversight of US-funded development projects is a major problem in Afghanistan—military commanders state that bad development is bad counterinsurgency, as it drives the population to the Taliban. The lack of US quality control yields a harvest of lousy projects. Badly graded roads paved over deficient roadbeds soon crumble. USAID-funded schools and hospitals built without sufficient rebar and supports are so unsafe they have to be demolished. And dams built with cheap cement can collapse. A military engineer later told me the problem with the Tani Dam was substandard Pakistani cement. "Elephant Cement," he sneered. "They used Elephant Cement on that dam." He showed me an empty bag, emblazoned with the warning, "For Export Only. Not for Sale in Pakistan." He says, "Now, we see empty bags of this stuff around one of our construction sites, we shut it down." Too late for Tani Dam, though. "I wouldn't want to live downstream of that dam," one US hydrology specialist in Khost told me with a rueful laugh.

Chapter 5

All Together

The Culture of Corruption

PERCHED ABOVE KABUL'S POSH OLD Wazir Akbar Khan district, grand new "poppy houses" crowd the lanes of the Sherpur neighborhood. A nouveau riche enclave of the Afghan opium Mafia, Sherpur likewise serves as the redoubt of Afghan government officials who can somehow afford houses worth hundreds of thousands of dollars on annual salaries of hundreds of dollars. It is also the neighborhood where many international organizations and NGOs spend up to $20,000 a month to rent the ornate mansions. Afghans, citing an old proverb, describe well-paid international development consultants as "cows that drink their own milk."[1] Kabul locals derisively pronounce Sherpur as "Char-pur," wordplay for "City of Loot."[2] It's the place where everyone's in on the Afghan corruption game.

When the Taliban fell in 2001, Sherpur housed a community of people who had lived there for decades, hunkered in their modest adobe houses on the site of the nineteenth-century British cantonment with its poignant little cemetery of fallen foreigners. But less than two years later, the newly empowered warlords connected to President Hamid Karzai grabbed the land, which government bulldozers and one hundred armed men had scraped clean. "The machines pushed down the wall and a wardrobe fell on my little girl," said an Afghan army officer who made $80 a month. "Our holy Korans were buried under the earth. I have worked for the army for twenty-six years, but now the powerful people with guns have humiliated my family and destroyed our home."[3] Investigations by the United Nations and the Afghan Independent Human Rights Commission revealed that twenty-nine highly placed Afghan government officials, including six cabinet members led by Defense Minister Mohammad Qasim Fahim and Education Minister Yunis Qanooni, the Kabul mayor and police chief, the Central Bank governor, and two former militia commanders had colluded in the land grab. Eventually all but four of the

84

thirty-two cabinet members nabbed plots. Calling the officials "land Mafia," Miloon Kothari, the UN special rapporteur on housing and land rights, said a "culture of impunity" allowed powerful Afghans to destroy the homes and seize the land.[4]

In spite of calls for resignations and a disingenuous presidential commission to investigate the land grab, candy-colored "poppy palaces" soon began to sprout on the Sherpur's bomb-cratered, sewage-befouled lanes. Four- and five-story marble- and granite-clad grandiosities with floor-to-ceiling windows and gilded columns rose behind high walls. Faux Taras, Roman villas, and even a mock cruise ship sprang from the fertile imaginations of Pakistani architects catering to the Afghan narco-crowd. Such accoutrements as enormous chandeliers, swimming pools, massage showers, and nightclubs in the basement were de rigueur. "Narco-tecture," the international development consultants laughingly called the mansions—but still leased them from the government-official owners for tens of thousands a month.[5] Wild real estate inflation had begun almost as soon as the Taliban fled Kabul in late 2001, triggered by the avalanche of aid money and the international development consultants who skidded in behind it. A house in the old consulate neighborhood of Wazir Akbar Khan that rented for $200 a month in September 2001 cost $3,000 per month just half a year later.[6] Sleek multistory apartment and office buildings began to rise beside the dirt streets. Through the years, Sherpur mansions morphed even bigger: one Sherpur property dealer listed a forty-seven-room behemoth that leased for $47,000 a month.

The Sherpur pattern repeated across Afghanistan's provincial capitals, where warlord/government officials owned more than 70 percent of the homes rented to the international groups. As the money piled up, many of the landlords moved on to owning even more luxurious seaside digs on Dubai's palm-shaped manmade islands, such as Palm Jumeirah and Palm Jebel Ali.[7] The Sherpur structures weren't just owned by influential Afghan citizens. According to Afghan reports, Afghan-born neocon Zalmay Khalilzad, the US ambassador to Afghanistan from November 2003 until June 2005, was the owner of a five-story Sherpur supermarket-cum-office-building.[8]

*   *   *

Sherpur was symptomatic of the corruption that began to grip Afghanistan after the frenzy of distracted US war making and development met the ravaged central Asian society accustomed to graft and fraud. Afghanistan's corruption may have some roots in central Asia's tradition of strongmen. In the view of some scholars, Afghanistan can be considered a Big Man society—one whose leaders attempt to dominate resources for their tribes and families in endless competition with other powerful men.[9] Throughout Afghanistan's early history of modern statehood, which began in the 1880s with the reign of Abdur Rahman Khan, the reach of Afghan central government was limited, as the state was forced to coexist with a vibrant and empowered tribal society that accepted little interaction or support. The government was dependent on foreign subsidies—initially from the British Empire's "protection payments." When the central state did intrude in the hinterlands in the late eighteenth and early nineteenth centuries, the result was "chronic and systematic abuse and exploitation of the rural and peripheral populations at the hands of government officials," as noted Afghan scholar and Indiana University professor Nazif Shahrani writes.[10] Shahrani quotes an Afghan, Mahmud Beg Tarzi, who lamented corruption early in the twentieth century: "Public morality has become poisoned, and this lack of morality among the people has produced such an undesirable effect that we have totally forgotten the Commandments of God, His Prophet, the Qur'an and our duty to the country, our national honor, our tribal/ethnic respect and dignity, the right of *'ibadullah* [God's slaves, i.e., Muslims], and our conscience and faith." Foreshadowing the issues that plague Afghanistan in the twenty-first century, Tarzi complained about corrupt government officials, so avaricious they became like "a man-devouring snake, an *azhdaha*, if you will! a shark, if you will! a demonic beast, if you will!" Tarzi charged the officials with grotesquely enriching themselves: "All this from the embezzlement of the public treasury and all from the blood of the citizens."

When the Cold War heated up, the Soviet Union and the United States dueled each other with competing foreign aid to King Zahir Shah's government. The king's government had a thin carapace of law-based civil service, but at its heart was still a medieval oriental court with a resplendence of nepotism and client–patron entanglements. While patronage and personal connections ran the country during the king's reign, most Afghan informants considered government corruption to be comparatively minor.

The subsequent Communist regime that began in 1973 attempted to introduce central planning and an expanded state presence into Afghanistan's tribal societies. But the injection of more government cash into the economy also presented greater opportunities for corruption. As the US-funded *mujahideen* resistance began to wrack the country after the 1979 Soviet invasion, deception accelerated. The US funding for the mujahideen attracted an unsavory cast of international weapons dealers, who dumped as many of their bad armaments and munitions on Afghanistan as they could manage. Israel, Egypt, Turkey, and Britain all unloaded obsolete weapons on the Islamic fighters. Pakistan's Inter-Services Intelligence (ISI) got rich selling the mujahideen US- and Saudi-donated weapons, but the mujahideen didn't care because they were getting rich reselling them.[11]

After the Soviets withdrew, the booming opium industry and the war-lords' anarchic civil war enabled corruption to metastasize through the society. The Taliban's draconian Islamic order sharply reduced corruption in the late 1990s—though the opium economy's endemic deceits continued.[12] It was only after the relatively honest Taliban fell in 2001 that the US-supported Karzai government took the traditional nexus of power and corruption to new—global—levels of kleptocracy.

* * *

Opium was the seed of the postinvasion corruption. Within a few years, opium-related corruption was rife, unfettered by the confused US counternar-cotics policy. By 2004, Afghanistan's narco-state matrix was complete. During the same period, poorly managed international aid and military logistics money was flooding the near-moribund licit economy. Endemic payoffs began to pervade every aspect of Afghan life, including schools, police, courts, and government agencies. *Band-bazi*—corruption networks within the Karzai government—managed a bazaar economy that bought and sold every favor, service, and administration position from cabinet members and provincial governors down to district police chiefs.[13] *Bakhsheesh*—Dari for "gift"—was the word of the moment. Officials bribed higher-ups with hundreds of thousands of dollars to get positions that paid official salaries of a few hundred dollars a year.[14] *Maslahti* was the term for the prearrangement of official positions awarded for money and connections rather than for merit or competence.[15] One district police chief on a narcotics trafficking route reportedly paid $150,000 for his job that earned a pittance of a salary.[16] District subgovernors overseeing drug-producing regions the size of small US counties likewise paid up to $150,000 for their positions, which they might hold for only a year. Even subgovernors administering poppy-free districts needed to pay $20,000 and more.[17] Honest officials were forced to make hard choices. A State Department cable out of the Kabul embassy reported that the governor of Khost was reasonably honest but probably wouldn't be there long because he told the

Americans he didn't have "the $200,000–$300,000 for a bribe" to hold the position permanently.[18] With the help of deal-brokering Afghan *commis-sionkars* who facilitated extortion, dirty government officials could rapidly reap a hefty return on their investment.[19]

At the top, there was "grand corruption."[20] Big deals for big fish. The minister of mines reportedly received a $30 million bribe from the Chinese for the Aynak copper mine concession.[21] Former minister of education Yunis Qanooni had numerous charges of corruption swirling around him, from a $30 million embezzlement scheme from a school desk deal to reports he received over $2 million a year from Britain's secret service to push its interests. When Hamid Karzai consolidated his power, the extended Karzai family developed a band-bazi of epic proportions, networks of corruption that included the Afghan government, the opium Mafia, the CIA, and the Taliban.[22]

US-funded public-works contracts were gold mines: after a healthy dose of graft to the right government official, the contractor always seemed to have a connection to one of Afghanistan's twenty powerful families. Once he hacked off a chunk of the development money, the insider quickly subcontracted the project. Some projects were "flipped"—aid-speak for subcontracted—numerous times (with skims at each juncture), till some woebegone construction company would slap something together with a shadow of the money. Tuft University researcher Paul Fishstein described a typical flipping deal in Balkh Province, where the ISAF military awarded a contract for 3,500 modular units to a politically powerful Afghan firm for a bid of $17,000 each. The Afghan firm immediately flipped it to a second company for around $13,000 a unit, grabbing $14 million dollars of profit for little work. The subcontractor immediately sold the contract for $9,000 a container, garnering his own tidy profit. When the flipping finally stopped, the work was done on a shoestring budget of $7,500 a unit, less than half the original cost, which meant the actual builder had to scrimp on materials to construct low-quality office structures. It was all business as usual.[23]

The British analyst and darling of the Washington Afghanistan policy crowd, Clare Lockhart, told another flipping story: In 2002, the United Nations awarded $150 million for a house-building project in Bamiyan Province. The donor countries transferred the money to an aid agency in Geneva, which kept 20 percent and flipped it to another NGO, which got its 20 percent before passing it on to a third agency, which took 20 percent and subcontracted implementation to yet another firm. With the pittance remaining, the fourth firm at least bought some Iranian wooden beams, which

Afghan warlord Ismail Khan's trucking company transported to Bamiyan for five times the normal rate. When the timbers arrived in the Bamiyan villages, the locals determined they were too heavy for typical Afghan mud-wall construction. So the villagers chopped up the beams for firewood.[24]

And the security contracts, which sometimes were as much as 40 percent of the total contract, were another great source of profits for the powerful families that controlled most of Afghanistan's private security firms—profits they shared with compliant warlords, police, and insurgents.

At the Kabul ministerial and provincial levels, there were plenty of opportunities to scam money in the areas of customs, transport, and natural resources. Reports estimated 50–70 percent of Afghanistan's customs revenues never made it to the central government treasury. Not surprisingly, one middle-level customs official in Herat was reportedly able to afford a $150,000 house after four years in his government position—a position that paid $50 per month. One border police chief in southern Afghanistan reportedly raked in $5–$6 million a month extorting the opium trade, according to a *Harper's Magazine* article.[25] Afghanistan's justice system was run on graft—judges being among the most likely public officials to ask for a bribe. It took thousands of dollars to a judge to get legal matters settled. Landownership disputes, common in Afghanistan where war and greed have clouded most every title, were a particularly rich vein. You needed bribes to the prosecutor to move a criminal case forward (or more often, make it disappear). Want to get your innocent relative or employee released from jail? Distribute some graft. The executive director of the United Nations Office on Drugs and Crime (UNODC), Antonio Maria Costa, stated the prevailing wisdom: "At the moment, the Afghan people are under the impression that it is easier to buy a judge than hire a lawyer."[26]

Corruption became a major part of the Afghan economy—almost a quarter of Afghanistan's Gross Domestic Product (GDP), nearly enough to rival the GDP share of opium. Bribes became an inextricable part of daily life in Afghanistan. There were shakedown "tolls" by the cops at the roadblocks.[27] It took a hundred dollars in *shirini*—Dari for "sweets"—to get a driver's license; four hundred to get connected to Kabul's electric grid; thousands to get a provincial business permit. Officials at the Ministry of Education needed graft to release government funds to provincial schools. Teachers demanded bribes for each child taught. Doctors and nurses had to be paid off to provide care and medicine. Petty thugs wanted some change to let you get bread. Bigger thugs kidnapped you for thousands of dollars. An Integrity Watch Afghanistan

(IWA) report in 2007 found that Afghans thought corruption was at "unprecedented levels." One Afghan said, "Despite the fact that we now have an apparently democratic state, the occurrence of corruption is much more frequent and on a larger scale than ever before."[28] The IWA survey revealed that over half of Afghan households had paid bribes to government officials in the previous six months. Researchers indicated that three-quarters of the Afghan National Police stole from the people.[29] The IWA estimated that the average Afghan paid over $100 a year in bribes—in a country where 70 percent of families live on $1 a day.[30]

In 2005, the respected anticorruption NGO Transparency International ranked Afghanistan among the world's most corrupt countries: the 117th worst out of 159 countries, the forty-second most corrupt country on earth. Just two years later, Afghanistan had leapt up the rankings. Transparency International ranked Afghanistan the ninth most corrupt country in the world. By 2008, Afghanistan was the fifth most corrupt.[31] With its ravenous, predatory government feeding on opium, aid, and its own people, Afghanistan had rocketed up the corruption charts—with a bullet, as the DJs like to say.

* * *

A lot of bullets, actually. Afghans claimed corruption was a major reason for the revival of the Taliban and other insurgent groups. The pervasive corruption undermined faith in the Karzai government, pushing Afghans to the insurgents for justice and order.[32] The late special ambassador Richard C. Holbrooke stated that "the massive, officially sanctioned corruption and the drug trade are the most serious problems the country faces and they offer the Taliban its only exploitable opportunity to gain support."[33]

The Taliban gained more than popular support from US-funded corruption. Like their coconspirators in the Afghan government, the insurgents soon learned how to score US taxpayer money for their own purposes.[34] A Pakistani journalist, Syed Saleem Shalzad, had great contacts with the insurgents until his murder in 2011—perhaps at the hands of the ISI.[35] In 2003, Shalzad interviewed Azmattulah, a tall, soft-spoken Taliban lieutenant in his twenties. Shalzad asked Azmattulah where the Taliban got its money. Azmattulah replied, "From US dollars from the US authorities!" He went on to explain: "You know they distribute dollars to the tribal chiefs, local administrators and other concerned people for welfare projects. What is your opinion of where it goes? Not every penny, but most goes into Taliban pockets to refuel their struggle."[36] The pattern persisted and grew over time. "American money is *haram* [unlawful in Islam]," a Ghazni Province elder told an Afghan journalist in 2006. "We could not use it to improve our lives. So we decided to give it to the Taleban [*sic*]. The most important thing we could do with this money was help the Taleban to pursue the jihad."[37] An elder in another Ghazni village told the reporter, "One day, the US troops gave us 50,000 afghani [$1,000 USD] for a construction project, but the Taleban came to us that evening and asked us what we were going to do with it. We told them it was their decision. They took the money and left." A mullah who served as the local Taliban representative told the journalist they bought weapons, explosives, motorcycles, and mobile phones with the aid money. "We are not allowed to keep a penny of that money for ourselves," he said.[38] At least the Taliban made honest use of the US taxpayers' cash.

There was, of course, also the loot of war: the black market was full of stolen US military gear from defecting Afghan police and soldiers. Sometimes, the insurgents hawked things too big for them to use. In the Ghazni City bazaar, the Taliban was selling parts of captured tankers and trucks.[39]

Then there were the malevolent partnerships that joined ostensibly US-allied Afghan leaders with the Taliban.[40] US military investigators and anti-corruption task forces came to call the partnerships "Malign Actors Networks," or MAN for short. The investigators charted the intricate webs that connected the highest levels of the government and economy down to jihadists in the mountains and villages.[41] Peter Galbraith, former US diplomat and the United Nations's deputy special representative for Afghanistan, told me, "I described this as a Mafia state. We see the Afghan state on one side, and the Taliban on the other. But the reality is they work together."[42]

American authorities were long aware that US funds were bankrolling the insurgency. Matthew "Mac" McLauchlin has been working as a US government official and senior strategist in Afghanistan since 2003. Beyond stints in the Kabul embassy, McLauchlin worked for the Special Inspector General for Afghanistan Reconstruction (SIGAR) as a senior adviser. He spoke over Skype™ with me in 2011 about US taxpayer money funding the Taliban. "We always knew. . . . First with the CERP [Commander's Emergency Reconstruction Program] and counternarcotics, but mostly having to pay bribes to get contracts done on the roads, etc."[43]

Gargantuan logistics contracts to provide fuel, water, and construction materials to the American military became conduits for illicit finances, with well-connected Afghans making deals with a broad range of malign actors, including politicians, dirty businessmen, and the Taliban. "The Taliban are businessmen," one highly placed international political analyst specializing in the Taliban told me. "Construction companies, transportation—there are thousands of ways for the insurgents to make money."[44]

Afghan road construction became the great American boondoggle—and also an important source of financing for the Taliban. Proceeding from the unproven assumption that development leads to stabilization, the US military and aid officials made road construction central to the American war effort. "Where the road ends, the Taliban begins," General Karl Eikenberry quipped in 2005. It became the catchy slogan that USAID and construction industry flacks endlessly flogged as they fished for lavish appropriations. Multinationals were soon planning roads thither and yon in Afghanistan—paved with US funds. As an important USAID "implementing partner," the Louis Berger Group landed a $665 million contract in September 2002 for a mammoth infrastructure-development project, which included the design and construction of more than 1,500 kilometers of roads. The projects included the legendary million-dollar-a-mile Kabul-to-Kandahar highway, a skinny, badly constructed, two-lane blacktop that cost as much as highway construction in the United States, even though it was built in a country where workers earn dimes on the hour.[45] Berger bragged that the road was 75 percent built by Afghan labor. Although international companies proposed to rebuild the highway for $250,000 a kilometer, Berger got the job at $700,000 per kilometer—and then deftly subcontracted the construction work out to Indian and Turkish companies. After President Bush decided to rush the road completion for a public-relations coup, Berger used the "accelerated construction schedule" to pump the take up to one million bucks a mile.[46] Thinly paved (after Berger got USAID to lower the required thickness of asphalt) and with a maintenance budget of zero, the road was soon falling apart. A 2004 USAID Inspector General audit called out Berger's failure to establish a quality control and assurance program or to "fully monitor the quality of the road construction," resulting in "defective work."[47] Former minister of planning Ramazan Bashardost claimed the Taliban built better roads when it was in power.[48] In 2008, then senator Joe Biden was still echoing the road rah-rah: "How do you spell hope in Pashto and Dari? A-S-P-H-A-L-T."[49] But the reality was much different. The highways not only provided a font of protection money to the insurgents, they also yielded shakedown money from the increased traffic at Taliban checkpoints. The road construction contracts themselves were a source of Taliban funding, facilitated by corrupt politicians and Afghan businessmen playing both sides of the game. "Each of the projects, you have to pay the Taliban," a political analyst told me. "If you don't pay them you can't do anything."[50] Development wasn't countering the insurgency; it was paying for it.

Among many cases of endemic collusion, the analyst documented one case in 2007, when the governor of Kapisa Province directed US-funded development projects to three Afghan businessmen who had long connections to the insurgents.[51] The report stated about the Kapisa Province governor, "He is extremely weak and corrupt, and there are credible allegations of his involvement [in] illegal taxation and [he] enjoys excellent relation[s] with AGEs [Anti-Government Elements] (HIGs) [the jihadist political party Hizb-I-Islami Gulbuddin] active in the province." The analyst's report noted that the governor had fought against the Soviets with the vicious US- and Pakistan-supported mujahideen commander Gulbuddin Hekmatyar.[52] In December 2002, Hekmatyar turned his Hizb-I-Islami Gulbuddin forces against the foreign forces and later voiced support for the Taliban. On February 19, 2003, the United States pronounced Hekmatyar a Specially Designated Global Terrorist.[53]

According to the political analyst's intelligence report, the Afghan businessmen who held the US contracts were also friendly with the insurgents: "the three mentioned businessmen give a part of the funds allocated for the reconstruction projects to the HIG and Taliban commanders in Kapisa Province and Sorobi District, Kabul Province." The report indicated one of the businessmen had the US-funded road contract to Sorobi: "He is close to both Taliban and HIG influential commanders in Kapisa and Sorobi District, Kabul Province." The insurgents made good use of the money. As the jihadists reconstituted their forces from 2004 to 2008, an amply funded insurgency exploded in both Kapisa Province and Kabul Province's Sorobi District. At one point in 2008, a top HIG commander stayed at the governor's house for three days. From the intelligence report, it appears that US taxpayers not only contributed to the insurgents' battle funds, but also paid for hospitality.

The security contracts for international NGOs and forces provided another great way to distribute American money to both sides of the conflict. In 2005, Ahmad Rateb Popal and Rashid Popal, two cousins of Afghanistan's president Hamid Karzai, started Watan Risk Mangement to sell security services to international organizations. Hamid Karzai's brother, Qayam, was reportedly also an owner, though he denied ownership.[54]

While the two Popals were unlikely candidates for security work (both had convictions for federal heroin charges in the United States), their company prospered. Watan quickly signed security contracts with a range of major international organizations including USAID-contracted international development companies, NGOs, and the American University of Afghanistan. Watan Risk was so cozy with USAID that the company bragged on its website that it paid for a USAID documentary. Watan staffed key positions with former Coalition military officers—particularly British special forces; the senior business manager rode the revolving door around from USAID to Watan.[55] Watan had clout. The website touted the company's "strong ties to the democratic government," as well as a "unique insider understanding of Afghanistan," and "strong tribal relationships."[56] All those assets came into play when Watan started nabbing profitable military security contracts to protect truck convoys hauling supplies to NATO and ISAF forces. The website promised, "Watan is able to use its unique tribal network and connections to gain access to areas that would otherwise be impassable. Watan also uses these contacts to keep costs low on behalf of the client, through minimising [sic] attacks and through careful use of the tribal networks to provide security in depth." The Popals' "unique insider understanding" and "tribal networks" turned out to be little more than buying off the Taliban. The Watan–Taliban protection racket grew so systematized that there was a price sheet for each truck and itinerary: "the current price to the Taliban is $500 per truck from Kandahar to Herat, $50 from Kabul to Ghazni," one US contractor told investigators. A congressional report concluded the Taliban's share of the US security money—millions of dollars per week—was potentially "a significant source of funding for insurgents," rivaling opium as a source of Taliban finance.[57]

As the central logistics hub for the US war effort, Bagram Airfield was a honeypot for the warlords and their friends. At least one Taliban family—that of Taliban provincial commander Mawlawi Abdul Raul—held trucking contracts directly, running a large transport company that hauled oil to the giant American military headquarters at Bagram Airfield. The infamous Tajik warlord General Baba Jan could see the opportunities at Bagram. After sequentially (or perhaps concurrently) being an Afghan Communist, an anti-Soviet mujahideen, a US-funded commander against the Taliban, and chief of police for Kabul and Herat, the effervescent Baba Jan slid over into the business seat, securing the primary logistics contract to supply Bagram Airfield.[58] Baba Jan's twenty-five-year-old nephew was the owner of Afghan International Trucking, which ran one of Afghanistan's major US logistics hauling contracts out of offices at Bagram Airfield. The company began sharing its good fortune in 2004 when it started bribing three US military contracting officials for favors. At one point, Sergeant Ana Chavez got a candy box stuffed with $70,000. Staff

Sergeant James Clifton got $20,000 a month from AIT, while a second trucking firm, Afghan Trade Transportation, paid Clifton another $15,000 monthly. The companies paid these bribes to Clifton in exchange for getting assigned just one additional day's trucking per month, a hint as to the profits to be harvested from the hauling contracts.[59]

Military-base security was another good business. Jan Baz Khan was a Khost Province warlord whom the US military hired in 2002 to provide security for Forward Operating Base Salerno near the Pakistani border. Khan was connected: Pacha Khan Zadran, the powerful east Afghan warlord and signer of the Bonn Agreement, was his uncle. Ex-mujahideen Pacha Khan Zadran was another of those almost–whimsically fickle Afghan warlords. After helping defeat the Taliban, he was awarded governorship of Paktia Province. When the locals chased him out of office, the Karzai interim government sent a replacement. Angered because his fiefdom had been taken from him, Zadran turned renegade, ordering his forces to attack the provincial capitals of Paktia and Khost. Arrested in Pakistan in late 2003, he was incarcerated in Kabul the next year. In 2005, Zadran was elected to the Afghan legislature.[60]

Zadran's nephew, Jan Baz Khan, was a chip off the old block. To increase his revenue stream from the US military for increased security, Khan ordered his militia to attack Forward Operating Base Salerno with multiple rockets, which he then claimed insurgents had launched. When the Americans offered him a bounty to find the perpetrators, Khan—ever the canny businessman—quickly turned over a dozen suspects. One was an innocent taxi driver named Dilawar, whom American soldiers tortured to death during an interrogation at the notorious Bagram Airfield prison.[61]

Senate investigators revealed that a private American security company, ArmorGroup, hired two local warlords (called Mr. White and Mr. Pink in the Senate report) to provide security for the sprawling Shindand Airbase in western Afghanistan, where the company had the contract to provide security. Unfortunately, Mr. White and Mr. Pink were thugs who engaged in "anti-Coalition activities." Despite reports that the two were Taliban, ArmorGroup continued to use them for base security for eighteen months, a period when there were numerous attacks, which climaxed with Mr. Pink killing Mr. White to "get a bigger piece of the pie." After ArmorGroup finally roused itself to fire Mr. Pink because of his "move to the Taliban," the US forces team leader confirmed that Mr. Pink was a "mid-level Taliban manager," who "posed a force protection issue for us."[62]

The Afghan government insiders and the insurgents had another slick operation: a "catch-and-release" system for captured high-level Taliban leaders, whom Afghan officials released in exchange for payoffs. The Taliban commanders then returned to the battlefield to again menace US soldiers. The system was so well organized that the Taliban eventually set up a standing "Freedom" committee to handle the bribery negotiations with government officials. A European policy consultant who deals with rule-of-law and security issues in Afghanistan told me on deep background about Karzai family members in the government running a "business assisting in the release process in return for payment," repeating for emphasis, "There's an active business racket releasing Taliban prisoners for money."[63] The consultant said an Afghan security source stated there were "thousands" of cases of Afghan political insiders intervening to arrange the release of high-level Taliban. The consultant told me, "This release of Taliban prisoners business—there are now remarkably few Taliban prisoners in detention—an American intelligence officer told me 'the cupboard's about bare.'" He further told me the Taliban pay off tribal elders to lobby in Kabul for the release of the captured insurgents. The government officials are predictably receptive to the elders' entreaties—probably because they've already gotten their cut.[64] The consultant documented cases as far back as 2005, when the Taliban in Badghis Province purchased the release of three notorious commanders captured by Coalition forces. After their releases, the men returned to making mines, ambushing convoys, and attacking ISAF forces. "They are now among the most dangerous Taliban commanders in Badghis," the analyst says. Over the next few years, Taliban and Afghan government insiders systematized the catch-and-release scam, which, according to the consultant, extended all the way up to "someone in the presidential office."

The insurgents even learned how to tap the relatively untainted National Solidarity Program (NSP), a community-based reconstruction program that spent hundreds of millions of US dollars across Afghanistan to win hearts and minds. According to British journalist Jean MacKenzie, in 2009 the Taliban fighters were skimming 40 percent of the NSP money coming into Farah Province.[65]

In the shadowland of Afghanistan, there were shadow Afghan government employees: Taliban-sympathetic ghosts who only materialized on payday. There were shadow structures: dams and schools and clinics that were purportedly built with (unsupervised) US development funds, but somehow the structures disappeared into the murk of corruption, never to be found. In the south and east, the insurgents ruled wide swaths of the region with their shadow government, which they financed with shadow taxes on opium and development—sometimes collected in shadowy offices. MacKenzie wrote of a "quite professional" Taliban office where contractors with US development money queued to pay the insurgents their cut: "A shadowy office in Kabul houses the Taliban contracts officer, who examines proposals and negotiates with organizational hierarchies for a percentage."[66]

An international scholar of the neo-Taliban spoke on background about the system, which he confirmed was "quite widespread" and included a broad range of international NGOs that colluded with the Taliban. "In Kabul, the NGOs approach Taliban agents. They submit a project for approval and then have to pay 20 percent to the Taliban. The NGOs are reluctant to circulate that they do this, because they will lose their support."[67] Echoing the complaint of the many Afghans who charged the international military and development community with being complicit in Afghanistan's culture of corruption, an international political analyst told me, "The corruption inside is terrible. They are all together: those who implement, the government, and the insurgents."[68]

*　　*　　*

In spite of corruption's pernicious impacts, the US government either ignored it or enabled it. With relatively few American troops on the ground, the US military depended on cheap, warlord-beholden security. The diplomats and development officials were propping up the dysfunctional Afghan government, whose officials were merrily divvying up the loot.[69] To curry favor with the Afghan officials, they needed to accomplish their career-enhancing missions; both US military and civilians colluded with Afghan politicians who were steering lucrative contracts to their cronies, their own Dubai bank accounts, and, in many cases, the Taliban.[70] The international logistics and development funds that poured into Afghanistan totally destabilized the destitute country, which had a pittance of a GDP—well under $30 billion a year.[71] The torrent of foreign money fueled corruption, exacerbated tribal conflicts, and supported the byzantine webs of codependent actors.[72]

The US military had the most money—and also had the biggest difficulty dealing with corrupt politicians, according to diplomat Peter Galbraith. He told me, "I watched them in the Balkans and Afghanistan. The military guys are not very tough—there's a natural tendency to suck up in a military culture. And they also need the cooperation of the head of the government for military operations."[73] Military logistics contracts were the largest source of money in Afghanistan, but the Army Corps of Engineers also awarded hundreds of millions of dollars in Afghan construction projects with the same lack of oversight and quality control that characterized US civilian reconstruction projects. Tales of failed, subpar, and wildly off-schedule Corps projects were common—almost acceptable.[74] Among American officers and staff, there was a casual acceptance of corruption, almost a sangfroid.[75] One US colonel working in development spoke for his colleagues when he told me, "We know there's corruption here. We just want to know what's the going rate. What is it—20 percent? We just don't want to overpay."[76] One US military officer working in Kabul with logistics contracting said, "We understand that across the board, 10 percent to 20 percent goes to the insurgents."[77] Echoing the sense of futility and acceptance that pervaded the US military, Major Carlos Moya, a civil-affairs officer operating in the powder keg of eastern Afghanistan, plainly told me, "The fact or the idea that a contractor is using funds that we're providing them to pay off insurgents or something like that is a serious issue we're trying to deal with here, and I don't know how soon that can really be fixed."[78] Among the soldiers on the ground, there was a cynical belief that the United States had lost the capacity to control the malignant symbiosis of poorly managed funds, a corrupt Afghan government, and a wily, deeply rooted insurgency. "Truly, I don't know if there is a fix in the long run for someone paying off the bad guys," Major Moya says. The attitude made for some interesting playmates.

In his exposé of Colonel Abdul Razik, the corrupt border police chief of the southern Afghanistan opium heartland, journalist Matthieu Atkins wrote about Razik's rise being abetted by "overstretched NATO commanders," and his "hand-in-glove cooperation with the local ISAF forces." According to Atkins, Razik made over $5 million a month in drug payoffs and sometimes dispatched his green border patrol trucks to haul drug shipments.[79] A State Department cable detailed the devil's bargain Western officials made with Razik, saying the officials "walk a thin tightrope when working with this allegedly corrupt official who is also a major security stabilizing force."[80]

USAID handled the next largest pool of appropriations—badly, as it turned out. As early as 2003, the USAID Office of Inspector General was calling out alarms about flawed development programs, a concern that the GAO and, later, the Special Investigator General for Afghanistan (SIGAR) amplified.[81] But as in the military, in these bodies there was an insouciance about corruption, and certainly almost no public acknowledgment that mismanaged aid and logistics funded the Taliban. Not wanting to mess up a good guns-and-aid gig, the international development organizations and NGOs pointed to many reasons for corruption, including opium profits, weak insti-

tutions, low public-service salaries, tribal patron–client mores, and poor security—always exempting themselves. When the development officials listed the
beneficiaries of corruption, they targeted Afghan powerbrokers and officials,
seldom identifying aid organizations, consultants, and multinationals among
those sharing in the booty.[82] Occasionally, an international agency would
begrudgingly note that some Afghans "believed" the international community
shared complicity in corruption. A UNODC report on bribery noted, "It is
believed that even foreign aid in many instances fueled corruption because of
mismanagement of assistance projects."[83] A USAID corruption report, written
by beltway bandit Checchi and Company Consulting, stated, "Afghans believe
that international assistance is also corrupt, due to inefficiencies in high-cost
delivery through international organizations, NGOs, and firms. Afghan perceptions of international 'corruption' criticize the high pay and overheads for
NGOs, contractors, consultants, and advisers as a form of corruption, irrespective of whether or not the applicable rules were followed in IC [interna-
tional community] contracting."[84] Not unexpectedly, the USAID/Checchi
report recommended anticorruption initiatives, requiring, of course, large
numbers of international development consultants to implement them.

The majority of Afghans saw the international development community
that thronged Kabul and some of the provincial capitals as corrupt, incompetent, and absurdly overpaid.[85] The private development companies billed out
full-time expatriate consultants at $250,000 to $500,000 a year, when most
Afghan officials made far less than a $1,000 a year.[86] Minister of Finance
Anwar-ul-Haq Ahady bitterly complained about the fifty international
advisers with half-million-per-year pricetags that BearingPoint, the US private
contractor holding the $98 million USAID modernization contract, foisted
on his ministry. After a long wrangle with USAID, Ahady managed to get rid
of half of them.[87] A former BearingPoint consultant, Rob Hager, said that US
private development contractors were far more interested in their margins than
in recruiting competent employees. "They can put in any bozo," he said. "Pay
them what they want and make their profit."[88] During the parliamentary election, Afghan parliamentarian and former minister of planning Dr. Ramazan
Bashardost called corrupt politicians and complicit international NGOs "a
mafia." Bashardost said, "From the tax money of Americans, these people are
living like kings. This money is donated so that it should be given to the hungry
people of Afghanistan."[89]

The Afghans' frustration with the international guns-and-aid crowd combusted in May 2006 when a riot erupted in Kabul. After a US military truck

crashed into a line of cars, causing a death, mobs of Afghan men and boys shouting "Death to Bush" and "Death to Karzai" began rampaging through the city with a clear focus on NGO- and US-affiliated structures. When the black billowing smoke began to clear a day later, there were more than one dozen dead, aid offices were smoldering (including CARE International and a French NGO called Acted), and the new five-star Serena Hotel—the preferred digs of the well-heeled development execs—was pocked with hundreds of AK-47 bullet holes.[90]

To do the actual development work, USAID was dependent on its "implementing partners," multinationals such as the Louis Berger Group, Checchi, Chemonics, and the Academy for Education Development, companies whose politically connected principals picked up goat-choking contracts with no competitive bidding and almost no adult supervision.[91] Large, often multiple overheads for headquarters in Kabul and America ate up the contract appropriations, so much so that the term *phantom aid* became part of the discourse.[92] Oxfam International reported that "vast sums of aid are lost in corporate profits of contractors and subcontractors, which can be as high as 50 percent on a single contract."[93] A 2005 study of international development aid by the charity ActionAid found an even higher percentage of US development money to be phantom aid that never benefited the intended recipients: "Eighty-six cents in every dollar of American aid is phantom aid, largely because it is so heavily tied to the purchase of US goods and services, and because it is so badly targeted at poor countries."[94] Beyond the reliance on high-profit US development companies and their high-priced consultants, USAID's "buy American rules" mandated that development projects had to favor American corporations, especially agribusiness and pharmaceuticals, even when the same goods were far cheaper in the host country. Many US aid projects in Afghanistan during the Bush administration reflected the neoconservative market-economy philosophy, with a great emphasis on funding complex infrastructure projects such as provincial international airports and international trade markets that were simply inappropriate and unsustainable for an impoverished agrarian society. To plan for an international airport in a place like Khost Province, where around 80 percent of the people were subsistence farmers who couldn't even afford a horse, was an exercise in Panglossian thinking—unless it was all about enriching the cabal of international and Afghan coconspirators.

Abysmal project management and oversight contributed to the corruption. A 2005 Integrity Watch Afghanistan report expressed the Afghans' mordant view: "In the case of construction companies it was reported that corruption takes place in a hidden manner, but with damaging consequences, such as the collapse of a school after one year of construction because of the low quality of the material which was used for the construction of the walls."[95]

One medical clinic that the Louis Berger Group built as a model for eighty-one clinics was so shoddily built and dangerous that the Afghan Health Ministry refused to approve it, citing unsafe chimneys and substandard plumbing. Just a few years after completion, the clinic was already falling apart—ceilings collapsing; the flimsy chimney a fire hazard; the stench of raw sewage pervading the facility.[96] "Afghan good," the US contractors and officials cynically called the lousy construction, physical evidence of American greed and arrogance that the Taliban used endlessly as fodder for their public-relations machine.

USAID officials were fully aware the agency was running the gargantuan US development programs in Afghanistan without a strategy, proper oversight, or effective metrics of performance. As early as 2003, the USAID Office of Inspector General's (OIG) risk assessment of the agency's major activities in Afghanistan highlighted the risks of overwhelming the insecure, badly governed country with poorly administered aid money. The audit included this prescient statement: "The OIG—and the mission's own assessment— concluded that, overall, the risks were high for program goals not being attained, noncompliance with laws and regulations, inaccurate reporting, and illegal or inappropriate use of assets or resources."[97] The OIG audit underscored "material weaknesses in its system of management controls," which translated into money being thrown around with little or no oversight.

US-funded development organization and oversight was laughable. In 2002 and 2003, the United States spent $900 million on Afghanistan humanitarian and redevelopment aid. In 2003, with the insurgency growing and the US presidential election looming, the Bush administration made the standard Washington response to a problem: throw money at it. With a whopping $1.4 billion appropriation, the Bush officials pushed through the ill-named Accelerated Success program. Of that, USAID spent about $538 million on humanitarian and reconstruction aid in fiscal year 2004. But it was a shoot-from-the-hip approach: three years into the huge redevelopment program, USAID still had no comprehensive strategy or meaningful metrics.[98] Sole-source, fixed-fee contracts to multinationals without any set-asides to ensure quality were the norm. "The problem is the outsourcing," Scott Arney, general counsel of the Project on Government Oversight, a nonprofit organization that investigates federal government corruption, told me.[99] "This is the first time we've seen a war outsourced at this level. The agencies were just handing the money over.

Where is the accountability? Where is the accounting? How are they tracking waste, fraud, and abuse?"

Though USAID justified the sweetheart contracts with the excuse that speed was essential, there were abysmal rates of completion. Despite its name, Accelerated Success was neither. For example, the plan was to build or rehabilitate 286 schools by the end of 2004, but the final tally was 8 new schools completed and 77 others rehabilitated. The plan to rehab or construct 253 clinics came out even worse: none rehabbed and only 15 built.[100] Were the Louis Berger–built structures expensive? You bet. The GAO stated that in 2004 CARE, an international NGO, built forty Afghan schools, which cost $10,000 to $20,000 each. The USAID-funded schools built by Louis Berger cost four times as much.[101] The small Louis Berger–built clinics cost on average $133,000 per building. Another NGO that also built clinics for USAID charged $85,000.[102] In a fairly common ploy, the private development corporations provided overdesigned plans for expensive structures wholly inappropriate for Afghanistan: buildings that couldn't handle snow loads and collapsed; structures that needed highly trained engineers to erect; buildings that were reliant on imported materials and technology.

And then there were the buildings that were just plain goofy. Randolph Hampton, a former USAID consultant with long international experience, was the first civilian hired for the initial PRT that stood up in Gardez. He e-mailed me about his experience in 2003, when a Louis Berger manager showed him a design for six hundred schools in Afghanistan.

> The structures looked identical to a Hardy's restaurant that one might find in small town southern US. The structure was to be prefabricated in Pakistan in iron frame and metal sides and shipped to Afghanistan. The buildings were totally metal and rested on 2 to 3 feet of concrete base. I immediately told Mr. Wilson (Bob) that this configuration would never be accepted by the locals. I asked if the design had been approved or introduced to any of the governors in Afghanistan. The reply was 'no!' I then asked how a concrete truck would make its way over the 11,000-foot mountain pass to Gardez (Paktia Province) or Khost. The reply was a blank stare. It was so obvious that no real consideration as to the where, how and what the impact of the proposed 600 units spread through Afghanistan would [be]. I was visibly disturbed that this organizational thrust at infrastructure development was so far off reality.[103]

And the quality of the construction when the buildings were finally finished? Much was on the level of the crumbling Kabul–Kandahar road and the

Louis Berger clinic. A GAO report found USAID measured input and activities but had few meaningful metrics that assessed quality and sustainability, and virtually none that measured the impact of aid on quelling the insurgency—USAID's main selling point. In the polite language of Washington, the GAO report stated that the agency and contractor "did not have systems in place to capture information for all measures."[104]

USAID was scarcely alone in failing to track the impact of development aid on the insurgency. The military didn't attempt to measure the critical aid-and-counterinsurgency metric either, leading one development symposium to question why "military contingents with otherwise strong traditions of robust after-action reviews," completely failed in this case.[105]

The USAID Inspector General's audits of programs costing hundreds of millions of dollars were likewise punctuated with bureaucratic tsk-ings: "no data," "lacked key deliverables," "unreliable contractor data," "lack of proper management controls," "did not fully monitor the overall quality," "deficiencies in the work," "overstated project results," "well behind schedule," "delayed," "concerns about sustainability," "long-term program was questionable," and most damning: "little impact on overall US strategy."[106]

Some of the mismanagement problems lay in staffing. It was hard to recruit civilian officials for Afghanistan, and the development officials who did go were understaffed to say the least. The average USAID staff member in the Kabul mission was managing $27.5 million in projects, while his counterparts in other countries were managing on average $1.2 million in projects.[107] And the staffers, commonly on short-term rotations, were most often sequestered behind blast walls and razor wire. With the simmering insurgency and millions of mines, Afghanistan certainly wasn't an oversight-friendly environment. Lacking their own independent protection force, the US agency staffers had to negotiate with the military to get secure transport out to jobsites. It took a convoy of armored vehicles carrying dozens of security soldiers for a civilian to inspect a roadbed or plumbing—especially as the insurgency exploded in 2004. Most staffers were happy to sit in their fortified bases anyway. It was a license to steal.

Adding to the problem, the revolving door between Washington agencies and private industry continued to spin in Afghanistan. Like the former USAID official who served as senior business manager for Watan Risk, George Ingram, the acting president of the Academy of Educational Development (AED), one of USAID's primary "implementing partners," was himself a former USAID deputy assistant administrator.[108] After handling hundreds of millions of dollars of USAID contracts, AED was eventually banned from further government contracts for "serious corporate misconduct" in Afghanistan and Pakistan. The cozy relations between the American contractors and officials led to abuses such as "descoping," a process by which government officials rewrote contracts after the fact to accept whatever work had been done as completed projects.[109]

In the parallel universe of Afghanistan at war, there were webs that connected American military, civilian agencies, and contractors with corrupt Afghan politicians, grifter businessmen, and the insurgents. The haphazardly conceived and ill-administered US programs and projects provided big paydays for the accidental conspirators and their fellow travelers, who included the Taliban. But in spite of the evidence, most American officers and officials wouldn't publicly acknowledge the US role in Taliban finance—whether because of self-delusion, denial, or a shared dirty secret.

Many people in Afghanistan knew anyway. One day in embattled Laghman Province, where the insurgency was growing in leaps and bounds despite years of full-scale US-funded development projects, an army sergeant squatted beside a HESCO® barrier, spit a Skol®-stained stream into a half-empty plastic bottle, and sardonically told me, "We're funding both sides of this war."[110] In a system of corruption that gave everyone a share, the main losers were the soldiers on the ground, innocent Afghans, and the US taxpayers.

*   *   *

Scene: Rabia Balkhi Women's Hospital, Kabul, Afghanistan. It was the perfect photo op: US Health and Human Services Secretary Tommy Thompson in Kabul to open the Rabia Balkhi Women's Hospital in April 2003. "Today is a new day in Afghanistan, where we now have a new hospital for women to receive top-notch healthcare," Thompson said at the opening ceremony of the maternal-care facility. Ah, were it only so.

Health and Human Services (HHS) had partnered with the Defense Department on a $5 million project to refurbish the hospital and train the staff in modern American medicine. With Rumsfeld's military now engaged in this nation-building thing, it was a chance to show what go-getter Americans could do to improve the lives of Afghans, who had world's second highest infant mortality rate. What could go wrong? Well, lots.

"I was informed that this was our signature project," says Colonel Dan Reyna, a civil-affairs officer from New Mexico, where he served as public-health offi-

cial.[111] *"We all know how this goes: you're always going to have agencies working the issues." Thompson and other American officials continued to toot their horns about Rabia Balkhi, claiming that infant mortality had dropped 80 to 90 percent. But the reality was grotesquely different.*

The HHS trainers had insisted that caesarian births were the way to reduce maternal deaths, but the hospital was operating without reliable electricity or even basic sanitation. There was no functioning plumbing. "People were defecating in corners," Reyna told me. "All the afterbirths were taken out in wheelbarrows and buckets and emptied in open-air trash bins in front of the hospital that were only emptied once a week." Women were birthing on the same plastic sheets, one after the other. As the caesarian sections climbed, so did the deaths of mothers and babies—a 67 percent jump in infant deaths.[112] *"It was just horrible," Reyna says. "There was a 100 percent infection rate." At the same time, Thompson was telling the Pan American Health Association, "We're bringing hope and health to Afghan women." Reyna says, "They weren't developing the Afghans, they were developing themselves. I hope I never have to see any of that again."*

Chapter 6

The Neo-Taliban
A Learning Organization

DEFENSE SECRETARY DONALD RUMSFELD flew into Afghanistan in late February 2004—his sixth visit since the US invasion. Under tight guard, he made a lightning stop in Kandahar and then headed to Kabul for security talks with his commanders and President Hamid Karzai. Puffed as a peacock with his polished glasses, dark suit, and brilliantined hair, Rumsfeld stood amidst his dun-colored commanders, telling them he was going to reduce US troop levels in Afghanistan.[1] At the press conference held at Karzai's worn, bullet-pocked presidential palace, Rumsfeld startled the assembled journalists by announcing, "I've not seen any indication that the Taliban pose any military threat to the security of Afghanistan."[2] Karzai seconded Rumsfeld, stating, "The Taliban doesn't exist anymore. They're defeated. They're gone."

Were it only so. The Taliban was alive and well—and close to the capital. The same day as the press conference, insurgents killed five aid workers in Kabul Province near an area described as a "Taliban nest." Three aid workers who escaped the killing said the insurgents belittled them for "living in luxury." The five dead development workers were among the hundreds of people whom the Taliban had killed in the previous six months.[3] Rather than gone, the insurgency was exploding.

* * *

The Taliban and other Islamic fundamentalist fighters never really left their homeland after the US invasion. In the winter of 2001–2002, thousands slipped over the nominal Afghan–Pakistan border to havens in Pashtun refugee camps, friendly villages, and Quetta's Taliban-controlled Pashtunibad district. Thousands of others just returned to their families in southern Afghanistan.[4] In the year following Operation Anaconda, the insurgents regrouped. With fresh money, recruits, and equipment, they began assaulting Coalition forward operating bases (FOBs) in eastern and southern Afghanistan in 2003 with mortar and rocket attacks.[5] Night after night, Coalition soldiers hunkered in slit trenches and bomb shelters as rockets rained down. One rocket even hit the ISAF headquarters in Kabul. The UN reported insurgent training camps in eastern Afghanistan. Ambushes and buried bombs increased, as did the discovery of large weapons caches. In April, US Special Forces in Khost captured two men and a donkey loaded with munitions. In many provinces, the insurgents installed shadow governments. The relentless attacks continued through 2003, with 220 Afghan soldiers and civilians killed in August alone. "It is a bloody August in Afghanistan," the *Economist* reported.[6] The American military admitted it was facing a far better enemy than the ragtag jihadis it had defeated less than two years before.[7] Sergeant Christopher Below said, "They've adapted to our body armor—they know where to shoot us. These guys may be hard-core survivors."[8] A Taliban commander said, "We have the American forces and the puppet regime of Karzai on the run. They will collapse soon."[9]

The attacks continued to spike through 2004—reaching fifty per month for most of that period. The use of improvised explosive devices (IEDs) increased, and suicide bombers began to appear. The Taliban moved at will throughout Kandahar and Helmand Provinces, where Mullah Omar and his officers issued battle orders from command centers.[10] The mountainous Deh Chopan region in Zabul Province became an insurgent redoubt, where hundreds of heavily armed Taliban fighters fought US Marines and Special Forces in pitched battles in 2003 and 2004. The Taliban killed twice as many US soldiers in the first half of 2004 as it had in *all* of 2003.[11] By mid-2004, insurgents controlled 80 percent of Zabul, and 50 percent of the four southern provinces.[12] Though the insurgents occasionally went toe-to-toe with the Coalition forces, they generally fought a patient guerrilla war. They were playing for time against the distracted, overstretched infidels.[13]

And so it went. With increasing popular and Pakistani ISI support, the insurgents continued their relentless campaign.[14] "Several things came together," Lieutenant General Karl Eikenberry said about the increasingly dire situation in 2005.[15] "The Taliban and al Qa'ida had sanctuary in Pakistan and conducted operations from bases. Local governance was not taking hold. Narco-threats to security. The planning and implementation of critical economic infrastructure projects—roads, power, and water management—were lagging." Faced in Iraq with mounting casualties, sectarian war, and the fallout from the Abu Ghraib scandal, the United States continued to skimp on Afghanistan. In the summer of 2005, as the Afghan insurgency grew in strength, there were only about nineteen thousand US troops with boots on the ground in Afghanistan.[16]

And then the Pentagon further reduced troop levels, pulling out a full battalion of infantry. Intent on grabbing US troops for Iraq, Rumsfeld tossed southern Afghanistan security into NATO's box. In the summer of 2005 NATO completed plans to take over security in Afghanistan. The deployment was the most ambitious operation it had ever attempted outside of Europe.[17] The under-resourced NATO forces were short on maneuver troops, helicopters, close air support, and even transport planes, while the Taliban was dramatically improving its numbers and its ability to fight.[18] Infiltration from Pakistan skyrocketed 300–400 percent, allowing the insurgents to man larger and larger units. In place of the small insurgent squads of 2002, the jihadis were operating in company- and battalion-sized groups of up to four hundred men by 2006 and 2007. One Taliban commander in the south claimed to have twelve thousand men under arms.[19]

The preeminent historian of the neo-Taliban, Antonio Giustozzi, is a slender, shaven-headed Italian with a cropped, grizzled goatee. He has been researching in Afghanistan for well over a decade. A research fellow at the London School of Economics Crisis States Research Centre and author of the seminal *Koran, Kalashinokov, and Laptop*, Giustozzi estimates the total number of insurgent combatants in 2006 to be about seventeen thousand men, further augmented by Pakistani and foreign fighters.[20] Compared to the million-dollars-a-year to keep an American soldier in Afghanistan, it was dirt cheap to field an Afghan insurgent—as little as $3,000 a year.[21] But ultimately, it was the combination of failed US strategy, flawed execution, and revived insurgency that was deadly. It was, as General Eikenberry put it, "a perfect storm."[22]

When the traditional fighting season heated up in the summer of 2006, violence was at its highest level since the invasion in 2001.[23] Across the south, bearded and black-turbaned Taliban manned roadblocks on the new highways, burned schools, and assassinated officials and collaborators. Roadside bombs doubled; suicide attacks increased fourfold. The revived Taliban shocked the freshly deployed NATO forces with ferocious attacks, sometimes in pitched battles. US and NATO casualties jumped 20 percent. One major NATO offensive in the south, Operation Medusa, narrowly averted the Taliban takeover of Kandahar city as the Canadian soldiers battled thousands of well-armed fighters who were poised in the Pashmul vineyard district to invade the nearby capital.[24] Though the Taliban lost to the overwhelming NATO firepower, it won the propaganda war through what Giustozzi termed the "Tet offensive effect." To the Afghan populace, the epic battles demonstrated the Taliban could engage the infidels and live to fight another day.[25] In Helmand Province, where overmatched British troops sometimes had to fix bayonets for hand-to-hand combat with the insurgents, the British forces began reaching "cessation of hostilities" agreements with insurgents, effectively ceding the area to the Taliban. While the US commanders were furious, the NATO commander, British Lieutenant General David Richards, coolly defended the move, saying it was the way of the future.[26]

In Washington, officials kept up a brave front. In May 2005, President Bush welcomed newly elected President Hamid Karzai to the East Room of the White House. Despite Afghanistan's alarming insurgency, corruption, and election fraud, Bush managed to stammer out, "It's a—it's a—democracy is—democracy is flourishing."[27] Robert Gates, who replaced discredited Rumsfeld as secretary of defense in 2006, claimed the US and Afghan governments were "producing solid results."[28]

In 2007, Bush and Karzai held a joint press conference on the Camp David lawn. The two presidents stood at their twin podiums with their helicopters behind them, as though ready for a getaway, Bush tieless in a sailor-blue shirt, Karzai with his jaunty karakul hat. It was another lovefest for the journalists. Bush thanked Karzai for his "stewardship" and "strong stance for freedom and justice." Karzai thanked Bush for "our liberation" and "our stability and prosperity," before veering into even more wishful thinking, calling the Taliban "a force that's defeated."[29] But like Bush's 2005 assertion, Karzai's statement seemed to speak more of psychopathologic denial than realpolitik. Perhaps it was wishful thinking. Or perhaps the statements were—in British journalist Norman Macrae's phrase—"astonishing lies."[30]

*   *   *

So who were these insurgents? After the *Economist* popularized the term in 2003, many pundits started calling them the neo-Taliban.[31] For the most part, these were not your father's Taliban. A new generation of jihaidis, the neo-Taliban was a regenerative aggregate of Islamic fighters who most often operated independently but also loosely cooperated in times of stress. One for all, all for one when there were infidels to fight. There were three major insurgent groups with the largest being the Quetta Shura Taliban, named after the Pakistani city where they were headquartered. Commanded by the one-eyed cleric Mullah Omar, the Quetta Shura Taliban fought mainly in Helmand and Kandahar Provinces. The second most powerful insurgent group was the Haqqani Network. Run by the aging jihadi Jalaluddin Haqqani, and his son, Sirajuddin, the Haqqani fighters wreaked havoc in Afghanistan's eastern provinces and launched spectacular attacks on Kabul. During the Soviet war, the United States provided extensive support to Jalaluddin Haqqani, and according to the Associated Press, Haqqani visited Ronald Reagan in the White House.[32] In the northeast, the CIA's favorite Soviet-era *mujahideen*, Gulbuddin Hekmatyar, commanded the lethal fighters of his party, Hezb-I-Islami Gulbuddin—HIG in the military parlance. Then there were the bottom-feeding neo-Taliban: "tribal malcontents, drug traffickers, and other ill-educated chancers," as the *Economist* termed them.[33] Lumber and gem smugglers allied with the group, as did criminal gangs. Extremists from Pakistan, Chechnya, and Arab countries slipped across Afghanistan's borders to join the insurgency. By 2005, reports linked the neo-Taliban to other jihadi groups such as the Islamic Movement of Uzbekistan (IMU) and al Qaeda, including in Iraq, where the neo-Taliban learned new techniques from Iraqi insurgents, such as improved IEDs and suicide bombs. Taliban leader Mullah Dadullah said of young Afghan jihadis traveling to Iraq in 2004 for "on-the-job training" with Iraqi fighters: "we have 'give and take' with the mujahideen in Iraq."[34]

The transnational training had a quick impact in Afghanistan: catching the Coalition forces off guard, the neo-Taliban more than doubled the use of IEDs from 530 in 2005 to 1,297 in 2006. Likewise, the numbers of suicide bombers in Afghanistan increased dramatically after the 2003 Iraq invasion. Prior to 2004, there were almost no suicide bombings in Afghanistan—most likely due to Islamic and *Pashtunwali* proscriptions against suicide. But in 2004, suddenly there were six. Then there were twenty-one in 2005. The following year there were 141 suicide attacks that caused 1,166 casualties. Calling the bombers "Mullah Omar's missiles" and "our atomic bombs," the neo-Taliban improved their efficiency: in 2007, there were 1,730 casualties, a 50 percent increase from the previous year, though the number of attacks declined slightly to 137.[35] The bombers penetrated security, blowing themselves up at the gates of American bases, in the midst of Canadian convoys, on Afghan army buses, and at a public meeting in Baghlan Province where five parliamentarians, a former minister, and fifty-nine children were among the seventy-two dead.

In January 2008, the neo-Taliban brought suicide bombers to the heart of Western commerce in Afghanistan: Kabul's posh five-star Serena Hotel, where four suicide bombers wearing Afghan police uniforms invaded with automatic weapons and hand grenades. Their target was the hotel's Maisha Mind, Body, and Spirit Spa, a foreigner favorite. Hurling grenades, one human bomb exploded in the courtyard. A car bomb went off, allowing the remaining attackers to rush into the luxurious marbled lobby. A floor below, Norwegian diplomats were meeting with the leader of the Afghan Human Rights Commission. One insurgent with a Kalashnikov took up a position in front of the elevators, shooting guests as the bronze doors opened. Security guards killed him. Another bomber accidentally locked himself on the hotel roof, where he blew himself up. If he was like many suicide bombers, he was an uneducated and impoverished young man from the sprawling Afghan refugee camps in Pakistan. Perhaps an orphan, perhaps a drug addict. Perhaps before he detonated himself, he followed the jihadi instructions to tuck his head and hands into his body to complicate identification.

The attackers killed six people, including a Norwegian journalist, an American woman, a Filipina hotel worker, and two Afghan guards.[36] A Western medic who arrived soon after the battle said, "The lobby was a gorgeous five-star hotel at one point. But when I went in the marble floor was covered with blood, broken glass, and furniture was upset. It should be easy enough to restore the hotel. We took the people we were working on to a hospital. Unfortunately, the woman I had attended to earlier died en route. I see a lot of this kind of thing in Afghanistan."[37]

Along with their use of bombs and suicide attacks, the neo-Taliban fundamentalists learned to overcome their predecessors' aversion to modern technology. In the 1990s when the Taliban took Afghan cities, the fighters festooned power lines with radios and televisions that they had "hung." But the neo-Taliban insurgents put that behind them, embracing radio, video, telephones, and the Internet to spread their message.[38] In the insurgency areas, members of the neo-Taliban operated dozens of mobile radio stations, tiny low-power rigs that they moved constantly to avoid capture—transporting the briefcase-sized transmitters by pickup and motorcycle, even by donkey.[39] Vikram Singh, a US Department of Defense official who headed the Department of State's "counterpropaganda" program in Special Ambassador Richard Holbrooke's office, told me there was a good reason why the neo-Taliban focused on radio: "If you look at Afghanistan today, it's a highly illiterate society, and radio is by far the media with the highest penetration. Over 80 percent of the households have radios."[40] And the United States had bought most of those: American soldiers distributed millions of durable hand-crank plastic radios across Afghanistan.

Jimmy Story, a State Department officer serving in eastern Afghanistan, told me in his soft South Carolina accent, "They last—pretty much last—forever. They're a perpetual-motion machine. If you've got the energy to keep turning the crank, you can keep getting your radio programming."[41]

So the new-wave Taliban DJs broadcast a popular mix of Koranic readings, Pashtun poetry, and unaccompanied martial songs called *Tarana*, which they interweaved with diatribes against the Afghan government and its Western allies.[42] Programming was also dispersed via CDs and cassettes. The über-modern insurgent could even download catchy Taliban songs as ring tones for his cell phone, which he could also use to text threats to Afghan government collaborators.

For the more visual-minded insurgent, the neo-Taliban produced increasingly sophisticated videos, which it distributed through DVDs and its websites, such as alemarah.org ("The Emirate") and shahamat1.org. In place of the old-fashioned taciturn Taliban commander, the technosavvy neo-Taliban leader learned to sit in a video studio to record passages from the Koran or exhort his followers to kill the crusaders. Taliban fighters carried video cameras into battle. The neo-Taliban was, in the military phrase, "a learning organization."[43]

Among the neo-Taliban rank-and-file, there were relatively few old jihadis. Many recruits came from the thousands of madrassas in the Pakistani tribal regions that US funds helped start during the Soviet war. But most recruits came from the Pashtun tribal communities of Afghanistan. Fiery mullahs inspired some recruits to join. Kinship ties motivated others. The Taliban was your cousin, your uncle, your son. Across the insurgency belt, a vibrant village underground assisted the fighters with intelligence, supplies, and support. The rebellion had classic Afghan motivations: revenge, honor, resentment of the corrupt central government, xenophobia, money—and *jang*, the Pashtuns' age-old love of battle.[44]

Opium was part of the picture. The neo-Taliban revival accompanied an upsurge in US counternarcotics activities. This undermined the Faustian deal that the CIA and special ops teams had made in 2001 with the powerful Afghan warlords connected to the opium trade. After the Bush administration decided to pursue an aggressive counternarcotics campaign in the southern Afghanistan poppy heartland, there was enormous blowback.

One day in eastern Afghanistan, an ambitious young US lieutenant connected to intelligence told me why "we'll never win in Afghanistan."[45] As we stood under the shade of a pepper tree near the airfield, where Apache* helicopters were flitting off like evil insects and Chinooks* winched giant bladders of water into the air to haul to isolated combat outposts, the tall, loquacious

Asian American lieutenant first wanted to tell me about his prestigious law school, his time on the Hill as a congressional aide, his decision to join the military to "kill some bad guys," and his frustration that the army was wasting his skills with staff work. That out of the way, he told me that opium was chief among the reasons why the United States was failing in Afghanistan: "Our counternarcotics policy is a big, destabilizing strategy. It's a stupid move right now," he says. "We told the warlords back in 2001, 'If you help us defeat the Taliban, you can have your opium back.' Then we reneged. The warlords were furious. They said, 'You made a deal.' And we said, 'Oh, that was *years ago*.'" To combat the counternarcotics campaign, the drug lords, powerful Afghan officials, and the Taliban solidified their relationships, which helped the insurgency take off. The lieutenant listed two other reasons that his "big brain" intelligence informants said would cause the US strategy to fail. First, Afghans have never wanted a strong central government and will fight to keep one out. Second, the US-led Coalition's financial support for the Afghan National Army and Afghan National Police was larger in 2009 than the entire Gross National Product of Afghanistan. It is nonsustainable. "Afghanistan is a beggar country; a client country," he said.

Attempting to devise a counterinsurgency strategy, Coalition forces tried to parse the neo-Taliban into "Tier One" and "Tier Two."[46] One Canadian military officer who was part of the NATO security forces defending Kandahar Airfield during the chaos of the 2006 Taliban offensive said, "Tier One, to put it simply, is the hard core."[47] A mix of old Taliban fighters and impassioned madrassa recruits, Tier One units were well-equipped with machine guns and rocket-propelled grenades to carry out coordinated attacks against Coalition forces, Afghan government targets, and NGOs. In the military's analysis, the Tier Two fighters were young locals hired on a day rate to fight the infidels and their Afghan clients. As it turned out, the Taliban paid better than the Afghan government: insurgents received two and three times more money than Afghan National Army soldiers or Afghan police. The Canadian officer said about the Tier Two Taliban, "We're basically talking about people whose main motivation is work. They are handed an AK-47 with a couple of magazines of ammunition and sent out to do damage." But whatever tier or motivation the Western military assigned them, the neo-Taliban fighters, succored by kinsmen and funded by Saudi and Persian Gulf donations, opium, and corruption from US aid and logistics, were proving to be formidable foes.[48]

* * *

Scene: Bak District, Khost Province, eastern Afghanistan. It's early June in "Indian Country," the soldiers' term for the Taliban-controlled Bak District. The Indiana National Guard's five heavily armored MRAP trucks creep down narrow dirt lanes that are bracketed by ditches and thin dusty poplars. In the wheat fields, turbaned farmers stare unblinking at the turret gunners manning the machine guns and grenade launchers. It's an aid mission: the development team is headed for a meeting to discuss agricultural education projects with Bak's tribal elders and the district governor, a wealthy Afghan landowner named Latifullah. As the convoy enters a mud-brick village with high walls on both sides of the road, the team tenses. Intelligence says insurgents have spiked the road with IEDs. Near here few weeks earlier, another National Guard convoy hit a trip-wire bomb that totally destroyed the 37,000-pound, $1.5 million truck.

As they slowly roll down the same constricted lane, the soldiers begin calling in reports. The intercom crackles: "The village seems deserted," one says. "There's no traffic," notes another. A bearded Afghan glowers as the convoy passes. A soldier calls out a metal teapot by the road. Is it a bomb? A gourd hanging from a branch triggers a truck commander's warning: "Gunner, get down!" he barks. A donkey in the road stops the convoy—the insurgents sometimes use animals to pack their IEDs. A wheelbarrow with a yellow bucket looks suspicious, till someone sees ice in the container. A lurking Afghan suddenly makes a cell phone call and ducks around a corner. "Hey, that guy in brown just took off," a driver yells. A second later a concussive blast rocks the convoy. "IED! IED!" echoes in the intercom.

This time a jury-rigged trip-wire catcher on the front of the MRAP sets the bomb off. No damage; no casualties. But up ahead the driver spots a second IED that blocks the way. As a Kiowa® helicopter rides shotgun overhead, the convoy detours up a wadi, *a dry streambed. The convoy eventually lumbers into the Bak District Center, a low-rent Fort Apache with a few hardened structures surrounded by tall HESCO® barriers and coils of glinting razor wire.*

The next morning, district governor Latifullah roars into the compound in a battered red Toyota® pickup perforated with two enormous ballistics holes. He leaps out in a flush of oily indignation. A plump, perfumed Pashtun with a silver watch, a fastidious black beard, and a black-and-silver turban that sports a rooster crest of pleated fabric and long cloth tail that drapes over his shoulder and down to his waist, Latifullah fulminates to the team commander. The team's Afghan interpreter—the terp—translates: "The Taliban try to kill him—see," as he points to two-inch holes, one precisely in the center of the truck's tailgate, the other deftly piercing the column behind the driver's door. I ask what kind of weapon makes that hole. The team commander tells me the US military gave a new Toyota to another district governor when insurgents destroyed his truck. The commander thinks someone punched Latifullah's holes with a power tool.

Later, in the courtyard, Latifullah sits with a smug smile, fingering his amber prayer beads. One of the terps translates for him, saying that Latifullah heads the village where the team hit the IEDs and he was concerned: "Yesterday, I try to talk to you, to lead you here. Your soldiers frighten me." I think, "They're right—this guy's Taliban."

The night before, the Bak police chief, a sun-darkened Pashtun with deep-set eyes and a brow of bottomless furrows, invited the National Guard commander for a chat in the concrete barracks. Under a buzzing florescent light, a feckless barefoot Afghan in a brand-new police uniform served green tea, dried chickpeas, and raisins, then naan and bendee—flatbread with a stewed okra-tomato mélange. Another policeman with a ponderous paunch painfully lowered himself to the carpet, saying that with two wives and a bad back, he slept at the district center.

The chief told us the Taliban drive around with impunity, but his policemen can't use the roads—too many mines for their thin-skinned pickups and second-hand Humvees. Instead they patrol on foot, using the fields. Two cops were killed last week, so not much patrolling by the thirty men holed up in the base. "Bak people are kind of crazy people," he said, tearing off a piece of bread. Glancing off, he offered that the district governor "is not very good—but his assistant is OK." The National Guard commander asked if the khan, the local tribal leader, is a "bad man"—aka Taliban. The chief said he'd check, but added that 90 percent of Bak people agree with the Taliban. He said out of the fifty thousand people in the district, there is not one government soldier or policeman, concluding, "If they help you, they will just cut off their heads." The National Guard commander asked, "Would they like to work with us, but are afraid?" "Exactly," the chief replied. The chat ended when an American intelligence officer boiled into the room cursing Latifullah's duplicity.

Latifullah's dramatic entrance the next morning augurs an eventful development meeting with the Bak khans and mashharaans (village elders). Throughout the meeting, one gray-bearded mashharaan holds his worn Kalashnikov with a tommy-gun canister at the ready. Another wears a Pancho Villa–style bandolier. Latifullah and the elders begin to press for free seed and fertilizer, complaining about the adulterated Pakistani fertilizer they use. Most improvised incendiary devices—the buried bombs that are the insurgents' weapon of choice—are home-made with fertilizer and fuel. I imagine the villagers thinking, "Yeah, we can't make decent bombs with that lousy Pakistani stuff. We need some good American fertilizer." One elder interrupts to say he hears on Radio America the Americans have spent billions in Afghanistan, but his village has gotten nothing. The National Guard commander says quietly, "I don't know where the money went, either." The subject returns to free seed and fertilizer. The commander tells Latifullah that only farmers in poppy-growing provinces get free seed and fertilizer so they can grow alternative crops. Bak District and Khost Province have virtually no poppy production.

When he learns they can't get free seed and fertilizer, Latifullah is at first purse-lipped. Then his sidelong glances focus into a glare, his pursed lips harden into a pout—and then he cracks a little smile. Maybe what we need to do here in Bak, Latifullah says, is start growing some poppy.

Chapter 7

Housecats of Kabul

OUT IN AFGHANISTAN'S FORWARD OPERATING BASES, where dozens of US State Department, USAID, and Department of Agriculture officials often live in austere, insecure conditions, they have many names for their American counterparts comfortably tucked into the Kabul embassy: straphangers, pogues, fobbits, or that enduring Vietnam-era insult, REMFs— Rear Echelon Mother Fuckers.

I heard another slur the night after Thanksgiving at FOB Salerno. Patrols of American soldiers were moving in the dark toward the perimeter of the base— rumors of a Taliban attack. In their tightly sequestered compound, the special ops team was loading up for its midnight counterterrorism raids. In the inky darkness, red and green flickers marked soldiers making their way across the blacked-out base with their hooded flashlights. Some headed for guard towers. Others threaded through the rows of hardened barracks toward the giant clamshell gym, where a nonstop symphony of grunts, clanks of Nautilus machines, and ESPN accompanied round-the-clock physical training (PT)— a necessary fetish on the embattled frontline bases. From specialists to commander, every soldier worked out. Marathons and road races were major social events. Like most Americans who ventured into the volatile province, I religiously did my daily hour of PT in hopes of keeping up with the troops climbing the mountains and *wadis* of the Hindu Kush. On this Spartan base where alcohol was forbidden, lean was the frontline physique—and the State Department foreign-service officers were no exception.[1]

That night as I negotiated the FOB's ankle-turning gravel chunks and unexpected ditches, I ran into a couple of skinny diplomats who were hitting the gym before returning to their office for several more hours of work. With their khaki tactical clothes, lug-soled boots, and military haircuts, they were a far cry from their striped-pants brethren. Out in the field, the workloads were staggering. Officers and officials typically worked seven days a week, often for twelve hours and more. On Thanksgiving, officers and officials scarcely broke pace for a plate of dining-hall turkey and the family Skype™ call. Then it was back to work. The foreign-service officers told me they counted on holidays to catch up on work, as they sure weren't going to be bothered by the Kabul embassy. "Oh, no," one diplomat laughed. "At the embassy, they take their holidays and weekends off—if they're not already on R&R. And, um, they sure don't work out much." A week or so before, a helicopter-load of plump embassy staff had dropped into FOB Salerno for a whiff of the front lines. Some could barely fit into their body-armor vests for the flight back. "We call them the housecats of Kabul," the diplomat told me.[2]

*　　*　　*

In the summer of 2009, it took scarcely forty-five minutes to fly on a tiny Blackwater-piloted mail plane from FOB Salerno to Bagram Airfield, and in that period I traversed eight centuries, flying through a thirteenth-century landscape of blue-gray mountains, barren rangeland, and huddled tribal villages to the twenty-first-century wonderland of Bagram Airfield, with its shopping centers, high-tech armaments, and a hierarchy so complicated that it defies comprehension. Then ten minutes of bumping through the murk of Kabul Valley air on a slender little Fairchild Metro® turboprop filled with sullen rangers, officers, and a few vagrant civilians to the Kabul airport. The fifty-kilometer distance between Bagram Airfield and the capital of Kabul is deemed too dangerous to travel by land, so almost all American passengers of import (read: government officials and military officers) have to fly the short distance from Bagram to the military side of the Kabul airport. Aerial testimony to the real security in Parwan and Kabul Provinces. Soldiers ruefully note the Kabul International Airport's acronym: KIA.

The US embassy in central Kabul was my destination, via one of the embassy's armored Chevy Suburbans®—essentially a rolling bank vault with bulletproof windows. The Afghan driver wearily handed out armored vests to the passengers for the ten-minute drive to the embassy down "Ambush Alley," so named because of the number of attacks. Located in northeast Kabul's tony Wazir Akbar Khan neighborhood, the embassy is a fortified encampment. The SUV entered through razor wire, twenty-foot-high HESCO® barriers, and high gates, and then passed through numerous security checkpoints, most manned by crisp, diminutive Nepalese and foul-tempered Americans. Because of Kabul's pervasive insecurity, the State Department began restricting the embassy staff from making unofficial forays into the city's lively expat nightlife in 2005 and required armed security details for official travel. Ambassador Eikenberry declared the security of embassy staff members to be "his highest priority," though not without a cost.[3] With the State Department's main concern being American staffers' security, the officials seldom went into the field to check on contracted projects, leading to uncontrolled abuses. Strategic success took a backseat to safety.[4]

The Department of State considered Embassy Kabul to be a hardship post, "a high-stress, high-pressure, high-exposure, high-stakes environment," as Secretary of State Hillary Clinton told embassy staffers.[5] To compensate them, most Americans serving in the Kabul embassy received an "Afghanistan Service Recognition Package," which paid them in excess of $150,000 a year plus virtually unrestricted overtime pay. Additionally, the recognition package provided them with holiday periods that totaled two months for their year of service, with international flights on business class tickets.[6] With the frequent breaks and staffers rotating out en masse each summer, institutional knowledge and continuity suffered mightily. Despite the service recognition benefits, however, a 2006 State Department inspection reported that Embassy Kabul staffers complained that living conditions were akin to a "minimum security prison."[7]

But Embassy Kabul was a very funny kind of prison, secured by some very naughty guards. Soon after my visit, the Project On Government Oversight (POGO) sent a letter to Secretary Hillary Clinton exposing the wild lives of the embassy security guards. The guards worked for ArmorGroup, a division of Wackenhut Services, Inc., which held a $180 million Department of State contract for embassy security. Things were a little loose: in POGO's phrase, the guards maintained a *"Lord of the Flies* environment." In its letter to Clinton, POGO included photos and videotapes that depicted drunken embassy security guards engaged in nude, homoerotic hazings. One e-mail from a guard described parties where ArmorGroup guards and supervisors were "peeing on people, eating potato chips out of [buttock] cracks, vodka shots out of [buttock] cracks." The guard noted, "there is video of that one." There were brawls, broken doors, threats, intimidation. The photos and clips, most thankfully censored, lit up the front pages, networks, and Internet, particularly when accompanied by reports of Kabul brothel-hopping, sex-trafficking, and hookers smuggled into the embassy.[8] I'd already heard about the gonorrhea epidemic among the guards.

The US embassy's main compound is about fourteen acres with an adjacent eight acres of leased ground known as the CAFE (Compound Across From the Embassy). The main chancery building is a red-gold modernist concoction built in 1967 and surrounded by several other office and apartment buildings that have arisen in the compound since the invasion. Warrens of white trailers serve as offices, stores, and dining halls. The embassy's legendary Duck & Cover pub is tucked into yet another trailer, identifiable by its trademark sign: a helmeted duck standing forthright in the Hindu Kush. After FOB Salerno, the embassy swimming pool seems like an unimaginable luxury. Then there's the coveted hooches—the living quarters. Looking like trailers with top hats, the hooches are white metal shipping containers capped with tall, sandbag-filled metal roofs to protect against incoming rockets. The eight-foot by thirty-foot containers are divided into two living quarters that are approximately one hundred square feet each—an almost opulent indulgence for officials who have been living in barracks and tents out in the provinces.

*   *   *

With civilian and military staffers flooding into Kabul, the overpacked embassy became a compression chamber of careerism, with daily climaxes at lunchtime in the embassy's DFACs—the cafeteria trailers where the embassy staffers cluster to complain, commiserate, and conspire. It's Little Washington in Kabul: military officers who live to brief; pudgy bureaucrats in pressed white shirts and cheap ties; aggrieved, self-important women with bad haircuts clustered together at one table. There's the air of the discontented convent, the unhappy cloister, the simmering hostility of valedictorian hostages packed together.[9] All clawing for the next rank, GS level, pay grade—certainly the next posting, anywhere but there.

The table of USAID officials are dissing the field officers. The embassy staff calls them "cowboys" and "corrupted by the military." The AID officials are flustered about the latest *Washington Post* exposé that outed a particularly scandalous development project: a $40 million plan to transform a plat of barren scrubland near Mazar-e Sharif into a prosperous commercial plantation with miles of strawberry fields and thousands of cashmere goats. But it was only after the project had sucked up enormous resources that USAID figured out the groundwater was far too saline to grow anything.[10] Another Bush-era neocon fiasco championed by free-market ideologues whizzing through the war zones.[11] Save for the bombast of the early press releases and the promulgators' deftly worded CV entries, the Mazer-e Sharif project was a multimillion-dollar failure. Fork in hand, the USAID section leader blusters that in the *Post* article's aftermath, one AID staffer is already PNG—persona non grata. Eyes widen. Will there be an available hooch?

Over on the cafeteria line, solemn Afghans with hair-netted beards serve a clutch of staffers bitching about Washington's unreasonable schedules for videoconferences. Don't they remember Kabul's eight-and-a-half hours ahead? Grumblings about lost sleep. One says his Friday-night dinner plans were ruined.[12] At a long table filled with men, a major grouses that someone took the new commander, General Stanley McChrystal, to Torkham Gate, the major's Kyber Pass command, without notifying him—costing him an opportunity to suck up. "They did the same thing with Petraeus," he fumes. A portly, pleased-with-himself bureaucrat in a straining short-sleeve white shirt—a fat cat—gossips about McChrystal's briefing earlier in the day at the embassy. He gloats that he got into the auditorium, though it was "jammed with stars" (generals) jostling for proximity to power. He stabs his salad and sniffs that the briefing "was 9.9 on the snooze scale, on a scale of 10." If he had a tail, it would be full and flashing. Young female diplomats and development officials—the "aid chicks," as the Jalalabhad PRT woman termed them—purl around the room, dropping their alma maters into discussions like pedigrees: Georgetown, London School of Economics, Yale.[13]

So many Yalies were in Kabul that the alums had a February bacchanal at the Duck & Cover: the Feb Club Emeritus party, where dozens of Yalies gathered to slug down many Kabul Cups—a stupefying combination of pomegranate juice, champagne, and five shots of orange vodka—from a large silver loving cup passed hand to inebriated hand, along with a stunning array of other booze. It was particularly stunning given that Afghans are prohibited by law from buying, selling, or consuming alcohol in Islamic Afghanistan, which makes booze a scarce commodity, particularly for embassy tipplers walled off from Kabul's black market.[14]

But the Kabul diplomats were indomitable in the face of adversity: charged with providing "important services that contribute to the morale and welfare of the embassy community," the Kabul Embassy Employee Association stepped into the breach by establishing a convenience store in some trailers, where each embassy employee can purchase up to one bottle of liquor, three bottles of wine, and two cases of beer per day. Not surprisingly, most of the association's sales were in alcohol.[15] When the Feb Club's party stash ran low, reported the enthusiastic Yalie correspondent who posted to the club's blog, the marine guards "graciously concocted a faux velvet cup with a variety of unidentified ingredients and two very rare cans of Guinness®!" The marines also brought their weapons for the Yalie women to sight down. According to the correspondent, the full spectrum of high-living expat Kabulis attended the party: "We had people from all Kabul walks of life: NGOs, the Canadian and British Embassies, the US Embassy, you name it! The Deputy Chief of Mission, Ambassador Chris Dell, came by to learn firsthand what all the hype was about!" The perky Yalie correspondent concluded, "Of course, fueled by the cups and good cheer, the dance party raged until 4 a.m."[16]

*　　*　　*

But that was nothing compared to the Kabubble—the ongoing party outside the embassy's blast walls, where the international guns-and-aid crowd reveled.[17] With one of the world's largest aid-and-development troughs located in Kabul, the city was awash with a floating pack of international diplomats, aid workers, journalists, spies, and shooters (aka security contractors)—most single, or pretending to be, with six-figure salaries (mainly tax-free) to burn.[18] The Kabul trough was uniquely deep and full.[19] In 2006, the head of the World Bank in Kabul, Jean Mazurelle, fulminated, "In Afghanistan the wastage of aid is sky-high: there is real looting going on, mainly by private enterprises. It is a scandal. In thirty years of my career, I have never seen anything like it."[20]

So when the loaded but lonely foreigners risk leaving their well-guarded bubbles, there are eight or nine happening *bôites* where they can socialize and spend their gelt. Places such as L'Atmosphere ("Latmo" to those in the know), the Grill, and the Gandamack Lodge's Hare and Hound pub, where stressed expats ease their ennui with the good sauce of home. At these expat hangouts, it's Western prices paid with US dollars: continental breakfast at Le Bistro for ten bucks; same price for a beer at Gandamack; another ten for a sandwich at the Flower St. Café; sixty dollars for a Latmo *prix fixe* French meal (vintage wines extra)—this in a country where people make a dollar a day. You need a foreign passport to get in. Be sure to check your weapons before entering. Most places catering to the bright young killer crowd have reminder signs outside the door depicting a cartoon AK-47 in a red circle slashed with a diagonal stripe. London-based journalist Heidi Kingstone wrote in 2007: "Kabul is party city. You can head from one reception to another, from the bar at La Cantina to Red, Hot, Sizzlin', and can always rely on the UN or other official organizations to host some nightly soiree, which makes networking fun and easy."[21]

Networking lubricated by precious stashes of Western liquor, Heinekens®, and vagrant reds and whites that somehow found their way through the Hindu Kush. Expat-only networking, because Afghans are generally barred from entering the premises—those alcohol laws, you know. So it's an alcohol-segregated crowd—a neoapartheid where Westerners canoodle under the influence while they wait for the Afghan aid boom to end. Latmo's summer-time pool scene is legendary: a balmy garden spot where beautiful young aid chicks and ripped mercs (mercenaries) commingle—particularly on Thursday nights. With Friday being the weekly Islamic holy day, Thursdays are Afghanistan's designated party night—for both expats and Afghans. One young British security exec wrote in *Kabul Scene*, the expat journal of choice, that his life was "day, day, day, Thursday night, day, day, day, Thursday night ..." With the Kabubble's decided gender imbalance, expat females are queen bees, though as the women often repeat when discussing the mating pool, "the odds are good, but the goods are odd."

To the American soldiers out in Pashtun provinces, Thursday nights mean something else: Man-love Thursdays, when Afghan males enjoy one another.[22] One FOB Salerno soldier returning from Thursday night watchtower duty shuddered when he told me about the scenes he witnessed with his night-vision goggles while guarding the truck yard where Afghan drivers waited to unload. According to a Wikileaks-published State Department cable, at least one American security firm, DynCorp, managed to underwrite some Man-love Thursday-type action. The June 24, 2009, cable described DynCorp (which controls almost $2 billion a year in US government contracts, including major Afghan police training projects) paying for a Kunduz Province *bacha bazi* pary—*bacha bazi* literally means "playing with boys." The party entertainment featured adolescent boys wearing makeup and dressed in women's clothes. DynCorp paid for the boys to sing and dance for a group of Afghan police recruits, who later had sex with them. The State Department cable summarized a meeting between an American assistant ambassador and Afghanistan's Minister of Interior Hanif Atmar, who insisted the US government had to help with a cover-up of the party because publicity would "endanger lives."[23]

*   *   *

The history of NGOs and private contractors in Afghanistan is relatively short. A few NGOs, such as the respected International Assistance Mission, began in the 1960s.[24] During the 1980s Soviet war, many NGOs set up shop in the Afghan refugee camps in Pakistan and Iran, often funneling money and supplies through the *mujahideen* warlord organizations. In the late 1990s, development analyst Michael Keating wrote about idealistic aid workers who labored in Afghanistan during the 1980s Soviet war: "They were prepared to endure terrible hardship and danger to bring basic services, usually medical, to embattled communities. There was an innocence about assistance that gradually evaporated as the 1980s wore on and as aid became less a gesture of solidarity and more enveloped in politics, particularly once the US stepped up its involvement in the war from the middle of the decade. Today, there is little innocence left."[25]

As US- and Saudi-funded aid money became abundant in the late 1980s, the Afghan warlords set up dozens of NGOs. Keating indicated that while sincere Afghan technocrats ran some worthwhile organizations, "many seemed to exist to soak up funds rather than to deliver any verifiable service."[26] In 1996, the Taliban government set up a department in the Ministry of Plan to coordinate the activities of the relatively few NGOs operating inside Afghanistan. As the NGOs gingerly tried to cooperate with the Taliban, Keating described this generation of aid workers as "less idealistic" and "more self-conscious."[27]

After the Taliban fell in early 2002, NGOs began to thunder into Afghanistan, attracted by promises of incoming international aid. By the end of 2002, there were already about eight hundred in the country.[28] But as the big reconstruction money began to appear, so did big numbers of NGOs. In 2008, a security analyst reported 2,400 NGOs were operating in Afghanistan.[29] The organizations were supposed to be coordinated through the Ministry of Economy's NGO Department, though even less effectively, it appears, than under the Taliban.[30] The NGO Department reported in 2009 that there were a total of 1,610 NGOs operating in Afghanistan. The list included everything from CARE, Oxfam, and the Catholic Relief Services to the TUTU Children's Cultural Center, Sports Sans Frontieres, and the Prosperity and Selfness for Afghan Women Organization.[31] There were giant international agencies, such as USAID and UNAMA (the United Nations Assistance Mission to Afghanistan), which operated outside the NGO list. Being little more than a contracting agency, USAID was almost completely dependent on expensive private contractors who certainly helped inflate the Kabubble. UNAMA was another massive development organization that operated almost as a self-funding parallel government with platoons of well-compensated international consultants and officials.

Journalist Michael Ignatieff contrasted the banks of computers in the UN compounds to the barren offices of the Afghan Assistance Coordination Authority, the government agency charged with coordinating development efforts, where men sat drinking tea as they awaited basic equipment—like desks. Setting the tone for the whole conflict, the Afghan officials estimated that in the first few years of the war, the UN agencies sucked up $700 million of the international aid funds for themselves—while the Afghan government only received $100 million. Afghan senior officials made $150 a month, while the international agencies paid their Afghan drivers $1,000 a month.[32]

There were plenty of Department of Defense (DOD) contractors hanging around Afghanistan. By June 2009, there were more private DOD contractors in Afghanistan than military personnel. There were so many, the DOD and the GAO weren't quite sure of the total number, though they were sure they included a lot of private shooters.[33] Though General Stanley McChrystal said private security contractors were "just not right for a country that is growing law and order," in 2010 there were over twenty-six thousand private security personnel, 90 percent under US government contracts or subcontracts, working in Afghanistan.[34] American guards for US security firms such as Global Risk, DynCorp, and Blackwater (formerly Xe Services, now Academi) earned up to one thousand dollars a day. Even USPI, a low-rent US security firm that held Louis Berger security contracts, paid its experienced (read: ex-military) American security contractors $200,000 a year. An American working as a private security contractor earned about 1,700 times more than an Afghan guard, who probably faced more danger.[35]

And then there were the logistics contractors. Many of them had time on their hands in Afghanistan. I knew a couple of American mechanics on FOB Salerno. I used to run into the friendly pair—one from Louisiana, the other from Texas—leaning on a concrete barrier near the dining hall. Their job was to maintain the MRAPs, the million-and-a-half-dollar armored vehicles Americans use to travel in mine-ridden regions. "We thought we'd be doing, you know, mechanical work," one laughed. But the military wanted to do its own maintenance. So the highly paid mechanics hung out by the dining hall. They were great boosters of their company's MRAPs, and had I been in the market for one, I surely would have bought their brand. The friendly mechanics had plenty of company. In 2009, a decorated ex-Army officer took a job with one of the American megacompanies that scarf up DOD logistics contracts. It was his second contract with the company. At a salary of $188,000 a year, he hired on to be a maintenance mentor for Afghans learning how to actually repair all the equipment the United States is dumping on Afghanistan. The ex-officer lived off-base in Kabul, the company paying big bucks for a residence and protection by some of those private security guards. But eight months after the ex-officer had arrived in Kabul to mentor Afghans, there were still no Afghans to mentor. To his credit, rather than hanging out at Latmo and Red, Hot, Sizzlin' like other underemployed contractors, he spent his time dispatching vans: "getting pd a 188 grand to be a Taxi Dispatcher." He says he wasn't alone: "There were several positions over there . . . that the employees do not have jobs because they don't exist and they spend their time doing Arts & Crafts." After the ex-officer told his supervisor before a briefing that he wasn't going to lie to the US Army "about positions that needed filled, that don't exist, thousands of positions and millions of dollars," the company fired him and seized his computer.[36] What did the company care about his actual productivity or about all the other contractors standing around Afghanistan on the taxpayers' dime? The company was on a cost-plus contract. Lord knows how much it billed for the $188,000 taxi dispatcher.

*   *   *

The expats' ubiquitous white SUVs roaring past constantly remind impoverished Kabulis of the iniquitous system. The Afghans are smart people. They see the high HESCO barriers and razor wire that herald aid agencies and expat residences; they talk about the grotesque disparities in incomes, the rampant corruption, the aid-fueled inflation, the drunken laughter spilling out of the bars, the bizarrely expensive Western-style supermarkets, the gun-waving shooters charging through town, the tales of promiscuous bikini-clad Westerners cavorting at the pools. They know it all too well. Aman Mojadidi serves as a director of the well-regarded NGO Turquoise Mountain, which supports Afghan arts development. In his bitter essay, "Era of the Well-Intentioned Dog Washers," Mojadidi writes of the guns-and-aid elite who have descended on Kabul, and their realization that the fin de siècle is fast approaching: "As a result, many internationals, Afghans, and Afghan expats alike have come to perceive of the reconstruction effort no longer as a means to an end, but rather as the end in and of itself; resembling a free-for-all, a country where everyone is out to get what they can before the foreign armies and international organizations begin to pull back and the country begins its rapid descent from atop the mountain of aid money that has sustained it for so many years."[37]

*   *   *

*Scene: US Embassy, Kabul, Afghanistan. "Everything's a struggle in Afghanistan,"
I think as I wrestle my hundred pounds of pack up the concrete steps from the deep
tunnel that runs under the street between the two embassy compounds. Used to be
the staffers could just cross the street, but rockets and ambushes put a stop to that.
Now they're tunnel people. Sweat in my eyes. Hands full of briefcases and bags. Big
itch under my body armor. Trying to keep up with the colonel who's leading me to
my hooch, my beloved hooch. Promises of a private bathroom. Oh, Lord.*

*The thought of a private bathroom with toilet and shower shimmers in the
imaginations of those coming from the hinterland bases, particularly the remote
combat outposts (COPs) where once-a-week cold showers and plywood outhouses
built oversized so you can shit in your body armor sharpens your appreciation for
indoor plumbing. After the COPs, where modern sanitation consists of a misbe-
gotten soldier burning scat in a fifty-five-gallon drum, even flushing seems luxurious. Military wives back home tell of husbands e-mailing rhapsodies about their
hooch toilet.*

*Manicured green embassy lawns—almost surreal after the hardscrabble
brown world of eastern Afghanistan. The hiss of sprinklers, snip of pruning shears.
A gardener bends over vivid red roses. A pair of diplomats confer at a courtyard
table, sipping cappuccinos from the espresso stand. Microwave towers climbing into
the fierce blue sky; every rooftop covered with satellite dishes aligned just so. Sandbagged allées winding between rows of bomb-protected hooches. A small copse of
shedding pine trees sheltering a couple of picnic tables and a collection of mismatched charcoal grills. At last, my Afghanistan trailer-town home.*

*The clink of glasses, laughter, and the smell of burning meat wakes me from a
fitful, drooling sleep. Out at the picnic tables, a clutch of development workers in
from Paktika, Kandahar, Farah, and Kunduz hammer down Heinekens.
USAID, USDA, Corps of Engineers, some acronym of a development company
that I don't recognize. They're wild-eyed, twitchy, a touch too loud: adrenal glands
pumping for months at a time, hard to slow down. Cigarettes and Bic® lighters.
Empty green bottles begin to fill the tables. Tales of close calls accompanied by
hoots. Side-flicking eyes and stories of failing projects. Quiet. Who hooked up. More
hoots. More green bottles. Seems miraculous that there's still beer in the world.
Someone sprints off to his hooch for more. Good idea. Then half-full Johnny
Walker® bottles. Vodka. Brandy. Empty bottles. A falling man. A struggle with the
hooch door. Sleep.*

Chapter 8

The Afterthought War
Zigzag Strategies

AFGHANISTAN WAS THE AFTERTHOUGHT WAR, waged with left-over resources.[1] As the war persisted year after year, each new US commander rotating into Afghanistan brought his own strategy, creating a merry-go-round of plans that often negated earlier efforts, confused allies, and strengthened the insurgents.

After the rout of the Taliban in 2001, the International Security Assistance Force (ISAF) troops mainly hunkered down around Kabul to protect President Karzai's toothless government. Out in the countryside, the dusted-off and refurbished Afghan warlords reestablished their tenuous control.[2] Through the summer of 2002, most of the eight thousand US troops billeted in tents at Bagram Airfield. Outside of the Kabul area, the American presence was generally little more than US hunter–killer teams stalking al Qaeda, punctuated with maneuvers such as Operation Anaconda.

But the tactical problems of Operation Anaconda and other miscues caused the military to reassess the command structure in Afghanistan.[3] In mid-2002, the Pentagon and the White House directed the establishment of Combined Joint Task Force-180 (CJTF-180) under the command of Lieutenant General Dan K. "Bomber" McNeill, who, befitting his name, began to pick up the pace of operations in the restive Pashtun regions of the south and east. In May 2003, McNeill relinquished command to Major General John Vines, who quickly passed it on to Lieutenant General David Barno in October 2003.[4]

With few planning resources, Lieutenant General David Barno had to literally wing it when he took over—writing his new strategy plan while flying to his new command.[5] Though Coalition forces were spread thin, McNeill and Barno launched large-scale "clear and hold" combat operations that relied on door-kicking tactics and heavy aerial and artillery support. Beginning in August 2003, the ISAF command dispatched massed Coalition troops into battle in four major operations. While the operations yielded relatively few Taliban casualties or prisoners, ISAF soldiers did seize large weapons caches, evidence of the insurgency's enduring power.[6]

The operations mainly served to alienate the Afghan population. The door-kickers—American and ISAF soldiers—crashed into Afghan houses, maddening the conservative Pashtuns, particularly when they separated the women from their male protectors. "That was explosive, gasoline on fire, in terms of cultural sensitivities out there," Barno said. "What I heard from the Afghans, which resonates with Americans as well, was, 'How is it that we, the Afghans, with a constitution that gives us all these rights, can have people barge into our bedrooms in the middle of the night and drag our wives and children out of bed and throw them on the floor and point weapons at us.' Darn good question."[7]

Even worse, the air support that accompanied these ballyhooed operations inflicted large numbers of Afghan civilian deaths—deaths the military often initially denied.[8] For example, Operation Mountain Avalanche commenced with more than two thousand Coalition troops and great hoopla. Military spokesman Lieutenant Colonel Bryan Hilferty proclaimed it as the largest ground operation yet in Afghanistan, designed to crush the insurgents: "We're going to operate simultaneously throughout the entire eastern and southern part of the country so we get inside the decision cycle; so we hit them before they can hit innocent men, women, and children." But when an A-10 warplane sprayed a village in Ghazni Province with 30-mm high-explosive rounds, the military killed a group of nine innocent children, none older than twelve. The military initially claimed the plane also killed a Taliban commander, Mullah Wazir, but the local villagers insisted Wazir was long gone and the dead man was his cousin, Abdul Hamid, an innocent laborer who had recently returned from Iran. Saying rival factions had fed bogus information to the Americans, the villagers railed against the careless use of America's military might.[9] President Hamid Karzai expressed his deep concern about the children's deaths. UN Secretary-General Kofi Annan announced he was "profoundly saddened" and called for an investigation. A few days later, military spokesman Hilferty apologized and told reporters the military had sent blankets, clothing, food, and toys to the village. "We accept blame. We offer our condolences to the village, but I will tell you the surveillance video shows no children there. But we're not trying to avoid blame in this," Hilferty said, going on to indicate the military was studying the victim's DNA to see if they got the right man.[10] "The biggest thing is we want to express our condolences no matter what happened," he said.

As media reports depicted blasted schools and houses, bloody schoolbooks, hunks of dead children, and wailing women hunched over small, mounded graves, angry Afghans protested the onslaught of civilian deaths.[11] Operation Mountain Avalanche's civilian deaths were hardly unique. In December 2001, the *Guardian* published a critical study that concluded, based on collating reports from the United Nations, aid agencies, and media, that US air strikes killed 3,767 Afghan civilians in the first two months of the war alone.[12] Barno admitted to an army historian that into 2004 there was "a tendency to use airpower more robustly than was probably appropriate for an environment where the civilian population was generally on your side."[13] Tabulations of civilian deaths varied wildly, with both the Coalition and Taliban PR machines blaming the other side for the deaths. Counting innocent civilians killed by Coalition military wasn't a high priority for the international forces, so it wasn't until 2007 that UNAMA and the Afghanistan Independent Human Rights Commission (AIHRC) began any kind of systematic collection of civilian fatality data. Even those figures are not fully accessible and "likely represent a substantial undercount," according to the *Guardian* website on Afghan civilian casualties, which indicates that combat actions have killed tens of thousands of Afghan civilians since the 2001 invasion.[14]

*   *   *

Confronting a growing rebellion in 2004, General Barno turned to a strategy of counterinsurgency—COIN in the military jargon. At that point, the US military had virtually no counterinsurgency doctrine, so Barno relied on his thirty-year-old West Point textbooks and British staff officers with experience in Northern Ireland for guidance. Barno theorized that the military had focused too much attention on the destruction of the insurgents, and not enough on winning the Afghans' support. With Barno's direction, the US military turned its attention from the Taliban to the Afghan population, which it termed the "center of gravity." Barno posited that the Coalition could succeed by binding the Afghan people to the Karzai government through a five-part strategy—"The Five Pillars" as they became known after Barno's oft-shown PowerPoint® graphic of a cartoon Greek temple with five columns. The pediment of the COIN temple was labeled, "Center of Gravity: The Afghan People," underscored with the declared "Unity of Purpose: Interagency and International." The first "pillar" was the defeat of the insurgents through "full-spectrum" military operations, which included combat, negotiation, and development. The second pillar was standing up the Afghan security sector—the army, the police, and the justice system. The third pillar was "Sustain Area Ownership," which necessitated stationing Coalition troops in the insurgent areas after operations, rather than returning to their bastions at Bagram, Kandahar, and a few other forward operating bases after maneuver operations. The fourth pillar utilized Provincial Reconstruction Teams to develop Afghan infrastructure and governance. These four pillars constituted essential elements of a "clear, hold, and build" strategy. The last pillar in Barno's strategy involved diplomatic engagement with Afghanistan's bordering countries.[15]

While the temple and its Five Pillars briefed well from the podiums of Kabul and Washington, the reality on the ground was far more troublesome. As it turned out, the COIN temple was as slapdash as everything else the United States did in Afghanistan. With its foundation laid in the shifty sands of the corrupt Karzai government, cobbled together with scraps of manpower and resources, supervised by distracted officers and officials, and undermined by deceitful Pakistani officials, Barno's grand COIN edifice began crumbling before it was even finished.[16]

*   *   *

Barno and Ambassador to Afghanistan Zalmay Khalilzad forged a strong relationship. To exemplify the "interagency unity of purpose," Barno moved his office into the embassy to facilitate civilian–military cooperation. But the Kabul embassy was extremely light on experienced diplomatic and development staff because of very short rotation schedules. The staff shortages prompted Barno to assign military planners to the ambassador to generate embassy mission plans. "It was arguably the second most important embassy effort in the world, and in a war zone," Barno said. "It was not resourced well during the entire time I was there."[17]

Barno's unity of purpose was tested when the neocon-dominated Bush administration decided to send a unique group to Afghanistan in mid-2003 to reform development.[18] Determined to incorporate free-market hardheadedness into the fuzzy world of nation building, neocons in the national security hierarchy organized a team of high-level American business executives and government officials into the Afghanistan Reconstruction Group (ARG). The diverse group highlighted the challenges of maintaining a unity of purpose in a rancorous interagency environment. By late 2003, the vanguard of the ARG-onauts, as they came to call themselves, were in the Kabul embassy, where the powerful private-sector executives anticipated using their expertise and moxie to force-feed market-economy ideas into US aid organizations and the new Afghan government.

It was an odd fit: very senior and very cosseted corporate and government executives dropped into a war zone. General David Barno recalled, "They were able to get COOs [chief operating officers] and CEOs [chief executive officers] and CFOs [chief financial officers] and other very experienced private-sector people and put them on a special contract for a year and have them come live like dogs at the embassy in Afghanistan in the trailer park, inside a minimum-security prison, inside a construction site, where we all lived—so some very, very dedicated Americans."[19] To further complicate the situation, the ARGonauts, accustomed to eager-to-please minions and staff, thought they would get the support of the State Department and USAID. But that was far from the reality. Indeed, the situation got so bad, the interagency bureaucratic war raging inside the embassy rivaled the insurgent war that was developing outside the compound.

In part, the Reconstruction War went back to ARG's origins in the Pentagon, where the new ambassador to Afghanistan, Zalmay Khalilzad, had deep connections. A neocon Vulcan with impeccable credentials, Afghan-born Khalilzad had earned his doctorate at the University of Chicago, a genesis point for the neoconservative movement.[20] With his leonine head and elegant suits, "Superman Zal" shambled his way to the top through positions in the State Department, the White House, and the Pentagon. After 9/11, Khalilzad helped overthrow the Taliban before serving as Bush's special presidential envoy for Afghanistan. In 2003, when the White House wanted the pragmatic neocon Khalilzad to serve as the first postinvasion ambassador to Afghanistan, he wanted help sidestepping what he perceived to be ineffective efforts by the State Department and USAID. "Ambassador Khalilzad wanted a group of experts," Patrick Fine, former USAID mission director in Afghanistan, told me. "He didn't trust the US government or USAID could mobilize the resources that the Pentagon could."[21]

Under former secretary of the army Martin Hoffman, the Defense Department began spinning up the ARG. But then came a fateful decision: National Security Adviser Condoleezza Rice chose to throw a bone to Secretary of State Colin Powell, who was smarting from lost fights with Rumsfeld. Rice decided to give the Defense Department's ARG to the State Department—without a budget. In essence, Rice gave the ARG to Powell as a sop—but Powell didn't want it. As ARGonaut Jeff Raleigh says, "That was a complete recipe for disaster."[22] The ARGonauts were orphans in a strange family and without resources. "In government, if you don't have a budget, you can't do nothing," Raleigh says. "In theory, ARG was a wonderful idea, but it was poorly executed."

It was high tide for the neocons, who thought free-market ideas should be injected into nation building. Out in Iraq, a coterie of young neocons was already helping L. Paul Bremer run the ill-starred Coalition Provisional Authority (CPA). Jeff Raleigh, a twenty-eight-year public-relations veteran, worked with both the CPA in Iraq and the ARG in Afghanistan. He told me of his fond memories of the "mostly blonde young women from Christian colleges" in the CPA development offices, where doctrinaire free-market ideas served as the operant wisdom. Bright young conservative Republicans blithely administered neocon "shock therapy" to Iraqi society. A twenty-four-year-old former ice-cream-truck driver was in charge of establishing the Iraq stock market; a twenty-one-year-old intern in Vice President Cheney's office became a management adviser to the Iraqi security forces.[23]

Jack Bell, a former transportation CEO and the ARG's new chief of staff, traveled with Khalilzad when he flew out to Afghanistan to begin his ambassadorship in November 2003. A former marine, Bell was serving as head of defense procurement when Rumsfeld sent him to Kabul to bring "business methods" to reconstruction. Coming in with the support of top Bush officials and Ambassador Khalilzad, Bell's team of high-powered ARG executives had a clear idea about the end-state they wanted: a market-economy Afghanistan.

But the ARG arrived on the front lines of the development war without any warning to the entrenched State Department and USAID bureaucrats. Not unexpectedly, there were some strong reactions to the newcomers. "The State Department people hated us with a passion that was only exceeded by USAID," Jeff Raleigh told me. "USAID believed we got together at this morning meeting and *prayed*. They said we had secret meetings. In their eyes, we were horned devils; Christian, right-wing Bushites. The reality was, we were maybe more Republican than Democrat, but we had all kinds of people, including some flaming liberals."[24]

Beyond the problem of being rejected by USAID and the State Department, and beyond the fact that they had no funding, the ARG members had yet another challenge: for the most part, they had no experience with development or nation building—a deficit that USAID jumped on with both feet. "They didn't get it," one former USAID official told me with vehemence, "They didn't understand what they were doing."[25] But despite their lack of reconstruction experience, Bell and his ARG team were soon fighting about infrastructure construction projects with the USAID staffers led by Director

Jim Bever, an AID official with decades-long experience in the Muslim world. The ARGonauts wanted things built fast—make an impact. USAID was aghast—standard aid practice included meticulous buy-in from the host nation, and a plan to use the projects to concurrently develop local human and logistic capacity. "They took reconstruction literally—they thought it was an engineering problem," the former USAID official snapped. "This obsession with engineering; this obsession with metrics." The official summarized: "It was just one long conflict after another."

Andrew Natsios, the former head of USAID, published a critique contending that the US military under the ARG's guidance built hundreds of schools that were not coordinated with the Afghan Ministry of Education and so were never staffed.[26]

The ARG members returned the hostile sentiments. "USAID—it's just turf and greed," Martin Hoffmann told me.[27] Another ARG official said, "Natsios didn't want any competition for AID. AID had gone out of the development business in the 1980s. They were focused on humanitarian aid and got rid of all the engineers." Relations with the State Department weren't much better. The ARGonauts had trouble getting body armor, transportation, even medical care for an ARG official who was seriously wounded in an IED attack. Calling his experience "a nightmare," the former ARG official told me, "Everything State could do to strangle ARG, to abort it before it got started, they did. That's how it began—very, very ugly."[28]

As General Barno and Ambassador Khalilzad continued to forge their whole-of-government alliance, the USAID staffers and ARGonauts continued their internecine war. Less than a year after arriving, Jack Bell was steaming out of Kabul, leaving a "blistering rebuke to USAID," as the *Washington Post* characterized his leaked memo. "The most important programs—including roads, schools, and clinics—are in serious trouble," Bell fulminated. "The health program is well on its way to becoming a disaster."[29] One ARG member told me, "The fact that we actually survived the launch period was an accomplishment in itself."[30]

Bell's successor, Lou Hughes, was a former top GM executive and Lockheed Martin executive. Hughes arrived in Kabul in September 2004. "By the time I got there," Hughes told me, "there was quite a conflict between ARG and USAID."[31] A collaborative guy, Hughes first asked the ARGonauts what they wanted to accomplish. "We had some very competent people from Wall Street, private industry, the military, and government," Hughes says. "They all wanted to make a positive difference. However, it was sort of like managing cats." Then he went to the USAID director, Patrick Fine, who also wanted a rapprochement. "I quickly sized up that they had a lot to offer," Fine told me.[32] "These were guys who get paid thousands a day to be consultants. I thought I needed to build bridges. Lou Hughes came in about a month later, and he was a bridge-builder too." A cautious working relationship developed between the two teams. "Familiarity bred collegiality," Fine says.

Though there was finally a truce between ARG and USAID, it wasn't like AID was going to take direction. So the ARGonauts began mentoring Afghan ministers. Ultimately, mentoring was to be the ARGonauts' greatest contribution. Before he was recruited for the ARG, Mitchell Shivers was a successful Wall Street investment banker. Son of a sea captain, Shivers had circumnavigated the globe at ten years old before serving as a marine officer in Vietnam. Not long before he was living in an ARG shipping container on the hardscrabble Kabul Embassy grounds, Shivers was domiciled on Jakarta's best street in a luxurious garden home tended by seven servants. In his capacity as the ARG's senior adviser to the ambassador and economic sector chief, Shivers mentored a number of Afghan ministers, including the respected minister of finance Ashraf Ghani and his successor, Anwar ul-Haq Ahady, as well as prominent businessmen such as Moby Media Group mogul Saad Mohseni, whom *Time* named as one of the world's one hundred most influential people. "Ashraf Ghani said ARG was invaluable," Shivers told me.[33]

With the military commanded by General David Barno cooperating with Ambassador Khalilzad, and ARG working with USAID, there was a momentary interagency unity of purpose. "It was a new approach—a whole-of-government approach," Fine says. Hughes echoes, "We had all the arrows aligned: Defense and State, ARG and AID, the USG and Government of Afghanistan. It was a heady and hopeful time."

But there were the realities of development in a dysfunctional system. Tom Berner was a high-powered Manhattan attorney with experience in modernizing Afghan law before he joined the ARG. "I read *The Ugly American* as a kid, and thought Americans went off to do good things. Then I found out otherwise," he told me. Berner told me about his project to sort out Afghanistan's tangled land-title problem, created by decades of war and multiple governments issuing conflicting titles, which prevented an effective mortgage system. "Fixing the land-title issue was really not a big problem," Berner says.[34] "North Carolina had a perfect system. Cost $200,000 to set it up. But no one at AID was interested in it. They awarded a contract to one of those six companies run by retired USAID. It was over $30 million just to consider the issue, and then the follow-on contract was going to be hundreds of millions of dollars more."[35]

While Berner witnessed the value of their experience and sacrifice, he also saw the ARGonauts' limitations. "You take a big corporate executive, he's effective, but if he doesn't have a big corporation under him, he's not so effective. They're used to snapping their fingers and getting things done," he told me. "They were a little bit of a fish out of water."[36]

But in the whirling world of two-war America, change was soon on the way for the ARGonauts. In May 2005, General Barno turned the military command over to General Karl Eikenberry, who had little time for whole-of-government approaches. Eikenberry quickly moved the military headquarters out of the embassy, where Barno had worked in conjunction with Ambassador Khalilzad. "That was a huge negative," Hughes says. In the summer of 2005, Ambassador Khalilzad was transferred to Iraq, replaced by Ambassador Ronald Neumann, who decreed that he wanted a "normal embassy." No more transformational diplomacy, no more Superman Zal antics. Just observe and report as good diplomats should do. In July 2005, Patrick Fine moved on, replaced by another USAID career foreign-service officer, Alonzo Fulgham. "All the arrows were in a line, suddenly some of the arrows were going in a different direction," Hughes says. "A pity—it could have been a great vehicle. It was a golden moment."[37]

The Afghanistan Reconstruction Group sputtered to a quiet halt in early 2007. "If you're tough on ARG," Mitchell Shivers told me, "it was uneven. By the end, I don't even think it was ARG." He concluded, "We had the right policies all along, but terrible execution."[38]

In the view of at least one American observer, the neocons left a painful legacy in Afghanistan: rampant corruption. Whitney Azoy first came to Afghanistan as a State Department foreign-service officer in the early 1970s. But rather than hopping from station to station like most foreign-service officers, Azoy decided to focus on Afghanistan as an anthropologist, becoming one of America's most perspicuous commentators on the often-opaque Afghan society. Azoy spoke to me from his winter home in Mexico, not long before he headed to his castle in Spain. He told me that it was laughable that the United States thought that the self-reliant Afghans needed development—or retired American CEOs to explain free-enterprise capitalism to them, for that matter. "The Afghans are the greatest free-market operators in the world," Azoy says.[39] He pointed out that corruption was always part of Afghan society, but fell within what he termed "culturally tolerated deviance." He says, "Afghans seem to agree that corruption was at its lowest level during the Marxist period. Most of those Afghan communist bureaucrats really did believe in the state and didn't steal much. Then come the Americans, and what happens—particularly in the neocon ideal—there's not much of a state at all. There's just the individual, and that's what happened in Afghanistan. Corruption exploded, and now we're dealing with it."

*   *   *

Barno's counterinsurgency strategy wasn't an easy transition for the US military, as few of Barno's fourteen thousand troops had any training or experience in the doctrine, making his first pillar, defeating the insurgency, complicated.[40] Rather than killing its way to victory, the military was now suddenly trying to concentrate on winning the Afghans' trust and support.[41] Soldiers conditioned to be warriors had a tough time adjusting to a "hearts-and-minds" campaign—though many gave it their best. A tall, lean career soldier who describes himself as a "former pipe-swinging infantryman," Lieutenant Colonel Michael Howard was the commander of a battalion in hostile Paktika Province. He was the ultimate counterterrorism soldier, determined to root out the insurgents. "We can't hunker down in the firebases," Howard said in January 2004, as he described his troops taking part in Operation Avalanche and engaging the enemy with warplane and attack helicopter support.[42] When Barno began promulgating the new COIN strategy in early 2004, there were few guides available to the almost-historical doctrine. As Howard tried to figure out how to implement this new strategy, he was forced to buy counterinsurgency books off the Internet. Barno remembered one conversation: "'Mike, we just changed your mission here from counterterrorism, which it was when you first got here last summer, to now a broad-based counterinsurgency approach. How did you get your platoon leaders and company commanders and first sergeants and platoon sergeants to be able to shift gears here in midstream and go from one to the other?' He goes, 'Easy, sir: booksamillion.com.'"[43] When Howard's books arrived at his post in the remote Afghan–Pakistan border region, he and his staff did a quick cram before heading into the wild Hindu Kush to apply the new tactics. Learning by doing.[44]

But not all of the US commanders accepted the importance of counterinsurgency. Many officers persisted with counterterrorism (CT)—killing as many insurgents as they could manage, without regard to hearts and minds. As the insurgency grew in strength in the east and south, the COIN versus CT debate complicated the Coalition's efforts—particularly as it played out on the ground.[45] Time and again, a Provincial Reconstruction Team's patient efforts to win over a district with development projects would be negated by an air strike or night raid that left dead innocents in its wake.[46] Speaking about the special ops teams' secrecy and separate command structure that commonly thwarted development efforts, Major General Peter Gilchrist, the British officer who served as Barno's deputy commanding general, said: "Most of the trouble tended to arise from that because the coordination wasn't there, because they're very secretive, and don't want anyone to know what they are doing. So you'd spend a long time sorting an area out, spending a bit of CERP [Commander's Emergency Response Program] money to get people to become compliant and so on, and the next night, you find that two houses had their doors blown in and the people were arrested and taken away, which you didn't know anything about, and it would then take another two or three months to recover from that."[47]

Lack of resources continued to bedevil the US commanders in Afghanistan. Barno complained, "The army was unhelpful, to be generous, in terms of providing us with resources and capabilities and people. They clearly had Iraq on their minds, but there was no interest whatsoever in providing us with anything but the absolute minimum of support."[48]

Rumsfeld, fixated on Iraq, tossed command of the ISAF forces over to NATO in August 2003, a decision that further complicated the war. The NATO ISAF commanders and their staffs rotated out with alarming rapidity—every six months. During his nineteen months as commander, Barno saw four different NATO commanders come and go, which naturally affected momentum and continuity. "You got some significant zigzags in terms of what ISAF was willing to do, what their direction was, where they played, and how they operated," Barno said.[49] Beyond the disruption caused by the rapid turnovers, the rotations also dismayed Afghan allies, who lived in a tribal society where long-term relationships were the coin of the realm. As their trusted Coalition comrades-in-arms rotated out, the Afghans learned that Western-style COIN was a different thing.

The decision to transfer ISAF to NATO made the order of battle even more complex, as dozens of uncoordinated military actors pushed multiple agendas. NATO took over operational responsibility in four steps, beginning with the north in 2003–2004. In May 2005, NATO took over the west, and—after much wrangling between the Bush administration and the NATO allies—assumed responsibility for the insurgency-infested east and south in 2006. Eager to pass off responsibility, Rumsfeld reassured NATO with that perennial American favorite: body counts. Rumsfeld told reporters, "If you look at the number of terrorists and Taliban and al Qaeda that are being killed every month, it would be hard for them to say that the Coalition forces and Afghan security forces were losing."[50] But the NATO allies were wary of all-out combat with the Taliban. The United States transferred ten thousand of its twelve thousand troops to NATO in the fall of 2006. The shift left in place the two—often uncoordinated—command structures in Afghanistan: the ISAF command and the continuing US Operation Enduring Freedom command that was primarily focused on high-value targets and insurgent concentrations.[51] By 2007, ISAF included troops from thirty-nine countries, the twenty-eight NATO countries and others including Australia, New Zealand, Sweden, and Jordan. There were sixty major donor institutions and hundreds of small NGOs jockeying for attention and resources. The ambassadorial staffs of the United States, the European Union, NATO, and the United Nations vied for power.[52]

The NATO military had trouble meeting its commitments. US officials grumbled the NATO allies weren't producing the numbers of troops, helicopters, and armored vehicles they had promised, or even enough transport planes to get them to Afghanistan.[53] While the COIN doctrine glowed with pixilated promise on Coalition computer screens, the plan needed soldiers and stuff to actually work. A Western ambassador said, "We can clear territory, but we can't hold it. There aren't sufficient numbers of NATO or Afghan troops."[54] British Army Colonel and counterinsurgency expert Alex Alderson fumed, "Presence matters, numbers are required, and plans need resources. Without them, in counterinsurgency, securing the population is an unachievable aspiration."[55]

The NATO military operated with long lists of national caveats imposed by their individual Western countries—seventy-six caveats by one count, enumerated in a document that was the size of a phone book.[56] The phrase "European cheese-eating surrender monkeys" entered the American soldiers' lexicon.[57] The Germans, for instance, demanded to be posted in the relatively quiescent north, where they were prohibited from executing combat missions, patrolling at night or on foot, or even returning fire if attacked. Deployed on three- and four-month rotations, their soldiers scarcely had time to figure anything out about Afghanistan. When the Germans did venture from their fortification in their buttoned-up armored carriers, an ambulance was required to accompany each convoy. The Germans' national caveats obviously isolated their troops, which some critics argued allowed the insurgency to spread to the north.[58]

The Netherlands deployed troops to the Taliban-infested southern province of Uruzgan, but operated under national caveats that required them to use force only when attacked and break contact as soon as possible, concentrating instead on redevelopment, with the motto, "Rebuild Where Possible, Fight Where Necessary." The Dutch pointed to their success in increasing NGOs, police, schools, and clinics, but critics maintained that the Dutch troops stayed huddled in secure areas, allowing the Taliban to control most of the countryside, where they had a booming narcotics trade.[59]

The French military initially declared it had no interest in redevelopment or the COIN strategy, instead focusing on training Afghan security forces. It did eventually soften its anti-COIN position. When a French battalion took over command of Kapisa Province in 2009, the commander embraced a Gallic version of COIN, making efforts to "protect, seduce, and convince" the population.[60]

The casualty-shy NATO allies also employed alternate tactics that led to unintended results. The British 2006 "cessation of hostilities" agreements with the Taliban in Helmand allowed the insurgents to return to the fight reinvigorated and refitted.[61] The Italians employed an even more direct approach: bribing the insurgents tens of thousands of dollars to not attack them. It was a successful strategy. When the Italians had the military responsibility for the Sarobi District east of Kabul, they only suffered one death before handing off control of the ostensibly quiet district to French forces in the summer of 2008. According to accounts, the Italians unfortunately neglected to mention their little financial arrangement to the French, who suffered ten dead and twenty-one wounded soldiers in an ambush less than a month after taking over. Hell evidently hath no fury like an un-bribed Taliban. French President Sarkozy was likewise furious, vowing never to send troops to Afghanistan again. The Italians were nonplussed—after all, they had paid the Taliban over $1.5 million in 2007 in ransom for the release of an Italian journalist.[62] As to why the Italians failed to fess up to the French, a Western military officer said the practice was "a bit shameful" and "never spoken about openly." Western officials subsequently said the practice of bribing the Taliban was widespread among NATO forces. One military officer reported Canadian soldiers did it in Kandahar; another outed the Germans in Kunduz. An Afghan officer tattled on the Italians, saying they also paid the Taliban in Herat. A senior Afghan official said, "I can tell you that lots of countries under the NATO umbrella operating out in rural parts of Afghanistan do pay the militants for not attacking them."[63] US troops in Nuristan Province used the same tactic, giving insurgent commander Mullah Sadig tens of thousands of dollars and hundreds of weapons to purportedly fight against the Taliban—not long after Sadig's men overran Combat Outpost Keating, where they killed eight American soldiers and wounded twenty-two. American officers eventually approved paying Sadig's fighters $25,000 a month to be village militia, though Mullah Sadig was a hard bargainer—holding out for another $150,000 in development projects.[64]

*　　*　　*

Barno's second COIN pillar, standing up the Afghan security sector, was likewise shaky. The Germans took responsibility for training the Afghan National Police, but the Afghan recruits typically were illiterate warlord militiamen accustomed to shaking down citizens to augment their low wages. The German efforts were halfhearted and underfunded, forcing the United States to pitch in. None of it went well. Rather than community protectors, the Afghan populace viewed the police as corrupt predators. Likewise, the Italian government's commitment to build a competent judiciary system faltered. A 2009 Congressional Research Service report tactfully concluded, "The court system remains in its infancy, with few capable jurists and attorneys."[65] More candidly, the Afghan judicial system was notorious for injustice and corruption. Barno's efforts to stand up an Afghan National Army tapped into the legendary Afghan fighting spirit, but the training was hobbled by lack of resources. Major General Gilchrist noted that Secretary of Defense Rumsfeld demanded quick results without providing the funding to accomplish the task: "So although we accelerated the training, the kit wasn't here; the barracks weren't there. So you had all these soldiers, but we didn't have any infrastructure or anything that made them an army."[66] As the insurgency grew in strength, US priorities vacillated until it was almost a multiple-choice strategy. Ahmed Rashid wrote, "One year [the United States] decided that the Afghan National Army had to be built up, and funding poured into it. The next year it was the police who were to be funded. Trying to get sustained money for any service sector project for any length of time was next to impossible."[67]

Barno's third pillar, establishing area ownership with forward operating bases and combat outposts, allowed tactical units to build relationships with local tribal elders, mullahs, and government leaders. "The one-year tour in a province is an immense, positive change from these two-week in-and-outs that we'd been doing before that," Barno said. But even the one-year rotations were problematic, as units seldom wanted to admit their mistakes to their replacements, so the learning curve started over with each deployment. "Every twelve months, it's the first day of school," Barno said.[68] Though they were now posted out in the provinces on FOBs, most American soldiers remained "fobbits"; 90 percent of US soldiers never "broke the wire"—left their bases. And the isolated combat outposts that the US military established across Afghanistan often became magnets for the insurgent *mujahideen*, as the tragedy of Combat Outpost Keating proved.

Barno's fourth COIN pillar envisioned using the military–civilian Provincial Reconstruction Teams to build Afghan infrastructure and governmental institutions. But US development was also a carousel of uncoordinated programs and groups. In the early years of the war, when the United States was still relying on its warlord strategy, *nation building* was a dirty word. As Donald Rumsfeld famously rebutted President Bush's stillborn "Marshall Plan" speech, "The last thing you're going to hear from this podium is someone thinking they know how Afghanistan ought to organize itself. They're going to have to figure it out. They're going to have to grab ahold of that thing and do something."[69] Accordingly, the development of Afghan infrastructure, security, and state institutions scarcely showed up on the US agenda, with the CIA and special ops teams often distributing what little US aid money that did arrive.[70]

As the 2004 American presidential elections loomed, the Bush officials got nervous. After years of failed promises, the Afghans were restive; the Taliban already renascent. The Bush team didn't want Afghanistan as another black mark on its record. So at a momentous National Security Council meeting in June 2003, the administration secretly decided to accelerate aid in Afghanistan. US spending appropriations skyrocketed from $740 million in 2003 to $1.9 billion in 2004.[71]

The US military elevated development as a key counterinsurgency tool. And the Congress went along with it. From 2002 to 2005, the Department of Defense's share of overall US-government development assistance jumped from 6 percent of the total to 22 percent. USAID's share concurrently dropped from 50 percent to 39 percent.[72] By the 2004–2005 period, $91 million in congressional appropriations was helping to fund twelve US PRTs concentrated in the rebellious south.[73] The typical PRT had only three civilians in the eighty-person unit. Given the shortage of civilian development expertise, the military had to reach out to the Army Reserve to staff the teams, giving rise to what army historian Donald Wright termed a "we own it all" philosophy.[74]

With the military dominating the PRTs, training was predictably heavy on combat skills. "I was gobsmacked how fucked up it was," Lieutenant Colonel Simon Gardner, an early PRT officer, told me about the training PRTs received at Fort Bragg.[75] "You don't have to train to be miserable." With the infantry in charge, the PRT role-playing to learn Afghan-appropriate development skills took a backseat to military drills—slogging through mud, surviving attacks. "The State Department officials would just get in a meeting to practice a negotiation with a governor and some asshole would run through and throw a grenade," Gardner says. "Or the convoy would be on the way to a meeting with a tribal leader and there'd be an ambush. And the meeting would never happen." It wasn't until 2009, when the military moved PRT training from Fort Bragg to Camp Atterbury, Indiana, that the army trainers concentrated on more appropriate development skills—though there were still plenty of fake grenades and authentic mud.[76]

The US military linked development and aid to tactical combat goals. In contrast, its European allies generally framed development in humanitarian terms. The American PRTs' heavy security protection and cooperation with the CIA and other US military intelligence agents hampered the teams' ability to gain the trust of Afghan communities. Critics contended that the military's war-zone development work was little more than patronage paid to warlords and Afghan officials and a quid pro quo for intelligence. Most Afghans felt that they needed security before meaningful reconstruction could begin.[77] As the US military persisted in trying to win hearts and minds, the Afghans were just trying to keep their heads down.

As congressional funding for the Commander's Emergency Response Program began to pulse into Afghanistan in 2004, military development increased. But CERP was another shoot-from-the-hip program at a time when George Bush's cowboy neocon policies ruled the range. Intended to provide funding to commanders for small relief and reconstruction projects, CERP had problems from the beginning. There was relatively little oversight as the commanders had the power to make quick decisions without higher authorization. There were few subject-matter experts, such as engineers or agricultural experts, to help assess the projects before they were launched, leading to welters of uncoordinated, unsustainable projects.[78] The insurgency often prevented appropriate supervision of even the small projects CERP was set up to handle, making ongoing implementation a security nightmare.[79] And even if the military commanders made the commitment to get to projects, there was an enormous shortage of contract oversight officers to actually manage them. As the congressional funding grew, CERP morphed into something else. Commanders and civilian aid officials increasingly used CERP money for large-scale projects such as road construction.[80] By 2009, Congress had funded over $1.6 billion for small-scale CERP projects in Afghanistan, but an investigation by the Special Inspector General for Afghanistan Reconstruction (SIGAR) found that the majority of the money was spent on large-scale projects—3 percent of the projects sucked up 67 percent of the CERP money.[81]

And small wonder they lost track: the military and USAID couldn't share information on development projects because they were on two different databases. One officer told the GAO auditors that the military lost historical data from CERP projects when the data was being transferred into another database system.[82] Another officer said that the military failed to note in the database the location of the districts and villages where they had done development projects, so there was no way to monitor or assess the impact of the projects on quelling the insurgency.[83] A PRT officer in Khost Province told me his team had essentially lost its institutional memory when an earlier PRT accidentally erased all of the electronic data that wasn't backed up. "There's a storage container full of hard copies," he told me as we sat in the hundred-degree heat, "but I need to wait for it to cool down before I can send anyone out there."[84] In the course of the rotations, the PRT even lost the locations of some of the schools and clinics they had built earlier.

The development metrics were no better than Rumsfeld's body counts as a measure of effective counterinsurgency. USAID, the Corps of Engineers, PRTs, and sundry other actors merrily counted spending, inputs, and sometimes even outputs, such as teachers trained or trees planted. But there was a dearth of longitudinal follow-up studies, particularly on sustainability. In spite of the supposed linkage between aid and counterinsurgency, there was a disconnect, as development officials very seldom measured security outcomes. "Statistical rubbish," security analyst Anthony Cordesman called development data gathered in a war zone.[85] Critics said PRTs mainly spent development money where it was safe enough to go—what the PRTs said was the "ink-spot" or "Go Green" strategy: rewarding good, progovernment villages and districts so that hostile adjoining territories saw the goodies they could get for docility. Critics claimed the development schemes that enriched Afghan insiders often alienated Afghans who didn't get their share of the booty. Sometimes the clear outcome of development projects was a dramatic spike in violence, as the insurgents and their Afghan tribal allies resisted the incursions of Coalition forces. However it went, the development metrics almost never showed a connection between aid and improved security.

As the years went by, development plans were adopted and abandoned at lightning speed. The Afghanistan Reconstruction Group was a short-lived experiment. The ill-fated Accelerated Success program left a legacy of overpriced, unsustainable development projects, many of which were implemented without any coordination with the United Nations or other Western partners.[86] The grandiose plans to stand up functioning Afghan ministries had risible outcomes. The redevelopment money and technical aid that the NATO countries promised never seemed to arrive in full.[87]

Barno's fifth COIN pillar, diplomatic engagement with neighboring countries, was the shakiest of all the supports, as Iran and Pakistan actively supported the Taliban and other insurgents.[88] Predominantly Shia Muslim Iran overcame its aversion to the Sunni Muslim Taliban in the interests of thwarting its archenemy America with continued chaos in Afghanistan.[89] With the collusion of Pakistan's Inter-Services Intelligence, army, and fundamentalist Islamic parties, the country's Federally Administered Tribal Areas became a vast insurgent staging area with over one hundred training camps. The Pakistani army provided advice, and sometimes even covering fire to the insurgents. Pakistan was more a support for the insurgents than a pillar of American counterinsurgency.

*   *   *

Saima Wahab is an Afghan American woman from the West Coast, a Pashtun who spent five years working as a linguist, cultural adviser, and research manager in some of the most volatile provinces in Afghanistan. She was there during the 2004–2005 period when Barno rolled out his counterinsurgency strategy. Proud of her American citizenship, blue-jeaned and T-shirted Wahab is also a proud Pashtun. Wahab still has family in Afghanistan. Though she was posted just a few miles from where they live, she couldn't contact them. The danger was too great. "They've gotten night letters from the Taliban about my work with the Americans," she told me.[90] "I keep in touch with them through my mother in the US. She'll tell me, 'Oh, your cousin is having a wedding,' or whatever. I'll be a couple of miles away." Wahab told me she is appalled by the military's failure to recruit Pashto speakers to translate between the Americans and Pashtuns, instead often relying on Farsi-speaking Afghans to interpret. In this tribal land, it is culturally insensitive—if not disastrous—to the mission to use interpreters from a tribe speaking another language. "I know why we are losing in Afghanistan," she says, "because we are losing the Pashtuns. You can't do this with Farsi-speakers. You can't do COIN without communication." Wahab sees the United States making the same mistakes the Soviets did. "We went into a culture we didn't understand. Our army didn't have the correct training—didn't know the history. We built a lot of buildings but didn't understand all the Afghans wanted was security. Spending millions on projects the

Afghans can't use because they can't come out of their homes. We turned a blind eye to [President] Karzai and corruption." As she mused on her experience with Barno's great counterinsurgency experiment, she concludes, "In some ways, COIN would have worked if the army had dedicated itself to it. But I don't even think they picked up on it."

In spite of the work of tens of thousands of Americans and billions of dollars spent, the first US counterinsurgency campaign in Afghanistan was a failure, doomed by duplicity, lack of resources, attention, coordination, consistency, and will. The Special Forces dictum states that if an insurgency is not shrinking, it's winning. When all was said and done, the Afghan insurgency regrouped and grew during Barno's short and poorly resourced counterinsurgency effort.

*   *   *

In May 2005, Barno transferred the command to Lieutenant General Karl Eikenberry, who promptly moved his office out of the embassy, signaling an end to the close civilian–military alliance that Barno and Khalilzad had formed to execute the counterinsurgency strategy. Barno's deputy commander, Major General Gilchrist, recalled the transition: "When General Eikenberry came in, he looked at the campaign plan, and he said, 'That is ridiculous. That is like a Soviet Five-Year Plan. We won't have any of that.'"[91] According to Gilchrist, Eikenberry quickly downgraded the interagency coordination and simplified the strategy into "three or four strands he could follow." Colonel David Lamm, Barno's chief of staff, said, "It was almost a de-Barnoification of the operation."[92] Instead of an ambitious civilian–military counterinsurgency campaign that reached out to the whole Afghan society and government, Eikenberry wanted to use traditional army ways to improve security, the inept Afghan security forces, and the woeful Karzai government.

In February 2007, the new secretary of defense, Robert Gates, replaced Eikenberry with General Dan "Bomber" McNeill. Bomber McNeill didn't have much interest in either population security or government reform and certainly had little sympathy for the NATO cease-fires or economic development. He wanted to hit the enemy, so that's what he did during his year-and-a-quarter command. The next commander, General David McKiernan, switched back to counterinsurgency, replacing Bomber's permissive rules of engagement with a restrictive policy that emphasized "restraint and the utmost discrimination in the use of firepower."[93] The vacillating strategies prompted Afghanistan expert Antonio Giustozzi to write, "It can be argued that changing strategy every six to twelve months is tantamount to no strategy whatsoever, particularly if that is not justified by changes in the insurgents' own strategy."[94]

As the military rotated strategies, the Pashtun-led insurgency expanded in the south and east. By 2007, Taliban attacks were up 27 percent from 2006. The culture of corruption had fully matured, with everyone in on the take. Using a robust cash flow from opium, crime, Gulf State and Pakistani support, and skims from US development and logistics, the insurgents certainly didn't have any problems financing their war. With Iraq at full boil, the Americans continued to under-resource the Afghan conflict. Speaking to the House Armed Services Committee in December 2007, Joint Chiefs of Staff Chairman Admiral Michael Mullen said, "Our main focus, militarily, in the region and in the world right now is rightly and firmly in Iraq." He emphasized, "It is simply a matter of resources, of capacity. In Afghanistan we do what we can. In Iraq, we do what we must. There's a limit to what we can do in Afghanistan."[95]

A few months earlier, an ambitious young senator from Illinois named Barack Obama gave a major foreign-policy speech at the Woodrow Wilson Center. Critiquing President Bush's rush to war in Iraq, Obama stated, "I was a strong supporter of the war in Afghanistan."[96] He went on to promise, "When I am president, we will wage the war that has to be won." He pledged to deploy additional troops to Afghanistan, as well as increase nonmilitary aid by one billion dollars to fund counternarcotics programs and improve Afghan governance with "tough anticorruption safeguards on aid, and increased international support to develop rule of law across the country." In many ways, he was planning to put George Bush's Afghanistan strategies on steroids. The question was: Would it make a difference?

*   *   *

Scene: Ali Daya, Khost Province, Afghanistan. We're on our way to the village of Ali Daya for an agricultural-development mission, our convoy of armored MRAP vehicles juddering down the primitive road while the turret gunners keep watch. Inside the sealed vault of the truck, I lurch back and forth in the seat safety harness that is designed to keep me in place when we hit a buried bomb. Ali Daya is a typical Afghan village, a collection of brown adobe houses sheltering three hundred families behind high, thick walls. Along dirt lanes and tiny canals, the leaves of slender poplar trees flicker green and gray in the breeze. Farm fields surround the village. Mountains rise in the distance. It's a government-friendly village, the Indiana National Guard Agribusiness Development Team (ADT) soldiers tell me. "We're going to show them some love," the ADT deputy commander, Colonel Cindra Chastain, says. A fit, blonde career soldier, Chastain is leading the mission. She's a good choice, as her ready laugh and quick mind are remarkably effective at defusing tense situations. She explains we're traveling to Ali Daya with a Fourth Brigade combat unit to do soil tests—and try to rewin hearts and minds.

I heard about Ali Daya several weeks ago when I interviewed Jamie Terzi, the deputy director of Afghanistan for the international aid organization CARE, at Kabul's expat hangout the Flower Street Café.[97] She told me how on the night of April 8, 2009—about eight weeks before our ADT mission—a team of American-led special ops soldiers crept into Ali Daya on a clandestine raid.[98] The military considered the village, located in the relatively quiescent Gorbuz District, to be pro-government and progressive. Notable in fundamentalist Khost Province, there was even a girls' secondary school supported by CARE. Even rarer in a province where teacherless girls' schools stand empty, the Ali Daya school had a teacher, the wife of an Afghan Army colonel named Awal Khan. The spec ops team crept into Ali Daya to capture a suspected insurgent. Surrounding the suspect's walled compound, the raiders climbed on adjacent houses, moving across the flat roofs to take up positions. But they neglected one important detail: to notify the inhabitants of the houses where they crouched. One of the houses was Awal Khan's. He was away on a mission, but his brother was there, guarding Khan's teacher wife, two children, and Khan's cousin, a young mother with a newborn. Hearing footsteps on the roof, the Khans thought the Taliban was about to attack them for their work with the Westerners. So they shot through the ceiling at the intruders above. The shots unleashed America's attack dogs. Thinking the insurgents were below, the soldiers responded with a firestorm. When the shooting stopped, Khan's wife, two children, and brother were dead. The four-day-old baby of Khan's cousin was also shot and killed.

In her British accent, Terzi told me that the military initially contended that four "armed combatants" had been shot dead. "Coalition forces go and make a mistake in a raid, kill one of our teachers, her daughter, who was a student, and three of her family members including a four-day-old baby, inside her house, which was one of our classes." Her voice rose, "I find it really hard to understand how a four-day-old baby is shot. I really just don't get it. I mean did you not look when you were firing? Because if it was for any other reason, but a four-day-old baby."[99]

In shuras (meetings) across the province, the enraged Khostis protested the civilian deaths. According to a study by an eleven-member NGO consortium that included CARE, there were 2,100 civilian casualties in Afghanistan in 2008, a

30 percent increase from the year prior.[100] *Only when the international media amplified the uproar from the Khostis, CARE, and the Karzai government did the military take responsibility and begin damage control. The big brass flew in, proffering generous condolence and solatia payments, promising an investigation and new procedures for night raids. Ali Daya got a new generator with lines to all the houses. Eager young US officers swarmed the village wanting to make nice. Our agricultural-development mission was another US effort at* consequence management—*that bland term for trying to fix things gone horribly wrong.*

Winning Pashtun hearts and minds is problematic at best. Famously vengeful, the Pashtuns are primed to exchange their hoes for weapons at the first sign of an affront or invader. When the coalition drops an errant bomb or attacks the wrong house, it loses that village for three generations. We are unclear about the reception we will get at Ali Daya.

But when the ADT dismounts in Ali Daya, they receive a warm greeting. Young men crowd around the soldiers as they walk to a village farmer's wheat field, where the ag specialists learn about his declining yields. He has plenty of water, the tribesman says. That's not the problem. They look at the small wheat seeds he provided the week prior. Then, he said they were bad seeds. Now he says they are fine. The specialists conjecture: Maybe a bad translation? ADT ag specialist Major Larry Temple stalks the field with his stainless steel soil probe, taking soil samples. As the ag specialists show their love in the farm field, the combat soldiers toss Frisbees with the young Afghans, who spin like tops trying to follow the discs' unfamiliar arcs. Fascinated by the smiling American woman in body armor, a throng of young men cluster around Colonel Chastain. She tells them her name is Leila, a common Afghan name that she used for role-playing during Pashto language classes. As the young Afghan males' adulation mounts to rock star levels, the sound of Derek and the Dominos' anthem, "Layla," begins playing in my head.

Over by the dirt road, the ADT security platoon distributes pens, candy, and stuffed animals to a gaggle of children, including a small girl venturing out from her family's compound. Emboldened by the booty, the boys become ravening wolves, beating up the little girl to get her toy. A slender, fair-haired security soldier, looking like a long-necked tortoise in his helmet and bulbous body armor, watches. "Makes you sick," he says. "Can't do a thing." A contingent of ag specialists and combat soldiers return from their love-showing session with tribal elders. An ag specialist reports the villagers really accepted them and their offer of an expensive hydrology project. As soon as the elders bought into the irrigation project, the combat soldiers pursued their mission—security—by asking, "So who are the bad guys in the village?"

The way back to the ADT base is the typical tense transit across an unpredictable, asymmetric war zone. Eyes scan for trip wires and disturbed roadbeds. An ADT driver laments, "What I want to know is, why can't we go back to the good old-fashioned war before IEDs?"

Chapter 9

The Broken Agency
USAID

INTENT ON IMPRESSING THE WINSOME French journalist with her pursed lips and slender white notebook, the burr-headed aid contractor leaned across the expat café's starched tablecloth. "It's not development anymore," he said. "It's civ–mil." He sat back as she wrote. The solicitous Afghan waiter appeared with more coffee. She looked up, and he leaned in again. "It's just thousands of guys working in security bubbles—hoping they don't blow us up. American people are seeing it as development. Maybe they're not even seeing it as development. We say it's nation building, using development organizations as weapons. USAID is a force multiplier." With an arched eyebrow, she bent her head to write again.

*   *   *

Since its inception as the primary US-government aid-and-development organization, the United States Agency for International Development (USAID or AID) has been an instrument of American foreign policy—charged with providing "economic, development, and humanitarian assistance around the world in support of the foreign-policy goals of the United States."[1] A Cold War baby that President John Kennedy begat in 1961 to deliver long-term US foreign assistance outside of the military–security aid matrix, USAID remained umbilically attached to American foreign policy. To endear USAID to the American public, Kennedy invoked the Marshall Plan, which helped to bond western Europe to democratic capitalism in the post–World War II period. In the congressional debates leading up to the Foreign Assistance Act of 1961, proponents touted USAID as a powerful foreign-policy tool that would consolidate four politically complicated aid-dispensing programs—deemed "haphazard and irrational" in Kennedy's summation—into one muscular agency. The new agency would carry America's aid-and-development flag into the bipolar world to stand shoulder-to-shoulder with the US military and security forces in battles for hearts and minds. Promoting the new aid agency in the Mutually Assured Destruction (MAD) era, Kennedy raised the specter of Communists taking over poverty-stricken societies, saying the falling dominos would be "disastrous." Kennedy said, "Thus our own security would be endangered and our prosperity imperiled. A program of assistance to the undeveloped nations must continue because the nation's interest and the cause of political freedom require it."[2] Congress passed the Foreign Assistance Act on September 4, 1961, establishing USAID.[3] But Kennedy and Congress never addressed the tension between long-term development needs and short-term security imperatives, creating an agency forever trying to please two, often squabbling, masters.[4]

The Vietnam War was the high-water mark for USAID. In 1962, there were 8,600 direct-hire USAID personnel, and when the US war effort was at its peak in 1968, USAID had 17,500 employees. USAID was also a vital element in a unique hybrid civil–military organization known as CORDS—Civil Operations and Revolutionary Development Support. Formed in May 1967 to coordinate the US civil and military pacification programs in Vietnam, CORDS included personnel from the military, the State Department, USAID, USDA, and CIA, who operated in joint teams throughout South Vietnam's forty-four provinces and 250 districts.[5] While USAID directed CORDS, it was William Colby, the CIA station chief in Saigon and later CIA director, who masterminded the "hearts and minds" program. CORDS included the infamous Phoenix Program that killed tens of thousands of suspected National Liberation Force members and "neutralized" many tens of thousands more.[6] But the intertwining of USAID's development work with the CIA and military's counterinsurgency campaign ultimately created a crisis for the aid agency. In the early 1970s, an antiwar Congress protested USAID's focus on short-term military goals and lack of demonstrable foreign-policy results by slashing appropriations. Congress's 1971 refusal to approve foreign-assistance funds for 1972 and 1973 was the first defeat of a foreign-aid authorization bill since the Marshall Plan.

*   *   *

Reform became the enduring USAID buzzword. In 1971, the chastened (and defensive) agency issued a self-assessment. The Stern Report blamed USAID's failures on a lack of clear direction and support from Congress and the American public.[7] Congress launched reform initiatives in 1973 and 1978 among what were to be seven major foreign-aid reform efforts in the post–World War II era.[8] The 1973 "New Directions" legislation refocused USAID toward the "basic human needs" of the developing world's poorest classes with agriculture, rural-development, health, nutrition, and family-planning programs, which were linked to the recipient countries' human-rights development.[9] The legislation that followed the 1978 reform initiative established the International Development Cooperation Agency, a "super" agency charged with coordinating the multitude of foreign-assistance programs that had sprung up after the 1961 Foreign Assistance Act. Concurrently, President Carter attempted to revivify the Development Coordination Committee. But by the Reagan administration, the International Development Cooperation Agency was a memory, a victim of bureaucratic turf battles, and the Development Coordination Committee was equally moribund. Through the 1980s, with Reagan officials focused on countering Soviet influence in the Third World, the aid emphasis was often security-related. Reagan's supply-sider officials were also pressuring USAID to accelerate privatization. But USAID's efforts to reform itself didn't do much good.

In 1989, the Task Force on Foreign Assistance chaired by the esteemed centrist Democrat Representative Lee Hamilton concluded USAID was so ineffective that the agency could no longer be saved. "US foreign assistance needs a new premise, a new framework, and a new purpose to meet the challenges of today. It is time to start anew," stated the report of what came to be known as the Hamilton–Gilman Commission.[10]

Lee Hamilton retired in 1998 after thirty-four years in Congress on the House Foreign Affairs Committee. Now nearly eighty years old, Hamilton remains a pillar of the foreign-policy establishment, serving on multiple national-security boards and councils and heading up the Center for Congress at Indiana University. In spite of his regular early-morning workouts, time has slightly stooped Hamilton's former basketball-star 6'4" frame, but his whipcrack mind and Jimmy Stewart folksiness continue to stand him in good stead among the globe's luminaries.

Hamilton told me that when the task force investigated USAID in the late 1980s, it found a troubled organization: "It was a very unfocused agency. Development is such a vast thing, with so many strands that AID tried to be all things to all people. When you gather together development experts—and we have a lot of them—they almost always will push forward certain ideas, certain aspects of development. The problem is you end up with a great number of very worthy projects, but no focus. And USAID had limited resources, so they sprayed the money around. You end up with a number of worthy projects being carried out, but of limited overall impact."[11] The 1989 Hamilton–Gilman report indicated USAID had 33 legislated objectives and 75 agency priorities, with 288 reporting requirements for more than 2,000 projects around the globe, further complicated by more than 700 annual project-change notifications and innumerable earmarks, directives, restrictions, conditions, and prohibitions. "The result," the report read, "is an aid program driven by process rather than by content and substance."[12]

In Hamilton's view, USAID suffered under a woeful lack of congressional support—some of which was deserved: "It lost the support because of its confusion and ineffectiveness of delivering results, I think." He spoke of AID's short rotations in the countries where the work was done, undermining the sustainability of the projects. "It's a short attention span," Hamilton says, "the inability to keep people in the field." The combination of USAID's weak resources, inability to prioritize, and failure to sustain efforts in the field eventually contorted the agency into a dysfunctional organization concentrating on appropriations-delivering politicos rather than the world's development needs. "I think you have a lot of well-meaning people," Hamilton says. "But USAID focuses on Washington and Kabul."[13]

Back in 1989, the Hamilton–Gilman report engendered a new foreign-assistance act, but the reform legislation failed to become law—twice passed by the House; twice rejected by the Senate.[14] In 1991, as the Soviet Union blew apart, the first Bush administration proposed yet another aid reform bill, but that measure likewise didn't make it through Congress. While lots of people in Washington saw the need to fix USAID, there was no consensus about the remedy beyond continued calls for free-market vigor to be injected into the sclerotic organization.

The end of the Cold War was a shock for USAID, already perennially besieged by congressional critics questioning the agency's short-term expediency and long-term foreign-policy value. A 1992 GAO study pilloried the agency for lack of strategic vision and leadership.[15] It was the beginning of a bad year for USAID. In 1992, the State Department nabbed the responsibility for US foreign-assistance programs in the former Soviet Union—after having been given development responsibilities for former Communist countries in Eastern Europe three years earlier.[16] And the White House Office of Management and Budget loosened a formerly ironclad rule that all foreign aid had to go through USAID, weakening the agency's control.[17] Congress began to combine sector-specific funding, which further impacted USAID's capacity to control aid funding.[18] In a 1992 *Foreign Affairs* article, James Clad and Roger Stone wrote that USAID was "a dispirited bureaucracy lacking leadership, resources, and rationale."[19]

The next year, a critical GAO report stated, "The Agency for International Development (AID) is at a critical juncture in its thirty-year history," going on to characterize its management as "poor," and its future imperiled in the post–Cold War era. In 1993, with globalization, privatization, and "reinventing government" on its mind, the Clinton administration proposed the Peace, Prosperity, and Democracy Act to replace the Foreign Assistance Act. For the most part, Clinton's drive to "reinvent government" met the standard bureaucratic buzzsaw.[20] The Clinton proposal never even got out of the House Committee—or into a Senate committee, for that matter.[21]

But with Communism no longer the existential threat that could be used to justify appropriations, USAID was frantic to find a new rationale. And the failure of the reform legislation meant AID had to muddle along without congressional direction. American politicians were dreaming about former Communist dictatorships being reborn as European-style market-economy democracies, so USAID officials suddenly transformed themselves into caped crusaders for civil society. The idea that development was essential to the growth of freedom meant there were lots of congressional appropriations for the promotion of free-market liberal democracy to soak up.

Privatization seemed to be another answer. Critics had long demanded free-market solutions. The calls for outsourcing aid contracts to private development companies began as early as 1965, when the consulting company Booz Allen not unexpectedly recommended that USAID should hire fewer government staffers and more private consultants. In 1969, President Richard Nixon picked up the refrain, calling for "innovative technical assistance"—aka private, free-market consultants. Study groups under Reagan, then Henry Kissinger, had evinced their belief that private-sector ideas would fix USAID.[22] With the Hamilton–Gilman recommendations and the Clinton administration intent on reinventing government, USAID officials figured a private-sector, free-market solution was the politically savvy way to go.

Accordingly, a 1990 USAID report recommended outsourcing development and aid work to private contractors rather than to other government agencies. Though Clinton's Peace, Prosperity, and Democracy Act didn't get legislative approval, USAID signed on to be a "reinvention laboratory," and as part of it, started the New Partnership Initiative, which strengthened its linkages with NGOs and private-sector companies—*especially* private-sector companies.[23] The agency argued that private contractors were cheaper and that the government could have greater control over private contractors than over other government agencies, avoiding the sandbox fights that inevitably erupted when multiple governmental agencies were involved. And there was a further, quietly stated benefit of outsourcing aid contracts to for-profit development corporations: the private companies could lobby Congress.[24]

USAID's privatization strategy depleted the agency's ranks. In 1980, the agency had 4,058 permanent American employees. By 2008, the number was down to 2,200. Equally debilitating, most of AID's technical staff left. By 2008, there were only six engineers and sixteen agricultural experts still on staff.[25] From 1997 to 2007, the number of USAID employees in Washington overseeing contracts plummeted nearly fivefold.[26]

It was the Beltway Bandits—a derisive name for the private development contractors headquartered around Washington's I-495 ring road—who picked up the slack.[27] USAID called them "implementing partners." Often run by former USAID officials, the for-profit corporations increasingly won the majority of development contracts. The notable bandits included the Louis Berger Group, BearingPoint (a KPMG spin-off), DynCorp, Chemonics, the Academy for Educational Development, and Creative Associates International—companies that all received major contracts in Afghanistan.[28] With President George W. Bush and the neoncons plotting their war against Saddam Hussein in 2002, there was even more development money for the Beltway Bandits. In his 2002 National Security Strategy, President George W. Bush elevated development to be an equal to defense and diplomacy as a pillar of national security. It became known as the 3D framework. In the 3D rubric, development was another tool to build free-market democracies. Bush's "New Compact for Development" speech in March 2002 announced his promise to increase development assistance by 50 percent over the subsequent three years, and the establishment of the Millennium Challenge Corporation (MCC). Inspired by studies from the conservative Heritage Foundation, the MCC bestowed development dollars on stable countries with low corruption and free markets—without answering why well-governed countries would need development assistance from foreign powers. And so, the Beltway Bandits got a boost. Not surprisingly, Chemonics's revenue grew at an average of almost 25 percent a year from 2001 to 2005. BearingPoint's public-sector division, which included USAID contracts, averaged $1.3 billion a year in revenues.[29]

But critics were soon pointing out the problems of outsourcing. The hoped-for efficiencies were still a dream, and the flaws of the contracting process were increasingly obvious. The problems began even earlier, when Wall Street insiders and Ivy League heavyweights thundered into post-Soviet Eastern Europe loaded with US taxpayer money courtesy of USAID contracts for spurious free-market development schemes, which became stinky scandals when the media honed in on the abuses.[30] Focused on their profitability, the small number of private US development companies learned to game the system to their advantage, sucking up most of the AID contracts, which were primarily cost-plus.

According to the development NGOs, which were increasingly pushed out of contention for the aid contracts, the for-profit companies ignored the need to engage the host countries in the projects. Rather than grow a developing country's human capacity to run its own society through the aid projects, the Beltway Bandits were focused on engineering and construction—a "git 'er done" mentality. Sometimes this philosophy led to slapdash and counterproductive results, such as the scandals that erupted over the badly built schools, clinics, and roads that Louis Berger foisted on the Afghans. The US contractors' overheads leached most of the money out of the contracts, resulting in high profits and substandard projects. With their cozy relationships and the bare-bones USAID oversight staff, the for-profit aid companies could dial in their own bottom lines with little real need to actually provide meaningful aid in the developing world.[31]

USAID faced other problems. In the larger scheme of things, the independent MCC also served to subvert USAID's beleaguered officials, as did Bush's Emergency Plan for AIDS Relief, which was also out of USAID control. "The Bush administration just wired around USAID completely," Lee Hamilton says.[32] The additional foreign-assistance agencies meant that the American aid effort was even less integrated, contributing to what foreign-affairs specialist Larry Nowels termed a "growing organizational incoherence."[33]

Even USAID's role in America's war against terrorism was questioned. At a USAID symposium in June 2002, Princeton economist Alan Krueger and a panel of peers debunked the idea that AID's development work could actually contribute to America's counterterrorism fight. "Any connection between education, poverty, and terrorism is indirect, complicated, and probably weak," Krueger said. USAID Assistant Administrator for Policy and Program Coordination Patrick Cronin agreed that the research indicated "no compelling link between poverty and terrorism."[34] So as USAID embarked on the great development crusade in Afghanistan, the leaders already knew there was no connection between aid and security.[35]

*   *   *

USAID's attempts at reinvention had failed to quiet the critics. Senator Jesse Helms, the irascible conservative from North Carolina, had introduced a bill in 1995 to eliminate USAID. Helms declared that foreign aid "is the greatest racket of all time" and "a rip-off of the American taxpayer," a scam that "lines the pockets of corrupt dictators while funding the salaries of a growing, bloated bureaucracy."[36] In Helms's hyperbolic view, foreign aid was "throwing money down foreign rat holes."[37] As the agency scrambled to reorganize yet again, Helms led another charge to merge AID into the State Department.

A 2003 GAO report on USAID read like a refrain to the critical 1992 and 1993 GAO reports, again recommending that USAID implement a strategic planning and management system to redress its glaring problems. The number of US direct-hire staff, including foreign-service officers, dropped 37 percent, from 3,163 in 1992 to 1,985 in December 2002, and the agency increasingly relied on institutional contractors to do the work. In the same period, the number of countries with USAID programming almost doubled, meaning the failing agency was spread even thinner. USAID had evolved from a government agency with US foreign-service employees implementing development projects to one with a shrunken staff letting out contracts. As direct-hire USAID staff continued to decline, mission directors outsourced even oversight to contractors. The profit-making corporations were in charge.

*   *   *

The smoke was still drifting from the last grenades as Ed Fox, a grizzled former USAID officer, sat with me near the derelict Indiana schoolhouse talking about the fall of AID. The rattle of automatic fire occasionally drifted over from the faux Afghan village near the center of Camp Muscatatuck, the former Indiana Farm Colony for Feeble-minded Youths that started in 1920 out on the Hoosier prairie. A team of muscular Navy SEALs pumped iron beside a moldering brick cottage. After the colony had been abandoned for a decade, the military repurposed the former home for developmentally disabled boys as the training center for military–civilian development teams deploying to Afghanistan. "We're returning it to its original purpose" Sergeant Brad Staggs laughingly said earlier in the day as he waved at a group of diplomats walking toward the dining hall, where we were heading to witness a fake ambush.[38] "There'll be kinetics at lunch," the sergeant said, using the military term for guns and such. "That's a nice place to get shot at."

At Camp Muscatatuck, the civilian diplomats and development officials learned basic war-zone survival skills through events such as their lunchtime ambush, as well as practicing negotiation skills with a troupe of Afghan Americans who role-played Afghans of various stripes, from provincial governors to Taliban. "We've got one guy who's the spitting image of Karzai," Sergeant Staggs told me. The camp, also used for disaster training, was crammed with blown-up cars, rappelling structures, burn houses, and a maze for serious paintball games. Pointing to a vast mound of demolished concrete that simulated a bombed building, the sergeant said, "That's a very popular rubble pile to get bodies out of."

Ed Fox, the former USAID staffer, now works for the McKellar Corporation, the private company that held the contract to train the development teams for Afghanistan. "When the Cold War ended," Fox told me, "the coalition that supported AID fell apart—people said, 'Where is the Peace Dividend?' There were funding wars in the 1990s. USAID had no constituency. State hated AID—they made a play to absorb USAID."[39] Fox told me about the torturous path that USAID took to survive the early nineties' funding wars, first through alliances with NGOs such as CARE and Save the Children, and then with the private development contractors. He spoke of the rise of military-controlled reconstruction and the new aid entities, as well as the endgame under Condoleezza Rice, who "lowered the boom," in his words. Speaking about Rice's policies that devastated AID, Fox said, "They cut the head off."

*   *   *

So it was an undermanned and overwhelmed USAID that stumbled into Afghanistan.[40] And reinforcements weren't on the way; it was hard to get anyone to sign on for the hardship post in Kabul. As the surge of American aid money began to engulf Afghanistan in September 2003, the Kabul Embassy had seven full-time staff and thirty-five full-time contractors—most Afghans. There were sixty-one USAID vacancies, including five unfilled openings for direct-hire foreign-service officers.[41] The agency went from twelve staff members in Kabul in 2002 to thirty-nine in 2003. By 2004, there were still only 101 total USAID staffers in Afghanistan. During that period, US spending on development skyrocketed from $214 million in fiscal year (FY) 2002–2003 to $1.1 billion in FY 2004–2005.[42] In June 2004, USAID staffers in Kabul were nominally managing $27.5 million in projects per person compared to the worldwide norm of $1.2 million. By September 2004, USAID had the nominal management down to $11.2 million per staffer versus the global norm of $1.3 million.[43] "Nominally managing" because, first, no one but a super-officer could manage that load; second, because concerns about the deteriorating security situation kept the USAID officers penned behind the embassy razor wire. The Pentagon required all US officials to have military escort to break the wire—but there were seldom enough soldiers to accompany them, so mainly they were stuck inside the compounds.

Mark Ward joined USAID's foreign service in 1986, serving in posts around the globe before becoming AID's post-9/11 mission director to Pakistan and later the acting assistant administrator for Asia. He chafed under the security rules that sequestered the USAID workers behind walls. Ward wrote in the *Washington Post*, "The principal provider of US assistance, the US Agency for International Development, is severely constrained in Afghanistan by security rules that tolerate no risk for our foreign-service officers. They are rarely allowed outside the fortresslike US embassy in Kabul. When they get out, to attend a meeting or visit the site of a project financed by USAID, they are often surrounded by heavily armed security personnel who make it virtually impossible to interact with the Afghan people they are helping."[44]

Ward created quite a stir in 2008 when he left USAID in frustration and moved over to the United Nations Assistance Mission to Afghanistan (UNAMA). Ward spoke to me in Kabul at UNAMA headquarters, where the security was just as tight as at the US embassy. But when Ward and other UNAMA personnel did emerge to do aid work, they had a much lower security profile—a lightly armed bodyguard and an armored car, compared to USAID staffers' guard of heavily armed security soldiers traveling in a convoy of hulking armored trucks with machine-gunners. Ward is a lanky, intense fellow with piecing blue eyes behind professorial wire-rimmed glasses. He laughingly claims to have jumped to UNAMA because the United Nations's blue helmets match his eyes. He expressed his concerns with the implementation and outcomes of US-funded development in Afghanistan, particularly military-directed development. "When the PRTs were first stood up in 2004, there was no buy-in. There was just a race to build things, to spend money in Afghanistan," he says, "There's the rush to spend money; the rush to send a report back; have a ribbon-cutting ceremony."[45] He told me he worried about the US government's push to run development dollars through Afghan ministries filled with corrupt officials: "I think the money might disappear if we dump it in the wrong place." With all his experience and inside knowledge, Ward had a sobering final assessment, "When we look back at the tremendous amount of money spent in the last seven years—for the amount of money invested in Afghanistan, there should be a success story or two, but sadly, there really aren't."

The tight US military security rules that isolated the USAID staffers precluded most supervision of the for-profit development corporations that had grabbed five out of six of USAID's Afghanistan reconstruction contracts in 2002 and 2003.[46] Ward complained in his *Washington Post* article that the "no risk" isolation contributed to AID projects was "out of sync with Afghan government priorities," and "poorly implemented by contractors because of inadequate oversight." The result was telling. In 2004, Afghanistan's finance minister, Ashraf Ghani, was so frustrated by the worthless services provided by hapless BearingPoint consultants that he demanded a number of them leave the country.[47] It was to no avail. In 2007, USAID awarded BearingPoint a five-year $218.6 million contract to provide "expertise" in Afghanistan to improve "the performance of ministries, businesses, nongovernmental organizations, universities, and local governments." There was no record of competitive bidding or even of whether there was a proposal.[48]

Cooped up—often willingly—in the walled American compounds, USAID officials sometimes defended themselves from criticism by contending that the CIA and the military, intent on using the Afghan warlords to pursue al Qaeda, purposefully sidelined the AID staffers. One former USAID official said, "DOD did not want us around to see how they were aiding the wrong guys."[49]

It wasn't like USAID didn't know what could happen when an avalanche of poorly supervised development money hits a corrupt and dysfunctional society. A 2004 USAID white paper laid out the agency's marching orders: "Conditions of instability and insecurity that arise from terrorism, transnational crime, failing states, and global disease must be mitigated for sustained economic and social development to take root and flourish."[50] The agency pledged to use US foreign aid to fight for national security, a lofty goal when it couldn't even staff and manage its own organization.

Then the USAID white paper delicately hedged its transformational bets, hinting that massive aid might have some unintended outcomes: "Not all countries enjoy the conditions needed for transformational development. In countries that are not committed to reform, conventional development programs are unlikely to advance development. In fact, assistance actually may mask underlying instability or contribute to state fragility." And that is the way it turned out in war-ravaged, graft-ridden, bullyboy-run Afghanistan.

One after the other, USAID's massive contracts for Afghan infrastructure, education, health, counternarcotics, agriculture, and governance fell under the shadow of scandal. Badly planned, poorly executed, and woefully unsupervised, the projects were often grotesquely unsustainable fiascos that wasted hundreds of millions of US taxpayers' dollars.[51] Equally appalling, the failed development projects fueled a pernicious culture of corruption that alienated the Afghan population and fed the insurgency.[52]

*   *   *

As it had been for decades, USAID remained Washington's whipping boy—in spite of Andrew Natsios taking over as USAID administrator in 2001. The Bush administration thought if anyone could turn around the troubled agency, it was Natsios. First, he was a conservative Republican with a long-standing friendship with Bush's chief of staff, Andy Card. A slender, bald career civil servant with a Mr. Peebles gray moustache, Natsios graduated from Georgetown and Harvard. Natsios gained some serious neocon street cred in 2000–2001 by manhandling Boston's out-of-control Big Dig to some level of order, leaving that post to take on USAID. For four years, Natsios was the public face of USAID, fending off the campaign by Senator Jesse Helms to absorb AID into the State Department and constantly battling other departments intent on encroaching on AID's territory. But by late 2005, even Natsios couldn't make it work. In December 2005, he announced he was leaving USAID to join the faculty at Georgetown.

In January 2006, Secretary of State Condoleezza Rice made the announcement: USAID was being absorbed into the State Department. With Natsios in the audience, Rice spoke at the Department of State's Benjamin Franklin Room. Echoing critics from almost the beginning of USAID, Rice stated that the US government's aid programs were too fragmented to be effective. "Let me be clear," she said, "the current structure of America's foreign assistance risks incoherent policies and ineffective programs and perhaps even wasted resources. We can do better and we must do better."[53] Rice announced the creation of a new position reporting directly to the secretary of state: the director of foreign assistance, who would also serve as the administrator of USAID. The new administrator would have authority over all State Department and USAID foreign assistance and would coordinate with the Office of Global AIDS coordinator and with the Millennium Challenge Corporation. After more than forty years, the primary US aid organization was effectively merged into the State Department.[54]

Announcing that Randall Tobias was to be the first combined director of foreign assistance and administrator of USAID, Rice led a round of applause for Tobias and his wife. Tobias came in with sparkling credentials, having been the chairman and CEO of AT&T International and then the chairman, president, and CEO of Eli Lilly and Co., where he turned the declining company around. In the previous two years he had served as the head of Bush's emergency plan for AIDS relief. In brief remarks, Tobias stated his intent to work with "the men and women of the Department of State and USAID, and with the rest of the foreign-assistance community as together we reenergize, reengineer, and refocus our commitment to achieving our foreign-assistance goals."[55] But Tobias soon learned that Rice didn't match her glib words about transformational diplomacy with resources. USAID and her supposedly transformational foreign-service officers continued to be substantially underfunded.

As Rice orchestrated the absorption of USAID into the State Department, events halfway around the world belied the argument that foreign aid helped bring order to underdeveloped countries. In 2006, the Taliban insurgency was raging across southern Afghanistan, where the United States had concentrated most of its aid money. The failed promise of development yielding security wasn't specific to Afghanistan. East Timor, which had received more aid money per capita that anywhere in the world, exploded into anarchic riots in the summer of 2006.[56]

Less than six weeks after he was sworn in as USAID administrator on March 31, 2006, Randy Tobias was in Afghanistan. According to the AID press release, he was there to "acknowledge the long-term commitment of the United States to help Afghanistan build a secure and prosperous future."[57]

But Tobias wasn't in it long-term himself. After scarcely six months at the helm, he was already talking about quitting. A steamy sex sandal involving an escort service connected to prostitution led to his early retirement in May 2007. He told reporters that he called the escort service "to have gals come over to the condo to give me a massage," later switching to another service that used Central American women.[58] Within minutes of the announcement of Tobias's resignation, his biography was removed from the USAID website.

USAID's days in the spotlight were far from over. In December 2007, the congressionally authorized HELP Commission released its report, which pilloried the agency. Testimony was unanimous: USAID was broken. The HELP commissioner, Eric Postel, said USAID was in a "death spiral."[59] The HELP Commission report indicated that USAID's failure to manage US government aid left a vacuum that the Department of Defense had filled. The report warned of the problems of the Defense Department doing development: "Even if its genesis is understandable, DOD's 'mission creep' comes with significant implications."[60] The report stated that the Department of Defense's expanded role "was complicating the already-complex interagency coordination in embassies overseas and would likely foment department turf wars in Washington." The report went on to indicate, "In addition, some host countries are quietly beginning to ask why the most prominent face of America is increasingly a military one. Even more problematic, the American military is being asked to carry out missions that deviate from its primary war-fighting and defense roles. Meanwhile, the civilian organizations that were created to address these concerns with sustainability in mind are denied adequate resources."

The Department of Defense was ambivalent about its new development role. The 2006 Quadrennial Defense Review, an overweening strategic blueprint for the Pentagon, included stability operations—aka development—for the first time, institutionalizing a role previously played by USAID. Upsurges in congressional appropriations followed.[61] The Pentagon's ambivalence led to Secretary of Defense Robert Gates's remarkable call in 2007 for increased funding for the State Department. In a speech at Kansas State University, Gates talked about the challenges of soldiers trained to be killers taking on reconstruction: "Forced by circumstances, our brave men and women in uniform have stepped up to the task, with field artillerymen and tankers building schools and mentoring city councils—usually in a language they don't speak," he said.[62] "The armed forces will need to institutionalize and retain these nontraditional capabilities. But there is no replacement for the real thing: civilian involvement and expertise." Gates noted that the State Department's entire foreign-affairs budget request of $36 billion for FY 2008 was less than what the Pentagon spends on health-care and called for greater support for the Department of State.

Other US leaders also questioned the wisdom of giving development responsibilities to the Defense Department. Representative Lee Hamilton, who led the Iraq Study Group with former secretary of state James Baker, told me about meeting an infantry captain in Iraq who was setting up a school system: "I asked him if he was trained to do that, and he said, 'Hell, no—I'm a killer. I'm a combat infantryman. My job is to kill people.' Something is out of whack there," Hamilton says. Hamilton went on to give the military credit for adapting to the new development responsibilities, though it has skewed the balance of power between the "3Ds"—diplomacy, defense, and development. "Defense has now become the biggest foreign-policy entity," Hamilton says. "The Defense Department has become the State Department."[63]

In spite of the increasing military role in development and USAID's "death spiral," the understaffed agency was still administering billions of dollars of programming, most done through for-profit corporations. In 2005 the agency's spending had doubled since 2000 to $14 billion, while its staff of 2,300 had grown by only one hundred.[64] In the next few years, as redevelopment money continued to pour into Afghanistan, there was little repair for the broken agency. In late 2008, as the Obama administration prepared its plans for foreign aid that included efforts to reenergize AID, longtime USAID critic senator Patrick Leahy of Vermont told an agency spokesperson in a Senate subcommittee hearing, "USAID's professional staff is a shadow of what it once was. We routinely hear that the reason USAID has become a check-writing agency for a handful of big Washington contractors and NGOs is because you don't have the staff to manage a larger number of smaller contracts and grants. Sometimes these big contractors do a good job, although they charge an arm and a leg to do it. Other times they waste piles of money and accomplish next to nothing, although they are masters at writing glowing reports about what a good job they did."[65]

* * *

When I arrived in eastern Afghanistan's Khost Province in the spring of 2009 to cover the role of development in counterinsurgency, I anticipated reporting on PRTs. With a typical civilian–military composition, the PRT I got to know included a large contingent of security and civil-affairs soldiers, as well as a smattering of USDA, State Department, and USAID civilian staffers. When we could arrange interviews between missions, most of the soldiers and civilians engaged in development were willing to speak to me about reconstruction in Afghanistan. But the woman serving as the team's USAID staffer was impossible to pin down. A small woman with darting, bespectacled eyes, she was a career foreign-service officer, having served in numerous postconflict countries including Cambodia and the Balkans. She was a hard worker, engaged, smart, and trying to do the right thing as the PRT dispensed reconstruction contracts across the embattled province. Whenever I would ask for an interview, she would flash a quick smile and say she was too busy or claim she was waiting for clearance from the Kabul USAID press official (who later told me she had approved the interview). When I encountered her on the forward operating base, I felt like she wanted to point at the sky and yelp, "Look, wild geese"—and then run when I looked up. Out in the insurgent-plagued province on military missions, I would occasionally run into this USAID staffer, hard-shelled in her Kevlar® helmet and body armor. She would quickly scuttle behind an armored vehicle or engage herself in the midst of a group—seemingly less afraid of the Taliban than of a journalist with a notepad. It was obvious there was enormous pressure on USAID staffers to avoid unfavorable media coverage. A former high-level US government official later told me that USAID administrator Andrew Natsios had instructed Jim Bever, the agency's country director, that "'there'd be no bad news out of Afghanistan.'"[66] It was just happy stories, the US official told me. "Photo ops—AID was famous for those," he said. I had seen plenty of USAID "Success Story" press releases about projects with glowing promise that didn't hold up to much scrutiny. But I just wanted to know the USAID staffer's assessments. What worked, what didn't, and why? After weeks of trying to arrange an interview, I finally confronted the woman. What was the problem? I just wanted to hear her viewpoint. She gave me a pained look and glanced around. "I don't want to get fired," she said. "I like my job."

*   *   *

Scene: Khost Province, Afghanistan. In civilian life, Bob Cline is an assistant prosecutor specializing in murder cases. He has cracked cases no one thought would ever come to court. He worked his way through law school driving long-distance trucks. He spent time as an undercover drug agent. Back home in rural Indiana, he juggles his demanding prosecutor work with a cattle farm, eleven kids (including two special needs adoptees from China), fifteen dogs, miniature horses, and a complicated menagerie of mismatched poultry. A burly, bald guy with pale-blue interrogator eyes, he's dogged, intense, used to getting things done, and used to getting to the bottom of things.

Captain Bob Cline arrived in Khost Province in 2009 as a member of the Indiana National Guard Agribusiness Development Team (ADT), whose mission was to help quell the insurgency by improving impoverished Afghan farmers' lives. Among a number of agricultural aid projects, the team planned to work with the Afghan government and tribesmen to build sustainable infrastructure, such as small dams and greenhouses, facilitate agricultural training programs, and improve animal health. Drawing on his civilian experience as a successful farmer, Captain Cline was focused on animal husbandry. He intended to use sixteen veterinarian clinics USAID had built in Khost Province two years before as local outreach and education centers.

"When we got here, we asked AID where the clinics were located," Cline told *me.[67] "They said they didn't know. When the previous group rotated out, the electronic data was lost and there wasn't a backup. I said, 'Hey, just give us the village names, a map marked with locations, the GPS coordinates, anything. We're the army—we'll find them.'" But even that information was lost; AID had no idea where the clinics they had built were located. Dogged Bob Cline, the hard-nosed prosecutor, spent a month bugging the USAID staffers about the vet clinics until they finally found printed reports with the locations. "But when we tracked the clinics down in the field," Cline told me with a wry smile, "almost all of them were abandoned, looted. In one place, the whole building was missing."*

Chapter 10

The COIN Flip

ON A FLAG-BEDECKED WASHINGTON STAGE, a phalanx of foreign-policy advisers backed up President Barack Obama as he explained his "comprehensive, new strategy for Afghanistan and Pakistan" on the morning of March 27, 2009.[1] Obama warned his audience that the interwoven security situation in Afghanistan and Pakistan "is increasingly perilous" and laid out the dangers radical Islamists posed to the Western democracies. Obama said, "So I want the American people to understand that we have a clear and focused goal: to disrupt, dismantle, and defeat al Qaeda in Pakistan and Afghanistan, and to prevent their return to either country in the future." Obama assured his listeners that "We are not in Afghanistan to control that country or dictate its future," auguring a stripped-down strategy of counterterrorism (CT)—basically, kill the bad guys and go home; forget nation building and counterinsurgency (COIN).

But by the end of the speech, Obama had also pledged to advance security, justice, and economic opportunities, particularly for Afghan women. "A campaign against extremism will not succeed with bullets or bombs alone," he said. Along with his announcement of billions of dollars in additional aid, Obama promised the United States would reform development efforts: "As we provide these resources, the days of unaccountable spending, no-bid contracts, and wasteful reconstruction must end." He promised strong measures to curb corruption along with "clear metrics to measure progress and hold ourselves accountable." It was a conflicted speech; some said confused. Diplomat James Dobbins stated the conundrum clearly: "There's a gap between the reason we're there and what we're doing. The rationale is counterterrorism. The strategy is counterinsurgency."[2] Whatever the rationale, Obama had flipped the US strategy in Afghanistan back to COIN—but according to the Obama administration, it was a bright, new, freshly minted COIN.

Obama's speech mirrored the tensions implicit in the new administration. Obama had boxed himself in with campaign-trail declarations that Afghanistan was "the war we need to win" through ramped-up attention and resources. But once he took office, his lack of on-the-ground knowledge about Afghanistan meant he had to rely on the advice of Bush-administration holdovers such as Defense Secretary Robert M. Gates and General David H. Petraeus, the counterinsurgency guru and hero of the Iraq surge who took over Central Command just before the election. The two men were part of the Bush-era personnel, policies, and military philosophy that Obama inherited and nurtured. Obama had ordered a strategic policy review of the Afghanistan war, which was led by Bruce Riedel, a CIA, Pentagon, and National Security Council veteran who favored counterinsurgency. But even before the rush review was completed, the military leaders were jockeying for an additional thirty thousand troops in Afghanistan.[3] Given his campaign promises, Obama had little choice but to accede to the Pentagon's eventual bargain request for twenty-one thousand additional soldiers.[4] And Obama had opted for the perennial policymaker's gambit: "This is a problem, so let's throw more money at it." Even as Obama agreed to the precipitous troop increase, a COIN versus CT fight continued in Washington among the foreign-policy officials.

Vice President Joe Biden led the charge for what he called "counterter-rorism plus," a less expensive strategy that emphasized spies, attack drones, and hunter-killer teams working with the conventional forces then in Afghanistan. Besides the Riedel report, the Pentagon's Joint Staff and Central Command also presented strategic policy reports that pushed for a counterinsurgency strategy, with many boots on the ground and a large hearts-and-minds compo-nent.[5] Petraeus's apparent success in Iraq with his updated COIN strategy pur-portedly made it appropriate for Afghanistan—an example of the dictum that generals fight the last war.[6] Since Afghanistan had served as a useful foreign-policy campaign plank for Obama, the military wasted no time in using it to maneuver him into a major escalation. In spite of Biden's vociferous CT advo-cacy, COIN—expensive, generally unproven, often ill-managed COIN—became the basis of the Obama strategy in Afghanistan.[7]

*   *   *

Beyond the Bush legacies of officials, policy, and mind-set, Obama had inher-ited a security mess in Afghanistan and Pakistan. In the summer of 2008, the Afghan Taliban had unleashed its largest offensive actions of the war. Multiple suicide bombers inflicted hundreds of casualties in ostensibly secure urban areas; insurgents attacked the Indian embassy in Kabul and attempted an assassination of Karzai; the Taliban sprung 1,100 prisoners out of Kandahar prison with a brazen raid. Large units of hundreds of insurgent fighters launched spectacular attacks on Coalition bases, including the increased numbers of small, vulnerable Combat Outposts (COPs) scattered in the volatile hinterlands.[8] "You can't commute to work in the conduct of counterinsurgency operations," General Petraeus said, explaining the rationale for COPs.[9] But the isolated COPs came with a price. In the summer of 2008, hundreds of insurgents, aided by local tribesmen enflamed by civilian deaths and the unresponsive Karzai government, unleashed a complex attack on a US combat outpost in Nuristan Province's Wanat Valley, wounding thirty-one soldiers and killing nine, the most combat deaths in a single battle since 2001. Three days later, US forces abandoned the base. Across Afghanistan, the insurgents relentlessly ambushed convoys and patrols and laid increasingly larger and more sophisticated IEDs. The losses mounted. "And most painfully," Obama said in his speech, "2008 was the deadliest year of the war for American forces."[10] NATO forces likewise suffered their highest death tolls.[11]

The erratic US military strategy and effort were failing through what Taliban expert Antonio Giustozzi diplomatically characterized as "extremely inefficient use of the considerable financial and technological resources available."[12] There had been glacial progress toward building an Afghan army that could stand up to the Taliban. The police force was little more than packs of government-condoned wolves. Coalition intelligence was close to an oxymoron. Reconstruction was a morass.

And the administration was questioning the military leadership in Afghanistan. The commander then in charge of ISAF, General David McKiernan, had taken over command from General Dan "Bomber" McNeill in June 2008. Like Eikenberry and McNeill, General McKiernan waged a generally conventional war, with little interest in chivvying Afghan governors, instituting local militias, or directing in-depth intelligence into Afghan tribal issues.[13] As time went on, the top Pentagon brass began to view McKiernan as a conventional soldier when they wanted a hotshot COIN warrior. It was a "long, slow boil," a Pentagon source said.[14] With the top brass preparing for the big COIN push, they determined that McKiernan wasn't "nimble or bold" enough.[15]

On May 11, 2009, Defense Secretary Robert Gates announced he was dismissing McKiernan, saying the United States needed "fresh eyes" and "fresh thinking" in Afghanistan.[16] Intent on staying for a full two-year rotation,

McKiernan didn't make it easy for his bosses by quietly resigning, instead saying they would have to fire him.[17] Which they did. With a quivering voice, Gates told reporters, "Our mission there requires new thinking and new approaches from our military leaders."[18]

McKiernan's replacement, Lieutenant General Stanley McChrystal, certainly represented new approaches. McChrystal was an austere former special-forces soldier—a "snake-eater" in military parlance—who had led the secretive Joint Special Operations Command (JSOC) in Iraq from September 2003 to August 2008, a period when JSOC commandos captured Saddam Hussein and killed Iraqi al Qaeda leader Abu al-Zarqawi. Considered somewhat of an outrider known for eating only one meal a day and running relentlessly, McChrystal was perfectly capable of articulating unconventional opinions. He had weathered the cover-up scandal surrounding the death by friendly fire of the former NFL player and army ranger Pat Tillman. At the time of the administration's disillusionment with McKiernan, Lieutenant General McChrystal was serving as director of the Joint Staff, a plum position that often leads to a fourth star. In spite of his experience in counterterrorism operations, McChrystal had embraced the counterinsurgency doctrine espoused by General David Petraeus, whom he had known since both were young captains in the early 1980s.[19]

Counterinsurgency had come a long way from when General David Barno was dusting off his West Point schoolbooks to patch together a COIN strategy for Afghanistan. In December 2006, General David Petraeus, then commanding general of Fort Leavenworth, Kansas, and the Combined Arms Center, oversaw the publication of *The US Army and Marine Corps Counterinsurgency Field Manual 3-24*, later famous as FM 3-24.[20] The year prior to the book's publication, Petraeus had returned from his second tour of duty in Iraq, where he became convinced the military needed to rapidly revise its counterinsurgency field manual, which hadn't been updated since the guerrilla war in El Salvador two decades earlier. Petraeus assembled a diverse group of officers, academics, human-rights specialists, and journalists to produce FM 3-24.

There was clearly a pent-up demand for the new COIN manual. FM 3-24 was downloaded 1.5 million times in the first month of publication, as soldiers deploying to Iraq and Afghanistan struggled to understand the new doctrine that placed protecting the civilian population over killing the enemy. The University of Chicago Press rushed out a paperback version within months—only the second time the army collaborated with a private press. In a foreward to the book, national-security expert John Nagl wrote that the section titled "Paradoxes of Counterinsurgency" would perplex soldiers trained to be door-kicking combat troops: "The nine maxims turn conventional military thinking on its head, highlighting the extent of the change required for a conventional military force to adapt itself to the demands of counterinsurgency."[21] The section concludes, "COIN is an extremely complex form of warfare. At its core, COIN is a struggle for the population's support. The protection, welfare, and support of the people are vital to success. Gaining and maintaining that support is a formidable challenge."[22]

FM 3-24 emphasized the need to "clear-hold-build," with a stress on the last element. In the new wars envisioned by FM 3-24, soldiers weren't combatants; they were a combination of kindly cops, nonjudgmental social workers, and honest contractors. As Nicholas Lemann wrote in a *New Yorker* review about the ideal COIN warrior, "He collects garbage, digs wells, starts schools and youth clubs, does media relations, improves the business climate. What he doesn't do is torture, kill in revenge, or overreact. He's Gandhi in IED-proof armor."[23]

While the military was proclaiming "the new counterinsurgency," there were broad similarities to Barno's strategy of five years before. It was now a "population-centric" doctrine, in place of Barno's "people as the center of gravity"—a distinction perhaps more important to press officers than to the Afghans. The "Green Villages" (government-friendly enclaves) of Britain's successful 1950s Malaysian counterinsurgency became the "ink-spot" COIN strategy in Iraq, later morphing into Afghanistan's "ink-stain" policy, which hoped to encourage secure villages with reconstruction projects. According to the COIN doctrine, the friendly enclaves would then spread like an ink stain to adjacent insurgent areas hungry for the Coalition development dough and the security that theoretically followed.[24]

With its emphasis on intelligence, nation building, and civilian–military cooperation, FM 3-24 restarted COIN in Afghanistan, where, after Barno's nascent counterinsurgency tactics, the next three generals had waged a generally conventional war.[25] Indeed, a fully articulated, vetted, and approved COIN doctrine was a big shift for the top levels of the US military, which had generally avoided wartime aid efforts since the Vietnam War pacification debacle until Iraq.[26]

But with Afghanistan beginning to look like a losing proposition, the US military leaders saw counterinsurgency as the best option—despite the need for substantial increases in troops, resources, and training to mold soldiers into nurturing COIN technocrats. Then again, maybe that's why COIN looked attractive to the military. Whatever the reason, the military leadership certainly rallied to the COIN cause. Reciting a litany of nation-building imperatives, chairman of the Joint Chiefs of Staff admiral Mike Mullen told the House Armed Services Committee: "We can't kill our way to victory, and no armed force anywhere—no matter how good—can deliver these keys alone. It requires teamwork and cooperation."[27] In June 2009, McChrystal talked to the *Wall Street Journal* about his Afghanistan strategy: "I know I want it to be an effective traditional or classic counterinsurgency campaign by getting down among the population."[28] He dismissed the effectiveness of conventional warfare in defeating terrorists, saying, "Since 9/11, I have watched as America tried to put out this fire with a hammer, and it doesn't work." McChrystal, the former leader of America's black ops ninjas, said, "You're going to have to convince people, not kill them."

General Stanley McChrystal unveiled his counterinsurgency campaign soon after taking command in June 2009. The summer of 2009 was even more violent than the previous year, with record numbers of insurgent attacks. Through the summer fighting season of 2009, the number and intensity of the insurgent attacks continued to grow. August 2009 was the deadliest month for US soldiers in Afghanistan, with forty-seven soldiers killed. As the violence mounted through 2009, McChrystal's COIN–training guidance memo instructed the troops to master a seventeen-part training guidance: "Everyone must understand this training guidance, be able to execute it, and become ISAF's ambassadors throughout the country."[29] The guidance included everything from "the People are the Prize," to intelligence gathering, driving instructions, language acquisition, counter-IED training, military development projects, and partnering with US civilian agencies and Afghan security forces.

Recognizing the problems of CERP being used indiscriminately for large-scale projects, McChrystal soon reduced the amount of CERP funds that could be expended without higher approval. McChrystal's restrictions on escalation of force and fire support, such as air strikes and artillery, caused the most grumbling, as the soldiers groused about being unable to defend themselves with the US arsenal's full power.[30] But the famously Spartan general's threat to ban the ubiquitous fast-food outlets—Pizza Hut, Burger King, Green Beans coffee shops, and the like—from the larger US bases created at least as much consternation.[31] Doing without smart bombs was one thing, but an after-patrol pizza slice or cappuccino—no way.

*   *   *

COIN looked good on paper, but McChrystal had a tough fight on his hands—not only with the enemy, but also with the dysfunctional system of command, mismanagement, corruption, and collusion that had evolved in the eight years since the invasion. First, he faced a rancorous Coalition force that was unprepared for counterinsurgency. McChrystal wrote, "ISAF is a conventional force that is poorly configured for COIN, inexperienced in local languages and culture, and struggling with the challenges inherent to Coalition warfare."[32] Beyond the issues of redirecting a cobbled-together war machine to be warmer and fuzzier, McChrystal was facing a fraying alliance, as a number of the NATO countries debated continuing their military commitment to Afghanistan.

McChrystal was also encumbered with decisions and structures made long before him. Though the Obama administration had dumped General McKiernan, it had kept some of his strategy. For instance, as the seventeen thousand additional troops began landing in Afghanistan for population-centric COIN work, many were headed to fight in Helmand Province, which had less than one percent of the population, because that was McKiernan's strategy to break the "stalemate" the revived Taliban had achieved in southern Afghanistan.[33] According to the COIN advocates, Afghanistan was still problematically under-resourced even with the troop surge. COIN's standard theoretical ratio called for one soldier or policeman to every forty to fifty people in the Afghan population, a goal that would require another one hundred thousand US soldiers—portending yet another troop request.[34]

US intelligence was woefully inadequate for a counterinsurgency effort that required intimate knowledge of the Afghans whom the military was now charged with protecting. As McChrystal took over, some 70 percent of the intelligence requirements were focused on the enemy, not the people.[35] American soldiers simply didn't know whom they were supposed to protect or how to go about doing it. McChrystal said, "Every day I realize how little about Afghanistan I actually understand."[36] And with a dearth of Afghan-language speakers and Afghan cultural specialists, the military had no shortcut to knowledge, especially since American soldiers and civilians only ventured out of their bastions in heavily armed convoys or helicopters. Afghans naturally tended not to open up to armed soldiers dressed like storm troopers.

But it was the abysmal Karzai administration that was the ultimate impediment to a successful COIN operation in Afghanistan. Rather than partnering with a legitimate host government—an indispensable "north star," in FM 3-24 lexicon—the United States was allied with an Afghan government that was largely ineffective and systemically corrupt.[37] The August 20, 2009, presidential vote count that gave Karzai an outright victory was widely seen as a grotesquely stolen election, a fraud so blatant it gave even the international Coalition, benumbed to Afghan malfeasance, reason to pause. "We are humiliating ourselves," one disgusted UN election official told me.[38]

In the run-up to the election, Karzai had already tainted his administration by trading cabinet posts and presidential pardons to warlords—many engaged in the opium trade—for political support.[39] The Afghans, particularly in the conservative Pashtun regions, were increasingly alienated from the predatory Karzai administration and the enabling foreigners. Polls often ranked corruption as one of the top problems contributing to the insurgency. Even the Coalition efforts to compensate for the weak Karzai administration backfired as the international power-mongering further proved the Afghan government's client status.[40]

Reconstruction, vital to the COIN strategy, was failing. McChrystal noted another problem, "Often, we will have a very clear vision that we're trying to bring stability and economic development to an area, but then we'll take an action which will be hugely misperceived. We will want to put in a school or a road or create some activity, and then we'll do it in a way that has the opposite effect."[41] McChrystal's comment dovetailed with critic Andrew Bacevich's view that the COIN doctrine was "social work with guns," akin to "imperial policing, combined with the systematic distribution of alms."[42] Bacevich saw COIN as an element of the Long War, an intractable, endless state of conflict that provided unlimited opportunities for advancement and gelt to corrupt locals, international military and civilian officials, politically connected defense corporations, and the tens of thousands of private contractors who thronged Afghanistan.[43]

Across the insurgency belt, it was obvious that the American counterinsurgency offensives often spurred rebellion, creating insecurity rather than dampening it. In the summer of 2009, the Afghan Army's spokesman, Major-General Zahir Azimi, confirmed it: "Where international forces are fighting, people think it is incumbent on them to resist the occupiers and infidels. This feeling is strong in the south and east and it may spread to other places."[44] In eastern Afghanistan, soldiers told me rebellion followed the road crews and PRTs, illustrated by the welters of graphic symbols representing IEDs and TICs (Troops in Combat) that clustered along the newly constructed roads on the military maps.

One day high in the mountains of Laghman Province, I patrolled with a tense military development team that was on a mission to inspect a new culvert, not far from where an IED had recently blasted an MRAP down the mountainside. We were dismounted in a hostile village that was filled with angry faces and portents of ambush. The security soldiers formed a cordon along the freshly paved road as an engineer gingerly peered into the new culvert, afraid the insurgents had already mined it. A white Toyota Corolla* station wagon crammed with scowling Afghan men passed us, and then laid on the horn as it careened around a curve, the unending wail drifting back over the hills. The children scattered; the soldiers checked their weapons. "Why are they honking?" an anxious medic on his first mission asked me in a high, strained voice. "These are all ambush signs," he said as he glanced up and down the road. The freshly paved road sure wasn't bringing peace and harmony to that part of Afghanistan.

Combat Outposts (COPs), intended to be bastions of counterinsurgency, instead became magnets for attack.[45] Tribesmen in the remote areas would take the humanitarian aid and then "give it to the muj."[46] Even areas that the United States touted as being pacified by development projects quickly devolved into rebellion. Counterinsurgency expert David Kilcullen wrote that in 2006 Kunar Province experienced a "significant improvement in security" through development, particularly road building—but within a few years those gains proved to be illusory.[47] In spite of the region's roads, clinics, schools, and irrigation projects built by the United States, the Korangal Valley insurgents became famous for their relentless attacks on beleaguered US outposts—in no small part because it became the destination of choice for incoming journalists determined to see action.[48]

The military insisted that Kunar's high, remote Pech Valley was another critical piece of turf, well worth the huge amounts of development money and dozens of American lives expended there. But while the Pech Valley tribesmen took the development money, they gave nothing in return—excepting unrelenting resistance.[49] In time, the US military abandoned the bases in both the Korangal and Pech Valleys.[50]

In the summer of 2009, as the policymakers in Washington squabbled over strategies and rationales, the cobbled-together and sometimes-conflicted US war machine in eastern Afghanistan ground on with the momentum of a vast flywheel. Colonel Mike Howard, the Paktika Province commander who had ordered his counterinsurgency manuals off the Internet back in 2005, when General Barno was launching his COIN strategy, was in his fourth rotation in Afghanistan. A thin, ascetic runner, Colonel Howard was now the commander of the Fourth Brigade Combat Team, which had combat operations in the wild border provinces of Paktia, Paktika, and Khost—P2K, as the area is known. An elder statesman of COIN, Howard told me his viewpoints had shifted from his earlier days in what he calls the "pipe-swinging infantryman's army," when the military's heavy-handed combat operations alienated Afghans.[51] Howard now embraced counterinsurgency and its emphasis on development and nation building. He says he wasn't the only one. "I would say that what we're doing is mainstream army now. We're not out there on the fringe doing crazy stuff. The army recognizes that we're not going to slug our way out of this war. We're going to out-govern, we're going to out-develop the enemy. In the meantime, we're going to smack him down so he leaves us alone so we can do the important things, like build rule of law, build government, build road structure, build healthcare systems, build education systems, peacefully transfer power with elected governments."

At Forward Operating Base Salerno in Khost Province, where the Fourth Brigade was headquartered, counterinsurgency and counterterrorism were neighbors. Convoys of development teams lumbered through the gates during the day for counterinsurgency hearts-and-minds work. At night, the hunter-killer teams' blacked-out Humvees crept out for counterterrorism raids and targeted assassinations. Sometimes COIN and CT came together, as when a CIA (OGA, Other Government Agencies, in the preferred jargon) agent rode along with the PRT. Sometimes the uncoordinated CT and COIN missions collided, as development teams doing hearts-and-minds work in a particular village encountered the aftermath of a special ops night raid. Angry Afghan villagers naturally didn't want to talk about aid projects when they were burying their dead.

*   *   *

The Obama administration was painfully aware that the American people, including its staunchest supporters, were wearying of war. Poll after poll showed declining support. Influential congressmen, such as Wisconsin Representative David Obey, chairman of the House Appropriations Committee, threatened to tie up the purse strings on the war.[52] Further complicating the discussion, nuclear-armed Pakistan presented the Obama administration with an intractable problem, as the American public was becoming increasingly aware that Pakistani military and intelligence services were providing a safe haven and support to the radical jihadists.[53]

As the military, politicians, and technocrats argued about the Afghanistan troop surge, Richard N. Haass, president of the Council on Foreign Relations, wrote a *New York Times* op-ed that questioned whether Afghanistan was truly "a war of necessity." Noting the difficulty of winning in Afghanistan and the other global threats facing America, Haass concluded, "There needs to be a limit to what the United States does in Afghanistan and how long it is prepared to do it, lest we find ourselves unable to contend with other wars, of choice or of necessity, if and when they arise."[54]

With Congress and the American public getting impatient, the Obama administration pushed the military for fast results. Not long after taking command in June 2009, McChrystal told his commanders in eastern Afghanistan, "Gentlemen, I am coming into this job with twelve months to show demonstrable results here—and twenty-four months to have a decisive impact. That's how long we have to convince the Taliban, the Afghan people, and the American people that we're going to be successful. In twenty-four months, it has to be obvious that we have the clear upper hand and that things are moving in the right direction. That's not a choice. That's a reality."[55]

But COIN wasn't quick. The counterinsurgency bible, FM 3-24, clearly stated, "COIN campaigns are often long and difficult."[56] Foreign-policy expert Seth G. Jones underscored that dictum with his RAND Corporation study of ninety post–World War II counterinsurgencies. Jones determined that it takes an average of fourteen years to defeat an established insurgency—and that victory is dependent on having effective indigenous security forces, a competent host government, and the ability to limit the insurgents' external support, especially sanctuaries. Obviously, with a hapless Afghan security force, a corrupt government, and cosseted insurgents in Pakistan sanctuaries, those variables for success didn't bode well for an imminent victory in Afghanistan.[57]

Congress began to demand that the administration provide metrics to track progress in the war. But counterinsurgency metrics are complicated—for a number of reasons. FM 3-24 had proclaimed, "Progress can be hard to measure."[58] And FM 3-24 was right: counterinsurgency progress was indeed hard to measure, in part because there was little data linking development with security. In a *Foreign Affairs* article entitled "Constructive COIN," economists Eli Berman, Joseph H. Felter, and Jacob N. Shapiro noted that there was little to no data to support the COIN advocates' theories that large-scale reconstruction efforts yielded a reduction in violence. If anything, the few studies done by reputable scholars indicated that large, expensive, internationally funded projects and programs administered by foreign contractors had virtually no violence-reducing effects. Likewise, cash-for-work programs, a cornerstone of

COIN strategy that was based on the assumption that the United States just needed to employ potential insurgents and they would forgo rebellion, was an unproven theory that was largely unexamined.[59]

Recognizing the political problem the lack of metrics presented, the Obama officials labored to devise a set of measurements that would satisfy the increasingly skeptical Congress. "The metrics are critically important to keep everyone's feet to the fire on this and for the public to know how we're doing and have some ways to measure it and not just have rhetoric," said Senator Carl Levin of Michigan, the chairman of the Senate Armed Services Committee.[60] By midsummer, the administration proposed a set of nine broad objectives to purportedly track progress in Afghanistan, with categories such as suppression of the insurgency, effectiveness of Afghan security units, economic revival, governance, corruption, support of the Kabul government, and international support for the war. When Congress received the Obama administration's military and nation-building metrics in September, the list had grown to fifty key measurements covering both Afghanistan and Pakistan.

Soon after wrangling the 21,000-troop increase from Obama, the military began lobbying for another major troop surge based on yet another strategic policy review—this time by General McChrystal.[61] The reports gathered by McChrystal's strategy-review team during the summer of 2009 were bleak. At an interim review meeting on July 4, team members told McChrystal that the best counterinsurgency in the world could still fail because of the feckless Afghan government.[62] The Pentagon delivered General McChrystal's assessment to the White House at the end of August. Though the actual report was highly classified, military officials began to work the media to try to pressure Obama into another troop surge—forty thousand was the oft-whispered number. The backchatter campaign climaxed on September 21, 2009, when the *Washington Post* published a leaked version of McChrystal's Afghanistan assessment, which stated that the Coalition was facing a "resilient and growing insurgency" as well as a "crisis of confidence among Afghans" out of patience with the government and the international community.[63] "The situation in Afghanistan is serious; neither success nor failure can be taken for granted," the report stated. It ominously went on to indicate, "Failure to gain the initiative and reverse insurgent momentum in the near-term (next twelve months)—while the Afghan security capacity matures—risks an outcome where defeating the insurgency is no longer possible." McChrystal stated that the United States needed to immediately implement a "properly resourced" counterinsurgency. "Properly resourced" meant an additional forty thousand US troops, a proportional "plussed-up" surge of American civilian officials, substantially increased hearts-and-minds resources, and more than double the number of Afghan security forces. McChrystal's assessment also addressed the problems caused by US complicity with corruption and failed development. Stating that the Coalition could no longer "ignore or tacitly accept abuse of power, corruption, or marginalization," the report indicated, "Problematic contracting processes and insufficient oversight also reinforce the perception of corruption within ISAF and the international community." The assessment confirmed what was widespread knowledge: "The narco- and illicit economy and the extortion associated with large-scale development projects undermine the economy in Afghanistan."[64]

What the McChrystal assessment didn't say was what was common knowledge in Afghanistan and Washington: the United States was financing the enemy. Behind the American bases' HESCO® barriers, the term "threat finance" was already being bandied around as strategists finally had to acknowledge that the insurgents were skimming poorly managed US logistics and development dollars to help fund their war.

The military pressure on Obama for the "plussed-up" COIN plan increased. During a speech at London's Institute for Strategic Studies on October 1, a relaxed General McChrystal again defended the counterinsurgency strategy, going on to dismiss Vice President Biden's counterterrorism strategy, which he said would result in "Chaos-istan." McChrystal told the audience that his military superiors were encouraging him to be blunt about the need for the increased troops and resources. But then he laughingly added there was no guarantee he would always be able to speak so frankly. "They may change their minds and crush me some day," he said.[65]

The same day as McChrystal's speech, General David Petraeus coyly told reporters in Washington that he had "not yet endorsed" the request for additional troops, though he agreed with the leaked assessment's bleak appraisal of the war. The day prior, Petraeus had been part of a three-hour strategy session at the White House, where the troop increase was hotly debated. Later, Petraeus's aides told journalists that he didn't want to "get ahead of the president."[66]

Through the fall, Obama appeared to waffle between COIN and CT, with commentators parsing his every move. Obama's assurance that he wouldn't reduce troop levels in Afghanistan was seen as supporting COIN. His visit to the "bat cave" at the National Counterterrorism Center, where analysts tracked global threats, was interpreted as a tilt toward counterterrorism.[67] Obama convened one lengthy policy review session after another at the White House, with McChrystal videoconferencing in his COIN rationales. Petraeus kept the heat on, telling a military conference that the president's strategy review was "moving quite quickly" and a decision was near.[68] "There is a recognition of the need to move through this," he said. Though Petraeus refrained from saying the president needed to approve the military's troop request, he said Afghanistan needed a "sustained, substantial commitment."

As the Obama administration debated in October 2009, fifty-five US soldiers lost their lives in Afghanistan, the war's highest monthly total to that point. The 316 US military deaths for all of 2009 were more than double the 2008 total. Despite the increased numbers of American and NATO troops, the Taliban was gaining ground across Afghanistan. The Taliban resurgence prompted begrudgingly positive articles about the movement and its leader, Mullah Omar. In the *New York Times*, foreign-policy adviser Bruce Riedel said about Mullah Omar, "This is an amazing story. He's a semiliterate individual who has met with no more than a handful of non-Muslims in his entire life. And he's staged one of the most remarkable comebacks in modern history."[69] Back in Washington, Obama was increasingly aware that the military was tightly circumscribing his options. During a November Afghanistan strategy-review session—the eighth on Afghanistan—Obama sparred with his military leaders. The officers, who included Mullen, Petraeus, and McChrystal, were offering the president the classic policymaker cocktail: two unrealistic alternatives, and two "reasonable," virtually identical, options, which constituted the policy they wanted—a 40,000-troop increase. Obama said, "So what's my option? You have essentially given me one option. You're not really giving me any option." After some hemming and hawing, Admiral Mullen finally admitted the Pentagon didn't see any other alternative to McChrystal's call for forty thousand additional troops. Obama demanded that the Pentagon provide another option, but an alternative never arrived.[70]

*   *   *

Scene: Bagram Airfield, Parwan Province. The development team's convoy of armored MRAPs rolls out of Bagram Airfield, the sprawling old Soviet base that serves as the US-led Coalition's fortified stronghold. Though on a humanitarian mission to nearby Ushashi village to improve irrigation, gunners manning machine guns and automatic grenade launchers keep watch up in the turrets. Inside the vaultlike MRAPs, the heavily armed Kentucky National Guard Agribusiness Development Team soldiers wear helmets and fifty pounds of body armor.[71]

As the convoy trundles down the dirt road to Usbashi, the high sun glints on the miles of razor wire topping Bagram's high-wire fences and blast walls. Fighter planes roar skyward; attack helicopters flit into the air. A couple nights before, Bagram's Giant Voice blared out alarms as the concussive booms of Taliban rockets shuddered the base.

The convoy winds through a dry, brown landscape to Usbashi. Walled farm compounds called qalats *stand in the distance, their thick mud walls speaking of Afghanistan's eternal need for defense. A line of painted red rocks beside the road demarcates a minefield. On the hillside above, Afghans in thick protective suits carefully clear mines, marking the now-safe fields with cairns of white-painted boulders. Near a woebegone village, the MRAPs slow to a stop beside a small, glittering river where tribal elders wait. On the bank, two Afghan boys skip stones across the water as Major Eddie Simpson, the rangy Force Protection leader, grabs his rifle and organizes his security soldiers into a defensive perimeter.*

Dr. Wazi, an educated villager, explains how water used to flow to Usbashi from three sides, allowing the villagers to farm the now-desiccated land, but the hydrology changed when the United States expanded the Bagram base in 2002. He shows the soldiers a dry irrigation ditch coursing through the bleak landscape, telling them it used to have eighteen inches of water. The team's engineer coordinator, Major Marion (Tobey) Peterson tells the elders abut the plan to pump two million gallons a day of gray water from Bagram's wastewater treatment plant into Usbashi's irrigation canals for the villagers' use. There's a lively interchange between the soldiers and the elders, Kentucky accents mingling with the tones of central Asia. "Y'alls" are sprinkled through the conversation—including translations by the team's interpreter, whose southern "all y'all" is Afghan-tinged.

Dr. Wazi is enthusiastic about the irrigation offer, saying Usbashi is a progovernment place, a peaceful place. "You can take off body armor here," he says. Major Simpson snorts, "Those rockets came from this village a few nights ago." Simpson had talked earlier about the Soviet Union's ill-fated experience in Afghanistan: "It didn't work out so good for the Russians here," he told me. "It ain't working out so good for us. These people don't like anyone."

"I'm going to do my best to get them water," Major Peterson tells the elders, "my very best." Dr. Wazi quickly replies, "Inshallah"—God willing. As Peterson and Wali confer, there's a thrum of approaching vehicles. A white Toyota Corolla and two motorcycles charge down the dirt track toward the team, then abruptly veer for the river. The two boys skipping rocks stop to stare as the vehicles plunge into the shallow stream and emerge on the far bank, charging up to an overlooking bluff. The security soldiers watch intently as a pack of men boil out of the car. The

cyclists dismount and saunter over to join the others. The Afghans stand on the bluff like a band of imperious Sioux warriors scouting the cavalry. "Taliban, checking us out," Major Simpson snarls.

Though Bagram and nearby Kabul are considered relatively secure, insurgent activity is still rampant. IEDs, ambushes, and rocket and mortar attacks are regular occurrences. In spite of the dangers, the Kentucky team has not suffered any casualties to this point. "We've been very, very fortunate," Simpson says, mentioning a close call when a sharp-eyed soldier spotted wires coming out of a culvert, signaling a large IED. "Would have done some major damage to an MRAP," Simpson says. Sometimes even stones are a menace. Just a few weeks before, the team had encountered a mob of rioting Afghans protesting an alleged Koran-burning by US troops. Softball-sized rocks rained on the MRAPs, breaking windshields and antennas. "It was kind of a hell of fire, if you will," says ADT commander Colonel Mike Farley. Though the soldiers could have defended themselves, Colonel Farley said they chose to "button up and move on," a maneuver that earned the team an accolade for composure and forbearance.

But back at Usbashi, Major Simpson is frustrated. He stands fingering his weapon, knowing his security team can't engage the Afghan men he considers Taliban because of the strict rules of engagement. The village elders appear nonplussed by the glowering men across the river, bespeaking the complicated relationships Afghans maintain with both the Americans and the insurgents. "Dr. Wazi, he's trying to be nice to us and get the water back that got taken away from the village," Major Simpson says. "But he knows there are people coming into the village to rocket us or whatever. He's got to deal with that."

Simpson says cooperation with the Americans and the Afghan government can be a death sentence—including beheadings. "The beheadings are pretty much for show-and-tell," Simpson told me. "The Taliban are trying to make a point. For the most part, they blow you up or shoot you and drive on." The intimidation is part of the larger culture of corruption that thrives in Afghanistan, where US development dollars pass through many hands, including the Taliban's. Major Simpson says, "The Taliban intimidation is like embezzlement—they're making sure they get their piece of the pie."

So there's an Afghan standoff beside the stream a half mile from the largest American military base in Afghanistan: the insurgents on the bluff insouciantly scouting the meeting while the Kentucky soldiers strain at their leashes. The insurgents suddenly rush for their vehicles, and roar across the river with rooster-tails of spraying water. Once the Taliban are on the other side, the Americans can only watch as they speed away, back down the track.

Chapter 11

The Realization

THE OBAMA TEAM FORGED AHEAD with its counterinsurgency strategy as security and rule of law continued to deteriorate in Afghanistan through 2009. Reflecting his conflicted support of COIN, President Obama had tried to finesse his position by declaring in his March 2009 speech, "We will not blindly stay the course," and we "will not, and cannot, provide a blank check."[1] But the military was raring to go. Admiral Mike Mullen crowed in May 2009 that the refurbished counterinsurgency was "a new strategy and a new commitment." Playing off his 2007 statement, "In Afghanistan, we do what we can. In Iraq, we do what we must," Mullen now said, "This isn't about 'can do' anymore. This is about 'must do.'"[2]

Given the previous commitment of American brainpower, blood, and treasure, Mullen's comment seemed a touch disingenuous, honed for a gullible media and an American citizenry preoccupied with the economic crisis. Eight years into the war, there were sixty-eight thousand US troops in Afghanistan. Well over five hundred American soldiers had lost their lives in Afghanistan, with several thousand wounded—many grievously.[3] The US government had spent hundreds of billions on military operations since the invasion, with additional hundreds of billions needed for ongoing veteran commitments.[4] Since 2001, the United States had expended well over $51 billion in Afghanistan on development, most invested in the still-inept Afghan National Army and Afghan National Police. USAID alone had spent $7.8 billion on reconstruction projects, with the military spending $10 billion of the Commander's Emergency Reconstruction Program funds on development since 2004. But many critics thought the money and lives had been wasted, including US leaders who admitted the war in Afghanistan had been a haphazard, distracted effort. In December 2009, Secretary of Defense Robert Gates made a remarkable confession when he stated, "But the United States really has gotten its head into this conflict in Afghanistan, as far as I'm concerned, really only in the last year." The statement amplified his own culpability as leader of the Defense Department for three years, under two presidents, with three different commanders in Afghanistan.[5]

It wasn't as though thousands of strategists, consultants, and analysts hadn't been thinking about the war in Afghanistan over the previous years. Famous for "death by PowerPoint®," the military leadership and staff continued to crank out increasingly mammoth decks of increasingly intricate slides in an attempt to graphically display the increasingly chaotic situation. The art form culminated in December 2009, when a graphic from the Office of the Joint Chiefs of Staff leaked out. Titled "Afghanistan Stability / COIN Dynamics," the multicolor graphic was a Gordian knot of interwoven arrows depicting the tangled relationships among tribal leaders, government officials, Afghan people of varying loyalties, soldiers, insurgents, development workers, drug dealers, warlords, and Western citizenry as they interacted through multiple institutions, cultures, policies, procedures, and (mis)perceptions. It was a snarled skein of confusion. One commentator called it "an assault on logic." General McChrystal remarked when he saw it, "When we understand that slide, we'll have won the war."[6] However risible, the graphic did colorfully illustrate the complexity of counterinsurgency and the difficulty of countering the hydra-headed insurgency and its codependent enablers and beneficiaries. What the graphic didn't address was the endemic problem of implementation and continuity that had plagued the US war effort in Afghanistan since 9/11. As Ambassador Ronald Neumann said, "Most people complained about policy. But what we lacked was an ability to implement."[7] Nor did "Afghanistan Stability / COIN Dynamics" ask the big question: Does it make sense to wage an expensive and enveloping COIN war in a remote country to protect domestic security from a half a world away? NBC's Richard Engel, who revealed the slide, wrote that COIN critics said the slide's "spaghetti logic" was the result of what happens when "smart people are asked to come up with a solution to the wrong question."[8]

*   *   *

Political scientist Abdulkader Sinno drew on his experiences as a humanitarian aid worker in Afghanistan to write *Organizations at War in Afghanistan and Beyond*, which dissected the resilient organizational structures of the Afghan insurgents. An impassioned and accomplished academic with a penchant for field research, Sinno, a Lebanese-born professor at Indiana University, spoke with me about the cautions he gave a congressional committee in 2009 on American strategic interests in Afghanistan and Pakistan. While Sinno thought some aspects of the Obama AfPak strategy made sense, including reframing the war in a regional context and increasing development aid, he told the congressmen there were many aspects of the strategy that were unrealistic or "grounded in false assumption." He thought the Americans' faith in being able to reconcile and reintegrate members of the Taliban through compensation packages was unreasonable. The strategy assumed Afghans joined the insurgency out of financial desperation or coercion, rather than a belief in the broadly inclusive Taliban ideology that tapped into a wellspring of religious, cultural, and nationalistic motivations. "In many parts of Afghanistan, the Americans are seen as the infidels, the Crusaders. The Taliban are the patriots," Sinno told me.[9] He thought the Americans' faith that they could negotiate with "moderate Taliban" was also delusional. "The Taliban are winning," he says, "Why would they negotiate now?"

Sinno saw potential problems with counterinsurgency, including the complications of development, the contradictory counternarcotics policies, and the failure to rein in unchecked corruption. The Afghan constitution foisted on the country presented a structural problem, as the highly centralized state with a strong presidency prevented political parties from forming and the provinces from sharing power in a manner congruent with Afghanistan's traditional governance pattern. Speaking about the troop surge, Sinno drew a simple graph on a napkin. "Obama's made a big gamble here," he says. "He's increased the number of troops and resources, but it's unsustainable." Sinno pointed to the vertical line. "That's resources," he says. Then the horizontal line: "That's time. So because of fiscal and political pressures, the more resources he puts in, the shorter time he has to succeed." Sinno drew a relatively flat line along the time line: "Less resources means the more time the US has to win." Then a steep line that climbed along the vertical axis. "More resources, less time. Time is the one thing that the insurgents in Afghanistan have that the United States and NATO don't have."

*   *   *

In the winter of 2009, ISAF director of intelligence major general Michael Flynn gave a briefing, "State of the Insurgency: Trends, Intentions, and Objectives."[10] It was a chilling reminder of the growth of the insurgency since 2007. Facilitated by

Afghans' frustration with corruption, failed development, and misuse of the Coalition's kinetic power, the Taliban-led insurgency had spread across Afghanistan, with shadow governments in thirty-three out of Afghanistan's thirty-four provinces. Four years prior, there had been only eleven provinces with Taliban shadow governors. The insurgency's previously diffuse leadership was coalescing. "Regional instability is rapidly increasing and getting worse," Flynn warned. Kinetic events—violent enemy attacks—increased 300 percent from 2007 to the end of 2009. IEDs were exploding across the Afghan landscape in record numbers. There were 81 IED events in 2003; in 2009, there were 7,228 IED events, causing 6,037 casualties—more than double the 3,308 IED casualties in 2008. Cheap and effective, IEDs had become the insurgents' weapon of choice. Like the surface-to-air missiles in the Soviet war, the progressively more powerful IEDs that could blast open armored vehicles represented a potential game changer. They increasingly isolated the Coalition troops in their bases, preventing them from engaging either the population or the enemy. Nor was the situation a short-term problem. With ample funding, recruits, and resources, "the Afghan insurgency can sustain itself indefinitely," Flynn indicated. In the face of the insurgency's burgeoning power, the Coalition security-force capacity was lagging far behind. "In COIN, catch-up ball does not work," one of Flynn's slides ominously read, "time is running out."

In the summer of 2009, the devastation of IEDs was obvious in the forward operating bases of eastern Afghanistan. At a Dining Facility Administration Center dining table, a stunned Provincial Reconstruction Team huddled. They had hit a massive IED that was buried in a dry riverbed the team was using to avoid the heavily mined roads. One soldier, his face laced with angry red-brown burns and welts, told me of the MRAP's vaultlike rear door being blown open; the medivac flying their grievously wounded off to the combat hospital. Through the day, the FOB's Giant Voice robotically called out the codes for incoming casualties; sometimes it was "Shamrock Black, Shamrock Black," the dreaded call signaling four or more wounded—often horribly wounded—soldiers were on the way. The combat surgeon at the hospital spoke of the relentless triage on the incoming, often Afghan soldiers who fearfully traveled the bomb-spiked roads in pickups and lightly armored hand-me-down Humvees; "God's Waiting Room," the repurposed shipping container parked adjacent to the hospital for those too damaged to warrant treatment; the many recovering soldiers on the bases who had had their "bell rung"—been concussed—by the blasts; the Combat Stress Counselors with their protocols for soldiers with no short-term memory due to the sequential brain traumas they had suffered from multiple IED incidents. In unit after unit's headquarters, ubiquitous IED casualty memorials: colored photos, plaques, sometimes handwritten notes. Flag-draped stretchers wheeled through lines of solemn comrades to planes waiting to fly the fallen back home.

*   *   *

The US government kept insisting that standing up the Afghan National Army was the key to solving the security situation. Accordingly, the United States had invested $20 billion in training, equipping, and sustaining the ever-growing Afghan army since 2002. The Coalition initially envisioned the ANA maintaining order with fifty thousand troops, but by the end of 2002 the military planners had upped the number to seventy thousand. That was before the insurgency exploded. By the London Conference in January 2010, the military was calling for the Afghan National Army to be increased to 171,600 by the end of 2011, with an interim goal of 134,000 Afghan soldiers within ten months. In a rare instance of beating an expectation, the Coalition announced in July 2010 it had met the goal of having 134,000 Afghan soldiers. Ah, but there were some problems with those soldiers.

There was the problem of soldiers actually being present. A GAO report noted that across the country, only 69 percent of the ANA soldiers were present for duty, with the numbers being lower in the insurgent areas of southern and eastern Afghanistan. The ANA suffered an almost 3 percent annual attrition rate. Those problems translated into a shortage of thirty thousand soldiers from November 2009 to October 2010. And many deserters took their equipment with them, potentially arming the insurgents. The GAO tactfully noted that the absenteeism and attrition rates could prevent the ANA from meeting its target goal, as recruiters simply couldn't keep pace with the AWOLs and other absentees. And the recruits they did attract were overwhelmingly illiterate. Only 14 percent of the recruits were literate at even a first-grade level. Further, there was a tremendous regional imbalance. Proportionately few ANA recruits—only about 3 percent—came from the Pashtun south, where the insurgency was strongest and resentment against Tajik and Hazara soldiers the most virulent. And in spite of the $20 billion, military assessments indicated that there wasn't one ANA unit capable of conducting an independent mission without substantive Coalition assistance.

In violent Khost Province, it was common knowledge that the ANA seldom ventured from its base at Camp Clark. In Laghman Province, I watched disheveled ANA recruits reluctantly shamble toward the FOB gate as their frustrated US Army trainer barked orders. Later that day at a premission meeting with a group of American security soldiers, the team leader played a popular YouTube® video of laughably uncoordinated ANA soldiers unable to do jumping jacks, cracking up the tough US soldiers.[11] "These guys are going to beat the Taliban?" one soldier hooted. A day later, a crowd of Pashtuns angry about deaths from a special ops raid protested in the nearby city of Mehtar Lam. When an ANA squad comprised of Tajiks and Hazaras managed to keep the Pashtuns contained, the American officers were ebullient, hailing it as a major breakthrough. But it was a relatively small crowd of unarmed civilians, and the Pashtuns were bound to resent other tribesmen suppressing them. Afghanistan is a nation of warriors. Even Najibullah's orphaned Communist army held off the *mujahideen* for three years after the Soviet army withdrew. Yet after eight years and $20 billion, the US-sponsored ANA still had its training wheels on.[12]

And then there was the cost of sustaining an army of 171,600. The 2010 GAO report noted that the United States had already spent about $5 billion to sustain the ANA. The Defense Department estimated it would cost about $4.2 to $4.5 billion annually to sustain the projected 171,600 Afghan soldiers. The total national revenue of Afghanistan was $1.5 billion, so US taxpayers were on the hook for most of the ongoing costs. And it was just going to get more expensive: in August 2009, Department of Defense and NATO spokespersons began to say that the ANA needed to increase in size to 240,000 soldiers.[13]

The Afghan National Police and the Ministry of the Interior (MOI) that administered the police and counternarcotics forces were equally dysfunctional —"the weak link in the security chain," according to Special Ambassador Richard Holbrooke.[14] The United States had little to show for the $6.2 billion that had been invested to professionalize the MOI and ANP since 2002. Many Afghans saw the police as little more than uniformed thieves. A 2009 GAO study succinctly stated, "The MOI and ANP have a history of corruption, and much of Afghanistan lacks a functioning judicial sector," also indicating "its police do not respect human rights."[15] According to the study, the ANP–MOI officer corps was grotesquely top-heavy, with nearly eighteen thousand officers, including more than three thousand generals and colonels. The US-mandated reorganization pared the corps down to nine thousand officers and reduced the number of generals and colonels by 85 percent. Almost half (about 45 percent) of the officers didn't even pass background checks. The officers were supposed to be leading eighty-two thousand personnel, but that number was conjectural, as there were untold numbers of "ghost employees" who only existed on pay rosters. The numbers were untold because of "limited" ANP cooperation with US efforts to verify the rosters. US contractors were unable to verify almost 29,400 ANP and MOI personnel who had been paid with US funds because of "a lack of cooperation from some ANP commanders."

The MOI was no better. The US embassy concluded that "MOI suffered from corruption, limited control over provincial police structures, and low institutional capacity at all levels," which contributed to "a lack of account-ability in ANP districts and provincial commands." It wasn't like Afghan policing was going to get better soon. With Afghan cops making less than army personnel—and suffering higher casualty rates than soldiers—recruitment was getting more difficult. Even if the recruiters did manage to attract new policemen, there were nowhere near enough qualified mentors to effectively train the new hires, let alone try to staunch corruption. Worse, the Obama administration's "new" strategy just continued the Bush administration's same failed bare-bones eight-week training program—but with bigger numbers. The ANP needed widespread reform, not more ill-trained predators. More of bad wasn't going to make things better.

The Afghan government's few reform initiatives to rein in endemic cor-ruption had clearly failed, partly by design. The General Independent Admin-istration for Anti-Corruption (GIAAC), which the Afghan government estab-lished in 2003, was defanged soon after the agency filed embezzlement cases against high-level officials. By 2007, the moribund GIAAC was being run by a convicted drug dealer who was reportedly a friend of President Karzai.[16] After establishing an interministerial committee to study corruption, Karzai abol-ished GIAAC. The new plan: the High Office of Oversight and Anticorrup-tion, with the owlish acronym of HoO, which began in 2008.[17] The estab-lishing legislation gave HoO responsibility to "monitor" corruption and "assist" with anticorruption enforcement, but the legislation failed to give HoO either authority or enforcement powers. Not surprisingly, the under-staffed, untrained, and ineffective HoO was soon deemed as impotent as GIAAC had been.[18]

As Obama took office, Afghanistan's opium industry continued to boom, a well-lubricated money machine for corrupt government officials, drug lords, and the insurgents. Areas of major cultivation, primarily in the south, were effectively narco-states. The expensive Bush-era counternarcotics strategy had failed miserably—Holbrooke called it "the most wasteful and ineffective pro-gram I have seen in forty years in and out of government."[19] He said, "We have gotten nothing out of it, nothing." In spite of almost $3 billion in congression-ally funded counternarcotics assistance from 2001 through 2009, Afghanistan was still producing over 90 percent of the world's illicit opium—6,900 metric tons in the 2008–2009 growing season, twice as much as world demand, leading experts to conjecture about vast stockpiles. The export value of the crop reached $3 billion, representing a third to half of Afghanistan's GDP. Experts estimated that the Taliban's take of about $70–100 million a year financed as much as half of the insurgents' income.[20] In place of the Bush administration's changeable counternarcotics policies that included erratic poppy eradication, interdiction, and Alternative Livelihoods programs that attempted to replace poppy with other crops (primarily wheat), Obama had another plan. Now the United States was going to stop targeting farmers with eradication and instead implement a comprehensive, multiyear rural-development program that would ostensibly wean growers off profitable poppy with other high-value crops and market-development tactics. But with Congress and the American public getting increasingly edgy, a long-term coun-ternarcotics fix was a tough sell.

With few exceptions, reconstruction in Afghanistan was looking grim. Nearly a decade of poor management and abysmal oversight left a legacy of unsound projects that primarily benefited corrupt politicians and careerists. The development careerists cycling through Afghanistan on quick deployments focused on spending their budgets—period. Oversight, continuity, and effec-tiveness had distinctly lower priorities. "In the past, there was a strong emphasis on getting projects out there," Major Carlos Moya, a civil-affairs officer in the RC-East command, told me one day inside the bunkerlike brigade headquarters, built to withstand the Taliban rockets that regularly descended.[21] "Somewhere along the line, we kind of lost the focus on ensuring QA," he says with a worried little smile. "I guess we kind of bit off more than we can chew."

Bad development had alienated the Afghan population and helped grow the insurgency. In March 2009, Secretary of State Hillary Clinton told reporters at The Hague that wasted US aid expenditures were "heartbreaking," going on to say, "There are problems of design, there are problems of staffing, there are problems of implementation, there are problems of accountability."[22] Clinton promised increased oversight. "We are looking at every single dollar as to how it's spent and where it's going and trying to track the outcomes."

The late Representative John P. Murtha, the powerful chair of the Defense Appropriations Subcommittee, was equally frustrated about CERP abuses. One of his congressional staffers told me, "Congressman Murtha has been hammering for scrutiny."[23] In a July 15, 2009, letter to the secretary of defense Robert Gates, Murtha called for a "thorough review" of the CERP program and a list of all proposed CERP projects over $1,000,000. Murtha railed, "Over the last five years, CERP has grown from an incisive counterinsurgency tool to an alternative US development program with few limits and little management."[24]

With all the undersupervised US-funded logistics and development money sloshing around Afghanistan, it was little wonder that wily Afghans seized the opportunity. The politicians were in on it. In November 2009, as Transparency International ranked Afghanistan the second most corrupt country on earth, President Hamid Karzai told a conference in Kabul: "All the politicians in this country have acquired everything—money, lots of money. God knows, it is beyond the limit. The banks of the world are full of the money of our statesmen."[25]

Like many other families connected to powerful Afghan government officials, the Karzai family was also in on it. Mahmoud Karzai, the older brother of the Afghan president, made a remarkable transformation from being a small-time restaurant owner in the United States to being one of Afghanistan's wealthiest businessmen, owning a major share of the ill-starred Kabul Bank, four coal mines, the country's only Toyota dealership, only cement factory, and grand real estate projects financed with millions of dollars in US government loans. One luxury project in Kandahar was built on ten thousand acres of former Afghan government land that authorities turned over to Mahmoud Karzai for free. Karzai also ran the Afghanistan Chamber of Commerce, a powerful position that gave him sway over an array of foreign deals. Ahmed Wali Karzai, the president's raffish half brother, whom US officials have long accused of narcotics trafficking and collusion with both the Taliban and the CIA, was likewise implicated in the land deal.[26]

Dozens of Karzai family members used their connections to tap into millions of dollars of US government funds.[27] "Family politics is part of the culture of this part of the world," author Ahmed Rashid said. "Right now, Afghanistan is going through a phase of very primitive capital accumulation by the country's leading families."[28]

President Hamid Karzai, in turn, blamed the corruption on Western officials and contractors who, in his view, foisted rich reconstruction contracts on his family and other powerful Afghans. "How come we are now so luxury-oriented today?"[29] he asked. "The transparency of the contracts is not there. Why is the US government giving contracts to the sons and relatives of officials of the Afghan government? We don't do those contracts. I don't have an authority over a penny of those contracts. . . . And we've been protesting against this for years." Harking back to the relatively corruption-free Soviet days in Afghanistan, Karzai said, "How come we were not so corrupt then? How come we are suddenly corrupt and everybody's corrupt? There must be a reason."

Powerful Afghans allied with the United States weren't the only Afghans benefiting from the American funds. The insurgents were also in on the take—in a very businesslike way. A spate of news stories finally began unveiling the widespread pattern. In a story that was picked up by a broad range of international media, journalist Jean MacKenzie revealed in the *GlobalPost* that the Taliban kept a business office in Kabul to facilitate payments from contractors with US contracts. A Taliban contract officer at the office reportedly examined the proposals and negotiated the fees, a process that MacKenzie indicated was "quite professional."[30]

Afghan journalist Anand Gopal reported that the Taliban leadership in Quetta levied "taxes" on major US-funded projects in Kandahar after a Taliban engineer analyzed the contract to determine the correct figure. A European journalist added that the local Taliban commanders took another 10–20 percent bite.[31] Investigative reporter Aram Roston dropped a bombshell in November 2009 when he revealed in the *Nation* that US logistics contracts were funding the Taliban. Roston wrote, "It is an accepted fact of the military logistics operation in Afghanistan that the US government funds the very forces American forces are fighting."[32] David Wood, the military correspondent for the web publication *Politics Daily*, reported that an American security contractor alleged that the Taliban used US protection money grifted from the Khost–Gardez Highway project in eastern Afghanistan to buy weapons and explosives. Wood quoted the contractor: "I have yet to find a security company that doesn't rely on payoffs to the Taliban."[33] The exposés seemed to catch the military off guard. General Stanley McChrystal complained, "The media is driving the issues."[34]

*   *   *

The revelations came amidst the congressional debate about a troop surge. Both the Senate and the House had convened hearings on the Afghanistan war in December 2009. At a Senate Foreign Relations Committee meeting, Secretary of State Hillary Clinton said, "We have to do a better job in the international side to coordinate our aid, to get more accountability for what we spend in Afghanistan. But much of the corruption is fueled by money that has poured into that country over the last eight years. And it is corruption at every step along the way, not just in Kabul."[35] Clinton spoke of the potential for graft along long supply lines from Pakistan: "You offload a ship in Karachi and by the time whatever it is—you know, muffins for our soldiers' breakfasts or anti-IED equipment—gets to where we're headed, it goes through a lot of hands. And one of the major sources of funding for the Taliban is the protection money."

A staffer for Representative John P. Murtha told me, "The stories about convoys paying off insurgents drives Congressman Murtha up the wall."[36] Representative John Tierney of Massachusetts launched a Subcommittee on National Security and Foreign Affairs investigation on the Taliban funding scandal that culminated in the report *Warlord, Inc.: Extortion and Corruption along the US Supply Chain in Afghanistan*, which detailed the insurgents' extortion of US logistics and development money.[37] The Senate Committee on Armed Services began an inquiry on private security contractors in Afghanistan. The House State and Foreign Relations Subcommittee began to sniff around US assistance to Afghanistan. The Committee on Homeland Security and Governmental Affairs set up an ad hoc Subcommittee on Contracting Oversight, which began hearings on Afghanistan in Spring 2009. Senator Claire McCaskill of Missouri convened subcommittee hearings on waste, fraud, and abuse in Afghanistan contracts in December 2009. McCaskill noted that auditors had already uncovered one billion dollars in wasteful spending in the relatively few contracts they had examined. "That's nearly one of every six dollars," McCaskill said. "Currently, there is a great deal we do not know about contracting in Afghanistan," she said.[38] "We do know, however, that the president's new strategy in Afghanistan will bring a massive increase in the number and value of contracts and contractors in Afghanistan."

With increased congressional attention on Afghanistan's corruption and graft, other government oversight agencies began to concentrate on the issue—though they still generally tiptoed around the politically explosive problem of the US inadvertently funding the Taliban. The GAO, the "congressional watchdog" of taxpayer dollars, had already produced dozens of scathing reports on the war in Afghanistan, from exposés on flawed development and deteriorating security to more discrete issues, such as calls for better open-pit waste burning (a lively topic for unlucky soldiers on latrine-waste burning details). Written in arid bureaucratese, the GAO's reports summarized hair-raising failures with bland descriptors: development progress was "impeded" by attacks; success was "threatened" by hapless Afghan security forces; US civilian agencies "face challenges" from a raging insurrection. "Improvements needed" was the recurrent theme.

The Commission on Wartime Contracting in Iraq and Afghanistan, the independent agency set up by Congress in 2008, published *At What Cost? Contingency Contracting in Iraq and Afghanistan*, which explored the problems of outsourcing a war with little oversight—though it didn't address the Taliban funding problem.[39] The Department of State Inspector General had conducted evaluations of the Kabul embassy and State Department programs, such as rule-of-law and police training, but diplomatically avoided scandals.

The Department of Defense Inspector General issued numerous Afghanistan reports, including investigations into contracting corruption and dangerously poor construction. One 2009 Afghanistan report was prompted by the death of a Green Beret who was electrocuted in a shower installed by KBR in Iraq. The Afghanistan report detailed dangerous electric hazards from untrained workers, such as exposed and undersized wiring, bad splicings, and lack of groundings. In a camp in Spin Boldak, inspectors found a sock being used as an electrical insulator.[40] Even as a nonelectrician, it was obvious to me that electrical construction being done by the defense contractors in Afghanistan wouldn't meet the National Electrical Code back home. "Jackleg" would hardly describe the exposed wiring snaking through the plywood B-huts; the dangling, cockeyed sockets; the splices that looked done by kindergartner electricians. Soldiers would wryly warn me against using particularly haphazard lavatory units: "Uh, you don't want to shower there . . ." But though they were incisive in some areas, these reports from the DOD Inspector General failed to address the issue of the Taliban funding.

In spite of the billions of reconstruction money invested in Afghanistan, Congress didn't establish the Special Inspector General for Afghanistan Reconstruction (SIGAR) until 2008, when the country's culture of corruption was already full-blown.

Major General Arnold Fields, a retired thirty-four-year marine officer, served as the first head of SIGAR. An imposing South Carolina native with a military bearing and a celebrated singing voice, General Fields told me that SIGAR had to scramble to catch up: "Flying an airplane while building it," he laughed. "I was flying a plane without any wings."[41] SIGAR was delving into a situation in Afghanistan that had been allowed to fester since 2002. When Fields arrived for his first oversight visit to Afghanistan in September 2008, he found there was no coherent, integrated strategy—"very disappointing," he termed it. "We were amazed there was not an organizational structure, and there was not the engagement external to the embassy with the people of Afghanistan at multiple levels that was needed for our activities to be commensurate with the amount of money that had been appropriated for Afghanistan," he says. "I was very surprised—there were staff members of the US embassy who told me and my colleagues that they had been there for four months and had not been outside the embassy compound, yet we are reconstructing a country and implementing policies costing billions of dollars. I was taken aback by that."

When SIGAR's initial funding was finally sorted out in the fall of 2008, Fields began hiring what came to be 120 auditors, investigators, and support staff. SIGAR had trouble getting traction, not publishing its first audit until May 2009, and its first inspection report the following July. A series of SIGAR inspection reports on schools and roads exposed a pattern of substandard construction, including serious structural flaws in the school buildings, but SIGAR persistently failed to name the US officers and officials responsible for the projects.[42]

Prosecutions have been glacially slow. Investigations move at a pace befitting the retirees that primarily staff SIGAR. One wag working in reconstruction investigation says Inspector General staffers laugh that they don't get the funding because the military and USAID just can't afford any more scandals right now.[43]

Nor was SIGAR looking at Taliban funding. Fields told me the media revelations about US money funding the Taliban caught SIGAR off guard: "When this concern broke in the news, SIGAR hadn't turned its attention to it. We were looking for low-hanging fruit." Fields spoke of the "skewed information, skewed perspective," that plagued the US leaders looking at an asymmetrical counterinsurgency through the prism of a conventional war. "But I don't think that there should ever be or ever condone paying off a Taliban entity for anything," he says. "Obviously, that's wrong; it's against the law and counter to any counterinsurgency or reconstruction initiative that we would like to see put in place in Afghanistan."

I asked Fields if the US strategy was working. He told me, "We are hoping that we will change the culture, change the mind-set, and put the provisions in place commensurate with what we would consider to be a normal democratic environment. Now, that's a very idealistic approach to this."

*   *   *

The USAID Office of Inspector General (OIG) began auditing and investigating USAID projects in Afghanistan in 2002. By fiscal year 2009, the OIG had done twenty-seven audits/reviews and saved and recovered $149 million out of the $7.9 billion of obligated US funds. The investigation was one of forty-six investigations OIG did in Afghanistan though FY 2009, which resulted in eight indictments and three convictions.[44] Against the broad background of failed USAID-funded development in Afghanistan, the totals appeared paltry. Like most of the US Inspectors General, the USAID OIG seldom recommended disciplinary or criminal actions against American officials, however corrupt or inept. But by late 2009, USAID OIG was increasingly concerned about the problems in Afghanistan.

"We follow the programs," OIG Chief of Staff Dona Dinkler told me in Washington. A no-nonsense Kansan who had served as a securities and consumer fraud investigator before joining USAID OIG as a criminal investigator in 1985, Dinkler acknowledged the problems the agency had in Afghanistan. "Doing development in a war zone is a very difficult thing to do," Dinkler told me.[45] "Providing oversight of development operations is equally challenging. It's hard." USAID was woefully understaffed with Contracting Officer's Technical Representatives, who monitored the contracts. "You don't have enough people, and they're not well trained," Dinkler said. She indicated the OIG was taking a "new approach," asking, "Are these programs working?" She said, "We're already seeing audits being produced that have indicated the likelihood of success on programs are not good." When I asked about the Taliban using American funds to finance their war, Dinkler's eyes flashed as she told me, "I think it's safe to say the American taxpayer doesn't want his or her taxpayer dollars going to the Taliban, and I know USAID does not as well. We're aware of these allegations, and OIG is looking into them."

*   *   *

Scene: Forward Operating Base Salerno, Khost Province. By helicopter and MRAP, US development officials arrive at FOB Salerno from all over P2K, the wild eastern Afghanistan provinces of Paktia, Paktika, and Khost. The brigade commander is there, along with the Indiana National Guard Agribusiness Development Team (ADT), which is hosting the confab. No one wants to miss the big meeting with the emissaries from the DC office of the SRAP—Special Representative for Afghanistan and Pakistan Richard Holbrooke. Holbrooke's two development experts and a Kabul embassy posse have flown to FOB Salerno to take the frontline pulse and give the SRAP's mandate for development. It is Washington policy meeting on-the-ground Afghanistan reality.

The meeting is at the squat masonry ADT headquarters, which has become a must-see destination for many officials on war-zone junkets. Sitting around a horseshoe table, the participants represent the panoply of the American counterinsurgency. There are hardened soldiers, led by brigade commander and veteran COIN warrior colonel Mike Howard and ADT commander colonel Brian Copes. Looking like superannuated camp counselors in their multipocketed tac clothes, there are the State Department, USDA, and USAID civilian advisers who are posted in the rebellious provinces. Then there's the embassy crowd, hovering around the SRAP emissaries like bees around the hive. The two emissaries, Dr. Otto Gonzales and Dr. Beth Dunford, are articulate and confident as they deliver the Washington message: make an impact and make it fast—and there is plenty of development money to make it happen. Colonel Howard throws them off when he insists, "Don't send me any more money without the people to spend it responsibly." [46] Howard notes there are only six engineers overseeing hundreds of millions of dollars already being spent in P2K. "Please don't send any more dollars without people to effectively spend it." Colonel Copes adds, "There's a pressure to build, buy, and spend."

The conflicting worldviews of Washington and Salerno collide. Dunford snaps, "So people are your problem—engineers, experts, contract supervision people?" Dunford and Gonzalez are informed by the new Washington policies for Afghanistan: there is to be a "civilian surge" to Afghanistan of several hundred American civilians to help turn the insurgent tide, and the United States is now going to put an "Afghan face" on development, pushing Afghans forward to lead and manage the projects. But the talking points that sound so good from Washington podiums hit the hard reality of development in a tribal war zone. Howard says the problem isn't just the need for more people; they need competent people. "Civilians are OK, just not informed." As to Afghan experts, there are miniscule numbers of technically trained Afghans, and few want to live in violent eastern Afghanistan. The ADT deputy commander, Colonel Cindra Chastain, says two Afghan advisers just quit because of Taliban intimidation. "One guy said ten Taliban surrounded his house and announced they would do him harm if he worked for the Americans." Teresa Miller, the USAID representative working in Khost, emphasizes, "Getting people to Khost is difficult. Getting qualified people to Khost is very difficult. It is a real problem."

Despite the Salerno warnings, the SRAP emissaries persist with the talking-point questions, moving on to the politically hot issue of failed oversight: Dunford forcefully asks if the contractors can go out and do improved quality control. Referencing the widespread violence that threatens the precious few trained Afghans available, Holly Hughson, the USAID adviser attached to the brigade, tactfully says, "This is delicate. There are a finite number of experts and contractors."

The groups parry about what works and what doesn't. Dunford cites policy; Gonzalez demands fast results, at one point saying it was "a happy coincidence" that one potential development project is in a "red" area—totally controlled by the Taliban. The soldiers try to explain the dangers of development work there. I'm in the back of the room thinking of the ambush-friendly defiles the convoys have to negotiate; the exposed security soldiers; the trails spiked with IEDs; the tribesmen who tell us in no uncertain terms they don't want our aid. Power and ignorance, I think. The SRAP representative from Washington persists, and the military eventually defers. Colonel Copes says, "Maybe it's worth getting soldiers killed. I'm not being cavalier. We're farmer-soldiers here. That's what soldiers do." A State Department adviser working in volatile Paktia states, "'Clear, Build, Hold' doesn't work. 'Clear' sometimes doesn't 'hold.' So when we come in to 'build,' we can't." Dunford asks pointedly, "So it doesn't work in insecure areas?" An ADT officer and a State Department adviser chime in together: "Yes, it doesn't work."

And then the rocket attack happens. The shriek of the base's Giant Voice announces incoming. "We're driving on," Colonel Copes says as he resumes talking—but he's clearly lost his audience. Worried looks and anxious whispers among the embassy crowd. As the pulsing screech continues, Copes finally says, "Oh, it means there is a rocket attack and we have to move to a hardened structure." No one says anything for a moment, and then a quaky little voice asks, "Is this a hardened building?" Copes says, "It is. We're going to drive on." A soldier says Taliban rockets are hitting the base. As the signal wails on, Colonel Howard says, "Welcome to our world."

Chapter 12

They Get That
Agricultural Development in Afghanistan

THE KANSAS NATIONAL GUARD Agribusiness Development Team walked out of Forward Operating Base Mehtar Lam in full battle rattle—body armor, helmets, ammo, and weapons. Their battle gear clinking and jangling, they hiked over to the demonstration farm to talk with the Afghans about flowers. Primarily comprised of Kansan soldiers with farming backgrounds, the ADT arrived in unstable Laghman Province about a year before on a mission to improve Afghan farmers' lives through modern agriculture. They were kind of a Peace Corps with guns.

With the security platoon in a defensive perimeter, agricultural specialist Lieutenant Colonel Roger Beekman spoke with Lalagha, the wizened village elder. "Once we found Lalagha—The Man—then we could get started, we could scratch out a little," says Beekman, a tall, genial wit from Topeka.[1] "Without him, we can't go ahead." A group of boys clustered, cadging stuff from the grunts; chasing one another across the plowed field. Through the interpreter, Lalagha told of the ADT providing financial support to set up this demonstration farm. The farm allowed conservative Afghan farmers see whether the Americans' new ideas actually could bear fruit in this harsh, unforgiving land, where families starve if a novel concept fails.

On the farm, the villagers grew vegetables, grapes, and fruit trees. But the crocus flowers, which yielded the valuable spice saffron, were the crown jewels of the ADT test farm. A terraced brown plot with small purple flowers huddled near the ground is the crocus field. Inside the crocus blooms, tiny red-orange threads called stigmas glowed. When picked and dried, the stigmas become saffron, which brings big bucks in the developed world—and even in impoverished Afghanistan the spice is worth $1,000 a kilo. Saffron can be used in cooking, fragrances, and even as medicine. "The more we mess with this stuff, the more we find new things it can be used for," Beekman told me. "Very useful crop—very profitable."

Khost Province is a semiarid plain ringed by the rugged Hindu Kush mountains. With only about twenty-five inches of rain per year, the Khost farmers are dependent on the often seasonally dry Shamal River, wells, and irrigation canals to sustain their small grain fields and orchards. Thirty years of war have devastated Afghanistan's traditional irrigation system, causing widespread erosion and desiccation. Taken from a Black Hawk® helicopter during a reconnaissance flight, this aerial photograph of a village and its adjacent fields graphically displays the critical role of water in this parched, mountainous land.

About 80–85 percent of the Afghan people are connected to agriculture for their livelihoods. While some farmers have access to small tractors for planting, many still turn the khaki-colored soil with beasts of burden and wooden plows. A typical Afghan farmer is trying to feed his large family from about half an acre to an acre of ground. In this calorie-deficient society, farm families often slowly starve in the winter. The per capita income is about $400 a year.

In the Pashtun villages of eastern Afghanistan, a shade tree at the edge of the village serves as the place for *shuras* (meetings). Under the shura tree of the village of Shobo Khel in insurgency-wracked Khost Province, Indiana National Guard 1-19th Agribusiness Development Team (ADT) agriculture specialists meet with village leaders as ADT security soldiers guard against attack.

The ADT deputy commander, Colonel Cindra Chastain, leads the discussion with the tribal leaders of Shobo Khel about a proposed system of small rock dams to reduce soil erosion and improve irrigation.

A Shobo Khel elder listens to the Americans' proposal as a younger tribal leader sits in the shadow.

Colonel Brian Copes served as the commander of the Indiana National Guard 1-19th Agribusiness Development Team in Khost Province.

Intent on partnering with Afghan leaders on agricultural development, the ADT drank endless cups of green tea in hundreds of KLEs (Key Leader Engagements). Here Colonel Copes meets with Subgovernor Latifullah in a fortified district center about agricultural development projects. Intelligence officers indicated Latifullah, like many Afghan government officials, had strong connections to the insurgents. US forces, including the ADT, encountered many IEDs in Latifullah's village.

Because of the danger of attack, the military development teams in eastern Afghanistan travel in convoys of armed MRAPs (Mine-Resistant, Ambush-Protected), 37,000-pound armored vehicles.

Even quality-control missions are risky. Here a team of soldiers hike toward a Laghman Province river to inspect the new bridge that the United States built for the villagers.

Development projects in Afghanistan are often complicated by tribal frictions and inadequate oversight by Afghan contractors. Here hydrologists Lieutenant Colonel Kevin Sari and Sergeant Richard Joyce confer with a Zanda Khel village headmaster about the failure of a corrupt contractor to manage the dam project.

Tribesmen rest beside one of the Shobo Khel/Zanda Khel dams, made of small stones with a deep causeway. Some of the dams had even deeper causeways, so the village donkeys using the stream as a trail would have easy passage.

The provincial capital of Ghazni City is a Taliban hotbed, considered the "reddest of the red"—totally Taliban controlled. This photo of downtown Ghazni City was taken from an MRAP as members of the Texas National Guard Agribusiness Development Team traveled toward a livestock project they administered.

Colonel Dan Harris, a Texas homicide detective in civilian life, commanded the Texas National Guard Agribusiness Development Team in Ghazni Province.

Sergeant Major Harlan Hardy from Marfa, Texas, inspects a new livestock building the ADT organized and funded.

Two US security soldiers stand guard near Bagram Airfield. A walled, adobe-brick farm compound called a *qalat* stands in the background, speaking to Afghanistan's eternal need for defense.

The Kentucky National Guard Agribusiness Development Team is headquartered at Bagram Airfield, the sprawling center of US military operations in Afghanistan. Here amidst the roar of departing fighter jets and helicopters, Sergeant Jo Lisa Ashley tends her bee hives, part of her women's empowerment program to provide cash crops to Afghan farm women.

Kabul's Massoud Circle is adjacent to the heavily guarded American embassy and other US military headquarters. It was near the September 13, 2011, insurgent attacks on the embassy and nearby NATO headquarters.

In spite of a deteriorating security in Kabul, central Asian life goes on. Here a Kabul vendor hauls his load of naan flat bread.

This Afghan jingle truck, nicknamed for its elaborate embellishments, is a standard transport vehicle of the type used to haul the untold thousands of tons of military logistics supplies to the hundreds of US bases across Afghanistan. Congressional investigations have confirmed that the US-funded security contracts for the transport convoys are helping to finance the Taliban.

Khost Province has been a hotbed of fundamentalist Islamic armed resistance for decades. The Pashtuns rely on their thousand-year-old tribal codes, which include the cultural cornerstones of *nang* (honor), *tora* (courage), and *badal* (revenge), as well as the equally important tenets of *melmastia* (hospitality) and *nanawati* (sanctuary to a defeated foe). This village leader in an insurgency-plagued district of Khost Province reflects this proud warrior culture.

Laghman Province was increasingly embattled as the insurgency grew. This photo of a graffitied security barrier was taken the morning after Taliban attacks in the province had the Forward Operating Base Mehtar Lam artillery and combat teams working through the night.

Beyond boosting farm income, the ADT intended for saffron to replace the area's other high-value crop: the opium poppy that financed the Taliban. But in the soldiers' oft-repeated phrase, "Nothing is simple in Afghanistan." Beekman told me if not properly administered, saffron profits could also fund the insurgency. "You got that much money concentrated in a small area, there's still going to be a way to figure out how to make money and finance the bad guys doing that sort of stuff—that's another concern we've got. It'd be better to have the place flooded with saffron than poppy, but it's what the money can do that needs to be remembered."

* * *

Agriculture is important in Afghanistan. Over 80 percent of the Afghan population depends on agriculture for its livelihood, and decades of war have devastated the country's traditional agricultural infrastructure. The Soviets, in an effort to drive the *mujahideen*-supporting rural Afghans out of the countryside, had destroyed ancient irrigation systems and cut tens of thousands of fruit and nut trees. With the farming population in refugee camps, the irrigation canals, essential in this arid land, silted up. Crucial agricultural knowledge was lost in the carnage of war. After the US invasion, the Taliban-led resistance took root in the farming regions of the Pashtun south and east. Despite the simmering insurgency and the dire poverty of the region, the United States spent relatively little on agricultural development.[2] When the insurgency exploded, the Bush administration begrudgingly began to increase agricultural funds, and the National Guard responded with the ADTs. Beginning in 2008 with the Missouri National Guard ADT in Nangarhar Province, the other ADTs came from Texas, California, Indiana, Nebraska, Kansas, Kentucky, Tennessee, Arkansas, Iowa, Oklahoma, and Wisconsin—all states with large agricultural industries and land-grant universities for technical support.

The ADTs' farmer-soldiers operated like extreme ag-extension agents. With their heavily armed Force Protection platoons and fleets of heavily armored MRAPs, the ADTs could operate in the frontline, "nonpermissive" insurgent regions of eastern Afghanistan, where they didn't have to compete with a rampant poppy industry that dominated the south. The ADT ag projects ranged from large, US-scaled industrial agribusiness endeavors to village-sized farms. As time went on, the teams emphasized education, particularly attempting to professionalize (as in "reduce corruption") the provincial agricultural ministers, whom the ADT officers mentored and supported.

By the spring of 2009, the ADTs were the flavor of the month for harried Washington hierarchies searching for a win. Secretary of Defense Robert Gates, Joint Chiefs of Staff Chairman Admiral Mike Mullen, and Special Ambassador Richard Holbrooke lauded the ADTs, Holbrooke gushing, "they are doing all these terrific projects."[3] Central Command's commander-in-chief, General David Petraeus, testified in a Senate hearing: "They get very good results. They have all the attributes of soldiers in terms of being able to secure themselves, communicate—move, shoot, and communicate—and yet they're also experts in agriculture." Other US officials were complimentary of the ADTs, but a little more cautious. Wary of the military doing long-term nation building, Secretary of Defense Robert Gates said, "The first stage of doing that, I think, can be done by our military forces and especially by the National Guard, but longer term, that mission has to go to the civilian side of the government."[4]

*   *   *

It took the US government quite a while to figure out that agricultural development was critical to counterinsurgency. Instead of agricultural development, the Bush administration was intent on building large-scale free-market systems and infrastructure, such as banking, telecommunications, and roads. In fiscal years 2002 to 2004, only about 6 percent of the total USAID assistance, $37 million out of $645 million, went to agricultural programs, and most of that money was for humanitarian aid and counternarcotics projects. There was little long-term agricultural development. In the broad scheme of things, the agricultural projects were little more than poorly administered afterthoughts —albeit expensive ones, given the paltry impact they had. The explosion of poppy cultivation from 2002 to 2004 prompted the Bush administration to appropriate a larger percentage of total assistance to agricultural programs, but ag was still a small proportion of total aid: 10 percent in FY 2005, 13 percent in 2006, and in 2007 it inched up to 16 percent, where it basically stayed through FY 2010.

The programs that *were* done were often disasters. Most of the $1.4 billion that USAID awarded from 2002 to 2010 for agricultural development went for counternarcotics alternative development projects (ADPs) to ostensibly reduce poppy production. From 2005 to 2008, 71 percent of USAID's agricultural program awards went for alternative development projects that many judged to be primarily effective in financing the Taliban.[5] ADPs were supposed to work in tandem with other US-funded counternarcotics initiatives that included eradication, interdiction, rule of law, education, and drug demand reduction, which cost another $2.5 billion from 2005 to 2010.[6]

Martin Hoffmann, the former secretary of the army who formed the Afghanistan Reconstruction Group, told me about USAID's first effort to grow wheat in Afghanistan: "But they grew the wrong wheat in Afghanistan. They grew soft wheat the first time. The Afghans were first convulsed, then they thought it tragic and pathetic."[7]

Richard Holbrooke outed the scandalous $30 million USAID agribusiness project outside of the city of Mazar-e-Sharif, a quixotic 25,000-acre megafarm proposed by the billionaire chairman of Dole Foods, David H. Murdock, to President Bush. Murdock envisioned a vast tract of vacant land would become fecund with miles of strawberries and thousands of cashmere goats. Giddy with the promise, the development consultants began to conjure "Baby Doles," regional agribusiness centers, across Afghanistan.[8] The only problem was the Mazar-e-Sharif land was unsuitable for agriculture—the underlying aquifer was far too saline to grow anything. After spending millions of dollars, USAID quietly let the project go dormant.

Special Representative Richard Holbrooke was such a tub-thumper for agricultural development that Secretary of State Hillary Clinton began calling him Farmer Holbrooke. The Obama administration downplayed poppy eradication, which alienated Afghan farmers. The focus was now on economic growth and job creation to provide legitimate alternatives to poppy cultivation. President Obama said, "And we will also focus our assistance in areas— such as agriculture—that can make an immediate impact in the lives of the Afghan people."[9] And then Obama made the typical policymaker move: he threw more money at the problem, tripling the appropriations. From $246 million for agricultural programs disbursed in FY 2009, the Obama administration requested $827 million for USAID agricultural-assistance programs in FY 2010.[10]

Developed by Holbrooke's experts in conjunction with the Afghan government's Ministry of Agriculture, Irrigation, and Livestock (MAIL), the Obama administration's new Afghanistan ag policy aimed to increase farm productivity with improved seeds, fertilizer, irrigation, and "effective extension services." The Afghan farmers' anticipated surpluses would then find customers through improved markets, credit, and new trade corridors.[11] The policy also intended to increase the Ministry of Agriculture's capacity through mentoring, salary support, and development. In an effort to empower the Afghan government, US officials announced they were going to "Afghanicize" development—increase the reconstruction funding being channeled through the Afghan ministries.

*   *   *

Professor Kevin McNamara headed the Advancing Afghan Agriculture Alliance at Purdue University. First introduced to Afghanistan as a Peace Corps volunteer, McNamara has maintained strong connections with the country since. A burly, bearded, hands-on academic, who veers from intense to affable in a heartbeat, McNamara is one of the foremost US experts on Afghan agriculture. Beyond mentoring Afghan graduate students and ministries, McNamara helped orient US development teams to Afghan realities.

With his long experience in Afghanistan, McNamara was critical of the new US ag policy. "Instead of channeling US money through contactors such as Chemonics, we are now going to run the money through the Afghan government," McNamara told me.[12] Speaking of the shortcomings of the Ministry of Agriculture, he says, "In MAIL, there is no capacity, no quality people, no systems. Will MAIL contract with NGOs, especially Afghan NGOs? My sense is it will be a disaster." McNamara thought the grandiose US plans for international market centers were out of scale to Afghan agriculture—"a complete failure," he termed the program. "I think it's silly. I don't think it's doing anything to help poor farmers produce more." McNamara listed the challenges of Afghanistan: the unimaginative US agricultural policies that continued many of the same failed Bush initiatives; the shortage of cultural understanding; the greedy development corporations; the Afghan corruption; the dearth of qualified Afghans; the conservative subsistence economy; the inept Kabul government. "There is a lack of a viable Afghan government. Nothing's going to happen."

*   *   *

The human capacity of the Ministry of Agriculture was still extremely low. USAID rated MAIL's capability in 2009 on a scale of 1 to 5, with 5 being able to perform ministerial responsibilities without help. MAIL was judged to be a 2—needing assistance to perform all but the most routine functions.[13] To build MAIL into a functioning ministry, the United States placed an enormous amount of trust in the minister of agriculture, Muhammad Asif Rahimi, an Afghan technocrat who made the international development officials swoon. "He's the darling of the international community," UNAMA official Mark

Ward told me one night in Kabul.[14] Rahimi had been educated at the University of Nebraska at Omaha, which had long-standing ties to Afghanistan, and spent many years working as a development consultant for CARE, the humanitarian aid organization. Now a polished international bureaucrat with elegant suits and bristly, well-cut salt-and-pepper hair, Rahimi brings to mind a sagacious, self-possessed badger. In 2005, he returned to Afghanistan to help run the National Security Program, considered the country's flagship community-development program. He was appointed minister of agriculture in 2008.

Rahimi told me war "totally destroyed" Afghanistan's agriculture, which declined three percent every year from 1978 to 2001, with drought killing half the livestock.[15] "So now we are rebuilding," he says. "We have some success in both rebuilding Afghanistan's agriculture and rebuilding livestock back." While Rahimi had success recruiting bright young administrators, keeping them at the ministry was difficult, as the high-paying international organizations were constantly poaching his best people.

*   *   *

Holbrooke's plans for "plussed-up" ag policies were subject to the same problems that plagued most US development in Afghanistan. For instance, in response to the exposés about failed oversight, USAID instituted "alternative monitoring" guidelines in 2008 for high-threat environments such as Afghanistan. The guidelines called for increased oversight and security personnel, as well as cooperative monitoring with the military and Afghan officials (who actually ventured into the provinces even less than USAID), as well as the use of Google Earth® and aerial photographs to replace on-site visits. Aside from questions of efficacy and implementation, there was one further impediment to the success of alternative monitoring for agricultural development: according to the GAO, USAID neglected to tell the Afghanistan agricultural staff about the guidelines until June 2010.[16] Oddly enough, USAID had already been using remote sensing and local nationals to oversee development projects in northwest Pakistan's tribal regions, where al Qaeda and an array of insurgent groups held sway. Hynek Kalkus, GAO's assistant director for international affairs and trade focused on AfPak issues, told me, "We asked AID, if you can do it in Pakistan, why can't you do it in Afghanistan?"[17]

USAID also lacked a performance management plan in Afghanistan until 2006, leaving the staff without effective tools to manage and evaluate program performance.[18] But the AID strategic objective teams stopped providing data after 2007, blaming insecurity and "changed" program priorities.[19] And there it sat. As the development funding soared in the next years, there was a notable paucity of performance indicators for the "implementing partners"—the Beltway Bandits.[20] Beyond some patchy metrics for input and activities, there weren't many measurements of results. Sometimes there were suspicious statistics touting remarkable achievements, such as the 2009 metric that indicated USAID's counternarcotics alternative development programs in the southwestern Afghanistan benefited 56,399 families, far exceeding the goal of benefiting 12,696 families, a remarkable 444 percent overachievement of the target. The statistic is particularly remarkable given the same study indicated the number of hectares cultivated in alternative crops missed the target by one-third. Another program, the Rebuilding Agricultural Markets Project (RAMP), claimed to have exceeded its goal by a factor of seven. RAMP projected to increase the market value of five commodities by $250 million with a "value-chain" approach. The agency reported the incredible market increase was more than $1.7 billion.[21]

The reality was USAID and its cronies were just spending money. That was the metric. No feedback loops for corrective action. No sustainability. No calls on the carpet. Just spend the money and ask for more. And metrics to determine the impact of agricultural development on counterinsurgency? Well, there still weren't any.

With the Obama administration embracing born-again COIN, the military also championed agricultural development. One of the early COIN adopters, Colonel Mike Howard, complained about the low funding for agriculture: "In 2008, we spent $200 million of CERP money in P2K [Paktia, Paktika, and Khost Provinces], and $7 million on agriculture. That's ridiculous."[22] Howard later told me he was depending on agricultural development to help subdue the Afghans. "I mean, we spent a lot of money on oil in Iraq because it was an oil-based economy. Well, we got to spend a lot of money on agriculture in Afghanistan because it's an agricultural-based economy."[23]

*   *   *

Both the US military and civilians played some unfortunate games of chicken—funding ill-fated poultry projects that left egg on their faces. One night, I was working in a military development-team office in eastern Afghanistan. It was a typical thrown-together military office, crammed with soldiers at abutting desks. Civilians bustled in now and then for hurried confabs. A British postconflict-development consultant sat at the desk facing mine as we both bent over our laptops. In a low voice, he told me he had "gone to the dark side," by taking a military development contract. Civilian aid workers typically pride themselves on maintaining distance from the military.

"What's your e-mail address?" he asked, and information on failed development projects began popping into my in-box. "Did you hear about that Dole farm up north?" he asked in his lilting accent. He smiled as he punched his send button. He began telling me about the Afghan chicken scam. Both USAID and the military gave millions of dollars to Western development consultants for contracts to train Afghans (primarily women) in basic poultry techniques. Most often a sketchily trained Afghan subcontractor would give a few days of chicken classes to a group of Afghan women, who often received money to attend. Following the training, the women would get a flock of chickens and a rooster. But things seldom went as planned in Afghanistan. In a pattern that followed many Afghan livestock programs of this nature, most of the women quickly sold their free chickens in the marketplace, and the majority of the surviving chickens soon died. The Brit glanced around and then leaned closer. He told me out of the corner of his mouth that 80–90 percent of the inordinately expensive poultry-development projects in Afghanistan have failed. Noting one particularly extravagant project, he snorted, "It would have been cheaper to have parachuted chickens out of an airplane, with a year's worth of food."[24]

*   *   *

Washington officials talked about the National Guard Agribusiness Development Teams as though they were a uniform group executing a consistent strategy with equal effectiveness, but the reality on the ground was considerably different. Depending on province, perspectives, and personalities, each of the ADTs had wildly diverse experiences and accomplishments. And like the rest of the US war effort in Afghanistan, each rotation of each National Guard ADT brought a new set of individuals and tactics to bear. Some groups flailed around; some made progress. The Texas Agribusiness Development Team was an example—almost a tale of two teams. Posted to volatile Ghazni Province, the first team arrived in May 2008 with Texas-sized ideas. Using satellite photographs, the Texans honed in on a place called Nawar, a vast tract of open land in a mountainous Hazara region. Thirty miles long by ten miles wide, the area was an enormous, nearly uninhabited rangeland. The soldiers quickly devel-

oped an ambitious plan: A Great Plains–style industrial wheat-seed farm high
in the Afghan mountains. The first ADT planned to plant twenty thousand
acres with hybrid seed, which the Afghans would harvest with giant combines
delivered by helicopter into the remote, impoverished region, where literacy
rates are barely in the teens. The team estimated the cost of the farm to be $7.5
to $9 million.

First, there was the sustainability issue: How were destitute tribesmen supposed to get hybrid seed or transport harvested wheat through a near-roadless war
zone, let alone maintain complicated machinery when they couldn't even read?
When the second team of Texas ADT soldiers arrived in the spring of 2009 to take
over in Ghazni, they began to discover some other problems with the first team's
megalomaniac plan. Colonel Dan Harris, a homicide detective in civilian life, told
me about his team's research: "When we went up there and did our analysis, it's
about eleven thousand feet. The growing season is extremely short." The Nawar
District was essentially a high mountain desert, more suited to grazing animals
than a giant farming operation. The second team soon discovered Nawar was
Ghazni Province's best grazing land, used extensively by the Hazara herdsmen.
Then there was the soil problem. Sergeant Alex Stewart, the second team's hydrologist and a university professor in civilian life, says the Nawar soil wasn't suitable
for farming. "So the soils there aren't your typical kind of soils. They have a tendency to be saline and have a lot of chemicals in them." And then there was the
ownership problem. The open land that the first ADT thought was available for
Texas-sized agricultural development was actually communally owned rangeland
for the Hazaran tribesmen's sheep, goats, and cattle. Lieutenant Brad Clark, an
ADT agricultural specialist from Belton, Texas, worked as a USDA Natural
Resource Conservation Service range specialist in civilian life. He told me, "It's
basically all community grazing areas, and that gets really complicated when you
start involving the various villages and tribes. I can tell you they've got it worked
out. There's no fences, no 'This is my land; that's your land,' at least on the surface."

So the second Texas team sorted through the options for Nawar and hit on
an Afghan-appropriate development project. Colonel Harris told me, "We want
to put in a livestock center of excellence in there, artificial insemination clinic,
veterinarian clinic, lots of things relating to livestock." So the Texas Agribusiness
Development Teams concentrated on working with Hazara herdsmen to
improve their livestock and rangeland management. Colonel Harris says the
ADT learned a valuable lesson: "In Afghanistan, even easy is hard."[25]

Though the National Guard ADTs were in Afghanistan to provide development assistance, there was always the threat of a TIC—"Troops in Combat."

It was often confounding for both the troops doing aid work and the Afghans whose hearts and minds they were trying to win. With the ADTs out in the field far more than average units, IEDs were a constant threat. Near the village of Ali Shang, the Kansas team suffered "a catastrophic kill" on an MRAP, though the soldiers inside suffered only minor wounds. The same thing happened to the Indiana team in Khost Province—twice in 2009. But the Texas ADT wasn't so lucky. In October 2009, a Texas ADT convoy of lightly armored Humvees was returning from a mission to mountainous western Ghazni Province; the mountain terrain prevented them from using their MRAP trucks. Near a red area known as Jaghato, an enormous explosion alerted the team medic, Specialist Thomas Kinney, he was going to be needed. The convoy's radio began to crackle with calls. Kinney told me, "I tried to calm myself down. You know, I'm a paramedic—it never fails, every time a call comes in, you get excited. And this was way over that. These were guys I know. This might be really bad from the radio traffic."[26] The third Humvee in the convoy was a chilling sight. He says, "So I went forward to the vehicle and there was really nothing left from the trunk forward. There were two seats in the back that are basically attached to the trunk and they were there, but everything in front of that and between was gone. There were many small pieces and some large pieces had flown fifty meters. Incredible impact." Kinney began looking for the men in the Humvee. He found one soldier under the gun turret, and then two under the ruins of the Humvee. "So I squatted down and put my hand on one of their backs to see if it maybe wasn't as bad, but I could see right away there wasn't any way anybody could live through that." The two fallen soldiers were agricultural specialist Sergeant Christopher Staats of Fredricksburg, a Texas A&M graduate who was an environmental scientist in civilian life, and Sergeant Anthony Green, a Yorktown, Texas, farmer, who served as an animal husbandry specialist.

Appropriately for a farmer-soldier team, the Kansas ADT fought a battle in an Afghan cornfield. An ADT detachment was on a development mission in Laghman Province at isolated Combat Outpost Najil, nicknamed "Little Roundtop," after Custer's Last Stand. When the post commander learned insurgents were planning to attack a vital supply convoy, he quickly enlisted the ADT to counter the ambush. The ADT soldiers hurried a kilometer down the road, where part of the team headed up to a ridgeline while the rest moved toward a large cornfield. The ADT medic and a former marine, Sergeant Lucas May, told me the soldiers on the ridgeline saw four or five guys. "Couldn't tell what they were carrying—could be shovels, could be rifles—but they were bounding through the cornfield, kind of moving in a military fashion."[27]

Apparently unaware the ADT was also in the field, the Afghan fighters fired rocket-propelled grenades at the fuel truck leading the convoy. "And from that time on it was game-on, and we went in looking for them," says May, in civilian life a chef with a penchant for French cuisine. A firefight erupted. Two Afghans went down. "We kept on moving through the fields, and this is cornfields—they're seven-, eight-feet tall, so [you] can't see more than a foot or two in front of you. So we kept trying to find the best places to fire from—where the corn would break and stuff like that." The Coalition forces killed four Afghan fighters that day. The ADT escaped without casualties. May protested when the soldiers began holding up the dead Afghan fighters for photos. "They were like Hemingway holding up a marlin," May told me. Speaking of the dead Afghans that his videogame-trained comrades were photographing, May says, "They're just pixels on a screen to those guys."[28] The California National Guard ADT posted to Kunar Province also engaged in a fierce firefight in August 2010.[29] May told me it didn't matter if the ADTs were in Afghanistan to help farm families—they were still part of the war. "Because there's no front line on this war; because everything's the front line in this war, any job that you do, you can expect to have some sort of interaction with the bad guys."

*   *   *

Members of the first Indiana National Guard ADT that arrived in Khost Province in early 2009 became the ADT poster children, often on the circuit of US officials being shepherded around the frontline FOBs. Loaded with brass to get its way in the hierarchical military environment of Afghanistan, the team had exceptional preparation. Beyond extensive combat training, the ADT took Afghan-appropriate agricultural classes at Purdue University and got Afghan language and culture training at Indiana University, renowned for its central Asian programs. The team was determined to focus on low-cost sustainable development done in conjunction with the Afghan government and people. They placed particular emphasis on education. "Knowledge is something the Taliban cannot blow up or burn down," ADT Commander Colonel Brian Copes repeatedly said. Copes, a Pashto-speaking polymath who grew up on a southern Indiana hill farm, says, "They get that. Every time I've thrown that out, they get that; they understand that."[30]

But even with outstanding leadership and team morale, the Indiana ADT faced harrowing challenges. Small-scale development still took a massive commitment of security assets. The endless interchanges with tribal elders, Afghan government officials, and the spiraling nebula of US military and civilian hierarchies sucked up enormous amounts of time and resources. Afghan contractors presented their own unique set of challenges. The oversight responsibilities were both demanding and dangerous—and often frustrating. And at the conclusion of the arduous process, there was the high probability part of the money spent helped finance local insurgents.

The dams of Shobo Khel served as a case study. One hot dusty day in November 2009, ADT agricultural specialists climbed a steep, dry riverbed, a *wadi*, in the rebellious Tani District. Loaded down with seventy-five pounds of armor and weaponry, the soldiers huffed up the inclines while they scanned the high hills for snipers. A Taliban-controlled village was three kilometers away. The team saw a giant crater in the road while driving from FOB Salerno, reminding them the insurgents were active. The team was overseeing a water project at Shobo Khel—the ADT's tenth visit to the construction site. The ADT had hired an Afghan contractor to build small rock dams to reduce soil erosion and improve irrigation. The $200,000 budget included money to hire local tribesmen, theoretically outbidding the Taliban for their services. But the team learned that instead of building dams, one hundred villagers spent twenty days building stone walls along the river. The soldiers were back at the wadi trying to figure out why.

The project had begun months before, when the ADT used satellite imagery to determine that this seasonal stream would be ideal for one of their sustainable development projects. The ADT hydrologists designed eighty-seven small, piled-rock dams to slow the mountain river, benefitting two adjacent villages, Zanda Khel and Shobo Khel, with reduced soil erosion and improved irrigation. But like most development in Afghanistan, it was a long and complicated process. "Afghan buy-in" was the name of the game in counterinsurgency development, so there was a series of meetings to sell the idea. The ADT first pitched the concept to the district subgovernor in a KLE, a Key Leader Engagement, held in the Tani District Center, a fortified Afghan government redoubt protected by high HESCO® barriers and endless coils of shining razor wire. While ADT force-protection soldiers guarded the small compound, hydrologist Sergeant Richard Joyce explained the project to the Afghan official, telling him the "picture from the sky" identified the site near the village of Shobo Khel. With the subgovernor's approval, the team moved on to Shobo Khel, where they met with village elders in a *shura* (meeting) under a small shade tree at the edge of the mud-brick hamlet. The thin silver trickle of a rare running brook stood out in the parched brown landscape. The villagers were enthusiastic, particularly about the jobs. The daily wage of six dollars was munificent—roughly triple what a farm laborer typically makes.

The ADT then commenced the complicated contracting process, using CERP funds. McChrystal's directives reined CERP-funded projects back to $200,000 of easily approved funds, so that became the budget limit. The ADT engineers used US dam construction costs to estimate the project would cost under $150,000, but when the seventy-five proposals came in from Afghan contractors, the team was surprised to see the bids were triple that amount. After throwing out most proposals for failing to meet minimum requirements, the project managers told the remaining contractors to sharpen their pencils. On the rebid, the Taranom National Construction Company (TNCC) skidded in just below the $200,000 CERP limit.

Recognizing that unbridled spending contributed to inflation and corruption—and financed the insurgents—the Indiana ADT focused on a "small dollars, big impact" philosophy. Colonel Copes told me: "A few years ago, the $450,000 probably would have flown." Copes mimicked a development official of yore: "'$450,000, great! Gets money flowing in the country!'" Wryly he concluded, "We taught 'em, we just didn't know what we were teaching 'em."

The contractor provided professional engineering drawings showing crisp keystone-check dams marching down the wadi, with the erosion-prone stream banks protected by riprap. It was easy to envision happy villagers working in their well-irrigated wheat fields, their precious arable land protected from the soil-devouring spring rampage of the un-dammed river. But the vision wasn't the reality. The team soon discovered Shobo Khel and Zenda Khel were feuding over rights to the wadi. It took numerous meetings and the subgovernor's eventual intercession to arrive at a shaky Solomonic compromise: each village would contribute half of the workers and get half of the development cornucopia.

The ADT also quickly discovered the TNCC construction work was lousy, though the Afghan contractor had provided US military references. Contracting companies, CCs in the argot, were a crapshoot in Afghanistan. Four-month-old Taranom National Construction Company was one of the thousands of Afghan contracting companies formed to sop up the torrent of development money that flooded into Afghanistan. The joke going around was that any Afghan with a wheelbarrow was a bid-flinging CC. But the ADT was concerned not only with the Afghan contractor's poor construction work. Far more troubling was his false ID he tried to use to enter FOB Salerno, and his subsequent failed biometric BAT-HIIDE identification scan. (BAT, Biometric Automated Toolkit, and HIIDE, Handheld Interagency Detection Equipment, allowed soldiers use a camera, a fingerprint scanner, an iris reader, and portable computer to identify known insurgents.)

The ADT had questions: Was the contractor Taliban? Was he funneling money to the insurgency? In spite of the US military presence in the Taliban-ridden Tani District, the dam project was counterintuitively free of attack. Maybe the slapdash work and the secure construction site were connected. Pay-offs? Colonel Copes told me, "The Taliban might have taken 30 or 40 percent right off the top, and now he's struggling to perform, because he's got less than 100 percent of budget because the Taliban took their cut right off the top."

The project glitches necessitated repeated quality-control missions out to the wadi. Security for the ADT was a constant, nerve-racking problem. "I don't need to *ever* . . . see Shobo Khel again," ADT deputy commander Colonel Cindra Chastain told me in exasperation. "I must have been there twenty times. Well, ten anyway." A thirty-year military officer, Chastain paid for her Purdue animal science degree by raising 4-H blue-ribbon hogs on her parents' farm near Crawfordsville, Indiana. A fit blonde woman with a ready laugh and compassionate nature, Chastain was a remarkably effective officer who often counseled troubled soldiers. She told me an earlier trip to pay Shobo Khel villagers almost ended in disaster. Payday complete, the Afghan contractor had sped back down the narrow dirt road. The ADT soldiers were climbing into the MRAPs to follow him when an unfortunate Afghan motorcyclist inadvertently tripped an IED set to blow up the convoy.

So on this quality-control mission back to the wadi, the ADT was prepared for the worst. Before leaving the FOB, the Force Protection leader, Sergeant Joe Carter, warned us: "It's as bad as it can be. Keep your eyes open." As we climbed the wadi, it was obvious the construction was not right. Instead of the taut check-dams that the TNCC drawings promised, there were meandering piles of rubble, some with deep notches for donkeys to use as passages. Specialist Malcolm Modisett, a muscular security grunt with a goal to be the mayor of his hometown, Gary, Indiana, stood scowling beside one of the dams. "Man, you and I walking over them a couple more times are going to do 'em in," he said. Even worse, instead of the specified riprap on the banks to slow the river down, there were now high rock walls lining the streambed, which would accelerate the flow and negate the project. In violation of Afghan law, there was no TNCC engineer on site. Instead, a tall, composed local schoolmaster with a majestic white beard was serving as the de facto volunteer foreman. He explained to the ag specialists that the villagers feared the dams would flood their fields, so built walls instead of dams. After venting to the ADT officers about the corrupt TNCC contractor, the schoolmaster asked when the villagers would be paid.

Still sweating from the climb, the ADT leaders now faced a dilemma: If they didn't pay the villagers, it would undermine the counterinsurgency effort. But if the dams weren't built right, it would give the Taliban another example of failed development to publicize. They first assured the schoolmaster that they would pay the villagers, then told him the rock dams were designed to be porous, so the water wouldn't flood their fields. They pledged to tune the contractor up. And then they listed the corrections the villagers needed to make to the dams before the next payment. In deference to the villagers' flooding fears, the officers decided to leave the stone walls, figuring once the dams were fixed, the barriers would slow the river to some degree, improving irrigation and erosion control. And maybe, just maybe, the villagers would feel more connected to the Government of the Islamic Republic of Afghanistan rather than the Taliban. "Baby steps," they told one another as they trudged back down the streambed, "We have to do this in baby steps."

*   *   *

Scene: Khost City, Khost Province, Afghanistan. It's a HAM stop in Indian Country—soldier talk for a hearts-and-minds mission to the insurgency-controlled Khost City bazaar, where the Indiana National Guard ADT agricultural specialists hope to ask Afghan vendors about produce. Leaving FOB Salerno for the short drive to Khost City, the soldiers "go red," load their weapons, and prepare for war. "Yea, bullets," calls one gunner as he clicks a cartridge belt into his turret-mounted machine gun. Locked and loaded, they combat-seal the heavy doors with a hiss of compressed air. Because of the high risk of attack, four heavily armed MRAPs roll out for this market-research trip.

It's a circumscribed view through small bulletproof windows as we rumble past golden wheat fields that stretch off toward the rugged dun-colored mountains. Turbaned farmers bent to scythe the grain straighten to watch the convoy. Mud-brick villages hunker on the landscape. A flock of fat-tailed sheep waggle by; a bedraggled camel lounges. Clad in body armor, Kevlar® helmets, Nomex® fireproof gloves, and blast goggles, and cinched tight with lap and shoulder harnesses so they don't go flying in IED blasts, the soldiers in the armored cabin are constricted; close to immobile. All communications are over headsets crammed under helmets. It's like traveling through Afghanistan in a portholed submarine.

The intercom distributes unending truck banter, the sacred and profane merrily commingled. Fast-food yearnings till our mouths water. War movie critiques; reminiscences of Barney, Power Rangers, Mary Poppins. *Some female anatomy talk; some bafflement about female psychology. Scatology of near-poetic levels. A little country-music singing, then a Christian pop song about "voices calling out to me," led by ADT Commander Colonel Copes. An upcoming Saturday night dance sponsored by the "Ladies of Salerno" generates conversation. There being few actual "Ladies of Salerno" back at the FOB, the men make alternate arrangements. One guy asks his buddy, "So who gets to lead?" Rejoiner: "I do." "No, I do." Some bass-voiced bickering, concluding with "Who's the girl?" After some negotiation, they resolve the temporary gender deal, but the "girl" makes one last requirement: "No dirty dancing."*

Khost City is a booming provincial capital of over one hundred thousand. As we approach the outskirts, five-story office buildings and maxi-mansions rise here and there—financed, soldiers say, by corruption and skimmed US development dollars. In the center of town, a tall government building stands scorched and windowless, the casualty of a recent Taliban attack on the governor's office. Bullet holes pock mud walls along the road. Packs of children boil from the alleyways to hurl rocks; clunks and thunks announcing hits. One glances off the windshield. "You little shit," the turret gunner calls as a rock flies close to his head. Scowling tribesmen with crossed arms watch the trucks pass. A henna-bearded man with a black turban and gray salwar kameez, *the Afghan tunic and trousers the soldiers call "man-jammies," glares at the convoy with fiery eyes. "I wonder if it pisses people off, us rolling through with these big trucks," the driver wonders. "Might," a grunt says. "We got to do what we got to do." The convoy slows as the MRAPs approach the deep, dry riverbed. The metal bridge is a perfect place to plant bombs. "I hate this bridge," the driver growls as we crawl forward. Colonel Copes warbles a lachrymose tune, something about "I'm a flower quickly fading." He looks up, smiling, "My wife and I sing that in church."*

The Khost City bazaar is a near-medieval warren of stalls and open-front shops selling everything from fresh fruits and vegetables, hanging red meat, brass cauldrons, and blocks of packed mountain snow to auto parts, pharmaceuticals, and electronics—the thirteenth century jumbled together with the twenty-first. The Khost City bazaar is also a battleground, where assassinations and IEDs are commonplace. One soldier tells me the US Army hadn't entered the market for years. An IED killed two Afghans near a cell-phone shop two days before; another killed an Afghan soldier. The recent attack on the governor's office spilled into the market, with fighters blazing at each other down the lanes. A few days earlier, I stood beside a charred gray SUV with a slender, bearded Afghan officer as he told me about visiting the bazaar. When his guards exited the SUV, they accidentally left the door open. Before he could close it, an insurgent threw a grenade between his legs—though the officer managed to dive out before the grenade detonated.

Given the danger, the ADT's security team decided that the agricultural specialists have exactly seven minutes to do their market research. Any longer and the risk of attack is too great. The convoy of MRAPs slows to a halt beside the bustling bazaar. The turret gunners cover the approaches. The security team piles out, fearsome with body armor and personal weapons. Some stand perimeter duty; others serve as bodyguards for the ag experts. "Seven minutes," the security head reminds the team as they hurry toward the Afghan vendors with their questions. "You've got seven minutes. Listen for the MRAP siren." Glares, disdainful glances, crossed arms, and pointing fingers face us as we cross a smelly drainage ditch on a teetery wooden gangplank. Small boys toss stones from the alleys. But as the ag specialists and their guards stride over to the nut and dried-fruit vendor at the corner of the market, the faces shift to incredulity. Shoppers, they realize, we are shoppers.

"Salam aleykom (peace be with you)," Colonel Copes says to the vendor. "How much are the walnuts—the matak?" The colonel's bodyguard waits behind him, solemnly scanning the marketers with his handgun's safety button glowing red, indicating off. The colonel asks, "How much for the shelled ones?" Attracted to the Americans, a crowd of Afghan men and boys begin to cluster, their turbans and skullcaps and visages reflecting the tribal diversity of central Asia.

The commander and his interpreter—the terp—order a half kilo of walnuts and some shriveled golden raisins. The crowd pushes closer. The guard keeps his eyes moving, checking for danger. The officers ask where the walnuts, pistachios, almonds, and chickpeas are grown. Peshawar and Mazar-e-Sharif mainly, the vendor tells them. Who shelled the nuts? How much were they? A security soldier spots a young man hurrying through the market with a metal pressure cooker in a wheelbarrow, headed for the crowd. An assassin with a bomb? Operating under strict "Escalation of Force" rules, the security team's dictum is to "be polite, be professional, be prepared to kill." But it's just a curious boy, drawn by the excitement. No threat.

The MRAPs' sirens begin to whoop as Copes and the terp haggle with the vendor. The seven minutes are up. The siren's honking with urgency as the terp chides the vendor for overcharging the Americans and negotiates for a better price. Seconds tick by as the security soldiers scan the growing crowd. We finally get our change and Copes says, "Let's go." The security commander's glare threatens to combust us as we totter back over the gangplank and clamber into the MRAPs. Buckling in, an officer says, "That was the best seven minutes of my deployment, sir." The security commander lets out a big sigh as the armored door hisses shut.

Chapter 13

Change-Management Strategy

SNOW WAS ALREADY DUSTING the blue mountains around FOB Sharana on December 1, 2009. During the day, the high sun and dry air gave the bleak mountaintop camp in Paktika Province a High Plains feel. Looking out from the camp, there was the sweep of central Asia; eternal flocks and shepherds hurrying below, almost as through the Great Khan's armies were going to come cantering out of the yellow-tinged dust. Nights were cold and windy on Sharana; jackets essential. For weeks the soldiers had been speculating about Obama's speech on the troop increase. How many? Where?

I sat in a plywood B-hut with some KBR contractors watching talking heads on Fox News predict Obama was sending thirty-five thousand more troops to Afghanistan, mainly to the south, along with another $75 billion for bases and infrastructure. But then the pundits asked: What is a winnable strategy? Most of the soldiers were just talking about tour extensions—another four to six months of Sharana? "Lot of building going on here," a short, red-headed Irish contractor named Simon told me that night as we hunkered in the dark beside a rocky helicopter pad, hoping the Black Hawk* out of Sharana was actually going to arrive. "They say ten thousand of the troops are coming here," he said. With Afghanistan eight and a half hours ahead of Washington, the soldiers weren't going to get the news of Obama's speech till the next morning. After we waited for another hour or so, the Black Hawk spun down out of the darkness with a cloud of dust as the throng of soldiers and contractors pushed forward. "Better tell them you're a journalist and need to get to your next spot," the Irishman told me, giving me a nudge with his elbow. "There's too many here and they say an attack is coming and nothing's going to move for a while."

For a brief period early that next morning, the ubiquitous televisions that usually blared ESPN in every military air terminal, dining facility, and gym in US-controlled Afghanistan were all tuned to President Obama's speech at

West Point. The president began, "I want to speak to you tonight about our effort in Afghanistan—the nature of our commitment there, the scope of our interests, and the strategy that my administration will pursue to bring this to war to a successful conclusion."[1] After a brief review of the war, Obama announced with little fanfare, "And as commander in chief, I have determined that it is in our vital national interest to send an additional thirty thousand US troops to Afghanistan. After eighteen months, our troops will begin to come home." Obama promised a fast deployment of US troops, a rapid turnover to Afghan security forces, and increased engagement with Pakistan. Obama also pledged a "civilian surge" to reinforce increased funding to Afghan government officials who "combat corruption and deliver for the people." Obama emphasized, "The days of providing a blank check are over." Addressing increasing American concerns about the cost of the war, then entering its eighth year, Obama stated the Afghans had to take responsibility for their own security, as "America has no interest in fighting an endless war in Afghanistan."

The day after the speech, Agribusiness Development Team commander Colonel Brian Copes reflected the sour mood of many as he waited at the FOB Salerno terminal for a helicopter to ferry him to Bagram Airfield for meetings about the new plan. A cutout of a green-faced Halloween witch still hung on the terminal wall. Beside the small terminal, desultory Afghan workmen reerected a large building that had fallen over during construction—while soldiers wagered on its next collapse. Looking down, Copes told me, "If the COIN strategy is to win hearts and minds, I'm sure the Afghans are comforted to think, 'Oh, the Americans are only going to be here for another eighteen months.'"[2] Speaking of Obama's mention of agricultural development in his speech, Copes retorted, "I can make crops grow better, but I can't make them grow faster."

*   *   *

Back in Washington, the media and congressional investigations were engendering change—at least in the language of the government staffers. "Change-management strategy" became the buzzword as the government scrambled to reorganize. I'd made the rounds of DC agencies a few months before returning to Afghanistan. Gray stone buildings, long corridors with hundreds of closed doors, meetings in small conference rooms, awkward interviews with uncomfortable staffers proffering press releases touting their "accomplishments" as their press handlers hovered. When the subject turned to corruption or

Taliban financing, there would be imploring looks to the press officers—*help us*. But if I introduced the term "change-management strategy" into the conversation, there was a dramatic shift of tone. Now we were going to talk about the bright shining future. No more uncomfortable discussions of those bad things that happened. What's the point in that? Let's talk about the *future* in Afghanistan. That's the subject.

So the US government departments swerved like a flock of starlings toward change-management strategies. One of the change-management strategies handed down from on high was the "whole-of-government" approach, which dictated "unprecedented levels of civilian–military cooperation."[3] As a sign of the times, the oversight agencies were among the first to change. In August 2009, the GAO, Special Inspector General for Afghanistan Reconstruction (SIGAR), and the Inspectors General of the Department of Defense, Department of State, and USAID announced a comprehensive oversight plan for Afghanistan–Pakistan.[4] While the whole-of-government concept briefed well, it represented an almost delusional hope given the prickly jealousies and prerogatives that permeated Washington culture—and played out vividly in Afghanistan. The State Department, USAID, USDA, Health and Human Services, and the rest had their ways and means. Within the military, the various services, and even *branches* of the same service, often skirmished amongst themselves for power and resources—though quickly closed ranks when they needed to defend their turf from civilians.[5] The "unprecedented levels of civilian–military cooperation," or civ–mil as it came to be known, promised to be a collision of cultures, particularly given how contentious the money fights were in Afghanistan. Riffing on Petraeus's axiom, "Money is a weapons system," Provincial Reconstruction Team commander Lieutenant Colonel Simon Gardner summarized the internecine budget battles when he laughingly told me, "Money is a fratricidal system."[6]

There was one area where civ–mil cooperation was apparent: neither the US military nor civilians in Afghanistan gave Washington the straight story. Before a cable went out, truth was often parsed and curried, scrubbed for career-tarnishing bad news. Metrics were crafted to tell a nice story. Phyllis Cox had been a Denver attorney and professor for twenty years before she decided to "get a new life."[7] She succeeded, serving in the Kabul embassy from 2004 to 2006 as the chief of party focused on governance and rule-of-law issues. Chief Justice Faisal Ahmad Shinwari, a deeply conservative Pashtun cleric and scholar, was so grateful for Cox's mentoring, he wanted to award her a medal. In 2009, Cox returned to Afghanistan to continue her rule-of-law work as the country director for the NGO Global Rights. Based on her long experience, Cox lambasted the Kabul embassy's dysfunction and duplicity. "I feel so strongly about this embassy," she says. She told me much of the bad news about Afghanistan was not passed on to Washington—"the conclusions are spun for domestic consumption," she told me. Staffers were required to adhere to the party line. "They are punished for getting out of line—made persona non grata, whatever. It's easier for them to just put in their time."

Former Bush administration deputy secretary of agriculture Jim Moseley did extensive work in Afghanistan. He confirmed Cox's assessment: "The point is they knew what headquarters wanted to hear. Things got sanitized," he told me. "They knew what Washington wanted to hear."[8]

And the US officials sure weren't telling the American public. The military called the press briefings at Kabul "feeding the chickens," gatherings where press officers handed out releases and briefers gave upbeat reports to hungry journalists. Unfortunately, the reports were often at variance with what was happening out in the provinces and with what was said amongst the officers and officials behind closed doors. As I made my way around eastern Afghanistan and into Bagram and Kabul, officers and officials were telling me a much different story: rising levels of popularly supported rebellion, rapidly deteriorating security, a corrupt and incompetent Afghan government, scandalously wasteful development programs that funded the insurgents. But you wouldn't know it from the happy talk and success stories scattered around by the chicken feeders.

*   *   *

Goaded by inquiry, directive, and increased resources, the ever-changing military began its latest change: reborn COIN. While there was a semantic COIN versus CT dispute, bet-covering administration officials made sure both strategies got plenty of resources.[9] By the end of 2009, US troop levels were at their highest. The Pentagon was rolling out heavily funded and manned "clear, hold, build" COIN plans that were directed by substantially larger general staffs of officers—with Iraq winding down, the commanders needed to punch their Afghan tickets.[10] But there was also a substantial increase in counterterrorism operations, including armed drones and special operations raids. Though the Obama administration pushed the rhetoric of a new approach, critic and Boston University professor Andrew J. Bacevich said, "the truth is they want to try harder to do what we've been doing for the last eight years."[11]

Obama's team found the armed drones to be an ideal tool to use in the Afghanistan–Pakistan insurgent areas. Unmanned high-tech warplanes that could destroy enemies without politically unacceptable American casualties, the Predators® and their even-more-lethal cousins, the Reapers®, became one of Obama's weapons of choice; targeted killing became official US policy.[12] By October 2010, not even two years into his term, Obama had ordered or approved 120 drone attacks in Pakistan. The number was spiking: Obama ordered twenty-two drone-mounted Hellfire® missile attacks in September 2010 alone. In eight years, Bush had ordered a total of sixty drone attacks.[13] Obama likewise stepped up special operations counterterrorism raids in Afghanistan. With small elite units such as Task Force 373 and Task Force 2-2, the special operations forces engaged in 125 to 150 missions a month in Afghanistan, most directed toward the "kill or capture" Joint Prioritized Effects List (JPEL) that included up to two thousand senior insurgent leaders.[14]

Under General Petraeus's direction, the military also emphasized the organization of village militias called *arbakai*. Emboldened by his momentary success with the "Sons of Iraq" militias, Petraeus implanted the concept in Afghanistan with initiatives such as the Afghan Public Protection Program (AP3), which armed and funded local militias for "static defense tasks" in their home districts, theoretically under tribal elders also on the US dole.[15] For many Afghans, the AP3 units were far too reminiscent of the anarchic post-Soviet warlord militias that led to the Taliban's rise. The US precedent didn't look too good to the Afghans, either. A 2006 initiative, the Afghan National Auxiliary Police (ANAP), was designed to back up the Afghan National Police (ANP) in insecure regions. But the poorly trained ANAP recruits, who were all-too-often petty criminals and drug addicts, proved to be even worse than the notorious ANP. Many ANAP defected to the insurgents or just went AWOL after selling their arms. The US military pulled the plug on the ANAP after scarcely a year.

The US military's development programs also underwent a change. Once he took over military command in Afghanistan, General Stanley McChrystal quickly reined in the scope of CERP projects, increased project scrutiny, and demanded dramatically improved quality control. The dictum that "bad QC [quality control] makes bad COIN" began to circulate. In mid-2010, the military established the anticorruption Combined Joint Interagency Task Force *Shafafiyat* (Transparency). Led by Brigadier General Herbert McMaster, the task force was fully operational by October 2010, charged with integrating intelligence with planning, operations, engagement, and communications to battle Afghan corruption. McMaster came to the job with a reputation for being a hard-charging commander with a penchant for independent thinking. During the Gulf War, he commanded the celebrated Second Armored Regiment's Eagle Troop that defeated several Republican Guard armor formations. With his doctorate in history and professorship at West Point, shaven-headed McMasters also received some notoriety for his 1998 book, *Dereliction of Duty*, which criticized military leaders for failing to challenge Johnson and McNamara's Vietnam War strategy. Under McMasters, CJIATF Shafafiyat worked in tandem with Task Force Spotlight, which scrutinized private security contractors' behavior, and Task Force 2010, which attacked insurgency financing sourced from US contracting dollars.

Set up by General Petraeus and Admiral Mullen, Task Force 2010 was tacit acknowledgment the Afghan insurgents were extorting vast amounts of money from US military logistics and civilian aid contracts to fund their war. Established in June 2010, the unit was originally commanded by Rear Admiral Kathleen Dussault, the former commander of the Joint Contracting Command–Iraq/Afghanistan. Dussault said her goal was, "to put a laserlike focus on the flow of money, and to understand exactly how money is flowing from the contracting authorities to the prime contractor and the subcontractors they work with."[16] Set up as an interagency military unit, Task Force 2010 included personnel from all four services, as well as the Defense Intelligence Agency, the Defense Contracting Auditing Agency, the Army Auditing Agency, the US Army Criminal Investigation Command, and the Defense Criminal Investigation Command.

But Dussault, one of the rare military flag officers who specialized in contracting, was on her way within four months—some said because she was disturbing business as usual.[17] She was replaced by Brigadier General Ross Ridge, an experienced artillery officer with a large skill set. He had served in Europe and Korea, as well in Thailand's Golden Triangle on counternarcotics missions and in Haiti's notorious Cité Soleil slum in civil affairs. But rather than contract management, Ridge's previous two commands were in the US Army Field Artillery Schools. Critics fretted that Ridge's lack of contracting experience, as well as his one-star rank (compared to Dussault's two), represented a shift in the administration's campaign against corruption. Journalist Spencer Ackerman stated, "the Obama administration is engaging in a Hamlet-esque debate about how central anticorruption efforts really are to the Afghanistan war."[18]

However, Ridge told me his artillery background gave him a system and a philosophy to concentrate resources on a problem, including threat funding. In

2007, Ridge served in Baghdad as General David Petraeus's chief of staff, Strategic Effects Directorate, which aimed at political and economic development in Iraq. As an effects coordinator—akin to an artilleryman fires coordinator, the term for the individual coordinating fire—Ridge was directing all of the US resources—not just things that blew up, but also financial and human resources—toward the overall mission goal. Ridge told me from Kabul, "It was looking at the strategic effects of our actions. What was the effect we wanted? How do we get it?"[19] A solid, sure fellow, Ridge says, "Now I find myself in Afghanistan, looking at corruption." After years of lackadaisical US contract oversight, Task Force 2010 faced a herculean task of research, criminal investigation, education, and enforcement. "If we don't have good oversight," Ridge told me, "it will undermine all of our efforts in Afghanistan." He says about Task Force 2010, "It's nothing we've ever done before. It's a lesson that will come out of Afghanistan: you've got to have oversight in place."[20]

*   *   *

Beyond the troop increase, Obama also committed to a "civilian upsurge" to improve governance and reduce corruption in Afghan ministries through mentoring and oversight. The US government announced with great fanfare that it was tripling the number of American civilians working in Afghanistan—"plussing up," in the insiders' phrase. But it was much ado about little: even when the civilian upsurge was at high tide in 2010, the total number of US civilian advisers was still only going to total 974—and many of those were destined to be newbies with little language or culture training, recruited for one-year rotations out of universities, extraneous government agencies, and industries. "The Afghans will stick those civilians in cubicles and let them write white papers," a former aid worker chuckled.[21] "They won't have a clue."

To underscore the importance the administration was placing on the civilian surge, Deputy Secretary of State Jacob J. Lew joined a team of civilians training for Afghanistan at Camp Atterbury, Indiana, where he experienced the full spectrum of muddy combat drills and diplomatic role-playing used to prepare them for their Afghan adventure. At a Washington press conference following the training, Lew boasted the 974 American civilians were going to make a big impact in Afghanistan, as the new people were now going to be "extraordinarily well prepared," unlike the earlier civilians whom were sent with insufficient skill sets.[22] Lew touted civ–mil District Development Working Groups, which would work in the district centers to assist with governance issues. Along with District Support Teams (DSTs), the State Department contended the civilian advisers would bring change to the volatile countryside where the insurgency was strongest. Lew indicated the Obama administration was allocating "quite a substantial amount of funding"—roughly $6 billion—for civilian-led foreign assistance in Afghanistan.

The faith that Lew and other administration officials placed in the 974 civilian advisers was charming but worrisome. The ill-fated Soviet venture in Afghanistan included ten thousand civilian advisers, many with central Asian language and culture expertise. Flocks of Soviet advisers assisted the Afghan ministries. Hoping to develop the Afghan economy, the Soviet advisers oversaw major construction projects, including hospitals, power stations, and an expansion of the Kabul airport. In a Communist version of winning hearts and minds, the Soviets and their client Afghan government thought using the 580 military checkpoints across Afghanistan to distribute food, fuel, and other necessities would woo the Afghans from supporting the *mujahideen*. Obviously, in spite of ten thousand civilian development advisers and billions of dollars spent, the Soviet campaign in Afghanistan came to a bad end.[23]

And no one seemed to ask the Afghans if they wanted more American advisers. A mid-2009 Afghan press story quoted Jelani Popal, the head of Afghanistan's Independent Directorate of Local Governance, who said the expensive and demanding civilian advisers could "create a chaotic situation," formulating unwanted and unsustainable projects and recruiting Afghan government specialists with high salaries.[24] The story stated many Afghans were concerned the American development experts included soldiers, as the soldiers doing aid work sent "mixed signals." Popal called for a complete reevaluation of the US strategy.

In his December surge speech, President Obama also called for greater emphasis on Taliban reconciliation: "We will support efforts by the Afghan government to open the door to those Taliban who abandon violence and respect the human rights of their fellow citizens."[25] A few days later, CENTCOM chief General David Petraeus told the Senate Foreign Relations Committee that reintegration of "reconcilable" insurgents was "a core objective of any sound counterinsurgency effort."[26] President Hamid Karzai had been calling for national reconciliation with the Taliban almost since he took office, and he established the Program Takhim-e Sohl in 2005 to attempt to get the insurgents to lay down their arms. Over the years, the program was known by a number of names, including Peace through Strength Program, Afghan Truth & Reconciliation Commission, National Reconciliation Commission,

National Commission for Peace in Afghanistan, and the Afghan Reconciliation Programs. But whatever the name, they didn't work very well. Relatively few insurgents, whether high officials or low-level fighters, reconciled with the Afghan government, as the ideologically driven jihadists simply couldn't be bought off.

Nonetheless, the United States threw its money into reintegrating "reconcilables," Afghan insurgents the United States contended were fighting for financial rather than ideological reasons. Both the military and the State Department jumped in. The military committed $1.3 billion in CERP funds to the reintegration scheme.[27] It led to situations such as the 2010 case in Nuristan Province, where the American officers were trying to reconcile Mullah Sadiq, the insurgent leader who six months before had led the murderous attack on Combat Outpost Keating, where eight US soldiers were killed and twenty-two were wounded. The US military offered Sadiq $25,000 a month for he and his fellow fighters to reintegrate as police. Mullah Sadiq held out for an additional $150,000 in development projects; then six hundred assault rifles, sixteen trucks, and two dozen machine guns and grenade launchers. "We want this more than the Afghans do," said Lieutenant Colonel Robert B. Brown, who led the negotiations.[28]

By the summer of 2010, the administration officials had moved their viewpoint far beyond buying off relatively low-level "reconcilables." State Department officials were now shopping for Taliban who would talk to them. With the US troop withdrawal already scheduled to begin July 2011, negotiated settlement was the word of the day. Not long after the United States helped Karzai convene what was to be a fruitless Taliban-boycotted "peace *jirga*" in May 2010, the State Department's special representative, Richard Holbrooke, told journalists the United States would accept "reformed" Taliban in the Kabul government. When reporters pressed him about those who said the war was unwinnable, Holbrooke snapped back, "What do they mean by win? We don't use the word *win*, we use the word *succeed*."[29]

For months, NATO officials met in secret talks with Mullah Akhtar Muhammad Mansour, one of the Taliban's most senior commanders. NATO had squired Mansour up to Kabul for meetings with high officials. For one meeting, NATO flew the Mullah from Pakistan for talks with President Karzai at the presidential palace in Kabul. The pace of the promising talks excited American officials. Mansour was remarkably moderate in his demands to end the fighting, unlike the other intransigent Taliban insurgents who demanded the foreign troops leave Afghanistan. There was at last a reasonable Taliban official at the other end of the bargaining table. Ah, but there was a glitch. As it turned out, Mullah Mansour wasn't Mullah Mansour at all. Red-faced Western diplomats had to admit Mansour was a total imposter, and the high-level negotiations had accomplished nothing. "It's not him," a Western diplomat who had taken part in the Kabul talks said.[30] "And we gave him a lot of money."

The State Department had been funding major legal-system-development projects since at least 2005, when it began funding the Justice Sector Support Program (JSSP). State contracted JSSP out to PAE, a wholly owned aid-and-development subsidiary of Lockheed Martin. Lockheed and PAE was an elegant symbiosis: Lockheed Martin contracted to blow it up; PAE contracted rebuild it. PAE's JSSP contract was formulated to "develop and strengthen the capacity of the Afghan criminal justice sector institutions and justice professionals."[31] JSSP was another of those wildly expensive, generally fruitless programs that seemed to have an ongoing life despite the lack of measurable positive impacts.

Five years later, with the corrupt Afghan legal system in even greater rapacity, the US State Department launched yet another effort to clean up the system. In July 2010, Ambassador Hans Klemm arrived in Kabul as the coordinating director of rule of law and law enforcement. "It's a very, very challenging environment here," Klemm told me from the Kabul embassy.[32] "This is the second most corrupt country in the world."

Klemm led initiatives to reform Afghanistan's judicial system, including the graft-ridden police force and judiciary, and a corrections system that Klemm called "almost medieval." Headstrong international actors had spent hundreds of millions of dollars on Afghanistan's deeply troubled rule-of-law system . . . with little to show for it. "They weren't being coordinated, they weren't being effective," Klemm says. "We didn't have any good metrics. We didn't measure impacts." Empowered with a joint directive issued by Ambassador Karl Eikenberry and General David Petraeus, Klemm coordinated civ–mil strategies and programs to curb corruption and narcotics through the Combined Joint Interagency Task Force 435 (CJITF435). The task force's civilian deputy, Michael J. Gottlieb, a former White House special assistant on national security, told me in December 2010 that the team made significant headway. "In the last six months under Ambassador Klemm's leadership, the change in rule of law has been breathtaking," Gottlieb said.[33]

Gottlieb and Klemm were among the heavy hitters the State Department assembled for CJITF435. Klemm had already wrestled with intractable conflict situations that prepared him for Kabul. Prior to Afghanistan, Klemm served as US ambassador to war-torn East Timor. "Very much like Afghanistan, it emerged from three decades of war," Klemm says, citing East Timor's anarchic violence, grinding poverty, high illiteracy and child mortality rates, and endemic corruption. On another battle front, Klemm served during the Iraq War as the director of the Office of Career Development in the State Department's Bureau of Human Resources in Washington, where he weathered another rebellion: the notorious Striped Pants Revolt.

During an emotional 2007 town hall meeting at the State Department, hundreds of foreign-service officers protested being forced to serve in "directed assignments" to Baghdad's Green Zone embassy. Evidently, hell hath no fury like a directed diplomat (particularly when directed to a hardship post far from his typical tony environs). The State Department crowd gave loud huzzahs to one foreign-service officer who insisted a Baghdad assignment was "a potential death sentence."[34]

Task Force 435 began in January 2010 as a joint military unit but transitioned to the civ–mil CJITF435 in September 2010. The task force focused on detainee, biometric-identification, reintegration, rule-of-law, and intelligence issues. Given the pervasive dysfunction of the Afghan legal system, as well as the catch-and-release Taliban-prisoner scam, the reform attempts were long overdue. Military scholars and officers Mark R. Hagerott, Thomas J. Umberg, and Joseph A. Jackson wrote in *Joint Force Quarterly* in 2010, "There is not a lack of effort or good intentions supporting rule-of-law development in Afghanistan. There is, however, a lack of strategy, resources, and, most important, accountable leadership. Without accountability, rule-of-law development efforts will continue to be executed slowly through a host of meetings and draft strategies that accomplish little in terms of real coordination or progress."[35]

The Obama administration's changes particularly impacted the USDA. Prior to Obama, the State Department funded the USDA's development work in Afghanistan. During the first Bush administration, Deputy Secretary of Agriculture Jim Moseley was instrumental in many of the USDA's initiatives. Before he accepted the USDA position, self-effacing Moseley was a successful Indiana farmer, cultivating over 2,800 acres where he and his family raised sixty thousand hogs a year. He first arrived in Afghanistan in April 2003. "It was still a war zone," he told me from his prairie farm near Lafayette, Indiana.[36] "Kabul was leveled."

Out in agrarian Afghanistan, farmer Moseley could speak plainly with the Afghan Muslim farmers, though he diplomatically called himself a "livestock" producer. "The Afghans all knew I raised hogs; they thought it was funny," he says. Moseley told me that Defense Secretary Rumsfeld had toured Afghanistan and determined that unless the United States addressed agriculture, "they weren't ever going to get out of there." Over the course of the next years, Moseley made eight or nine trips to Afghanistan to try to rebuild the shattered agricultural infrastructure and provide training. It wasn't easy. The infrastructure was shattered by war; traditional knowledge was lost. "The Soviet and civil wars killed off two generations of farmers," he says. Beyond the extreme poverty and lack of resources, Moseley's efforts to revive Afghanistan's longstanding agricultural-extension agent service met with virulent opposition from USAID, which abhorred ag-extension programs since its ignominiously failed in Africa in the sixties and seventies.[37] Moseley told me, "A young woman with USAID put her finger on my chest—we were standing on the steps of the embassy in Kabul—and said, 'There will be no ag-extension agent program in Afghanistan.'"

With Holbrooke's new agricultural policy, USDA at last got its own budget, which was expected to jump to $25 million by 2010. Like most of the US civilian agencies, USDA had a scant few people actually on the ground in Afghanistan—fifty-six foreign-service officers from 2003 to 2009, which the civilian surge then increased to sixty-four in the last three months of 2009. While almost all the USDA specialists had been assigned to PRTs before the surge, now more were being placed in national and provincial ministries and in the US regional commands. But the USDA faced the same recruiting problems as other civilian agencies and had to reach out to universities, state ag departments, and agribusiness to find specialists willing to go to Afghanistan.

Like the rest of the Afghanistan development enterprise, USDA metrics were relatively sparse through 2009. "I have to say in the 2003 to 2009 period, there weren't highly scientific metrics," says Babette Gainor, the team lead for the USDA's Fusion Cell for Afghanistan and Pakistan.[38] A tall, slender, fourteen-year foreign-service development veteran in Africa and Southeast Asia, Gainor was now assigned to Afghanistan. "Change management is needed throughout the entire government," she told me in Washington. She hastened to tell me that prior to the USDA's new authority and funding, the agency didn't have responsibility for oversight and monitoring"—the USDA specialists were just advising. "*Now*," she emphasized, "as we are entering this period of whole-of-government approach, it's important we be part of the measuring." Without offering specifics, Gainor assures me there are a "whole host of things used to measure our progress in Afghanistan."

As the lead civilian development agency in Afghanistan, USAID was under particular scrutiny. President Obama spoke about eliminating USAID's no-bid contracts that facilitated some of the Beltway Bandits' worst excesses.[39] The March 2009 White House Afghanistan–Pakistan policy review stated international consultants and their overhead gobbled up "a large portion" of development assistance, and "virtually no impact assessments have yet been done on our assistance programs."[40] Eight years in and billions spent, and no one had asked if US development money had an impact on quelling the insurgency.

The congressional uproar over US-funded Taliban operations finally forced USAID to formulate some reform programs. In late 2010, the new USAID administrator, Dr. Rajiv Shah, announced the USAID Forward agenda, which included a new Bureau of Policy, Planning, and Learning (PPL) that would theoretically serve as "the intellectual nerve center for the agency," a kind of Lessons Learned Center to solve development problems.[41] Shah also instituted the division of Compliance and Oversight of Partner Performance (COPP), charged with tracking USAID's "implementing partner" performance and malfeasance.

Concerns with corruption were relatively new for USAID, as the agency had generally turned a blind eye to the problem in the prior decades. As a creature of foreign policy through the Cold War and beyond, USAID worked with the designated US ally, no matter how crooked or corrupt the leader might be.[42] But anticorruption was the hot issue, and USAID needed to show change management. The agency's Assistance to Afghanistan's Anticorruption Authority (4A) was a three-year, $27 million program that USAID contracted out in 2010 to the development company MSI, which operated out of modernist office buildings that floated on the Potomac.

The 4A project was funded to support Afghanistan's anticorruption agency, the High Office of Oversight (HoO), which was widely criticized as a powerless poodle of President Karzai. A trained poodle, actually. HoO was led by Azizullah Ludin, infamous for his role as the head of the Independent Election Commission that was implicated in Karzai's tainted election. "HoO lacks all capacity," a rule-of-law consultant told me, "except the capacity to be devious."[43] Though USAID insiders say there were serious efforts to kill the useless 4A project before it began, 4A staffers and consultants commenced work in late 2010. But 4A was more about generating contracts for the Beltway Bandits and spinning good press than actually impacting corruption and security.

Pressured about insurgent funding, USAID finally established the Accountable Assistance for Afghanistan (A³) program in early 2011. A³ was devised to try to reduce the Taliban take with new contracting procedures. But even after it was instituted, A³ didn't take off in a flash: The one-page A³ fact sheet wasn't promulgated until July 2011, and there was little evidence much was happening in the field. The sheet tacitly admitted USAID had problems monitoring aid programs in Afghanistan and preventing "potentially corrupt individuals and institutions" and "the Taliban or other malign groups" from grabbing US taxpayers' dollars.⁴⁴ Nonetheless, the fact sheet stated, "Accountability in the provision of development assistance is among USAID's highest priorities in Afghanistan." According to the sheet, the A³ program was going to tighten contract procedures for more visibility and restrict multiple subcontracting, the source of much Taliban funding.

USAID knew Islamic terrorists were using US development funds at least as far back as 2006, when the GAO warned the agency about the leakage of aid funds to Palestinian terrorists in Gaza. GAO specifically called out subcontractors as a prime source of terrorist funds.⁴⁵ The USAID Office of Inspector General followed up with a 2007 audit of the agency's antiterrorism vetting procedures and found them distinctly lacking. The OIG report plainly stated, "The audit determined that USAID's policies, procedures, and controls are not adequate to ensure against providing assistance to terrorists."⁴⁶

In response, USAID required its prime contractors in Gaza to report monthly on their subcontractors, who officially had to undergo mandatory antiterrorism vetting before any contract award—officially. But the reality was that the vetting was just another checkbox for the contractor and USAID's contracting officer's technical representative, who was charged with monitoring the program. A 2009 GAO study found extensive failure: a random sampling determined that around one-fifth of all the subawards in FY 2008 "did not contain sufficient evidence" to determine if the subcontractor had even been vetted.⁴⁷ Despite the Afghan jihadis' obvious parallels to Palestinian terrorists and the widespread knowledge that the Taliban-led insurgency was methodically skimming US development funds, USAID remained in deep denial.

As part of A³, the agency also formulated the Vetting Support Unit (VSU) to address Taliban funding by running security checks on contractors. Alex Thier, director of USAID's Office of Afghanistan and Pakistan Affairs, stated in an April 2011 press release, "The VSU opens a new level of investigation and transparency for USAID that will make it more difficult for those individuals who plan to extort or employ corruptive actions to succeed."⁴⁸ But the VSU only checked Afghan and other non-US companies and individuals with primary contracts worth more than $150,000, though most Afghan-held contracts were under $150,000. Nor did the VSU program propose vetting subcontractors. In 2011, USAID instituted the Sub Award Vetting System to theoretically snab hostile subcontractors working farther down the contracting chain. But like other US government vetting programs, they were just checkboxes.

Jeff Mallory, a longtime AT&T executive who served as a contracting officer overseeing defense logistics contracts in both Iraq and Afghanistan, most recently at Camp Leatherneck in Helmand Province, termed the Excluded Parties Listing System "rather dysfunctional" and the Sub Award Vetting System "a USAID adventure."[49]

Staunching the flow of US government funds to the Taliban seemingly still baffled officials eight years into the war. While publicly horrified that US taxpayer dollars might be financing the enemy, off the record, officials were often sanguine about the leakage. A congressional staffer on the late Representative John P. Murtha's powerful subcommittee also referenced Petraeus's "Money is a weapons system" dictum when she told me, "Money's fungible—when you add it into a system, you are offering a resource to the enemy. I don't know how you get it back. That's the price we're willing to pay."[50]

To determine if an Afghan contractor was an insurgent, the US military and civilian officials did little more than make perfunctory checks on the web-based Excluded Parties Listing System (EPLS), which notated about seven hundred thousand terrorists, and CENTCOM's Vendor Vetting Reachback Cell, the "vetting cell," which compiled background checks and intelligence reports.

There were a number of problems with the vetting-cell system: First, the vetting system wasn't established until August 2010, long after the United States had began handing out money to the Taliban. Second, like USAID's vetting program, the military vetting cell only investigated Afghan contractors awarded large contracts, though most of the contracts awarded to Afghans were relatively small—under the military's $100,000 vetting minimum. Critically, the vetting-cell system did not investigate any of the Afghan subcontractors, who handled the majority of the contract money in Afghanistan, where projects went through multiple layers of subcontracting so everyone got a cut—including the Taliban. Even with just limiting investigations to Afghan contractors, the Vendor Vetting Reachback Cell had little chance of keeping up with the enormous volume of contracting in Afghanistan. The vetting cell reported it averaged vetting fifteen Afghan contractors per week. In FY 2010, the United States awarded contracts over $100,000 to 1,042 Afghan contractors, meaning it would take another fifty-three weeks just catch up with FY 2010, all the while more vetting requests were piling up for FY 2011 contracts.

And an Afghan contractor with Taliban ties just needed to get his brother or cousin to front for the company. If engineer Abdullah had gotten arrested as an insurgent and scanned into the system, then Brother Hamed was the contractor of record. The vetting system was essentially a farce.[51]

Veteran contracting officer Jeff Mallory dismissed the vetting systems as "cursory," easily evadable by insurgents. He told me the system failed to adequately investigate past performance or true ownership. "It's a checkbox on the front of the contract. 'We checked to see if the Afghan contractor was Taliban. Check.'" He says the overwhelmed US contract managers were seldom concerned with the problem of threat funding. "They say, 'I'm not that interested.' Means and methods—you hear that a lot—'the means and methods belong to the contractor.'"[52]

And the contractors didn't seem to care. International Relief & Development (IRD) was one of USAID's largest implementing partners. In 2010, IRD's revenues jumped to $710 million, a 40 percent growth from the previous year; much of the increase due to a spectacular increase in the IRD's contract with USAID for the Afghanistan Vouchers for Increased Production in Agriculture Plus program, or AVIPA, which jumped from $58 million to over $275 million. The program brought highly criticized AVIPA-provided vouchers for wheat seed and fertilizer to almost three hundred thousand Afghan farmers.[53] The IRD also had major contracts for road projects, and since 2004, a contract for Human Resources and Logistical Services, which provided project management and quality assurance for the much-maligned USAID construction projects that included schools, clinics, roads, and water projects. According to the company website, the IRD provided good benefits to its employees, including fully paid medical, dental, disability, and life insurance, fully vested immediate retirement plan, and liberal holiday and sick pay benefits.[54] The pay was also good, as development companies at the level of the IRD typically billed out their aid consultants at up to $500,000 a year. The company has numerous former USAID staff in leadership positions, including its vice president for strategic business initiatives, Alonzo Fulgham, who served as USAID's mission director to Afghanistan in 2005–2006, served as the agency's chief operating officer, and in 2009 became the organization's top executive as the acting administrator. The IRD's director of the Afghanistan–Pakistan Task Force, Richard Owens, was another USAID veteran. He rotated over to the IRD in 2008 after a twenty-four-year USAID career that including three postings in Afghanistan and Pakistan. "I chased disasters all over the world," Owens told me when we spoke in 2011.[55] When I asked him about US taxpayer dollars funding the insurgents, he told me, "We don't think there were any significant problems with this." Talking about the contractor vetting system, he says, "This was something you *had* to do." Referencing the layers between the US primary contract holders, such as the IRD, and the Afghan subcontractors who made the insurgent payoffs half a world away, Owens distanced IRD from the problem: "Everything's at arm's length to us."

*   *   *

In mid-2009, the US government stood up the Afghan Threat Finance Cell (ATFC) to combat insurgency funding from US logistics and development money. The multiagency ATFC was comprised of about thirty specialists on loan from the Department of Drug Enforcement, the Department of Treasury, the Department of Justice, the Department of Defense's CENTCOM, the CIA, and the FBI. "Our job is to identify and disrupt sources of funding for the Taliban and other insurgent groups," an ATFC spokesman told me one sunny Kabul day as we sipped coffees at the US embassy's courtyard espresso stand.[56] Over at the security checkpoint, cranky armed guards glowered at faces and IDs. The ATFC specialist explained the insurgents fund their operations from a number of sources, including opium, Persian Gulf donations, and crime. "We also focus on corruption, part of the thrust to protect the Afghans, both from the Taliban and [from] their own government." Leader of the ATFC, US Treasury Department Assistant Secretary for Terrorist Financing David Cohen, had e-mailed that the cell used a "multipronged approach" to disrupt Taliban funding through investigations and building the capacity of Afghan authorities.[57] The ATFC strategy included a scrutiny of the *hawala* networks, the informal banking system of Afghanistan and much of the Islamic world. Though the vast majority of the banking done through the hawalas is legitimate and essential to the economy, insurgents use the system to move massive amounts of cash around the world quickly and inexpensively.

Taking a sip from his tall coffee, the burly ATFC official told me, "We're looking hard at the hawalas," explaining the cell's initial steps, which included trying to get the Afghan government to institute uniform licensing and to identify hawalas involved with insurgent activity. He told me there had been a major bust of three hawalas connected to the drug trade and insurgents the day before. As the hawalas are essentially opaque to outsiders, the ATFC and other embassy attachés also pushed support for Afghanistan's US-backed formal banking system, so development and logistics funds could theoretically be tracked to spot corruption and extortion. Facilitating electronic flow of US funds through the formal banking system would also, in the military phrase, "get cash off the battlefield," where insurgents easily accessed the flood of currency. But even that seemingly positive step of setting up formal banking was complicated in insider-controlled Afghanistan. Powerful Afghan families, most often connected to warlord-politicians, dominated the banking system. Beyond having a reputation for being voracious and chaotic, the Afghan banks also were known to pay the insurgents protection money. In support of the "cash off the battlefield" campaign, the United States began paying its Afghan government support as well as logistics and development contracts through the Afghan banks, especially the well-connected Kabul Bank, the country's largest. But with only a tiny percentage of Afghans having bank accounts, officers and officials were often forced to pay contractors as they had since 2002: by handing over hundreds of thousands of dollars in bags and suitcases.

Recognizing the HoO was ineffective, the ATFC worked with a trio of new Afghan anticorruption organizations: the Major Crimes Task Force (trained by the FBI and DEA), a unit within the Afghan National Directorate for Security, was given responsibility for investigations and arrests. Afghanistan's Attorney General's office created the elite Anticorruption Unit for prosecution of the cases. Within Afghanistan's Supreme Court, the Anticorruption Tribunal tried the cases.

A US embassy official in Kabul told me that US government officials estimated the insurgents' annual budget to be in the hundreds of millions of dollars. "Is it $1 billion? $500 million? The total amount is a tail people are going to chase until the end of time," he told me.[58] "We know they are raising substantial amounts of money; they can finance their operations. If you take away the Gulf money, they can make it up. If you take away the narco money, they can make it up. It's like punching jello." He confirmed the reports from the ATFC, the military, and other embassy officials that the insurgents used extortion of US development money for their funding. He cited the supply-convoy shakedowns, construction-protection rackets, Taliban "taxes" on corrupt officials, payoffs from NGOs and major Afghan businesses—such as cell phones, utilities, and banks—as well as skims from poorly overseen government projects of the National Solidarity Program. "The more money that comes in here, the more opportunities, and then there's a lot more exploitation, more corruption," the embassy official says. "And there's a lot more money coming in here." He spoke of the difficulty of balancing counterinsurgency needs with the challenge of monitoring funds in a corruption-ridden war zone. The official echoed many when he told me, "I don't know if it can ever be airtight, but we've got to take some risks."

*   *   *

Scene: FOB Salerno, Khost Province. Colonel Cindra Chastain is the deputy commander of the Indiana Agribusiness Development Team deployed in Khost, Afghanistan's most violent province. Perversely proud of working in the crosshairs, the ADT soldiers boast that General McChrystal's interim report identifies Khost as a key insurgent objective. Chastain's telling me about the problems of contractor payment in Khost, where virtually no one has a bank account. Earlier I had talked to a civil-affairs officer who told me up to a year or so prior there weren't even any banks in Khost. "Cash-in-hand payments were the *way; there was no other way," he says. "Guy walks away, he's got a suitcase full of money. As he's driving away, he's got to pay off all the bad guys so he doesn't get hurt."*

Chastain talks about a recent payment on an ADT project. She explains the team tried to pay villagers directly so their tainted Afghan contractor couldn't slip money to the insurgents, but that didn't go so well as the convoy almost got blown up. So, concerned about security risk and the need to pay the village workers, the ADT reverted to the time-tested method of payment: The Afghan contractor came to the base gate, where the ADT purser handed over a big, green garbage bag stuffed with millions of afghani *bank notes worth about $50,000. "We did it, we paid him the money in a big, green garbage bag," the Colonel says with a sigh. "He signed for it, but we did it."*

Chapter 14

The Complexities

THE BLACK HAWKS® LANDED THE TEAM in besieged Combat Out-post Sabari, located in a Khost Province district the soldiers called "the reddest of the red"—totally Taliban controlled. The Indiana National Guard ADT was on an aid mission to advise Sabari farmers. The ADT planned to meet with the local tribal elders in a Key Leader Engagement to discuss improving their agricultural yields. We had flown the fifteen or so miles from FOB Salerno because the roads were so insecure the journey by armored vehicles could have taken all day—or maybe we wouldn't have arrived at all.

We trudged past a sandbagged guard post, where a glinty-eyed soldier scanned the rocky landscape. "Little Beau Geste here, huh?" an officer said. Our helicopters—"birds," the soldiers called them—had barely swooped away when a soldier ran up to say a special ops team had hit Sabari the night before and killed two local men. A retaliation attack was expected soon. "373 here last night," a soldier said with a shrug. The tribal elders had already come to the COP to protest—insisting the dead men were innocent. We hunkered down in a bullet- and shell-pocked courtyard as the elders raged at the COP commander and his Human Terrain Team (HTT) advisers—frontline US anthropologists trying to decipher Afghanistan's complicated tribal culture. We could hear the frustration boiling out of the concrete room, Pashto and translated English alternating. An intense, blue-eyed anthropologist named Wesley was suddenly squatting beside us, saying the elders were done talking to the commander and were willing to speak with the ag advisers. We crowded into the room to talk to the angry tribesmen. It was a short meeting. The ADT interpreter translated the tribesmen's message: "We really don't need anything from you guys—no training, no nothing. In the day-time you guys give us something, in the nighttime the Coalition forces are coming and killing innocent people. That is why we are sad with Coalition forces. We don't want anything from Coalition forces."[1]

Operating with separate command structures, the spec ops counterterrorism mission had trumped the ADT's counterinsurgency mission. After the tribal elders stormed out of the COP, we waited by the rocky helipad, hoping the Black Hawks could land before the attack started. After the Black Hawks had returned us to FOB Salerno, ADT commander Colonel Brian Copes said, "It was an odd set of circumstances, but I characterized it later, just musing about *Alice in Wonderland* and *Through the Looking-Glass*, and simply said the environment here just gets curiouser and curiouser, which is about as apt a characterization I can offer you right now." Later that day, when the retaliation attack hit Combat Outpost Sabari, Wesley was running for a bunker when shrapnel from a mortar shell hit him in the head. He was airlifted to Germany, where the doctors still hoped to save his remaining eye.

* * *

Though the Obama administration had launched a new counterinsurgency offensive, and though Washington agencies and departments had instituted change-management strategies, American officials were facing a complicated situation. They were dealing with a deeply entrenched system—primarily of their own making. And after eight dysfunctional years of stutter-step strategies and quick fixes, the US efforts looked to be far too little, far too late.

While the military had dispatched great numbers of troops to Afghanistan, there were substantially more support troops than combat soldiers. It was the enduring "tooth-to-tail" ratio: the infantry—the "grunts" doing the fighting—constituted less than ten percent of the US Army and US Marines. In Afghanistan, 90 percent of the US soldiers never "broke the wire," never left their bases. The soldiers who did emerge from the bases were often constrained by their leaders, who were intent on keeping US military and Afghan civilian casualty counts low. Accordingly, the insurgents were often left unimpeded out in the countryside, where they controlled wider and wider swaths of territory.[2]

And when the US military did initiate operations, they precipitated violent responses from the populace. Once riled, the Pashtun warriors turned American outposts into bullet magnets—transformed the US-funded roads into linear bomb routes. The major US maneuvers became recruiting drives for the insurgents. "American soldiers were an irritant to the people," General Stanley McChrystal said about the futile operations in the Korengal.[3] "There was probably much more fighting there than there would have been [if US troops had never come]." Speaking of the futility of America trying to kill its way to victory in Afghanistan, McChrystal said, "You can kill Taliban forever, because they are not a finite number."[4]

The military plan to win over the Afghans with WHAM, winning hearts and minds, development projects, had lots of complications. CERP was out of control. Even successful reconstruction projects often resulted in more instability. The military's focus on short-term development for battlefield intelligence often yielded information that was at best questionable. "You can't get good intelligence at the point of a gun," one aid worker snorted.[5] The military's commingled combat–development model confused the Afghans, who saw soldiers being warm and fuzzy one day and warriors the next. It was common for military and civilian intelligence officers to accompany aid missions, buzzing around the villagers asking about "bad guys." The civilian agents were sometimes OGA, Other Government Agencies, the frontline euphemism for the CIA. It wasn't like the Afghans didn't know who they were. One USDA development specialist who worked with a PRT in eastern Afghanistan told me, "Yeah, the Afghans, they'd ask, "So who is the man without insignia and name tag?"[6]

The mixed development and combat roles also confused the American soldiers, who weren't trained to be aid workers. When given the opportunity, the Force Protection platoons attached to the military development teams were more than happy to revert to being pipe-swinging infantrymen. In Laghman Province, I watched a PRT security force giddily jettison its development mission when it had the chance to suppress a riot. The snipers were giggling as they loaded their M40 rifles into the MRAPs. They wanted to be soldiers. When the Afghan National Army was able to control the mob, the PRT soldiers were crestfallen.

The clash of counterterrorism and counterinsurgency at Sabari was emblematic of the Americans' larger problem of coordination. The US allies certainly weren't coordinated. Pakistan was always the big challenge.[7] Both the United States and Pakistan had been playing a too-clever-by-half, double-dealing game since the seventies, and the two ostensible allies were typically at cross-purposes. Still tethered to their constraining caveats, the NATO allies were leaving the unpopular war. The Netherlands became the first NATO country to end its combat mission when it pulled out 1,900 soldiers in 2010. It was widely predicted that Germany, Britain, Canada, and Poland were going to withdraw their major contingents of troops sooner rather than later. Holding the US-led coalition together till the planned handover to the Afghan security forces in 2014 was looking increasingly unlikely. Further complicating the handover, NATO had shorted the number of trainers it was supposed to provide to the Afghan National Army.[8]

While the United States had spent more than $25 billion to stand up the Afghan National Army (ANA), military planners had failed to adequately coordinate construction of Afghan security bases.[9] A military contracting officer working in southern Afghanistan told me about base contracting: "We're building megabases and infrastructure out here—Camp Leatherneck, Camp Dwyer, Camp Delaram. They are small cities. Inside the defense line, the processes for contracting are done very well. Taxpayers are getting a good bang for the buck. There's lots of competition. The problem was outside the wire."[10] The contracting officer said that with all the resources concentrated on American posts, planning paid little attention to bases for the ANA and the Afghan National Police (ANP). "The ANA and ANP just had to wait," he says. "We surged with a major muscle movement in 2010, and we're pushing into 2011 and we're just now getting around to building infrastructure for the Afghan security forces. The contracting piece is always left out of the doctrine. Contracting is always an afterthought." And when the US military did contract to build Afghan security bases out in the insurgent-controlled hinterlands, they added to another problem: "The Afghan contractors in bed with the Taliban were the only ones who'd bid on these," the contracting officer says.

Even intelligence, crucial to a counterinsurgency, was lacking in coordination. The military had long had trouble coordinating information-sharing in intelligence, surveillance, and reconnaissance operations, according to the GAO.[11] As far back as 2005, the oversight agency noted problems with collating and sharing data collected from drones. Though the insurgents had been using improvised explosive devices (IEDs) as their main weapon against the Western and Afghan forces for several years, the Defense Department was unable to coordinate a wide range of intelligence programs set up to defeat IEDs. From 2005 to 2010, the Defense Department spent over $25 billion on anti-IED programs, but still hadn't compiled goals and timelines to ensure "progress and accountability," according to the GAO.

In early 2010, Major General Michael T. Flynn, ISAF's deputy chief of staff for intelligence, published a scathing report on the state of intelligence in Afghanistan. Excoriating the stovepiped and sequestered US intel operations, Flynn's report stated, "Eight years into the war in Afghanistan, the US intelligence community is only marginally relevant to the overall strategy."[12] Flynn's report criticized US intelligence for obsessing with insurgents without inquiring into the culture that supported them: "Ignorant of local economics and landowners, hazy about who the powerbrokers are and how they might be influenced, incurious about the correlations between various development projects and levels of cooperation between villagers, and disengaged from people in the best position to find answers—whether aid workers or Afghan soldiers—US intelligence officials can do little but shrug in response to high-level decision-makers seeking the knowledge analysis and information they need to wage a successful counterinsurgency."

On December 30, 2009, US intelligence operations in Afghanistan suffered a staggering loss when a suicide bomber detonated an explosive vest at FOB Chapman in Khost Province. Though it was a highly secure FOB, the CIA had allowed a Jordanian double agent, Humam Khalil Abu-Mulal al-Balawi, to enter the base for a meeting with a number of key American agents without being searched. When the agents gathered near the base gym to welcome their informant, he killed seven Americans intelligence officers, including the base chief, a special debriefer brought in from Kabul, and a Jordanian intelligence officer. The blast was so large it could be heard miles away, including at FOB Salerno. The ADT convoy from FOB Salerno often rendezvoused at Camp Chapman with the PRT stationed there. It was an open secret that the CIA used Chapman as a HUMINT (human intelligence) base for attacks into Pakistan's adjacent tribal regions. Some sources posited that the CIA launched helicopter raids and drone attacks from Chapman's Soviet-built, 9,000-foot runway. One intelligence officer told me, "There are things that fly out of there that you don't want to know about." The shared PRT–CIA base made Chapman a graphic illustration of the commingled intelligence–development model that the United States had constructed in Afghanistan.[13]

Chapman's ill-fated CIA operation was also another example of American careerism trumping national interests, according to *Washington Post* journalist and author, Joby Warrick. In his book about the Chapman fiasco, *The Triple Agent*, Warrick reported the relatively new CIA base chief, Jennifer Matthews, was an ambitious officer who had taken the Chapman assignment because she had lacked the frontline experience required to move into the CIA's upper echelons, the high-paying senior executive service. "If Matthews really wanted to move up, she had to go to war," Warrick wrote about her career decision.[14] And she could punch her ticket quickly in Afghanistan. Because of the danger and discomfort of Khost Province, the CIA administrators deemed a one-year assignment at Camp Chapman to be equivalent to three years anywhere else. Eager to slingshot her career with an intelligence coup, inexperienced Matthews allowed the breakdown in basic security that facilitated Humam Khalil Abu-Mulal al-Balawi's devastating attack.

The US command also got more complicated. Scarcely a year after General

Stanley McChrystal had taken command, he and his staffers made derisive comments about the top civilian leadership in the presence of a *Rolling Stone* reporter. The subsequent exposé, "The Runaway General," ignited a firestorm.[15] Soon afterward, Obama summarily dismissed McChrystal as he had the previous commander, General David McKiernan. Afghanistan was starting to look like the graveyard of American generals. Six months after the McChrystal debacle, the marine general serving as the special investigator general for Afghanistan reconstruction, General Arnold Fields, stepped down under pressure from critical senators who accused him of failing to follow the $56 billion spent on development in Afghanistan with sufficient zeal and effectiveness.[16]

And the Afghans were certainly complicated. Nancy Hatch Dupree, a legendary anthropologist and activist, began working in Afghanistan in the 1960s. She was a longtime collaborator of her late husband, Louis Dupree, considered the preeminent anthropologist of Afghanistan. Still actively writing and organizing at ninety-three years old, Nancy Hatch Dupree was leading Kabul University's Afghanistan Centre, an award-winning research center and library, when she talked to me. The Afghanistan Centre coordinates a remarkable outreach program, which provides portable libraries, "libraries in a box," to hundreds of communities across Afghanistan. With her long perspective stretching back to US development in Afghanistan during the Cold War, Dupree was critical of the current counterinsurgency development efforts that imposed unsustainable projects on the Afghans with little understanding of the culture. "This is driving me nuts," she said. "The US military and government officials come out for such a short time. The contractors are worse."[17] Dupree said that the international money destabilized Afghanistan: "We never had corruption like this. Now it's astronomical."

She told me the unfettered international money and corruption was tragically transforming a once-independent and self-reliant people into a nation of hostile clients demanding handouts. "We are undermining a major Afghan attribute: their belief in self-sufficiency," she says. "This is lethal." And she told me the Afghans retained a great capacity to glom onto the right chance when it came around: "Louis used to say, 'the Afghans are great opportunists,' but in a positive way. For instance, in Pakistan, the Pakistanis complained the Afghans had taken over their transport business. Louis argued that the opportunities were always there—the Pakistanis could have taken advantage of them, but didn't—while the Afghans saw the opportunities and went for it. The flip side is, of course, corruption—they've certainly taken to that when presented with so many opportunities to make a fast buck. Very sad."

In contemporary Afghanistan, opportunism started at the top. The Karzai government became one of the world's great kleptocracies, overseeing a grand and pervasive extortion racket that took the country to the pinnacle of global corruption. Instead of benefiting the populace or calming the insurgency, the international aid and logistics money literally flew out of Afghanistan. According to investigators from Afghanistan's Central Bank, $190 million dollars in cash transited through the Kabul International Airport on its way to the safe haven of Dubai in one single day in July 2010.[18] The *Wall Street Journal* revealed that more than $3 billion packed into suitcases flew out of the airport from 2007 to 2010. US officials stated the cash flow included money skimmed from US and NATO development and logistics contracts.[19]

The US-abetted Kabul Bank, controlled by politically connected Afghan leaders (such as President Karzai's older brother, Mahmoud, and Haseen Fahim, the brother of warlord and vice president Mohammed Qasim Fahim) became a symbol of greed in 2010 when investigators discovered that insiders had scammed over $900 million dollars from the institution.[20] The tendrils of the massive fraud reached from inside the bank to the top levels of the Afghan and US government and included the bank's auditors, Pricewaterhouse-Coopers, Afghanistan's Central Bank, and DeLoitte, which had a $92 million USAID contract to advise the Central Bank. DeLoitte billed the US government $657,000 each month for five advisers it assigned to the project. Though the DeLoitte advisers saw evidence of fraud, they kept it buttoned up. Perennially overwhelmed USAID had only one junior contract officer overseeing the $92 million contract. The scandal triggered a financial crisis as the International Monetary Fund moved to block aid funds to Afghanistan.[21]

The Afghan justice system was a predation machine; detention was a shakedown gambit. The Taliban catch-and-release scam run by Afghan politicians and insiders became so systemized that Canada's Minister of National Defence Gordon O'Connor said on national television in 2007 the Afghan prisons "had quite a revolving door system."[22] US Deputy Ambassador to Afghanistan Francis J. Ricciardone cabled Washington in August 2009: "On numerous occasions we have emphasized with Attorney General [Muhammad Ishaq] Aloko the need to end interventions by him and President Karzai, who both authorize the release of detainees pretrial and allow dangerous individuals to go free without ever facing an Afghan court."[23] The cable noted a dramatic increase in pretrial releases after April 2007, when President Karzai established the Aloko Detainee Commission. From one pretrial release in 2007, the number of releases ballooned to 104 in 2008, and by Ricciardone's August cable there had already been forty-five releases in 2009.

Many of the insurgents released from Afghan custody were high-value detainees held by the National Directorate of Security (NDS), Afghanistan's CIA-funded intelligence service, leaving only "small fry," as one source termed them, in custody. A European rule-of-law and security consultant told me about the high-level releases, "ISAF security people say, 'We don't have anyone else; they've all been released.'"[24] High-level detainee releases made good business for the NDS. "The big bad Taliban buy their way out. The NDS guys are stunningly corrupt," Amir Attaran, University of Ottawa law professor and detainee rights activist, told me. "They simply let the high-value Taliban walk—then torture the low-level Taliban to extort money from the families."[25]

According to a US human-rights consultant, Afghanistan's abysmal rule of law allowed the NDS to operate their detainee-release scam: "The problem at the NDS is the rule-of-law vacuum allows for them to be open for corruption. The NDS rule-of-law reform has been the black sheep of the international rule-of-law initiative—until recently, almost entirely ignored as a problem."[26] A Kandahar-based international human-rights researcher told me that the corrupt release system also increased the Afghans' distrust of the government: "This catch-and-release pattern completely contributes to the problem. At a checkpoint, an Afghan policeman's not going to stop a Taliban riding by on his motorcycle with an AK-47 slung on his back. He knows the Taliban will most likely be released and take revenge. The series of assassinations that happen downtown everyday in broad daylight—the killers just walk away. No one stops them. There's no arrests."[27]

Even those Taliban inside the detention facilities were often allowed free rein. The notorious Pul-e-Charkhi prison had an entire cellblock wing of Taliban detainees, who planned the Serena Hotel attack from there via cell phone.[28] Sarposa prison in Kandahar was the site of two great Taliban jailbreaks. In 2008 over 1,200 prisoners escaped, and in 2011, after ISAF had allegedly strengthened prison security, five hundred Taliban insurgents scrambled through a half-mile-long tunnel and were spirited away. Western officials called it "an inside job."[29]

One source told me about President Karzai's notorious half brother, Ahmad Wali Karzai (or AWK, as ISAF noted him). According to the source, AWK spent $30,000 to secure the release of Anwar Shah Agha, an important Taliban commander who controlled all of the attacks from the western edge of Kandahar to Herat on the Iranian border. After Agha's arrest, AWK got to work, getting

Anwar Shah Agha transferred to NDS custody in Kabul, where he was released approximately nine months after custody with the help of other Karzai family members. According to a Kandahar intelligence source, Anwar Shah Agha soon was "again back and doing the same things," masterminding attacks on an *arbakai* progovernment militia that the US Special Forces had helped establish. A suicide attack at a wedding in the village of Nagaan killed three arbakai leaders, along with thirty-six others, and wounded seventy-three.[30]

"It's basically about money," says the European rule-of-law and security consultant, explaining that the Taliban and other insurgents gave money to AWK and Afghan government officials, who brought Afghan elders to President Hamid Karzai to vouch for the detainees as good citizens. President Karzai then released the detainees to garner future favors. As a kingpin in the Kandahar heartland of the Taliban, AWK had additional reasons to work with the Taliban, according to the analyst: "Ahmed Wali Karzai has a more direct interest in forming relations with the Taliban—he gets protection from the Taliban to pursue his deals."[31]

The Taliban-release problem contributed to the formation of the Combined Joint Interagency Task Force 435 (CJITF435), charged with improving detention operations. But because of the colliding counterinsurgency needs, international observers questioned CJITF435's ability to reform the deeply rooted Taliban–NDS release racket. On the one hand, allowing the corrupt Afghan government officials to run the catch-and-release trade helped the insurgency, but on the other, disempowering the Afghan government was equally risky. "The ultimate challenge for counterinsurgency is stuck between building the right system for the long-term—basic security forces or the judiciary—at the same time dealing with a situation where rapid demonstrable results are the rule of the day," said Nathan Hughes, director of military analysis at STRATFOR, a global intelligence company.[32] "You're trying to do contradictory things here."

While US officials often referred to the Taliban's "shadow government" that operated in virtually every province, the term was a misnomer.[33] It was actually Karzai's Government of the Islamic Republic of Afghanistan (GIRoA) that was the shadow government, because in provinces and districts across the country the GIRoA official was most often absent, not the insurgents' counterpart. In Khost, the director of agriculture refused to visit the countryside because of security fears, despite US military offers to transport him and guards by helicopter. Khost's director of women's affairs decamped for Kabul after her car was blown up. These officials weren't unusual. Across the east and south, provincial and district officials "governed" from secure capitals, occasionally venturing out for ribbon-cutting ceremonies and bribe collection. The celebrated "government in a box" campaign that US officials promised for Marja was a bust.[34]

Wikileaks cables indicated that governance was lacking even in Parwan Province, site of the sprawling US military headquarters at Bagram Airfield: "The provincial governance is weak and does not interact with the public regularly. If they continue to turn a blind eye to the public, there will be a significant increase in enemy activity in the province and a prominent civil uprising."[35] President Karzai remained the mayor of Kabul, his power and authority operating in tight concentric circles around a few semisecure areas. In many ways, it was the traditional way. With a few notable exceptions, the government of Afghanistan never held much sway in the hinterlands. But the Karzai government had even less reason to try to exert power outside Kabul. The international community was providing virtually all the government's money—97 percent of Afghanistan's GDP was foreign aid and logistics.[36] Karzai didn't need the pittance of revenue he could garner from his impoverished countrymen.

"Crazy Karzai" the Western officials began calling him, floating rumors of deep psychological instability.[37] Ambassador Karl Eikenberry was particularly critical, cabling Washington in late 2009 that Karzai was "not an adequate strategic partner," and "continues to shun responsibility for any sovereign burden, whether defense, governance, or development. He and much of his circle do not want the [United States] to leave and are only too happy to see us invest further."[38]

So perhaps Karzai was crazy like a fox. When Obama tried tough love early in his administration, Karzai lashed out, and the US diplomats and officers scuttled to assuage his distress. In spite of Karzai's larcenous 2009 presidential election and his relentless campaign against his own government's anticorruption and election-reform agencies, the US government decided Karzai was the best option it had. After the brief tough-love experiment, Obama and Karzai were soon playing pretty again, and the powerful river of cooperating interests kept flowing.[39] As accommodating US officials mouthed platitudes about "putting an Afghan face" on development, Karzai demanded the international community channel half of its donor assistance through his grasping Afghan ministries.[40] A European rule-of-law and security consultant indicated that Karzai's bluffs spooked the international community: "The usual reaction is to be terrified he is holding a gun to his head," he e-mailed. The consultant thought the international community should stiffen its resolve. "I think he would fold. But his game plan is to acclimatize the West to giving guns and money and let him run the show."[41]

The US complicity with the Karzai kleptocrats' blatant greed alienated the Afghan populace.[42] A former Afghan deputy minister said, "The West cries about corruption now, but they didn't care before. They're ready to fight the Taliban, but they've been indifferent to the snakes and scorpions which bite Afghans. Only when corruption started to affect the international community did they became [*sic*] ready to act."[43] Already outraged by civilian casualties from air strikes and spec ops raids, Afghans began to compare the American military to the Soviets. US development projects sometimes prompted deadly reprisals from the Taliban—unless they were in on the take.[44] The Afghans felt caught in the middle between the insurgents and the Coalition forces—"on the fence," as American military officers said about the Afghans' wavering allegiances. "Who should we react to or complain to?" an Afghan father in Kandahar asked as his two sons' bodies were prepared for burial after a suicide attack. "We are feeble against both forces, whether Taliban or government. We cannot stop them; we can just bear the consequences."[45]

Caught in the middle, stuck on the fence—the problem extended all through the Afghan society. In Khost Province, the ADT forged a relationship with Shaikh Zayed University. Because of security, the ADT traveled in armored MRAPs to the university for meetings. The armed ag experts walked across the modern campus in the middle of a fast-moving security cordon, the Force Protection riflemen sighting rooftops and Afghan students in their everyday clothes. After scouting out the administration building hallways, the grunts hustled the ag experts up the stairs into Chancellor Gul Hassan Walizei's office. A stolid, dignified professor with an organic chemistry doctorate from a German university, the chancellor waited patiently as the ag team dropped body armor and M16s, the sound of ripping Velcro® and clattering metal filling his spacious office. The secretary brought tea.

Some weeks later, the chancellor canceled a follow-up meeting because the insurgents sent a threatening *shabnamah*, a "night letter."[46] After some negotiations, the chancellor agreed to meet at FOB Salerno, where he explained the university's dilemma: "Two weeks ago we had one night letter from the Taliban side. Today we canceled the meeting; we did not want that. If you guys come over, some people will kill us. So we try to protect from both sides. . . . To protect your life and protect the university, so we, the chancellor, decide to have the meeting here, *Inshallah* (God willing)."[47] But it soon became clear that, while Chancellor Walizei did not want the ADT to come to the university, he was fine with taking the American money.

The increased aid and logistics money the Obama administration directed to Afghanistan accelerated the pandemic of corruption that began in the Bush era.[48] "The more money that comes in here, the more opportunities, and then there's a lot more exploitation, more corruption," a US embassy official in Kabul told me in early 2010. "And there's a lot more money coming in here."[49] And the Obama "Afghanicizing" strategy put the system on steroids. The US troop withdrawal deadline that accompanied the Obama troop surge then sent the whole organism into a feeding frenzy.

Quite simply, WHAM didn't work. Winning hearts and minds with development, a key element of the counterinsurgency doctrine, was a stabilization failure.[50] Indeed, the rising insurgent attacks tracked upward right along with the post-2009 increases in development funds and troops.[51] Critics pointed to the plethora of reasons for the COIN failure: lack of cultural understanding, oversight, and sustainability; bad planning and coordination; Afghan corruption and international greed; wild overfunding. "We've been like Santa Claus, going through money, whatever you need," said Navy Commander William B. Goss, who led the Kunar Province PRT.[52]

In spite of ample evidence that US development and logistics money funded the enemy, most American officials avoided the subject. It was "a blind spot," according to a congressional staffer for Representative John Tierney, whose subcommittee later published the scathing *Warlord, Inc.* report.[53] Maybe it was a "see no evil" kind of blindness. Aram Roston, whose groundbreaking investigative articles for the *Nation* unveiled the nexus between US logistics trucking contracts and Taliban funding, said that after eight years of war, "people should know everything about where the American funds are going, because it's not a new war."[54] Roston said, "People have to know. There's a lack of that. People simply don't—the American military in many cases isn't aware of how the process works. If they are aware, they're turning a blind eye to it."

The Taliban wasn't deluding anyone about where its money originated. A former Taliban Foreign Ministry official, Waheed Mojda, told the *Washington Post* in 2009, "The international community and the Americans have been deceiving themselves for the last seven years, saying the Taliban has been getting all of their money from drugs."[55] The article cited funding from smuggling, crime, and extortion of US contracts. When finally forced to confront the chaos, American leaders were often quick to excuse it. General McChrystal said, "We were in a hurry, we were ignorant, we created a business environment, and now it's come back to haunt us."[56] Too hurried, that is, to see if Afghan contractors were members of the Taliban. Almost a decade into the war, the State Department still had virtually no vetting, and the Defense Department and USAID vetting programs were weak and understaffed.[57] Too hurried to coordinate or plan beyond the laughably short rotations. "Who's leading the choir?" was an oft-repeated civ–mil refrain. Too hurried to oversee or determine if a project was sustainable. Too hurried to see if programs were little more than sops to politically connected Beltway Bandits. Faced with the facts, US officials begrudgingly began to admit what was common knowledge in Afghanistan.[58] Secretary of State Hillary Clinton told the Senate Armed Services Committee in late 2009, "There's a lot of evidence, that, in addition to funding from the Gulf and illegal narcotics trade, that siphoning off contractual money from the international community . . . is a major source of funding for the Taliban."[59]

US taxpayer dollars supported the Taliban in the smallest things: villagers gave humanitarian aid blankets distributed by American troops to the *mujahideen* and sold USAID-funded wheat seed and fertilizer in the markets to underwrite the insurgency.[60] Afghan National Police gave their American weapons and ammunition to the jihadis. Supported by the CIA and US spec ops, Afghan government satraps ran fiefdoms they shared with the Taliban.[61] US-supported Afghan cell companies and banks paid off the insurgents. Aided by corrupt insiders, the insurgents grabbed giant takes from road, transport, construction, and development projects. Representative John Tierney called the transportation security scam "a vast protection racket" that "may be indirectly funding the very insurgents we are trying to fight."[62] An American security contractor was more certain. He stated, "I have yet to find a security contractor that doesn't rely on payoffs to the Taliban."[63] US Army commander Larry Legree, who in 2008 worked with road construction in the Korengal, the valley later infamous for its violent resistance to the Americans, stated, "My view is that the locals were pragmatic. They wanted the money and they knew I was the checkbook."[64]

The Gardez–Khost Highway seemed to encompass the whole mess. I had flown in a fast-moving Black Hawk above the highway—fast-moving because it was a distinctly unsafe place to do much hovering. At one point over the K-G Pass, the bird veered and the pilots deployed antimissile flares and chaff, a sign that insurgents were taking pot shots with their rockets. The Gardez– Khost Highway construction was legendary for grotesque costs and overruns. The original 2007 estimate of $69 million was judged to be scandalously high, given that the highway, contracted out by USAID to the Louis Berger Group and Black and Veatch, was mainly following a functional roadbed built decades ago by the Germans for a fraction of the cost. As of the spring of 2011, the sixty-four-mile-long road had cost the American taxpayers $121 million, with final costs estimated to be $176 million—$2.8 million per mile.[65]

Security for the Gardez–Khost construction route, which impinged into an insurgent-controlled region in northern Khost and southern Paktia Provinces, ate up about a third of the total cost—$43.5 million. The South African security subcontractors, ISS-Safenet, had signed up a local warlord named Arafat to handle security. The problem was Arafat had ties to the Haqqani Network, among the most brutal of the jihadis. Wanting to maintain the Gardez–Khost cash cow, both American and Afghan officials hushed up Arafat's shady connections. Even after military intelligence placed Arafat on the "kill or capture" Joint Priorities Effects List, the infamous tabulation of insurgent leaders, he continued collecting $160,000 a month for road security, ostensibly because the contractors said he was keeping "relative peace."

Down in Helmand Province, the Kajaki Dam and hydroelectric plant once again figured in the narrative of America in Afghanistan. Begun in the 1950s, the enormous US-financed and US-built project was the cornerstone of the Cold War–era development race between America and the Soviets. In the years after the 2001 invasion, the US-led coalition fought the Taliban to control the dam and powerhouse—and then the US military and USAID fought between themselves about how to repair it. The work included the 2008 delivery of a new Chinese-built 18.5 megawatt turbine that took five thousand British troops and one hundred vehicles to get through the Taliban-controlled region. However, the Taliban quickly seized control of the access road, blocking delivery of cement and other equipment needed for installation. The turbine remained in its crates, forcing NATO in 2010 to consider spending $200 million on unsustainable diesel generators for Kandahar to make up for the power shortfall. The United States eventually spent over $100 million to repair and upgrade Kajaki to provide power to Helmand and Kandahar Provinces, again touting Kajaki as a glittering centerpiece of American aid.[66] Power lines again snaked across southern Afghanistan, bringing electricity to thousands. But in 2010, researchers discovered that over half the electricity went to areas controlled by the Taliban, which sent out utility bills and dunned late payers with quick-snipping collection agents who summarily cut them off.[67] Naturally, a good many of the insurgents' customers utilized the electricity to irrigate their fields of opium poppy. Once an icon of US assistance to the Third World, Kajaki now served as the symbol of America's distracted aid to the enemy. "The more electricity there is," an Afghan tribal affairs officer said, "the more money the Taliban make."[68]

*   *   *

Scene: Jalalabad Air Base, Nangarhar Province. The helicopter to Jalalabad lifts off in the dead of night, rising from the brightly lit Oz of Bagram Airfield into the darkness of Afghanistan. Cinched-in machine gunners at the open front and tail. Cold air rushes past soldiers packed into the bird. We fly over a vast landscape, tiny dots of light here and there announcing isolated outposts. Knife ridges slice into the slate gray sky. The front gunner suddenly starts firing, thumps reaching back through the fuselage, a thin torrent of tracers arcing down toward the ground. A few seconds later, the tail gunner chimes in. An Apache yell from the front gunner. Is he hit or triumphant? Tension flows through the bird, waiting for bullets, rockets to tear through the bird's thin skin and pierce our own. Will we make J'bad? We fly on.

After the stygian countryside, Jalalabad looks like an amusement park with its boulevards, cars, and tall buildings with rooftop warning lights. But the Chinook® lands outside of town in a bleak, unlit landing zone. The airmen wave us out impatiently, the bird too loud for speech. A lost stumble through a maze of boulders and HESCO® barriers. "Where do we go?" we shout in one another's ears. "Is this Jalalabad?" a soldier asks.

A battered minibus eventually delivers us to the tiny Jalalabad Air Base PAX terminal, where a military press officer collects me. He guides me across the quiet blacked-out base to a long, empty asphalt runway where a pedestrian-crossing traffic light is incongruously flashing red. "Stop here," he says. "Even if you don't see anything. Even if you don't hear anything. If the red light's on, wait." A Predator® suddenly swoops to the runway like a returning wraith and disappears into the gloom. Black night; white drone; gray halftone memory; gone. A golem; a spectre. Cold night in a weather-beaten tent, odd dreams of playing war as a boy.

Chapter 15

The Perfect War

ENSCONCED BEHIND HIGH WALLS in the heart of Kabul, the Gandamack Lodge is a fortified hotel favored by war correspondents and contractors on the make. It's a ferro-cement pile with colonial pretensions, replete with
English cottage prints and tattered copies of *Country Life*, and home to the
Hare and Hound Watering Hole, where Westerners thirsty from alcohol-
banned Afghanistan hammer down scotch and Heinekens®. But the collection
of battered old tribal rifles, planters made of mortar shells, and rangy Afghans
patrolling with Kalashnikovs signify that Gandamack's a long way from the
Cotswolds. Outside the breakfast-room windows, armed tribesmen prowl the
cheerless garden in its mid-December decline. Bedraggled roses and marigolds
cling to leggy stalks; the yellowed grass stretches patchy to the blast wall.

Inside, Kabul regulars down their bangers and eggs. At one table, a fleshy
former oil field contractor from Louisiana and his nubile California assistant
enthuse about the potential in Afghanistan for his new project-management
company. They are in Kabul trolling for development contracts. "There are just
so many opportunities here," the assistant chirbles. At the long table at the end
of the sunroom, raffish photojournalists flaunting Arab *keffiyas* that mark them
as Iraq War vets swap combat tales. The Gandamack owner, Hassima Syed,
sleek in her designer clothes, presides over the table closest to the wood-
burning stove. The well-connected daughter of an Afghan official, Hassima is
the young wife of the Gandamack's founder, the dashing former British war
journalist Peter Jouvenal. She intently pores over spreadsheets of her burgeoning empire that caters to the arms-and-aid crowd: the Gandamack, a construction company, a travel agency, a vegetable farm, a bedding shop, and a
security company called Angel Human Resources. A gasoline business is next,
she tells journalists. Across the room, a multinational exec in a pink London
suit pecks away on her PowerPoint® presentation for a USAID proposal she is
soon to give at the embassy. As the season slips toward 2010, it should be a

good year—the eighth of the war. A boom pulses through the hotel. A bomb has exploded nearby, destroying an international hotel. Eight dead; dozens wounded. The smooth Afghan manager reassures a guest: "It is normal, sir."

*   *   *

Everyone was in on the take one way or another—the Afghan insiders, the international consultants and technocrats, the politicians, the military, the Taliban. For almost a decade, this collusion of beneficiaries was running an expedient, ADD-afflicted war for their mutual profit.[1] "Out of chaos comes cash," a veteran conflict-zone contractor told me.[2] How else did an impoverished, largely illiterate society manage to dupe the world's greatest superpower? They had help. Phyllis Cox, the rule-of-law expert who began working in the Kabul embassy in 2004, says, "In my opinion, the US government is the leader in Afghan government corruption. It is an enabler. But in addition to being an enabler, it is really a primary actor, and the United States does not seem to be willing to take the actions necessary to call itself and the Afghan government on the carpet and stop this."[3] Karzai himself blamed the international community for the corruption, saying all the mismanaged development money was responsible.[4] Afghan parliamentarian Daoud Sultanzoi also blamed the US-led coalition for the corrupt Afghan government, saying Karzai would not be able to run his predatory government without US assistance. "Your president has given him the teeth," Sultanzoi said, "so it's your teeth that he's biting the people of Afghanistan with."[5]

Afghanistan continued to excel in the human-misery and corruption indexes. In its 2009 ratings, Transparency International ranked Afghanistan as the second most corrupt country on earth, trailing only anarchic Somalia. Despite all the US change in management, a year later Afghanistan was still among the top three most corrupt countries. An embassy official connected to the Afghan Threat Finance Cell said corruption actually got worse following President Obama's December 2009 speech, which committed more troops but announced the withdrawal. "The government people who were corrupt figured they better grab everything they can while the getting's good," the official said.[6] "The government officials who weren't corrupt are now grabbing, because they figure they are going to have to get out of here after we leave and Karzai falls." By April 2010, an increasingly erratic and self-empowered Karzai was threatening to join the insurgency if the United States and NATO continued to push him for reforms, reportedly telling a member of his parliament,

"If you and the international community pressure me more, I swear I am going to join the Taliban."[7]

But many people realized Karzai and his henchmen had already effectively joined the Taliban. In Washington, the Senate Foreign Relations Committee report *Afghanistan's Narco War: Breaking the Link between Drug Traffickers and Insurgents* summarized the sad history of America's post-9/11 support of the warlords who parlayed their political power into opium dynasties.[8] In spite of the billions spent on counternarcotics programs, Afghanistan was producing 90 percent of the world's opium, which profited the opium dealers, Karzai government officials, and the insurgents. The US-facilitated opium industry was just one source of insurgent funding. Beyond skimming the US logistics contracts, the insurgents were tapping corruption, graft, and payoffs from US development contracts.[9]

*   *   *

By mid-2010, it appeared the much-ballyhooed whole-of-government civilian–military cooperation scheme had died aborning. The "Unity of Effort" public-relations announcements failed to salve the endemic sniping between the civilian agencies. As for civilians and the military—well, despite the press releases, there were still a lot of unresolved issues. In April 2010, civilian and military groups gathered for a convention on Afghan agricultural development at Indiana's Camp Atterbury, the primary training facility for Afghanistan-bound development teams. USAID development adviser Steven Welker was dapper in his blazer as he faced the Camp Atterbury audience of two hundred stone-faced military officers, most of them development team commanders. Flipping through his PowerPoint slides, Welker exuded confidence, having just returned from testifying before the Senate. Trying to get a laugh, he termed the ongoing interagency–military conflicts "nonlethal fratricide." It didn't bring many smiles. He was facing a tough crowd.

Welker dived into the well-burnished USAID accomplishments: agricultural fairs where international representatives pondered Afghanistan's scant exports; agricultural vouchers for six hundred thousand farmers; 3.2 million saplings planted. An army commander sitting next to me whispered, "In east Paktika, they planted 250,000. Big problem: 90 percent died. How many of those 3.2 million trees are still alive?" But when Welker trumpeted the multitudes of schools built across Afghanistan, a commander from a Texas unit challenged him on teacherless USAID-built schools standing empty. Welker interrupted him, "USAID won't build any more schools in Afghanistan. The emphasis is now on teacher training," quickly flipping to his next PowerPoint slide, one of those polychrome graphics with rainbows of colors, curvilinear arrows flying various directions, and text reassuring that all is well.[10]

Talking about the 2010 USAID agricultural-development budget of $472 million, he noted the agency was requesting an additional $350 million in supplemental spending. Welker contrasted the US government's $250 million commitment to agricultural development in the poppy heartland of Helmand and Kandahar Provinces to the $125 million committed to the whole of Iraq, which at the time was the largest agricultural-development project in the world. "This is an enormous amount of money for two provinces," he proudly said. In the land of development, budgets are king.

The National Guard commander in charge of ADTs, Colonel Marty Leppert, called out, "There's a lot of people out there with a lot of money, tripping over each other. This takes a lot of coordination." Another commander asked about USAID's propensity to tabulate input, such as trees, rather than the impact on the insurgency. The commander pointedly said, "What are the outcomes? It's easy to measure input. What's the outcome? What do we get for all that money?" Welker weakly defended the programs with, "Well, this just started," and then spun on the stage as though he were preparing to dodge a bullet. When Welker started talking about USAID's implementing partners, a Texas colonel put his hand up and snapped, "We had trouble figuring out what USAID was doing." So much for "unprecedented levels of civilian–military cooperation." The commander next to me said, "There was seldom a week that went by that we didn't discover new USAID projects." As he walked off the stage, Welker gave a little laugh and said, "This is tougher than the Senate."

*   *   *

The military-industrial complex certainly continued getting theirs. By 2010, there were 104,000 private contractors working in Afghanistan—more civilian workers than soldiers. According to a Congressional Research Service report, contractors made up a full 62 percent of the Department of Defense's workforce in Afghanistan. And with the upsurge of thirty thousand more troops, the Congressional Research Service estimated they needed an additional twenty-six thousand to fifty-six thousand contractors to do laundry, fix meals, haul garbage, clean latrines, provide security, and tend to the vast webs of technology that connected the global web of war.

American civilians plucked out of tenuous financial and personal situations jammed Afghanistan. A fat, surly plumber at the Jalalabad Air Base grousing about child support and reduced R&R time in Qatar, the go-to getaway place. An Afghan American interpreter from California returned to Afghanistan to work as a translator because her husband's dire medical conditions had devoured their savings. She hoped her salary of well over a $100,000 would put them back on an even keel. Though a Dari-speaker who had fled Kabul in the 1970s, she was assigned to the Pashto-speaking regions of eastern Afghanistan, where she often bent over Pashto-language textbooks for on-the-job learning. A contract manager in southern Afghanistan said he had been downsized out of a corporate executive job. His age and the US economy forced him to war-zone contracting work. A kitchen worker from Texas dreamt of Dallas as she flipped eggs on the Pakistan border. A Xe (formerly Blackwater, now Academi) security guard talked bitterly of onerous alimony and the perfidy of the military for drumming him out of the army. But they were just picking up small change. Experts estimated in 2009 that the United States spent $23 billion on contractors in Afghanistan since the invasion—the experts had to estimate because the United States only started keeping records on contractor spending in 2007. Senator Claire McCaskill contended that $950 million of the $23 billion are "in questioned and unsupported costs."[11]

Eight years into the war there was still no central database of all the development contracts and contractors. The military and civilian electronic databases were incompatible, rendering central coordination beyond the ken of the supposedly cooperating groups—and beyond the easy scrutiny of investigating bodies. The investigators couldn't follow the money. A GAO audit found none of the "cooperating" agencies would vouch for the accuracy of the information: "The agencies could not verify whether the reported data were accurate or complete."[12]

The shortage of contracting officer representatives (CORs) led to the horrific lack of oversight. Trained to read contracts and assess contractor performance, CORs traditionally served as the frontline watchdogs for the taxpayers' money. But in the draconian post–Cold War cutbacks, the CORs were the first to go. And then Afghanistan and Iraq happened. In 2007, then senator Barack Obama said, "we cannot win a fight for hearts and minds when we outsource critical missions to unaccountable contractors."[13] And so, we didn't.

The Obama administration had cast its lot with a risky and expensive counterinsurgency strategy that was financially unsustainable over the long term. But there were portents of problems even in the short term. When the marines arrived in Helmand Province in early 2010 as the spearhead of the troop surge, they attacked Marja to shut down the thriving opium market funding the Taliban. But in the accompanying media hoopla, a critical fact was lost: less than a year before, on May 19, 2009, Coalition forces had already attacked Marja, and the Coalition press officers had already blared that *that* battle was a momentous victory: sixty militants killed, one hundred tons of drugs destroyed, and a cache of weapons seized.[14] Alas, with little Afghan government follow-up or security, the insurgents were soon back in Marja.

When the Americans attacked Marja again in 2010, the Coalition brought in a "Government in a Box," Government of the Islamic Republic of Afghanistan administrators who were supposedly going to rule. But it was a media event. Well-compensated Afghan officials in body armor scurried out of helicopters for Marja photo ops and then whickered away to safe havens in fortified bases and Kabul. The Taliban quickly returned to Marja—if indeed they ever left. Some reports indicated militants had lined up for Coalition financial assistance. The insurgents knew where the money was. The *New York Times* reported that the Taliban told the populace they would confiscate the wages of any Afghans now working for the Americans. The Taliban even got a share of the battle-damage and condolence payments the US forces made to aggrieved Afghan civilians. Once again, the United States was financing the enemy.[15]

*   *   *

As the skims and scams and corruption schemes continued, frustration grew among American soldiers. They could see firsthand the equipoise of rapacity in Afghanistan, where ravenous contractors, consultants, civilian careerists, mission-creep military, venal congressmen, corrupt Afghan officials, and opportunistic insurgents fed on the bleeding carcass of the American taxpayer. *The Mouse That Roared*, a 1959 Peter Sellers comedy, became popular with the troops through YouTube®. The movie was about a tiny bankrupt principality that cynically declared war on the United States, because the principality leaders knew after the Americans conquered them, they would be flooded with snatchable reconstruction money. One National Guardsman told me he found himself thinking about his own children's impoverished elementary school as he worked on miniscule Afghan orchard projects that cost tens of thousands of dollars. He asked me, "How can we spend hundreds of thousands of dollars— millions—here, when we can't afford books for our own children?" The soldiers were well aware that US money was leaching over to the Taliban. "We are financing our own enemy," a Force Protection sergeant sardonically told me. Colonel Brian Copes, the pithy commander of the Indiana National Guard ADT, was fond of saying, "In the words of the immortal Pogo, 'We have met the enemy, and he is us.'"

The Texas National Guard ADT was trundling through Ghazni Province in its convoy of MRAPs on a quality-control mission. The soldiers had their game faces on. They had already lost four of their team to an insurgent IED. Who knew what was next? Traveling through the Taliban stronghold of Ghazni City, they saw angry faces and averted looks. Inside the armored vehicles, the soldiers called out threats. "See that burgundy Toyota"—wasn't there a warning about a suicide bomber in a burgundy Toyota?" The gunner called out, "Man, this car is getting too close." A navy-blue Toyota edged closer. Someone held up a fuzzy photo, trying to see if it was the same car as in the intelligence report. The gunner plaintively called again, "Can someone keep eyes-on?"

Ghazni City triggered memories of hauling their IED-demolished vehicle back through the insurgent city—and recollections of their fallen comrades. To calm themselves as they rolled past the hostile glares, the soldiers reverted to their default truck banter, the intercom crackling with jibes, sexual bluster, and complaints about the corrupt Afghan officials. Captain Arie Kinra, an Indian American with a big dip of snuff contorting his lower lip, told me Ghazni City was run by a power elite, "who just want to keep things the way they are." A dip, and, "They're just like Mafioso, getting their cut." Another soldier chimes in, "It's like we're financing the Taliban. The road contractors are paying the Taliban for road contracts; the PRT talks about it all the time. We had a veterinarian truck hijacked. Had to pay $6,000 to ransom the workers. We think the contractor was working with the Taliban. They just *took* the truck."

At FOB Mehtar Lam in Laghman Province, the insurgency was growing and corruption was rife in December 2009. It had been a rough couple of days: IEDs were everywhere; local Afghans rioted over special ops raids that killed villagers; insurgents resolutely probed for weaknesses. The thinly manned combat teams were constantly on alert or on the move. Even the defensive security soldiers assigned to the development units were pulled into combat roles. The base artillery boomed through the night in support of operations out in the darkness. In their MRAPs, hooches, and chow halls, the soldiers groused about the graft and corruption that surrounded them.

Captain Douglas Seymour, a burly, lantern-jawed cop from Las Vegas who served as an intelligence officer, stood on the porch of a moldering plywood hut built by the multinational KBR. He looked ragged, as though long-term sleep deprivation and adrenaline rushes had taken their toll. Echoing the satiric tone of his fellow soldiers, Seymour compared Afghanistan to Las Vegas—everyone getting their cut, just enough excitement to keep the rubes engaged. Noting that the American casualties over eight years of war in Afghanistan were below the numbers killed in military training, Captain Seymour said, "The Afghans know just the right amount of fighting to keep us here. Not too many casualties or we'll bolt. Can't let peace break out or we'll lose interest. Just the right amount."[16]

In the jaded GI view that Captain Seymour voiced, everyone wins: "The military gets all these combat commands and combat patches. I get all this cool equipment. I started back when the Russians were the enemy. I never got all this cool equipment. The military-industrial complex, they're all making money. All this stuff." Pointing back at the small delaminating plywood hut, he asked, "What's that cost—$28,000? It's a playhouse. The government here, they're like the Mafia, always getting their cut. The Taliban gets their cut. It's the perfect war, everybody makes money."

*   *   *

Scene: Kabul International Airport. To fly out of Kabul International Airport I first need a trustworthy driver; kidnapping journalists is lucrative. Smiling, trusted Pazel negotiates the SUV out of the walled hotel compound through two steel gates. Before opening the final gate to the street, a guard with an AK-47 peers out a peephole to see if there is a lurking assassin. When the guard opens the gate, Pazel roars into a tangle of traffic, men with howling mouths leaning out of windows, shaking fists. Pazel lurches through a hole in the stream and we're off to the airport through warrens of blast walls and razor wire. There's a whoosh around an exposed roundabout as Pazel looks for suspicious vehicles and then heads down Ambush Alley, the Westerners' rueful nickname for the airport road. A white Toyota station wagon stuffed with Afghan men roars alongside. I look away.

At the airport's first guard post, a half mile or so from the terminal, I have to get out of the car for a total-body search—an everything-out-of-pockets, no-kidding, total-pat-down-including-there search. A bomb-sniffing dog leaps in the car, snuffling for explosives. A lingering crotch sniff. Then on to the next checkpoint for two more full-body searches. "Nogin? Nogin?" a Hazara guard kept asking. Finally he made a gun out of his fist and fingers. "Nogin?" Ah. No. No gun. He smiles. On to the luggage inspection.

Now only a quarter mile from the terminal. A feckless soldier in a woolen uniform begins a veeeery slow inspection of my four bags with a sly smile. "You give him $5," *Pazel says out of the corner of his mouth. A fiver slides over and security inspection is now complete. So much for rigorous security. Then bags back in the SUV, a run through more blast walls to a parking lot, where a porter with a rickety cart takes my bags. Pazel tells me to pay no more than $2 per porter. More guards, searches, inspections. A bus with two porters, each demanding baksheesh. "Baksheesh, you give baksheesh," says one, barring the way, "you give baksheesh." A thirty-second ride to another porter—baksheesh—but I can actually see the terminal, where a line of anxious passengers snakes out into the bright cold sunlight. Everyone knows a snowstorm is coming in the next day, so there's the-last-plane-out-of-Kabul tension in the air.*

Inside it's a melee as throngs of hard-bodied, turbaned Pashtuns jostle for the counter. Another search, baggage scan, porter, baksheesh. I go for the smile-and-wave technique, making friends like a nice Midwestern boy. Two tough Pashtuns from Khost Province decide to adopt me after they learn I was just there. They demand the other tribesmen be cordial. I get to enter the fray. There seem to be way too many people for the limited number of seats going out. Lots of us wanting to get to Dubai. Forty-five anxious minutes of deep breathing in a total crush of people edging forward. At last I get a handwritten boarding pass and the guy tagging my luggage demands . . . baksheesh. "You give me money," he mouths as he holds my bags hostage.

An old Afghan man in a rumpled suit jacket stops me at the gate to the passport checkpoint. I need a visitor registration card, which I couldn't get when I arrived in Afghanistan—the airport office was closed. I had a $100 bill ready for a bribe—no way I was getting stopped now. But instead the man smiles and says, "When you come back next week, you will get, yes?" Yes, yes, I definitely will.

Passport checks and more security. This time a complete disassembly of my carry-on luggage done by smiling and efficient Afghan women—cheery as they confiscate this and that. Another total pat down by a polite Afghan man with excellent English.

Departure lounge jammed with people. Three flights leaving in short order for Dubai—Sakai, Kam Air, and Pamir, which was my airline. No loudspeaker, no scheduling board, just a guy wandering through saying "mumble, mumble, mumble—Dubai!" Was that Pamir or Kam Air? Sounds the same. The passengers query one another—"Did you hear? Pamir? Kam Air?" Periodically we rush the gate with our precious boarding passes, only to be turned back. Eventually the Pamir passengers with lime-green tickets buddy up, as do the blue-ticketed Kam Air passengers—the tickets sticking out of people's pockets like some color-coded tribal identification.

But there's too many people, nighttime coming, snow ahead. Would the airport get shut down for security? Rumors of rocketeers out in the surrounding mountains. "They oversold the flights," someone says. First Sakai, the expensive flight, leaves. Then the horde of blue-ticketed Kam Air passengers thunder for the narrow doorway, pushing and shoving to get on the plane. It looks like madness.

Then it is just us. Too many of us. A man with a flat central Asian face from one of the -istans on his way to London with his wife and small son says he doesn't know how it will go. I'm dreading the fight for the seats. Evening shadows. Time for prayers. The Pashtun tribesmen rise as one and make their way to a striped wall of the lounge, where they lay their tiny traveling prayer rugs down at a slight angle to the wall, aimed toward Mecca. Three rectangular, lighted advertising signs hang on the wall. Two read Advertise Here, *the other is missing its face, just burning florescent tubes. "Maybe they'll call the flight now," the -istan man says. "I don't think so," I say, barely getting the words out of my mouth before they actually do call the flight. It's a frantic race for the gate before the Pashtuns can rush back from the wall. The -istan family and I manage to squirt through the gate just ahead of the mob.*

Down the halls, out onto the tarmac, where we board a bus out to the waiting plane. Night descending; fog coming in; worried faces on the flight line. Almost to the plane, where passengers are already going up old-fashioned metal stairs. I am right behind the -istan folks when an Afghan soldier rushes up with a rifle, howling in Dari for me to stop. The Pamir flight crew starts yelling back. The soldier steps on the stairs and bars my way with his rifle. I'm thinking, "There's no way you're stopping me now, buddy," but pfft, *he's got a gun. I fall back on my smile-and-wave ploys.*

But after a last passport check and requisite scowls, the soldier steps aside. I find my seat and look out on the tarmac where there are throngs of people. Way too many, I think. This isn't over. Sure enough, as the plane fills, here comes a flight attendant to challenge my handwritten boarding pass. Perhaps my size, lack of Dari, or guilelessness make him decide to find an easier passenger to displace. We sit rigid, staring forward, no talking, hoping the plane will get off. God, I want to get back to a saner world. But Inshallah—*God willing—is the name of the game out here. Somewhat to my surprise, we eventually lift off, sailing across the nighttime blackness of Afghanistan, Iran, and the Gulf, to the bright lights of Dubai.*

Final Kabul International Airport tally: seven bribes, five body searches, four luggage inspections, one bomb-sniffing dog, and more than one scare.

Chapter 16

The Way

IT WAS JUST PAST MIDNIGHT on May 2, 2011, when the first of the Navy SEALs' MH-60® helicopters swooped down on Osama bin Laden's compound in Abbottabad, about a mile from Pakistan's West Point. A blast and gunfire began a forty-minute firefight that ended on the third floor of the main building, where one of the SEALs shot a double tap—boom, boom—into Osama bin Laden's body.[1] Though bin Laden was dead, the strategy he formulated over a decade before was still succeeding in Afghanistan.

The United States was spending $120 billion dollars a year in Afghanistan on military operations alone. Almost one hundred thousand American troops were stationed there. Since the invasion, the United States had spent over $60 billion on Afghanistan reconstruction. Bin Laden's strategy was always economic: have an al Qaeda operative wave a flag, and watch the generals stampede over to that spot; wave an al Qaeda flag over there, and watch the generals rush there. He called it his "bleed-until-bankruptcy" plan.[2] With all the international and Afghan collaborators, bin Laden's plan was working like a charm.[3]

In some ways, it was all part of the death of hope in Afghanistan. Within a few months of bin Laden's killing, the assassination of President Karzai's half brother, Ahmed Wali Karzai, precipitated a crisis of control in southern Afghanistan.[4] Assassins had already killed numerous high-level Karzai kingpins, both important government officials and members of the informal power elite that included businessmen, tribal leaders, and drug dealers. A week after Ahmed Wali Karzai's death, assassins killed another powerful warlord, Jan Muhammad Khan, followed by the killing in September 2011 of former president Burhanuddin Rabbani, who was heading the Taliban reconciliation effort.[5] Rabbini's assassination was only a week after an audacious attack on the US embassy and ISAF headquarters in the heart of supposedly secure Kabul.[6] It all called into question whether Karzai's precarious government could even survive until the 2014 US troop withdrawal.[7] Karzai was already juggling a half dozen crises, among them the banking scandal, an election-fraud battle with parliament, and a widening border war with Pakistan.[8] The rampant corruption that linked together the Afghan insiders, the international colluders, and the insurgents had alienated the Afghan populace.[9]

The rising number of jihadi attacks in 2011 proved the special forces dictum: if an insurgency wasn't shrinking, it was winning. With attacks spiking 15 percent above the previous violent year, insurgents killed governors, soldiers, police, road builders, and NGO aid workers.[10] The insurgents attacked in the north, the west, the east, the south. An attack in the southern metropolis of Kandahar shut the city down for thirty hours.[11] In early 2011, the insurgents began striking Kabul with impunity, assaulting an upscale supermarket in the tony international neighborhood of Wazir Akbar Khan.[12] In May, a medical student, an ANA soldier, and a Pakistani helped launch a suicide attack on a Kabul hospital that killed six and wounded twenty.[13] Then in June, heavily armed gunmen that included nine suicide attackers stormed the five-star International Hotel, penetrating several rings of security as police guards raced away from the fighting. At least twenty-one people were killed. In the aftermath, there was general despair about the Afghan national security force's capacity to maintain order. Nariz Amini, an expatriate Afghan who survived the attack, said, "If they give the security responsibility to the current government at 10:00 a.m., the government will collapse around 12 noon. They cannot live without the foreigners."[14]

The audacious insurgent attacks in the capital reached a new peak on September 13, 2011, when fighters launched complex attacks across Kabul, including an assault on the heavily guarded US embassy and nearby NATO headquarters, the two primary symbols of American military and diplomatic power in Afghanistan. "This is not a drill, this is not a drill," the embassy loudspeakers blared. "If you are not in a secure location, do not move."[15] It took twenty hours for the Afghan security forces, which took over responsibility for Kabul security the previous July, to kill the last of the six attackers, who held out through the night in a fourteen-story building overlooking the embassy. While militarily inconsequential, the sophisticated and coordinated attacks demonstrated both the insurgents' capacities and their powerful sympathizers in the capital. The attacks also underscored the impotence of the Afghan security forces, whose spokesmen claimed they were protecting the capital in a "ring of steel." Poorly trained, erratically led, and ethnically riven, the Afghan security forces continued to be notable for their ineffectiveness.[16]

Efforts to reach a political solution with the insurgents were failing. Few insurgents took advantage of the US-funded reconciliation and reintegration offers, and even fewer fighters from the rebellious south and east.[17] The US programs to lure Taliban leaders to the bargaining table weren't working. At a peace *shura* in eastern Afghanistan, a tribal elder managed to besmirch both the US reconciliation programs and development projects when he said, "This peace process is like one of these reconstruction projects, where much money changes hands, but no results are achieved."[18]

A 2011 Afghanistan intelligence analysis concluded that the counterinsurgency development projects, including the billions spent on improving the Afghan government, had failed to produce a positive impact.[19] At best, the unsustainable US development projects had transitory impacts on security.[20] A district governor in Helmand said, "If the Americans end their cash-for-work programs, the people will go back to fighting for the Taliban."[21] As the old saying went, "You can't buy an Afghan's loyalty, but you certainly can rent it."

Afghan journalist Abdul Rahim Mohmand reported from eastern Afghanistan that Afghan government officials were systematically paying off the Taliban with both money and weapons. Abdul R., the brother of a senior law-enforcement official in Jalalabad, told of paying the insurgents $2,000 to $4,000 a month on behalf of his brother. He said, "We pay so they don't kill us. And the Taliban are happy with the sum and leave us alone." Just south of Jalalabad, the Taliban had reestablished itself in Tora Bora, where in 2001 the United States outsourced to double-dealing Afghan warlords what could have been the climactic battle against al Qaeda and bin Laden. In a phone interview, the Tora Bora Taliban spokesman, Qari Sajjad, confirmed government officials paid them off. He told the journalist, "Our mujahedin [fighters] and elders do not make people send them money and weapons. Some do so because they fear us, while others do so out of Islamic and Afghan sympathy [for our cause]."[22]

Through the spring and summer of 2011, there was anti-Western rioting in cities across Afghanistan, reflecting increasing anger over civilian casualties and the predatory Afghan government.[23] The increasing number of air strikes and spec ops night raids triggered the Pashtuns' deeply held tenets of *Pashtunwali*.[24] In villages and towns across the Pashtun regions, the age-old concepts of *nang* (honor), *tora* (courage), and *badal* (revenge) again animated the tribesmen into resistance against the infidels. Many Afghans still believed the United States was systematically funding the Taliban to justify continued military occupation.[25] The stated US counterinsurgency mission, to bind the people of Afghanistan to the Government of the Islamic Republic of Afghanistan, had failed. It was the death of COIN.

The powerful Afghan warlords who had been bribed and coerced into the Karzai government certainly figured the jig was up. With Obama's 2014 troop withdrawal deadline looming, a group of Tajik, Uzbek, and Hazara warlords formed an opposition alliance against Karzai. The warlords included Ahmad Zia Massoud, brother of the legendary Tajik commander Ahmad Shah Massoud, who fought the Soviets and then the Taliban. In kind of a Civil War–redux, the other warlords included Uzbek leader and ANA commander in chief General Rashid Dostum and Hazara warlord Haji Mohammad Mohaqiq.[26] The old warlords, including Marshall Mohammed Fahim, the Tajik warlord embroiled in the Kabul Bank imbroglio, were slouching away from the Kabul government to gird up for Civil War 2.0.[27] The insurgent groups were likewise positioning themselves for the power struggle.[28]

After the mixed reviews on the summer 2010 surge offensives circulated, many Americans began to conclude that counterinsurgency had failed.[29] Through the winter and early spring of 2011, American public support continued to dwindle. "The American people have Iraq and Afghanistan in the rearview mirror," Congressman Lee Hamilton told me in April 2011.[30] With the American economy still bumping along the bottom, the cost of the war was getting greater scrutiny. In 2011, the war in Afghanistan was costing US taxpayers about $10 billion a month. Beyond the one hundred thousand US troops and eighty-seven thousand military contract personnel in Afghanistan, there were another thirty-two thousand support troops deployed nearby. More than 1,100 civilians were assigned to the Kabul embassy.[31] Since 9/11, the United States had spent nearly one trillion of mostly borrowed dollars on the Afghanistan war. At a time when the United States was slipping in global rankings in education, health, and other human services, and the nation's infrastructure was alarmingly derelict, Nobel Prize–winning economist Joseph Stiglitz estimated the total cost of the Iraq War alone would eventually reach $3 trillion.[32] A Brown University study published in June 2011 concluded the cost of the wars in Afghanistan, Iraq, and Pakistan will reach $4 trillion.[33] Critics noted the $120 billion appropriated for Afghanistan in FY 2011 would pay for 1.9 million elementary school teachers, 16 million Head Start slots, or 15.5 million university scholarships.[34] The United States Conference of Mayors stated in June 2011 that American taxes should be paying for bridges in Baltimore and Kansas City, not in Baghdad and Kandahar.[35]

That was just the money and lost economic opportunities. The nation was also coping with almost 1,700 soldiers killed and over 11,000 wounded in Afghanistan, part of the 225,000 lives lost in America's post-9/11 wars.[36]

Untold thousands of soldiers with post-traumatic stress disorder and mild brain traumas were threatening to overwhelm the VA system. Soldiers' and contractors' families were often left to deal with their war-damaged loved ones. While the endless wars were militarizing American society, the conflicts were also rending the social fabric, as less than 1 percent of Americans were bearing the brunt of military duty. And then there was America's loss of moral stature in the world.[37]

Within a month of Osama bin Laden's death, American public opinion shifted dramatically. The Pew Research Center reported in June 2011 that for the first time a majority (56 percent) of Americans favored bringing US troops home as soon as possible, an eight-point jump from the previous month.[38] Two years earlier, only 38 percent of Americans favored withdrawing the troops as soon as possible.[39]

*   *   *

COIN architect General David Petraeus kept up a brave front, campaigning for long-term troop commitments, coupled with accelerated transition to Afghan security forces.[40] He told David Frost it was "arguable" the United States was winning. But public and governmental support was slipping away. The White House issued an assessment that stated security progress was "uneven" and Afghan governance was "unsatisfactory." US intelligence officials were leaking their misgivings about the Pentagon's rosy reports, which increasingly relied on body counts as a key metric.[41] Ever the bellwether, the *New Yorker* ran a cartoon of three glum generals talking at a briefing table. One said, "Well, I'm an optimist—I still think peace can be avoided."[42]

In Afghanistan, the US military strategy seemed increasingly erratic: abandoning some areas, vigorously assaulting others; talking COIN, but increasing CT. A colonel talked of "the great disconnect" between the heroic efforts of small tactical units and the larger strategic picture. "You can keep trying all different kinds of tactics," he said. "We know how to do that. But if the strategic level isn't working, you end up wondering: How much does it matter? And how does this end?"[43]

President Obama began juggling his war cabinet in April. Defense Secretary Robert Gates, an ambivalent counterinsurgency warrior, was retiring. A few months before, Gates told an audience of cadets at West Point that any future defense secretary who advised the president to invade Asia, Africa, or the Middle East with a large army should "'have his head examined,' as General

MacArthur so delicately put it."[44] CIA Director Leon Panetta, a staunch counterterrorism supporter, was named to replace Gates. Ambassador Ryan C. Crocker was tapped to take over the Kabul embassy from Karl Eikenberry. General Petraeus was going to head up the CIA, to be replaced by Lieutenant General John R. Allen, who had worked on insurgent reconciliation in Iraq.[45] Petraeus stepped down earlier than planned, in July during the summer fighting season. In his last interview as commander, Petraeus remained hopeful about security in Afghanistan. "It is very hard," he said, "but it is doable."[46]

But the US juggernaut was already turning. A bipartisan congressional consensus emerged to slash defense spending, the first deep cuts since 9/11.[47] Evidence that the administration was downsizing the Afghanistan nation-building campaign were manifest. Funding for development was cut.[48] After the Senate Foreign Relations Committee estimated the United States was spending $120 billion a year on the war, the Obama administration reportedly cut costs by limiting Afghanistan's security forces, previously deemed vital to transition, to 352,000.[49] Military development teams on the ground began to report that CERP funds were drying up, a story repeated up the chain to division level and to Washington, where CERP appropriations were being slashed from $400 million in 2011 to $200 million in 2012. USAID's funding for Afghanistan was cut 40 percent. Plans to shift US combat troops from the south to the RC-East command in the eastern borderlands were put on hold. "Everything is under review," a lieutenant colonel working on eastern Afghanistan development told me. "RC-East is no longer a priority."[50] With their ever-sensitive antennae, the Washington foreign-policy crowd was looking for a new gig. "Everyone I know is now working on Libya," one foreign-policy wonk brightly told me.[51]

On June 22, 2011, a little less than seven weeks after the killing of bin Laden, President Obama addressed the nation on "the Way Forward in Afghanistan." With bin Laden's death momentarily muting the political opposition, Obama announced a rapid withdrawal of ten thousand troops, with a total withdrawal of thirty-three thousand by the following summer. Though less in the headlines, the administration also pulled the plug on the much-touted civilian surge by sharply reducing the numbers of US government civilians assigned to Afghanistan from almost 1,000 to 450 by late 2012, to 150 by 2014. *Surge recovery* and *transition* quickly became the new buzzwords, as US military and civilian leaders raced to strip down their forces and assets. Like Gorbachev before him, Obama had given the military a free hand with its strategy for a year before announcing the withdrawal.[52] The speech was tacit acknowledgment that Obama's great hearts-and-minds experiment in Afghanistan was over. The United States couldn't kill its way to victory, nor could it buy it. Though some administration officials insisted the nation-building work would continue, Obama made no mention of the civilian surge or Afghan development in his speech. He did, however, reference the almost one trillion dollars the United States had spent in Afghanistan and said, "America, it is time to focus on nation building here at home."[53]

*　　*　　*

The American soldiers knew COIN wasn't working. While the happy news and success stories continued to pour out of the Washington and Kabul press offices, the grunts on the line were far less upbeat. Soldier after soldier shared his or her misgivings with me. A marine officer in southern Afghanistan told me in mid-2011, "Among the marines in Afghanistan, there's low morale. They say, 'This is such a waste of time. This is a drug and tribal war, with the ISI and Iranian intelligence involved. These people will never pull their heads out of their asses.'"[54] He says the senior military and civilian levels "know COIN is way too expensive and never successful," and the United States is "throwing a *lot* of good money after a *lot* of bad money." The marine officer told me, "On an operational level, the soldiers are saying, 'I'm going to go over there and try to not get my legs blown off. My nation will shut this bullshit down.' That's the feeling of my fellow soldiers."

The soldiers had long since lost faith in the hearts-and-minds stuff—"marines say, 'fuck this,'" the marine officer remarked. He wasn't alone. Even civil-affairs officers had reservations. "The thing about aid and CERP is it's short-term," veteran civil-affairs commander Lieutenant Colonel Simon Gardner told me. "There's a limit to how far largesse will go."[55] Lieutenant Colonel Jeff Madison, an intelligence officer with the Fires Center of Excellence, said, "We are not being very effective. We got off the plane, saw what needed to be done. Did it, built it. Found an Afghan leader, gave him a big pair of scissors. Put an Afghan face on it. Then we found an Afghan leader, asked him, 'Do you want a water project?' 'Yes,' they always say. Bring the leader out, give him a big pair of scissors to cut the ribbon. But the insurgency is still growing."[56] Some counterinsurgency experts, such as David Kilcullen, disputed the COIN doctrine that development spending created stability.[57] Brigadier General Patt Maney, who had worked in reconstruction, told me, "Never embark on a vast idea with a half-vast plan," laughingly slurring "half-vast."[58]

One day I walked back from the FOB Salerno airfield with Colonel Brian Copes, the commander of the first Indiana National Guard ADT. Raucous jackdaws in slender-leaved pepper trees cawed out their territories as we talked about America's demand for quick counterinsurgency results compared to the generations needed to resolve Afghanistan's problems. Copes told me about the pitfalls of an asymmetrical war, where US technological might is matched against an adaptive enemy fighting on its own turf. While ever-focused on the ADT mission to help bind the people of Afghanistan to their government, Copes had earlier told me, "The environment has by no means crushed my optimism, but it has tempered it."[59] We strode out of the dappled shade into the harsh central Asian sun, turning down graveled alleys between windowless bomb-hardened barracks, soldiers snapping salutes as we passed. Returning the salutes, Copes told me about the crucial need for patience in this culture clash, and the Taliban's exploitation of America's cut-and-run reputation. He turned to me and said, "You know the Taliban leaders' favorite saying? 'The Americans have the watches, but we have the time.'"

By the autumn of 2011, the Indiana ADT was on its fourth deployed unit in Khost Province, with two more scheduled to deploy through 2014. "Armed farmers," the Afghan called them. As the top brass parsed "surge recovery," the fate of ADTs with their dedicated security platoons was up in the air. Also up in the air was the impact of the US development initiatives on the Afghan insurgency. The second ADT unit deployed to FOB Salerno survived a nine-hour assault by one hundred insurgents, including three suicide bombers who penetrated the base defenses.[60] "The helicopters were shooting down inside the base," ADT commander Colonel Michael Osburn told me. "Shot one right by Green Beans—the coffee shop by the airfield," Command Sergeant Major Pat Fromme added.[61] After the US military and civilian officials spent hundreds of millions of dollars over the previous years to win hearts and minds in Khost Province, it was a reality check. The small dams of Shobo Khel and Zanda Khel, built by the first ADT with much travail and danger, worked as they were designed, slowing down the river to catch silt and improve irrigation. But when it came time to maintain their small rock dams, the villagers refused. They wanted the Americans to pay them to do it.[62]

*   *   *

The debate about the war continued past Obama's withdrawal speech. What was the way to go in Afghanistan after ten years, ten commanders, and seven ambassadors? Should the United States go sideways with a revised counterinsurgency strategy, as many COIN pundits recommended?[63] The COIN proponents argued that anticorruption change management, battalions of new contracting officer representatives, better metrics, and the tens of billions spent on the Afghan security forces were suddenly going to bear fruit. Some critics said we needed a consistent strategy that lasted longer than an election cycle. As soldiers liked to say, "We haven't fought a ten-year war, we've fought ten one-year wars."[64]

Though development experts and soldiers on the ground disabused the notion that development increased security, the COIN strategy persisted in the swollen budget lines and thousands of US war-zone development contracts. WHAM was a faith-based doctrine, supported by a wealthy and powerful congregation. USAID and the State Department signed one thousand contracts for Afghanistan in the year prior. The Kabul embassy announced in June 2011 that USAID was pumping $90 million in Afghan First reconstruction funds through the Afghan ministries, though American diplomats warned the ministries had a "narrow skill level" and a high propensity to steal.[65]

As part of the heralded USAID Forward restructuring program that began in late 2010, the agency methodically began a procurement-reform pilot project—certainly something needed in Afghanistan, where out-of-control procurement fueled a culture of corruption and helped fund the Taliban. But USAID specifically avoided including Afghanistan or any other conflict-zone country in the pilot program because of concerns it would "skew" the results. The procurement-reform plan included an emphasis on using "host-country systems" and increasing local capacities, as in the $90 million of Afghan First funds USAID committed to the Afghan ministries.

After speaking with USAID Senior Development Aide in Legislative and Public Affairs Ginny Barahona about the complexities of using "host-country systems" in corruption-rampant Afghanistan, she stated to me: "Procurement reform that's part of the USAID Forward agenda takes time and might not work in Afghanistan today. Maybe we can't pilot using the host-country system in Afghanistan right now."[66] In spite of the massive amounts of US development money still pouring into Afghanistan, USAID appeared to have few substantive programs for improved administration and little appetite to tackle the challenges of doing development in a war zone. Earlier in the spring, USAID Deputy Administrator Donald Steinberg stated at a Washington event sponsored by the Center for American Progress and the American Enterprise Institute, "You simply cannot achieve or even adequately address the fundamental goals of promoting governance, sustainable development, and international stability and cooperation in the presence of conflict and violence."[67]

In July 2011, Task Force 435 confirmed that $2.16 billion in US military logistics trucking contracts financed the Taliban. Though the House oversight committee's report, *Warlord, Inc.*, had revealed the connections between the Taliban and the Afghan transportation contractors a year earlier, all eight Afghan prime contractors remained on the US payroll.[68] The building crews at Bagram and the other four-hundred-odd US bases continued their frantic pace. A contracting officer in southern Afghanistan complained to me that he was overwhelmed with work in July 2011. It was near the end of the fiscal year, and the military was frantic to "burn" money, lest it get cut from the next budget. It was business as usual.

After Obama's speech, counterterrorism was touted as the way forward: drones and hunter-killer teams operating out of fortified operating bases.[69] Forget the hearts and minds, go for something farther down, they said. That worked so well in Vietnam, it was sure to be a winner in a Pashtun warrior culture with generations-long ideas of revenge.

But after thirty years of making Afghanistan the devil's playground, war-weary Americans weren't looking for a way forward. They were increasingly looking for the way out.[70] While many said the United States was done with Afghanistan, there was still a butcher's bill to pay. It took the Soviets three years to get out of Afghanistan after Gorbachev announced the Communist withdrawal. Held in thrall to timetables dictated by electoral politics, the United States was still engaged in the Vietnam morass years after President Richard Nixon announced the American troop withdrawal.[71] A mutually benefitting collaborative had built up an immense momentum in Afghanistan, and it was going take an equally forceful effort to extract the United States from the pernicious situation.

There was broad consensus that the government needed to reduce the US funds flooding Afghanistan. Critics thought the revolving door between the military and the defense industry should be closed, as well as the one between USAID and the Beltway Bandits. Though Secretary of State Hillary Clinton continued to support USAID, some critics thought triage was the answer for the broken agency.[72] Diplomats conjectured about a de facto balkanization of Afghanistan into the tribal entities that existed during the warlord period.[73] Others talked of the Western powers regrouping north of the Hindu Kush, leaving the south and the east to the intractable Pashtuns.[74] Officials began to argue that the United States should spend its diplomatic capital to resolve Pakistan and India's differences rather than trying to improve the Karzai government. Others said the United States should rethink the military and development funds given to Pakistan, as the billions certainly hadn't bought friendship or reduced the nuclear risk.

*   *   *

None of it looks promising. Decades of American arrogance and cupidity have brought us to this point. And millions of Afghans have paid for it. "Let's face it, we threw Afghanistan under the bus," former deputy of agriculture Jim Moseley told me.[75] But doing more of the same isn't going to fix things. The hundreds of billions of US dollars and millions of ruined lives haven't made Afghanistan safer or less desperate. As America has upped its bets in Afghanistan, the insurgency has continued to grow in power and in influence. And the US intervention certainly hasn't made Afghanistan more honest or democratic. On a corruption scale of 0 to 10, Transparency International ranked Afghanistan at 1.4—the worst in south Asia.[76] On a widely used democracy index, Afghanistan was categorized as an authoritarian regime, ranked 150 out of 167 countries.[77]

Change has got to come from concerned Americans. The beneficiaries of the war-and-development system, both Afghan and American, are not going to want change. And the bureaucracies' self-serving inertia will just keep sending good money after bad. The United States needs to follow the lead of its NATO partners and draw down its troops as soon as tactically possible. And America needs to prepare to help with the enormous humanitarian crisis that will predictably follow the inevitable fall of the corrupt Kabul government to the Taliban. But we need to go now. "The American populace is done with this," the marine officer in southern Afghanistan told me. "The juice ain't worth the squeeze."[78]

Acknowledgments

I am indebted to the many experts who shared their knowledge of America's war in Afghanistan and the cultures, institutions, and organizations that underpin it. Because of personal and job security concerns, a number of informants have requested to remain nameless. Their contributions remain vital to my inquiry and my appreciation goes out to them. None of my informants, of course, bear any responsibility for my errors of fact or interpretation.

I would particularly like to acknowledge the support of the Fund for Investigative Journalism and the Inner Asian and Uralic National Resource Center, as well as Indiana University's Center for the Languages of the Central Asian Region, Department of Telecommunications, Voices and Visions, and Office of International Programs. The Indiana Farm Bureau and Kansas Farm Bureau also supported my research into the role of agricultural development in counterinsurgencies.

Many thanks to the experts who graciously shared their wisdom with me, including David Kilcullen, Nancy Hatch Dupree, Clare Lockhart, Marin Strmecki, Martin Hoffman, Antonio Giustozzi, Steve Coll, Peter Galbraith, Terry Mason, Kevin McNamara, Rensselaer Lee, Thomas H. Johnson, Andrew Wilder, Andrew Natsios, Ahmed Rashid, Stephen Carter, Amir Attaram, Daphne Eviatar, Alex Strick van Linschoten, Jonathan Horowitz, Tina Foster, Jean MacKenzie, Nick Swellenbach, Scott Arney, Robert J. Bebber, Nazif Shahrani, Abdulkader Sinno, Nick Cullather, Joel Hafvenstein, David Izadifar, Whitney Azoy, and Beth Cole. Former congressman and foreign-policy luminary Lee Hamilton was kind enough to provide his long perspective on the Afghanistan war and USAID. Clarine Nardi Riddle, Vance Serchuk, Mike Dubois, Andy Wright, Scott Lindsey, Mathew Mazonkey, and Celeste Hughes all expanded my understanding of the ways of Washington.

Many members of the US military took the time to explain the strategy and everyday realities of waging a counterinsurgency in central Asia. I would particularly like to thank General David Barno, Brigadier General Ross Ridge, Brigadier General Mark Martins, Colonel Mike Howard, Colonel Kirk White, Colonel Marty Leppert, Colonel Howard Schauer, Colonel Jeffrey Milhorn, Colonel Dan Renya, Commander Wilson Marks, Lieutenant Commander Paul Abbott, Lieutenant Colonel Simon Gardner, Lieutenant Colonel Mike Brady, Lieutenant Colonel Ben Ungerman, Major Peter Simon, Major Theron Ritzman, Major Sid Rosenquist, Major Carlos Moya, Captain Dan Still, Captain Nicholas Allen, Captain Matthew Miller, Captain Christopher Hormel, Lieutenant Mark Handoff, and Sergeant Jessica Sera.

I owe a particular debt to the soldiers of the National Guard Agribusiness Development Teams who permitted me to cover their complicated missions in volatile eastern Afghanistan. My sincere thanks to those associated with the Indiana National Guard Agribusiness Development Teams, including Adjacent General Martin Umbarger, Colonel Brian Copes, Colonel Cindra Chastain, Colonel Mike Osburn, Colonel Walt Colbert, Colonel Shane Halbert, Lieutenant Colonel Gary Thomas, Lieutenant Colonel Paul South, Lieutenant Colonel Kevin Sari, Major Shawn Gardner, Major Ron Crane, Major Larry Temple, Major Mary Shaw, Captain Robert Cline, Captain Brian Pyle, Lieutenant Melissa Gutzweiler, Lieutenant Ben Wegner, Lieutenant Brad Lomont, Sergeant Major Robert Goodin, Sergeant Major Daren Hudson, Sergeant Major Scott Bassett, Sergeant Major Patrick Fromme, Sergeant Major Dan Jensen, Sergeant Brendon Wilczynski, Sergeant Shawn Tharp, Sergeant Lance Murphy, Sergeant Joe Carter, Sergeant James McCool, Sergeant Robert Lee, Sergeant Phillip Jacks, Sergeant Charles Felts, Sergeant Richard Joyce, Sergeant Melissa McCoy, Sergeant Adam Coakley, Sergeant Edmund Crabb, Sergeant Chris Zeis, Chief Warrant Officer Reed Gossman, Sergeant Mathew Wheatley, Sergeant Darvin Moore, Sergeant David Shaner, Sergeant Chris Pyle, Sergeant Mark Frettinger, Specialist Joshua Lovell-Ramey, Specialist Nathan Jones, Specialist Vivian Ryan, Specialist Jerry Peavey, Specialist Malcolm Modisette, and Specialist Sean Roberts. I also want to thank the Indiana ADT families who shared their experiences back on the home front, including Audrey Cline and the Cline children, Maxie Gardner, Kim Goodin, and Donna, Eugene, and Norvella Copes.

Thanks also to the Kentucky National Guard Agribusiness Development Team's Colonel Mike Farley, Lieutenant Colonel Carney Jackson, Lieutenant Colonel Tobey Peterson, Lieutenant Colonel Ruth Graves, Lieutenant Colonel Todd Ewing, Major Eddie Simpson, and Sergeant Lisa Jo Ashley, as well as the

Texas National Guard Agribusiness Development Team's Colonel Dan Harris, Major Michael Brown, Lieutenant Alex Baker, Lieutenant Brad Clark, Sergeant Major Harlan Hardy, Sergeant Mario Quinones, Sergeant Martin Conticote, Sergeant Alex Stewart, and Specialist Thomas Kinney. My thanks also to the Kansas National Guard Agribusiness Development Team in Laghman Province, including Colonel Eric Peck, Colonel Roger Beekman, Major Troy Price, Captain Jeffrey Mann, Captain Clint Townsend, and Sergeant Lucas May.

My sincere appreciation to ambassadors Zalmay Khalilzad, Charles Dunbar, Ron Neumann, and Hans Klemm for taking the time to share their experiences and visions, and I would also like to thank the US State Department's James Story, Boots Poliquin, Mike Gottlieb, Otto Gonzales, Quintin Gray, Beth Dunford, Vikram Singh, Thomas Praster, and Patricia Kushlis. I appreciate the help extended to me by USAID's Lane Smith, Michelle Parker, Mark Ward, James Bever, Jeannie Pryor, Nick Marinacci, Alonzo Fulgham, Richard Owens, Michelle Schimp, Diane Ray, Heather Sullivan, Jim Carey, Ginny Barahona, Jodi Rosenstein, Richard Scott, Ed Fox, Harry Edwards, J. Randolph Hampton, Mark Leverson, and Patrick Fine, as well as the assistance of the USAID Inspector General's chiefs of staff, Dona Dinkler and James Charlifue.

Former deputy secretary of agriculture Jim Mosely provided important perspectives on the early efforts to increase US agricultural assistance to war-ravaged Afghanistan, and USDA's Bobby Richey, Babette Gainor, Robert Curtis, Brian Guse, Peter Benson, John Mott, Gary Domian, and Linda Habenstreit provided valuable insights in the current US-supported agricultural efforts in Afghanistan.

The GAO's Charles Johnson, Hynak Kalkus, Davi D'Agostino, Margaret Morgan, Thomas Baril, Erika Prochaska, and Valerie Grasso illuminated that oversight agency's Afghanistan investigations. The Special Inspector General for Afghanistan Reconstruction's John Brummet, Raymond DiNunzio, Guy Sands-Pingot, and Susan Phalen gave me an overview of their agency's responsibilities and aspirations. My thanks to former Special Inspector General for Afghanistan Reconstruction Major General Arnold Fields, who provided thoughtful perspectives on the challenges of Afghanistan oversight. Afghan Threat Finance Cell's Kirk E. Meyer and R. Stuart Jones explained their unit's efforts to staunch the flow of funding, including US taxpayers' dollars, to the Taliban.

Many international development officials and conflict-zone contractors gave me the benefit of their experience, including CARE's Deputy Country Director for Afghanistan Jamie Terzi, Lisa Schnellinger, Human Terrain Team anthropologist Alex Metz, Mike Woodgerd, Gary Norton, Jeff Mallory, Troy Mallory, Gary Gaertner, Dr. Heidi Knock, Phyllis Cox, Nate Hughes, Saima Wahab, Thomas Berner, Jack Bell, Lou Hughes, Patt Maney, Derek Hodgson, Donagh Houlihan, Mac McLauchlin, Doyle Peterson, Jeff Raleigh, Mitchell Shivers, Edward M. Smith, Chris King, Ben Krause, Brian Murphy, and Stephen Casapull.

My appreciation to Afghans who provided their perspectives, including Minister of Agriculture Mohammad Asef Rahimi, diplomat Ashraf Haidari, Shaikh Zayed University Chancellor Gul Hassan Walizei, and Hamed Karimzada. Also, a particular thanks to the many Afghans working with the American forces and studying in the United States who asked to remain anonymous because of fears for themselves and their families. May your beautiful land again be peaceful and secure.

I am fortunate to work with agent extraordinaire Jill Marr at the Sandra Dijkstra Literary Agency. She has been a resolute and compassionate champion of the book from the beginning. My heartfelt thanks to her and the rest of the fine Dijkstra team. Also, my thanks to Prometheus Books's editors Steven L. Mitchell and Linda Regan, who have ably shepherded *Funding the Enemy* into publication. Revered journalism professor and writer Carol Polsgrove was instrumental in this book. Emma Young and Laura DeCamp served as invaluable editorial and research assistants, corralling errant commas and hunting down arcane facts. Thanks also to Carol Sklenicka, Sandi Clark, and Mark Hood for their support and their willingness to share their expertise. Dmitri Vietze of Rock Paper Scissors was a great help, as were David Zivan of *Indianapolis Monthly*, the *GlobalPost*'s Charles Sennott, and the *American Legion* magazine's Jeff Stoffer and Brandy Ballenger. A warm thanks to Kimberly Gray for her steadfast support and close reading. Thanks to my sons, Dylan and Seth, and my sister, Bunny Ostendorf, for enduring my long Afghanistan focus.

Notes

PROLOGUE: OUTSOURCING AND INCOMING, 2001

1. Senate Report No. 14 at 4-7 (2009); the Senate report quoted Osama bin Laden's February 11, 2003, audio: "The bombardment was round-the-clock and the warplanes continued to fly over us day and night. Planes poured their lava on us, particularly after accomplishing their main missions in Afghanistan." Peter Bergen, "The Battle for Tora Bora," *New Republic*, December 22, 2009; Benjamin Lambeth, *Air Power against Terror: America's Conduct of Operation Enduring Freedom* (Santa Monica: RAND, 2005), pp. 149–61; Steve Coll, *Ghost Wars: The Secret History of the CIA, Afghanistan, and bin Laden, from the Soviet Invasion to September 10, 2001* (New York: Penguin Books, 2004), p. 199, noted the CIA's familiarity with the Tora Bora region during the Soviet war, as the company agents visited mujahideen operations there.

2. Dalton Fury, *Kill Bin Laden: A Delta Force Commander's Account of the Hunt for the World's Most Wanted Man* (New York: St. Martin's Press, 2008), p. 173.

3. Bergen, "Battle for Tora Bora." There was a third commander, Hajji Zahir, who led lesser forces. Zahir was a somewhat callow twenty-seven-year-old son of Hajji Abdul Qadir, Yunis Khalis's military commander who had welcomed bin Laden to Jalalabad in 1996. In spite of Qadir's connection to bin Laden and the Taliban, the United States was reappointing him to the governorship he had relinquished only weeks before when the Taliban passed power to Khalis's caretaker government. Philip Smucker, *Al Qaeda's Great Escape: The Military and the Media on Terror's Trail* (Washington, DC: Brassey's, 2004), p. 89; Mary Anne Weaver, "Lost at Tora Bora," *New York Times Magazine*, September 11, 2005.

4. Bergen, "Battle for Tora Bora," reported that there were about one hundred journalists at Tora Bora, more than the US, British, and German soldiers and agents combined.

5. Senate Report No. 111-35 at 11 (2009); Philip Smucker, "On the Case in Tora Bora," *Asia Times Online*, April 10, 2009, http://www.atimes.com/atimes/South_Asia/KD10Df01.html (accessed September 5, 2010).

6. Weaver, "Lost at Tora Bora"; Khalis was also a Khogyani tribal leader.

7. Philip Smucker, "How bin Laden Got Away," *Christian Science Monitor*, March 4, 2002.

8. Seth G. Jones, *In the Graveyard of Empires: America's War in Afghanistan* (New York: W. W. Norton, 2009), pp. 197–98.

9. Weaver, "Lost at Tora Bora."

10. Fury, *Kill Bin Laden*, p. 85; Smucker, "How bin Laden Got Away."

11. Smucker, "How bin Laden Got Away."

12. Gretchen S. Peters, "The Taliban and the Opium Trade," in *Decoding the New Taliban: Insights from the Afghan Field*, edited by Antonio Giustozzi (New York: Columbia/Hurst, 2009), pp. 7–21, depicted the collusion between US-empowered Afghan officials and major Afghan drug smugglers, who provided financing and equipment to Afghan insurgents.

13. Fury, *Kill Bin Laden*, p. 130.

14. Gary Berntsen, *Jawbreaker: The Attack on bin Laden and al Qaeda: A Personal Account by the CIA's Key Field Commander* (New York: Crown Publishers, 2005), p. 280.

15. Fury, *Kill Bin Laden*, p. 217.

16. Ibid., pp. 210–11.

17. Senate Report No. 111-35 at 11; Smucker, *Al Qaeda's Great Escape*, pp. 121–22.

18. Senate Report No. 111-35 at 8.

19. Fury, *Kill Bin Laden*, p. 217.

20. United States Special Operations Command, *United States Special Operations Command History: 20 (1987–2007): Proven in the Past, Vigilant Today, Prepared for the Future* (MacDill AFB, FL: US Special Operations Command, 2007), p. 101: "The general consensus remained that the surviving AQ [al Qaeda] forces had either fled to Pakistan or melted into the local population."

21. Fury, *Kill Bin Laden*, pp. 233–34.

22. Senate Report No. 111-35 at 2.

23. The date of bin Laden's escape from Tora Bora is the source of some debate. Smucker, *Al Qaeda's Great Escape*, pp. 123–26, contends bin Laden escaped Tora Bora in late November, before the US-directed ground offensive began. Bergen, "Battle for Tora Bora," concludes bin Laden used Zaman's December 12–13 "surrender" negotiations to escape Tora Bora, though told Senate investigators that he fled on December 14; Senate Report No. 111-35 at 21; Fury, *Kill Bin Laden*, pp. 244–45: as late as December 14, Fury was still pressing forward in pursuit of bin Laden at Tora Bora, as he didn't know whether or not he was still there; Senate Report No. 111-35 at 2 stated, "On or around December 16, two days after writing his will, bin Laden and an entourage of bodyguards walked unmolested out of Tora Bora and disappeared into Pakistan's unregulated tribal area"; Weaver, "Lost at Tora Bora," agrees with the December 16 escape date.

24. Jon Krakauer, *Where Men Win Glory: The Odyssey of Pat Tillman* (New York: Doubleday, 2009), p. 131; Weaver, "Lost at Tora Bora"; Fury, *Kill Bin Laden*, pp. 263 and 273, mentioned the rumor of a Pakistani helicopter that landed near Tora Bora on about December 8: "Could it have picked up a special passenger and whisked him away?"; Peter Bergen, "The Long Hunt for Osama," Atlantic, October 2004, states the Pashtun Ghilzai were "paid handsomely in money and rifles for their efforts." Berntsen, *Jawbreaker*, p. 308, agrees the Ghilzai were "paid handsomely in money and rifles." Smucker, *Al Qaeda's Great Escape*, pp. 110–11.

25. Peter Bergen, *The Osama bin Laden I Know: An Oral History of al Qaeda's Leader* (New York: Free Press, 2006), p. 335.

26. Krakauer, *Where Men Win Glory*, p. 129; Michael Scheuer, *Marching toward Hell: America and Islam after Iraq* (New York: Free Press, 2008), p. 112. This twenty-year CIA veteran and chief of the bin Laden desk wrote that Khalis was "instrumental in facilitating bin Laden's escape from Tora Bora in 2001."

27. Berntsen, *Jawbreaker*, p. 306.

28. Ibid., p. 275; John F. Burns, "10-month bin Laden Mystery: Dead or Alive?" *New York Times*, September 30, 2002; Smucker, "On the Case in Tora Bora," and *Al Qaeda's Great Escape*, p. 111, discussed Ali's delegation of closing off the Pakistani passes to devious Ilyas Khel, whose soldiers were "firing cover for escaping al Qaeda."

29. Bergen, *Osama bin Laden I Know*, p. 322.

30. Ron Suskind, *The One Percent Doctrine: Deep Inside America's Pursuit of Its Enemies Since 9/11* (New York: Simon & Schuster, 2006), p. 60.

31. Robin Moore, *The Hunt for Bin Laden: Task Force Dagger* (New York: Random House, 2003), p. 246.

32. Suskind, *One Percent Doctrine*, p. 61. According to Suskind, Henry Crumpton (a counterterrorism expert) warned Bush, "we're going to lose our prey if we're not careful," and urged Bush to rush US troops to Tora Bora. "'How bad are these Afghani troops, really?' asked Bush. 'Are they up to the job?' 'Definitely not, Mr. President,' Crumpton replied. 'Definitely not.'" In Fury, *Kill Bin Laden*, p. 209, Fury wrote, "It was just over two months since 9/11, and for the most important mission today in the global war on terror, our nation was relying on a fractious bunch of AK-47-toting lawless bandits and tribal thugs who were not bound by any recognized rules of warfare or subject to any code of military justice short of random executions and firing squads." Jonathan Randal, *Osama: The Making of a Terrorist* (New York: Knopf, 2004), p. 256, wrote about the Pentagon's unwillingness to even let British commandos try to close the back door to Pakistan. Fury, *Kill Bin Laden*, p. 256: "Leaving the back door open gave the rat a chance to run."

33. Senate Report No. 111-35 at 2, p. 12.

34. James Risen, *State of War: The Secret History of the CIA and the Bush Administration* (New York: Free Press, 2006), pp. 168–69. Jones, *In the Graveyard of Empires*, pp.

197–98, discussed Ali's 2005 scams with $70.1 million of USAID counternarcotics funds for "alternative development" programs to replace poppy fields with other crops.

35. "Afghan War Diary, 2004–2010," WikiLeaks.org, July 25, 2010, http://wikileaks .org/wiki/Afghan_War_Diary,_2004-2010 (accessed September 5, 2010). "Meeting-Security," report dated December 12, 2006, regarding a meeting with Afghan Border Police commander general Abdul Zahir Qadir in Jalalabad: "We spoke at length about the recent campaign by Attorney General Sabit to arrest and prosecute government officials in Nangarhar for corruption.... General Sabit will be in Jalalabad tomorrow and expects... Hazrat Ali (former mujahideen commander and current parliament member) to be arrested for corruption next."

CHAPTER I. TRUE PEACE, 2002

1. George W. Bush, remarks at the Virginia Military Institute in Lexington, Virginia, April 17, 2002, http://www.gpo.gov/fdsys/search/pagedetails.action?browsePath =2002%2F04&granuleId=WCPD-2002-04-22-Pg642-2&packageId=WCPD-2002-04 -22&bread=true (accessed September 8, 2010); James Dao, "A Nation Challenged: The President; Bush Sets Tone for US in Afghan Rebuilding," *New York Times*, April 18, 2002.

2. Frank L. Holt, *Into the Land of Bones: Alexander the Great in Afghanistan* (Berkeley: University of California Press, 2005), pp. 45–57.

3. Ibid., p. 15.

4. Ibid., pp. 31, 57, 97, 99, 107, 111, 132. Alexander the Great colonized Bactria with twenty-three thousand Greeks—mainly infirm former soldiers, but it was an inhospitable posting. Many revolted and tried to return home to Greece. The posts Alexander established included Begram, which he colonized with three thousand soldiers and seven thousand locals. Begram is the site of today's Bagram Airfield, the US-led Coalition's headquarters.

5. Abdul Sabahuddin, *History of Afghanistan* (New Delhi: Global Vision Publishing House, 2008), p. 20, http://books.google.com/books?id=XfDYtxfOvTYC&source=gbs _navlinks_s. (accessed September 18, 2010); Holt, *Into the Land of Bones*, pp. 81–82. Holt wrote that the war in Bactria and Sogdiana is typified by "charismatic leadership, fierce local loyalties, shifting alliances, guerilla tactics, gritty endurance, and inborn xenophobia." According to Holt, a tactical victory in Afghanistan can be a strategic defeat. The soldiers who invaded Afghanistan to liberate it from the Taliban do not have history on their side.

6. Stephen Tanner, *Afghanistan: A Military History from Alexander the Great to the Fall of the Taliban* (New York: Da Capo Press, 2002), pp. 95–98.

7. Ibid., pp. 101, 107.

8. Peter Hopkirk, *The Great Game: The Struggle for Empire in Central Asia* (New

York: Kodansha, 1994), pp. 123, 237–42, 260–69; William Dalrymple, "The Ghosts of Gandamak," *New York Times*, May 8, 2010, http://www.nytimes.com/2010/05/09/opinion/09dalrymple.html (accessed September 18, 2010).

9. William Dalrymple, "The British Army Overwhelmed by Afghan Warriors—in 1842. So Can We Learn the Lessons of History before It Happens Again?" *Daily Mail*, June 17, 2010, http://www.dailymail.co.uk/news/article-1287227/The-British-Army-overwhelmed-Afghan-warriors—1842-So-learn-lessons-history-happens-again.html (accessed September 18, 2010).

10. Hopkirk, *Great Game*, p. 393; Karl E. Meyer and Shareen Blair Brysac, *Tournament of Shadows: The Great Game and the Race for Empire in Central Asia* (Washington, DC: Counterpoint, 1999), pp. 196–97, discussed the growing middle-class rejection of the colonial wars that were prompted by the Afghan, Zulu, and Tibetan wars; Tanner, *Afghanistan*, pp. 189–219.

11. Garen Ewing, "The Second Anglo Afgh an War 1878–1880," AngloAfghan War.info, 2005, http://www.garenewing.co.uk/anglo afghanwar/biography/malalai.php (accessed September 20, 2010).

12. Hopkirk, *Great Game*, pp. 383–91; Meyer and Brysac, *Tournament of Shadows*, pp. 180–201.

13. Meyer and Brysac, *Tournament of Shadows*, p. 199.

14. Lester Grau, *The Bear Went over the Mountain: Soviet Combat Tactics in Afghanistan* (Portland, OR: Frank Cass, 1998), p. xxvi, noted in the Anglo–Russian Treaty of 1907, the Russians agreed Afghanistan was in Britain's sphere of influence while Britain agreed to not station troops in Afghanistan or annex any part of the country. The agreement lasted until 1919, when the British invaded.

15. Tanner, *Afghanistan*, pp. 218–19.

16. Steve Coll, *Ghost Wars: The Secret History of the CIA, Afghanistan, and bin Laden, from the Soviet Invasion to September 10, 2001* (New York: Penguin Books, 2004), p. 50; Tanner, *Afghanistan*, pp. 226–27; Gilles Dorronsoro, *Revolution Unending: Afghanistan: 1979 to the Present* (New York: Columbia University Press, 2005), analyzed the confrontation between the Western-educated elites and the religious authorities.

17. Karl Meyer, *The Dust of Empire: The Race for Mastery in the Asian Heartland* (New York: Century Foundation, 2003), p. 131.

18. Grau, *Bear Went over the Mountain*, p. 203. The preeminent American military historian of the Soviet–Afghan War, Lester Grau wrote, "Once the Soviet Armed Forces were in Afghanistan, it was very difficult to get out." Gregory Feifer, *The Great Gamble: The Soviet War in Afghanistan* (New York: Harper, 2009), also used Soviet sources to portray the Soviet–Afghan War.

19. Robert S. Crews and Amin Tarzi, *The Taliban and the Crisis of Afghanistan* (Cambridge, MA: Harvard University Press, 2008), pp. 38–40; George Crile, *Charlie's War: The*

Extraordinary Story of the Largest Covert Operation in History (New York: Atlantic Monthly Press, 2003), p. 408.

20. Crile, *Charlie's War*, pp. 368, 370.

21. Ibid., p. 126.

22. Ibid., p. 474.

23. Thomas H. Johnson and M. Chris Mason, "No Sign until the Burst of Fire," *International Security* 32, no. 4 (Spring 2008): 41–64, has a particularly lucid description of *Pashtunwali*. David Kilcullen, *The Accidental Guerrilla: Fighting Small Wars in the Midst of a Big One* (New York : Oxford University Press, 2009), p. 75.

24. Johnson and Mason, "No Sign until the Burst of Fire," p. 63.

25. Tanner, *Afghanistan*, p. 113, quotes Sir Olaf Kirkpatrick Kruuse Caroe's translation.

26. Bergen, *Osama bin Laden I Know*, p. 315.

27. Coll, *Ghost Wars*, p. 180, noted there were in 1971 only about nine hundred official Pakistani madrassas, mostly clustered along the Afghan–Pakistan border, but by the summer of 1988, there were eight thousand official madrassas and an estimated twenty-five thousand unofficial ones.

28. Ibid., p. 111; Antonio Giustozzi, *Koran, Kalashnikov, and Laptop* (New York: Columbia University Press, 2008), pp. 12, 14, 43–44, 49; Ahmed Rashid, *Descent into Chaos: The US and the Failure of Nation Building in Pakistan, Afghanistan, and Central Asia* (New York: Viking, 2008), p. 57; Johnson and Mason, "No Sign until the Burst of Fire," p. 70, notes the Pakistani desire to counterbalance Pashtun tribal leaders agitating for a nation-state of Pashtunistan with conservative Islam, represented by newly empowered mullahs and their endowed madrassas.

29. Grau, *Bear Went over the Mountain*, pp. xii, 202.

30. Ibid., pp. xiv, 202.

31. Tanner, *Afghanistan*, p. 269; Crews and Tarzi, *Taliban and the Crisis of Afghanistan*, p. 16, stated 9 percent of the population lost their lives, 11 percent became internal refugees, and 33 percent left the country.

32. Coll, *Ghost Wars*, pp. 177, 198. Coll notes the CIA hand-delivered $900,000 to Tajik leader Massoud's brother, Ahmad Zia, for humanitarian aid projects in northern Afghanistan. Massoud provided photos of road and irrigation projects supposedly done with the money, "though the agency's officers doubted the projects shown had been directly stimulated by their funding." Tanner, *Afghanistan*, p. 273, notes that by 1989 the Soviet Union aid was still approaching $300 million a month while US support had slipped to between $40 and $50 million. Coll, *Ghost Wars*, p. 194, states the Soviets were providing $300 million a month, "at least twice as much as the amount of aid being supplied by the CIA and Saudi intelligence to the mujahedin [*sic*]." Tanner, *Afghanistan*, p. 273, quoted Mohammad Yousaf and Mark Adkin, *Afghanistan the Bear Trap: The Defeat of a Superpower* (Havertown, PA: Casemate Books, 2001): "Both sides wanted a stalemate on the battlefield."

33. Coll, *Ghost Wars*, pp. 193, 196. Coll cited a dissenting State Department official, Edmund McWilliams, who argued that "self-determination" funding empowered Hekmatyar, who was hostile to American interests.

34. Ibid., pp. 165, 181, 182, 191, 201, 202; Coll quoted one secular Afghan from the proroyalist camp, warning American agents about their support of the Islamic radical Hekmatyar, "For God's sake, you're financing your own assassins."

35. Ibid., p. 238; Coll reported from 1979 to 1992 the Soviets spent $36 to $48 billion for arms to Afghanistan, with the United States, Saudi Arabia, and China spending another $6 to $12 billion there, providing more arms to Afghanistan than any other country on earth in the 1980s.

36. Martin Ewans, *Afghanistan: A New History* (Richmond, Surrey, UK: Curzon Press, 2001), quoted in Tanner, *Afghanistan*, p. 277.

37. Coll, *Ghost Wars*, p. 233; Tanner, *Afghanistan*, p. 278; Ahmed Rashid, *Taliban: Militant Islam, Oil, and Fundamentalism in Central Asia* (New Haven, CT: Yale University Press, 2001), pp. 49–50.

38. Rashid, *Taliban*, pp. 49–50.

39. Kenneth J. Cooper, "Taliban Rebels Take Hold as Streets of Kabul Revive," *Washington Post*, October 3, 1996; Kenneth J. Cooper, "Conquered Afghan City Takes Good with Bad," *Washington Post*, October 3, 1996; Kenneth J. Cooper, "Kabul Women under Virtual House Arrest," *Washington Post*, October 7, 1996; Kenneth J. Cooper, "Taliban's Takeover of Kabul Spurs Educated Afghans to Flee," *Washington Post*, October 8, 1996; Rod Nordland and Tony Clifton, "The Islamic Nightmare," *Newsweek*, October 14, 1996; Rashid, *Taliban*, p. 178.

40. Rashid, *Taliban*, p. 182, noted the pressure applied by three hundred women's groups, trade unions, and human-rights organizations that organized a signature campaign.

41. Steven Erlanger, "In Afghan Refugee Camp, Albright Hammers Taliban," *New York Times*, November 19, 1997; Madeleine Albright, *Madame Secretary: A Memoir* (New York: Hyperion, 2003), pp. 362–64; Kenneth Katzman, *Afghanistan: Current Issues and US Policy Concerns* (Washington: Congressional Research Services, 2001); Amy Belasco, "The Cost of Iraq, Afghanistan, and Other Global War on Terror Operations Since 9/11," Congressional Research Service Report 7-5700, http://www.fas.org/sgp/crs/natsec/RL33110.pdf (accessed December 13, 2011); National Commission on Terrorist Attacks upon the United States, "Statement of Madeleine K. Albright, Secretary of State of the United States," March 23, 2004.

42. Michael Rubin, "Taking Tea with the Taliban," *Commentary*, February 2010, http://www.commentarymagazine.com/viewarticle.cfm/taking-tea-with-the-taliban-15344 (accessed October 4, 2010).

43. Barbara Elias, "The Taliban Biography: The Structure and Leadership of the Taliban 1996–2002," National Security Archive, November 13, 2009, http://www.gwu.edu/

~nsarchiv/NSAEBB/NSAEBB295/index.htm (accessed November 16, 2011); a confidential US embassy in Islamabad cable dated March 10, 1997, is summarized and quoted: "The Department comes to grips with the reality of US–Afghan relations by plainly stating 'the Taliban are a fact of life in Afghanistan and will not soon disappear . . . [US policy] will inevitably be messy and the policy we follow will be ridden with inner tensions, as we simultaneously engage with the Taliban and criticize their abuses.'"

44. Tanner, *Afghanistan*, p. 286; Coll, *Ghost Wars*, pp. 410–11; Rashid, *Taliban*, p. 134.

45. "Barnett Rubin on the Soviet Invasion of Afghanistan and the Rise of the Taliban," Asia Society interview, August 19, 2001, http://asiasociety.org/policy-politics/strategic-challenges/intra-asia/barnett-rubin-soviet-invasion-afghanistan-and-rise-t (accessed October 10, 2010).

46. Michael Rubin, "Tea (and Prejudice) with the Taliban," *Jerusalem Post*, June 19, 2000, http://www.michaelrubin.org/1177/tea-and-prejudice-with-the-taliban (accessed October 10, 2010).

47. Ibid. An October 1999 UN resolution imposed sanctions on the Taliban regime, including prohibition of arms to the Taliban and freezing of assets. In December 2000, the UN stiffened the sanctions by restricting international travel by Taliban leaders and closing Ariana Afghan Airlines. Elias, "Taliban Biography."

48. The Taliban's March 2001 destruction of the giant seventh-century stone Buddhas in Bamiyan Province triggered international condemnation, further isolating the Islamic radicals and pushing bin Laden and Mullah Omar closer together.

49. Tanner, *Afghanistan*, pp. 294, 307.

50. Ibid., p. 293.

51. Howard Fineman, "A President Finds His True Voice," *Newsweek*, September 24, 2001.

52. Katzman, *Afghanistan*, pp. 16–17. The Bonn Conference followed numerous international meetings stretching back to 1997 under the moniker of the "Six plus Two" contact group comprised of the United States, Russia, and the six states bordering Afghanistan, all of which had interests in bringing peace to Afghanistan. With the "Six plus Two" contact group's lack of progress, a second group, which included Italy, Germany, Iran, and the United States, began meeting in Geneva. Another Afghan-related multilateral mediating group of Islamic countries under the auspices of the Organization of Islamic Conference also met. On November 14, 2001, the UN Security Council adopted Resolution 1378, which called for a "central" UN role in the establishment of a transitional Afghan government and called on member states for peacekeeping forces and humanitarian assistance. On US emphasis on the leader selection: M. Nazif Shahrani, "President Obama's 'New' Afghanistan–Pakistan Strategy: Why It Is Unlikely to Work" (lecture at Centre for Arab & Islamic Studies [The Middle East & Central Asia], Australian National University),

http://easterncampaign.wordpress.com/2009/11/02/shahrani-on-bushobama-and
-afghanistan/ (accessed October 4, 2010).

53. Katzman, *Afghanistan*, p. 16; the Rome Group began in June 1999. In May 2000, members of the group visited Washington and soon received a formal statement of US support. On October 24, 2000, Senate and House resolutions (S. Con. Res. 150 and H. Con. Res. 414) expressed congressional support for King Zahir Shah's proposed loya jirga to establish a peaceful, representative government.

54. Coll, *Ghost Wars*, p. 287.

55. Ibid., p. 289.

56. Transitional Islamic State of Afghanistan, "List of the Members of the Cabinet of Ministers," Ariaye.com, December 6, 2001, http://www.ariaye.com/english/bonn.html (accessed October 4, 2010).

57. Rashid, *Descent into Chaos*, p. 86.

58. Ibid., p. 95.

59. "Filling the Vacuum: The Bonn Conference," *Frontline*, November 27, 2001, http://www.pbs.org/wgbh/pages/frontline/shows/campaign/withus/cbonn.html (accessed October 10, 2010).

60. James Dobbins, "Our Man in Kabul," *Foreign Affairs*, November 4, 2009, http://www.foreignaffairs.com/articles/65669/james-dobbins/our-man-in-kabul (accessed November 17, 2011). In late 2009, as Karzai was sinking into a mire of corruption charges, Dobbins, who was the Bush administration's first envoy to Afghanistan, contended the Northern Alliance leader and presidential candidate Abdullah Abdullah first suggested Hamid Karzai as president to the United States in mid-November 2001. In the Foreign Affairs article, Dobbins wrote that Abdullah had already lobbied for Karzai with India, Iran, Russia, and several other European countries, whose diplomats also supported Karzai as the best candidate. Dobbins states, "The selection of Karzai is often attributed to the United States. But, in fact, Washington provided me no guidance on the subject, and I had never met Karzai." Dobbins did not address in his article the dramatic CIA-enabled Karzai speech that opened the conference or any of the other strenuous efforts the United States made to ensure the conference chose "our man in Kabul."

61. Archived at "A Sittar Sirat: The PM 4 Interim Govt," http://groups.yahoo.com/group/afghaniyat/message/1643 (accessed November 17, 2011); the link was no longer active to the original UN Wire page, http://www.unfoundation.org/unwire/util/display_stories.asp?objid=22283 (accessed on October 7, 2010).

62. "The Afghan Talks," *Washington Post*, November 25, 2001.

63. Peter Symonds, "Major Powers Pull the Strings at Bonn Talks on Afghanistan," World Socialist Web Site, November, 29, 2001, http://www.wsws.org/articles/2001/nov2001/afgh-n29.shtml (accessed October 18, 2010).

64. Rashid, *Descent into Chaos*, p. 104; "Campaign against Terror: Behind the Scenes

at Bonn," *Frontline*, July 12, 2002, http://www.pbs.org/wgbh/pages/frontline/shows/campaign/withus/cbonntheme.html (accessed October 10, 2010).

65. Nazif Shahrani, e-mail message to the author, October 11, 2010. An Afghan scholar and authority with deep connections with Bonn Conference delegates stated, "I have heard from people who were delegates that in the actual election for the President Sirat got the overwhelming majority of the vote and Karzai had only a small number of vote[*sic*]. However it was decided that Sirat (an Uzbek who had denied his ethnicity all his life and even changed his name not to be identifiable and had married a daughter of a prominent Pashtun religious scholar from Ningrahar) was not acceptable for not being a Pashtun."

66. Rashid, *Descent into Chaos*, p. 96.

67. Transitional Islamic State of Afghanistan "List of the Members of the Cabinet of Ministers."

68. Rashid, *Descent into Chaos*, pp.136–37, 185–86; Katzman, *Afghanistan*, pp. 26–30, for US aid to Afghanistan, 1999 to 2001. From $76.6 million (much of it donated wheat) in FY 1999, aid rose to $113.2 million in FY 2000, to $182.6 million in FY 2001, before dropping to $118.3 million in 2002. In October 2001, President Bush announced aid to Afghanistan would total $320 million in FY 2002. Katzman writes, "The Senate version of the FY 2002 foreign-aid appropriation (HR 2506) contains a sense of the Senate provision that the US should contribute long-term reconstruction and development assistance to the people of Afghanistan, although no dollar figures are mentioned."

69. Rashid, *Descent into Chaos*, pp. 97, 134.

70. Rod Nordland, "Afghan Warlord with Many Enemies, and Possibly One Notorious Ally, Killed by Suicide Bomber," *New York Times*, February 23, 2010. Zaman was reportedly involved in 2002 with both the bombing of former defense minister Fahim's convoy and the murder of a drug rival, Hajji Abdul Qadir, who was Afghanistan's vice president; David Mansfield and Adam Pain, "Counternarcotics in Afghanistan: The Failure of Success?" *Afghanistan Research and Evaluation Unit Briefing Papers Series* (2008): 12.

CHAPTER 2. THE CREEPING MISSION: DEVELOPMENT AND THE MILITARY

1. Sean Naylor, *Not a Good Day to Die: The Untold Story of Operation Anaconda* (New York: Berkley Books, 2005), is the most extensive inquiry into Operation Anaconda. Philip Smucker, *Al Qaeda's Great Escape* (Washington, DC: Brassey's, 2004), pp. 145–206; Benjamin Lambeth, *Air Power against Terror: America's Conduct of Operation Enduring Freedom* (Santa Monica: RAND, 2005), pp. 163–221; Linda Robinson, *Masters of Chaos: The Secret History of the Special Forces* (New York: PublicAffairs, 2004), pp. 177–82; Robin Moore, *The Hunt for Bin Laden* (New York: Random House, 2003), pp. 269–95.

2. Naylor, *Not a Good Day to Die*, pp. 27, 76, 100, 143, 236 facing.

3. Moore, *Hunt for Bin Laden*, p. 272.

4. Naylor, *Not a Good Day to Die*, pp. 26, 71, 72.

5. Michael O'Hanlon, "A Flawed Masterpiece," *Foreign Affairs*, March/April 2002, wrote about Tora Bora and the aftermath, "It is supremely ironic that a tough-on-defense Republican administration fighting for vital national security interests appeared almost as reluctant to risk American lives in combat as the Clinton administration had been in humanitarian missions—at least until Operation Anaconda, when it may have largely been too late."

6. Cesar G. Soriano, "Afghan Fight Nearly Finished," *USA Today*, May 9, 2002, http://www.airforcetimes.com/legacy/new/1-292925-903829.php (accessed December 9, 2010).

7. Lambeth, *Air Power against Terror*, pp. 166, 167, 186.

8. Ibid., p. 204; Naylor, *Not a Good Day to Die*, p. 271.

9. Naylor, *Not a Good Day to Die*, pp. 197–203.

10. Moore, *Hunt for Bin Laden*, p. 290.

11. Naylor, *Not a Good Day to Die*, pp. 41–42, 276–81. It took several days of cajoling to get Zia's fighters back to Shah-i-Kot, long after they could have made a difference. US operatives had already experienced the untrustworthy character of the "friendly" Afghan fighters recruited for Operation Anaconda when Afghans on a reconnaissance mission prior to the Anaconda commencement alerted an al Qaeda–aligned village "there was going to be a big fight."

12. Ibid., pp. 301–12, 322.

13. Lambeth, *Air Power against Terror*, p. 199.

14. Naylor, *Not a Good Day to Die*, pp. 372–73.

15. Smucker, *Al Qaeda's Great Escape*, p. 192.

16. Naylor, *Not a Good Day to Die*, pp. 138, 377.

17. Brendan O'Neill, "The Strange Battle of Shah-i-Kot," *Spiked Politics*, March 22, 2002, http://www.spiked-online.com/articles/00000006D851.htm (accessed October 25, 2010); Geoffrey Mohan and Esther Schrader, "Back at Base, US Troops Say Afghans Failed Them," *Los Angeles Times*, March 11, 2002.

18. Anonymous [Michael Scheuer], *Imperial Hubris: Why the West Is Losing the War on Terror* (Dulles, VA: Brassey's, 2004), p. 51.

19. Ibid., p. 51, 177.

20. O'Hanlon, "Flawed Masterpiece."

21. Michelle Parker, "Development in Chaos: The Challenge of Providing Assistance in Afghanistan 2001–2006," in *International Peace-Building for the 21st Century: The Tswalu Protocol and Background Papers*, edited by John Mackinlay, Terence McNamee, and Greg Mills (London: Royal United Services Institute, 2008), http://www.rusi.org/publications/whitehallreports/ref:O48BFCC6FAA32E/ (accessed November 2, 2010).

22. Barnett R. Rubin, *The Fragmentation of Afghanistan: State Formation and Collapse in the International System*, 2nd ed. (New Haven, CT: Yale University Press, 2002), p. xi.

23. Nick Marinacci, interview by the author, November 4, 2010.

24. Lieutenant Colonel Simon. C. Gardner, interview by the author, September 24, 2010; Robinson, *Masters of Chaos*, pp. 182–83.

25. Michelle Parker and Mathew Irvine, "Civilian–Military Integration," in *Understanding Counterinsurgency: Doctrine, Operations, and Challenges*, edited by Thomas Rid and Thomas A. Keane (New York: Routledge, 2010), pp. 230–41; Oskari Eronen, "PRT Models in Afghanistan: Approaches to Civil–Military Integration," *Civilian Crisis Management Studies* 1, no. 5 (2008): 2–9; Markus Gauster, *Provincial Reconstruction Teams in Afghanistan* (Garmich-Partenkirchen, GER: George C. Marshal Center, 2008), pp. 19–20; *PRT Handbook: Tactics, Techniques and Procedures* [Handbook No. 07-34] (Leavenworth, KS: Center for Army Lessons Learned, 2007), pp. 1–6; Robert M. Perito, "The US Experience with Provincial Reconstruction Teams in Afghanistan: Lessons Identified," *United States Institute of Peace Special Report* no. 152 (October 2005): 2–8.

26. For more information on the "3Ds," see "3D Security: Development, Diplomacy, Defense," http://www.3dsecurity.org (accessed December 12, 2011).

27. *PRT Handbook*, pp. 1–6.

28. Gauster, *Provincial Reconstruction Teams in Afghanistan*, p. 11; Sven Gunnar Simonsen, "Ethnicizing Afghanistan? Inclusion and Exclusion in Post Bonn Institution Building," *Third World Quarterly* 25, no. 4 (2004): 719, stated, "However, the utility of the PRTs in the areas with the most difficult security situation seems questionable." He went on to note the PRTs' small military capacity precluded much impact on the security situation, and "they can not substitute for the work of humanitarian organizations and democratically accountable institutions."

29. Captain Dan Still, interview by the author, Forward Operating Base Salerno, Khost Province, Afghanistan, June 5, 2009.

30. Richard A. Hunt, *Pacification: The Struggle for Vietnam's Hearts and Minds* (Boulder, CO: Westview Press, 1995), pp. 82–132, 235, 236.

31. Perito, "US Experience," p. 14.

32. Hunt, *Pacification*, pp. 1–2, 276.

33. Marc Leepson, "The Heart and Mind of USAID's Vietnam [*sic*] Mission," American Foreign Service Association, 2000, http://www.fsjournal.org/apr00/leepson.cfm (accessed April 4, 2011).

34. Nina M. Serafino, *Peacekeeping and Related Stability Operations: Issues of US Military Involvement* (Washington, DC: Congressional Research Service, 2007), pp. 2, 7, 11, 12; Secretary of Defense, "Report to Congress on the Implementation of the DoD Directive 3000.05, *Military Support for Stability, Security, Transition and Reconstruction (SSTR) Operations*," April 1, 2007, p. 5; Hunt, *Pacification*, p. 82. Nick Marinacci, interview by the

author, November 2, 2010: A USAID veteran of early PRTs in Afghanistan, Marinacci said the military had little to offer in terms of institutional memory of the CORDS program.

35. USAID official, interview by the author, October 23, 2010.

36. PRT civilian official, interview by the author, February 7, 2010.

37. Nick Marinacci, interview by the author, November 4, 2010.

38. Joel Hafvenstein, *Opium Season: A Year on the Afghan Frontier* (Guilford, CT: Lyons Press, 2007), pp. 11, 269.

39. Lieutenant Colonel Simon C. Gardner, interview by the author, September 24, 2010.

40. Parker and Irvine, "Civilian–Military Integration," pp. 230–41.

41. Nick Marinacci, interview by the author, November 4, 2010.

42. Gary Domian, interview by the author, May 1, 2009.

43. PRT civilian official, interview by the author, September 29, 2009; Nick Marinacci, interview by the author, November 4, 2010. Marinacci said about the heedless well drilling, "We were worsening conflicts rather than mitigating them."

44. Peter Marsden, *Afghanistan: Aid, Armies, and Empires* (New York: I. B. Tauris, 2009), pp. 139, 224.

45. Gauster, *Provincial Reconstruction Teams in Afghanistan*, pp. 19, 34–35.

46. PRT civilian official, interview by the author, February 7, 2010.

47. Gauster, *Provincial Reconstruction Teams in Afghanistan*, p. 9; US Department of State and the Broadcasting Board of Governors Office of Inspector General, "Report of Inspection, Embassy Kabul, Afghanistan, Report Number ISP-I-10-32A," February 2010, p. 23.

48. USAID official, interview by the author, October 23, 2010.

49. Parker, "Development in Chaos."

50. Staffer for Rep. John P. Murtha, interview by the author, January 7, 2010.

51. GAO, *Report to Congressional Committees: Securing, Stabilizing, and Reconstructing Afghanistan: Key Issues for Congressional Oversight* [GAO-07-801SP] (Washington, DC: GAO, 2007), http://www.gao.gov/htext/d07801sp.html (accessed November 4, 2010); Nima Abbaszadeh, Mark Crow, Marianne El-Khoury, Jonathan Gandomi, David Kuwayama, Chirstopher MacPherson, Meghan Nutting, Nealin Parker, and Taya Weiss, Provincial Reconstruction Teams: Lessons and Recommendations (Princeton, NJ: Woodrow Wilson School of Public and International Affairs, 2008).

52. Parker, "Development in Chaos," writes, "Because there are no agreed upon metrics to determine the effectiveness of PRTs the results are difficult to identify and analyze." Abbaszadeh et al., *Provincial Reconstruction Teams*, pp. 14, 17, states, "Under the current system, most metrics are input-based (e.g., number of dollars spent). These are easier to develop but far less valuable than impact-based metrics. Those metrics which have sought to quantify output (i.e., number of schools built, number of wells dug) have usually failed

to measure truly desired outcomes (i.e., improved opinion of US forces or increased percentage of local children in primary school)."

53. Edwina Thompson, "Winning 'Hearts and Minds' in Afghanistan: Assessing the Effectiveness of Development Aid in COIN Operations" (report presented at Wilton Park Conference 1022, Steyning, West Sussex, UK, March 11–14, 2010). The summary states, "Development aid is becoming an increasingly important tool to 'win hearts and minds' and promote stability in counterinsurgency (COIN) operations. Given its centrality to current COIN doctrine and strategy, there is still a surprisingly weak evidence base for the effectiveness of aid in promoting stabilisation [*sic*] and security objectives."

54. USAID official, interview by the author, October 23, 2010.

55. Lieutenant Colonel Simon C. Gardner, interview by the author, September 24, 2010.

56. Ibid.

CHAPTER 3. MAKING SOME ARRANGEMENTS: THE UNITED STATES, OPIUM, AND THE AFGHANS

1. Rensselaer Lee, "Perspectives on Narcoterrorism" (testimony prepared for hearing on narcoterrorism, Senate Judiciary Committee, May 20, 2003), quoted in Robyn Dixon, "Opium Again Hooks Struggling Farmers," *Los Angeles Times*, October 5, 2003, http://articles.latimes.com/print/2003/oct/05/world/fg-opium5 (accessed November 15, 2010).

2. Barnett R. Rubin, *The Fragmentation of Afghanistan: State Formation and Collapse in the International System*, 2nd ed. (New Haven, CT: Yale University Press, 2002), pp. xvii–xviii, xxiv, states that the Taliban's July 2000 opium-poppy ban, which created enormous hardships for impoverished Afghan farmers and alienated the powerful drug lords, "constituted for the Taliban a final test of the goodwill of the international community." The Taliban leaders thought the counternarcotics campaign was the one international demand that they could meet without violating their religious strictures. The ban was a dramatic gesture, as there had been a boom harvest of 4,581 metric tons of opium harvested in 1999. The tepid international reaction to the opium ban led to a hardening of Taliban attitudes and helped bond the Taliban to al Qaeda.

3. Gretchen Peters, *Seeds of Terror: How Heroin Is Bankrolling the Taliban and al Qaeda* (New York: St. Martin's Press), p. 8.

4. Barnett R. Rubin, "Afghanistan's Fatal Addiction," *International Herald Tribune*, October 28, 2004; Alfred W. McCoy, *The Politics of Heroin: CIA Complicity in the Global Drug Trade*, 2nd ed. (Chicago: Lawrence Hill Books, 2003), p. 521. McCoy gives details

about several of the US druglord allies, including Uzbek warlord General Abdul Rashid Dostum, who controlled a large part of the Northern Alliance's heroin trade.

5. James Risen, *State of War: The Secret History of the CIA and the Bush Administration* (New York: Free Press, 2006), p. 157; Frédéric Grare, "Anatomy of a Fallacy: The Senlis Council and Narcotics in Afghanistan" (Waterlook, ONT, CAN: Centre for International Governance Innovation, 2008), p. 31; Peters, *Seeds of Terror*, p. 101.

6. Quotes in the following paragraphs attributed to "Lee" are from Rensselaer Lee, interview by the author, November 17, 2010.

7. Peters, *Seeds of Terror*, pp. 191–92.

8. United States Senate Committee on Foreign Relations, "Afghanistan's Narco War: Breaking the Link between Drug Traffickers and Insurgents" (report to the Committee on Foreign Relations, United States Senate, 111th Congress, 1st session, August 10, 2009, pp. 4–5).

9. See McCoy, *Politics of Heroin*; Eric Wilson, ed., *Government of the Shadows: Parapolitics and Criminal Sovereignty* (New York: Pluto Press, 2009); George Gavrillis, "The Good and Bad News about Afghan Opium," *Foreign Policy*, February 10, 2010, http://www.cfr.org/publication/21372/good_and_bad_news_about_afghan_opium.html (accessed November 24, 2010); Jonathan Goodhand, "Corrupting or Consolidating the Peace? The Drugs Economy and Post Conflict Peacebuilding in Afghanistan," *International Peacekeeping* 15, no. 3 (2008): 405–23; Byrnn Jacobs, "Drugs, the CIA, and Afghanistan," *Dangerous Intersection*, October 27, 2009, http://dangerousintersection.org/2009/10/27/drugs-the-cia-and-afghanistan/ (accessed November 24, 2010).

10. Wilson, *Government of the Shadows*, p. 1.

11. McCoy, *Politics of Heroin*, pp. 466–87.

12. Peters, *Seeds of Terror*, p. 35.

13. Ibid., pp. 49, 51, 53, 55.

14. Rubin, *Fragmentation of Afghanistan*, pp. 261–62.

15. Peters, *Seeds of Terror*, p. 59.

16. Rubin, *Fragmentation of Afghanistan*, p. xxiv; Joel Hafvenstein, *Opium Season: A Year on the Afghan Frontier* (Guilford, CT: Lyons Press, 2007), pp. 10–11.

17. Peters, *Seeds of Terror*, pp. 60, 81, 93. Most of the seventy-four tons produced came from the small territory controlled by the Northern Alliance, which the United States still supported.

18. McCoy, *Politics of Heroin*, p. 518, notes the United States awarded the Taliban $43 million for humanitarian aid in May 2001, which was announced by Secretary of State Colin Powell.

19. United States Senate Committee on Foreign Relations, "Afghanistan's Narco War," p. 5.

20. Risen, *State of War*, pp. 155–56; Hafvenstein, *Opium Season*, p. 11.

21. Peters, *Seeds of Terror*, p. 4.

22. Risen, *State of War*, 156–66; Barnett Rubin, *Road to Ruin: Afghanistan's Booming Opium Industry* (Washington, DC: Center for American Progress, 2004), pp. 10–11. Rubin cited "the United States' continued alliance with warlords and militia commanders involved in trafficking," as one of the three main reasons the international community was failing to counter the Afghan opium industry.

23. Anthony Loyd, "Corruption, Bribes, and Trafficking: A Cancer That Is Engulfing Afghanistan," *Times*, November 24, 2007; Peters, *Seeds of Terror*, p. 186. In 2007, President Karzai topped it all by appointing Izzatullah Wasifi as his anticorruption chief. Wasifi was a convicted heroin dealer, caught twenty years prior trying to sell $2 million worth of heroin to an undercover agent in Las Vegas. Wasifi termed it a "youthful indiscretion."

24. William J. Kole, "Afghanistan Opium Industry Down in North, Up in South," *Contra Costa Times*, March 10, 2007, http://www.afghanistannewscenter.com/news/2007/march/mar102007.html (accessed November 16, 2010).

25. Thomas Schweich, "Is Afghanistan a Narco-State?" *New York Times*, July 27, 2008; see also Thomas Schweich, "US Counternarcotics Strategy for Afghanistan," US Department of State, August 2007.

26. Eric S. Margolis, "The Murder of Haji Qadir," *Dawn*, August 5, 2002.

27. James Risen, "Reports Link Karzai's Brother to Afghanistan Heroin Trade," *New York Times*, October 4, 2008; James Risen, "Kin Uses Tie to Afghan Leader to Weave a Web of Influence," *New York Times*, October 6, 2010; Philip Smucker, "Afghan Opium Crop Booms: More People Doing Illicit Trade, Corruption Cited," *Washington Times*, March 16, 2007; "US Military Links Karzai Brother to Drugs," ABC News, June 22, 2006, http://blogs.abcnews.com/theblotter/2006/06/us_military_lin.html (accessed November 26, 2010); Seth G. Jones, *In the Graveyard of Empires: America's War in Afghanistan* (New York: W. W. Norton, 2009), pp. 195–96; Peters, *Seeds of Terror*, pp. 136–37; Scott Shane and Andrew W. Lehren, "Leaked Cables Offer Raw Look inside US Diplomacy," *New York Times*, November 29, 2010. Ahmed Wali Karzai reportedly operates under the protection of the CIA, and McCoy, *Politics of Heroin*, p. 526, notes the global propensity of the CIA to protect its drug-king assets from prosecution. "Such implicit tolerance allowed covert war zones to become enforcement-free areas where drug trafficking could expand without limit."

28. Loyd, "Corruption, Bribes, and Trafficking."

29. Hafvenstein, *Opium Season*, p. 9.

30. Ibid., p. 313. Hafvenstein's book on buccaneering aid work in insecure Helmand Province in 2004–2005, when the Taliban insurgency was reviving, offers a window into the professional aid racket. Like many private development companies, Chemonics chased aid contracts all over the world, figuring if the company got the contract, the executives would cobble together a team with a few veterans and a bunch of young "aid tourists," as one critic termed the inexperienced development workers eager for adventure (Hafvenstein, *Opium Season*, pp. 9–10, 141). Hafvenstein, who was the second-in-command of a pro-

gram slated to dispense millions of dollars to thousands of Afghan workers for 2.5 million workdays, described himself as painfully inexperienced, but "exhilarated" by the "adventure" in Afghanistan.

31. Ibid., pp. 214, 312–13.

32. Schweich, "Is Afghanistan a Narco-State?"; Hafvenstein, *Opium Season*, pp. 129–32, 150, 192–93, 229, 312–13.

33. Loyd, "Corruption, Bribes, and Trafficking."

34. Ibid.; Peters, *Seeds of Terror*, p. 186.

35. Schweich, "Is Afghanistan a Narco-State?"; Hafvenstein, *Opium Season*, pp. 129–32, 150, 192–93, 229, 312–13; McCoy, *Politics of Heroin*, p. 523.

36. Hafvenstein, *Opium Season*, p. 215.

37. Michael Scheuer, *Marching toward Hell: America and Islam after Iraq* (New York: Free Press, 2008), p. 105, states, "And in a case of tragic poetic justice, the US Drug Enforcement Agency reported in January 2007 that Afghan heroin is for the first time beginning to enter the United States in significant quantities."

38. Peter Bergen, "The Long Hunt for Osama," *Atlantic*, October 2004.

39. Michelle Parker, interview by the author, October 23, 2010.

40. McCoy, *Politics of Heroin*, p. 521.

41. Jones, *In the Graveyard of Empires*, pp. 197–98.

42. Michelle Parker, interview by the author, October 24, 2010.

43. Peter J. Middlebrook and Mark Sedra, "Revisioning the International Compact for Afghanistan," ed. John Gershman (Washington, DC: Foreign Policy in Focus, 2005), http://www.fpif.org/reports/revisioning_the_international_compact_for_afghanistan (accessed November 15, 2010).

44. Risen, *State of War*, p. 162.

45. US officer, interview by the author, Forward Operating Base Salerno, Khost Province, June 20, 2009; McCoy, *Politics of Heroin*, pp. 517–18.

46. "Joint Statement of Lantos and Ros-Lehtinen on Announcement of Revised Counter-narcotics Strategy in Afghanistan," http://www.prnewswire.com/news-releases/joint-statement-of-lantos-and-ros-lehtinen-on-announcement-of-revised-counter-narcotics-strategy-in-afghanistan-58013887.html (accessed January 7, 2012).

47. Richard Weitz, "New US Counternarcotics Strategy for Afghanistan Leaves Critics Dissatisfied," *World Politics Review*, August 15, 2007, http://www.hudson.org/index.cfm?fuseaction=publication_details&id=5181 (accessed November 26, 2010); Thomas Schweich, *US Counternarcotics Strategy for Afghanistan* (Washington, DC: Department of State, August 2007).

48. On Taliban funding, see Thomas H. Johnson, "The Origins and Financing of Afghan Terrorism: Thugs, Guns, Drugs, Interlopers, and Creative Movements of Money," in *Terrorist Financing and State Responses: Comparative Perspective*, edited by Harold A.

Trinkunas and Jeanne Giraldo (Palo Alto, CA: Stanford University Press, 2006). See Jones, *In the Graveyard of Empires*, p. 192, for opium-poppy cultivation figures for 1991–2008.

49. Peters, *Seeds of Terror*, pp. 133, 136.

50. United States Senate Committee on Foreign Relations, "Afghanistan's Narco War," p. 10.

51. Hafvenstein, *Opium Season*, p. 221.

52. Risen, *State of War*, p. 162.

53. Schweich, "Is Afghanistan a Narco-State?"

54. Ibid.; Hafvenstein, *Opium Season*, p. 273.

55. Schweich, "Is Afghanistan a Narco-State?"

56. Ahmad Zia Massoud, "Leave It to Us to End the Poppy Curse," *Sunday Telegraph*, September 4, 2007, quoted in ibid.

57. Hafvenstein, *Opium Season*, p. 275.

58. Ibid., pp. 278–79.

59. Ibid., p. 258.

60. Ibid., p. 100.

61. Ibid., p. 224.

62. RC-East PRT development adviser, interview by the author, March 3, 2009.

63. Hafvenstein, *Opium Season*, p. 146.

64. Ibid., p. 203.

65. David Mansfield and Adam Pain, "Counternarcotics in Afghanistan: The Failure of Success?" *Afghanistan Research and Evaluation Unit Briefing Papers Series* (2008): 12.

66. Hafvenstein, *Opium Season*, p. 269.

67. Nick Cullather, "Damming Afghanistan: Modernization in a Buffer State," *Journal of American History* (September 2002), http://jah.oxfordjournals.org/content/89/2.toc (accessed November 23, 2011); Hafvenstein, *Opium Season*, pp. 82–83.

68. Eric Newby, *A Short Walk in the Hindu Kush* (New York: Penguin Books, 1986), p. 72.

69. "Bombing of Afghan Hydro Plant Could Cause Disaster, says UN," International Rivers Network, November 8, 2001, http://www.rivernet.org/prs01_21.htm#081101 (accessed November 15, 2010).

70. "Taliban Flee Battle Using Children as Shields—NATO," Reuters, February 14, 2007, http://www.alertnet.org/thenews/newsdesk/SP287758.htm (accessed November 14, 2010); Jones, *In the Graveyard of Empires*, pp. 185, 187–88. In 2005, only 6 percent of the Afghan population had access to electricity from an electric grid.

71. Jon Boone, "Taliban Stalls Key Hydroelectric Turbine Project in Afghanistan," *Guardian*, December 13, 2009, http://www.guardian.co.uk/world/2009/dec/13/afghanistan-turbine-taliban-british-army (accessed November 14, 2010).

72. United States Senate Committee on Foreign Relations, "Afghanistan's Narco War," pp. 18–21.

73. Hafvenstein, *Opium Season*, pp. 216–17.

74. Ibid., p. 157.

75. Rajiv Chandrasekaran, "Marines Plan Joint Mission to Eject Insurgents from Last Helmand Stronghold," *Washington Post*, February 10, 2010, http://www.washingtonpost.com/wp-dyn/content/article/2010/02/09/AR2010020903511.html (accessed November 10, 2010).

76. Foodcrisis, "Five Questions for Nick Cullather," *Foreign Policy Blogs Network*, December 2, 2010, http://foodcrisis.foreignpolicyblogs.com/2010/12/02/five-questions-fornick-cullather/ (accessed February 18, 2011). In this interview, historian Nick Cullather stated, "When the marines moved into Marja earlier this year, only one report mentioned that the concrete trenches the Taliban were firing from had been built by Americans half a century before": Rajiv Chandrasekaran, "US Launches Major Surge against Taliban in Afghanistan," Washington Post, February 13, 2010, http://www.washingtonpost.com/wp-dyn/content/article/2010/02/12/AR2010021203563.html (accessed December 5, 2010). On the lack of evidence to link development aid with stability, see Edwina Thompson, "Winning 'Hearts and Minds' in Afghanistan: Assessing the Effectiveness of Development Aid in COIN Operations" (report presented at Wilton Park Conference 1022, Steyning, West Sussex, UK, March 11–14, 2010).

77. Rajiv Chandrasekaran, "'Still a Long Way to Go' for US Operation in Marja, Afghanistan," *Washington Post*, June 10, 2010, http://www.washingtonpost.com/wp-dyn/content/article/2010/06/09/AR2010060906214.html (accessed November 15, 2010); "McChrystal Calls Marja 'a Bleeding Ulcer' in Afghan Campaign," *St. Petersburg Times*, May 25, 2010, http://www.tampabay.com/incoming/mcchrystal-calls-marja-a-bleeding-ulcer-in-afghan-campaign/1097412 (accessed November 15, 2010).

CHAPTER 4. LOSS OF FOCUS

1. George W. Bush, "President Bush Announces Major Combat Operations in Iraq Have Ended," White House Archives, April 25, 2004, http://georgewbush-whitehouse.archives.gov/news/releases/2003/05/print/20030501-15.html (accessed July 30, 2011).

2. Vernon Loeb, "Rumsfeld Announces End of Afghan Combat," *Washington Post*, May 2, 2003; "Rumsfeld: Major Combat Over in Afghanistan," CNN World, May 1, 2003, http://articles.cnn.com/2003-05-01/world/afghan.combat_1_provincial-reconstruction-teams-afghanistan-afghan-president-hamid-karzai?_s=PM:asiapcf (accessed December 10, 2010); Ahmed Rashid, *Descent into Chaos: The United States and the Failure of Nation Building in Pakistan, Afghanistan, and Central Asia* (New York: Viking, 2008), pp. 240–61; Seth G. Jones, *In the Graveyard of Empires: America's War in Afghanistan* (New York: W. W. Norton, 2009), p. 246.

3. "US Casualties in Iraq, March 2003–December 2009," GlobalSecurity.org, http://www.globalsecurity.org/military/ops/iraq_casualties.htm (accessed July 30, 2011).

4. Rashid, *Descent into Chaos*, pp. 240–61; Jones, *In the Graveyard of Empires*, p. xiv; Luke Harding, "Elusive Mullah Omar 'Back in Afghanistan,'" *Guardian*, August 30, 2002, http://www.guardian.co.uk/world/2002/aug/30/afghanistan.lukeharding (accessed December 15, 2011); James Risen and Dexter Filkens, "Threats and Responses: Slippery Foe; Qaeda Fighters Said to Return to Afghanistan," *New York Times*, September 10, 2002, http://www.nytimes.com/2002/09/10/international/asia/10QAED.html (accessed December 15, 2011); Colum Lynch, "Al Qaeda Is Reviving, UN Report Says; Wave of Volunteers Said to Inflate Terrorist Group's Membership, Capabilities," *Washington Post*, December 18, 2002, http://www.highbeam.com/doc/1P2-396626.html (accessed December 20, 2010).

5. Donald P. Wright, James R. Bird, Steven E. Clay, Peter W. Connors, Lieutenant Colonel Scott C. Farquhar, Lynn Chandler Garcia, and Dennis van Wey, *A Different Kind of War: The United States Army in Operation Enduring Freedom* (Fort Leavenworth, KS: Combat Studies Institute Press, 2010), p. 189, http://documents.nytimes.com/a-different-kind-of-war#p=1 (accessed December 15, 2010).

6. David Kilcullen, *Accidental Guerrilla: Fighting Small Wars in the Midst of a Big One* (New York: Oxford University Press, 2009), pp. 12, 32.

7. Ibid., p. 29.

8. Bob Woodward, *Bush at War* (New York: Simon & Schuster, 2002), p. 80.

9. Bob Woodward, *Plan of Attack* (New York: Simon & Schuster, 2004), p. 8; Jones, *In the Graveyard of Empires*, p. 316.

10. Woodward, *Bush at War*, p. 80. Woodward also writes about how neocon proponents of the Iraq invasion argued an easy victory in Iraq would satiate a fickle American public, which might be soured by an intractable war in Afghanistan. "Wolfowitz seized the opportunity. Attacking Afghanistan would be uncertain. He worried about 100,000 American troops bogged down in mountain fighting in Afghanistan six months from then. In contrast, Iraq was a brittle, oppressive regime that might break easily." Wolfowitz told Bush, "war against Iraq might be easier than against Afghanistan" (*Bush at War*, pp. 82–84). Former CIA director George Tenet wrote that there were no real discussions among the top policymakers about the implications or wisdom of an Iraq war in the run-up to the invasion, including among members of the National Security Council, the Departments of State and Defense, the Joint Chiefs, the vice president's office, the Treasury, and the CIA. "In none of the meetings can anyone remember a discussion of the central questions. Was it wise to go to war? Was it the right thing to do? The agenda focused solely on what actions would need to be taken if a decision to attack were later made. What never happened, as far as I can tell, was a serious consideration of the implications of a large US invasion." George Tenet, *At the Center of the Storm: My Years at the CIA* (New York: HarperCollins, 2007), p. 308.

11. Critics of the "golden hour" theory point to large gains made by Pakistani conservative religious parties in the fall 2002 parliamentary election. The religious parties' upsurge was a popular reaction to the US invasion that was facilitated by Pervez Musharraf, who suffered a dramatic plunge in popularity following his acceptance of the post-9/11 US actions in Afghanistan. A successful Pashtun insurrection in Pakistan's northwestern tribal areas soon followed, setting the stage for the revival of the Taliban and other Afghan insurgents. These critics contend any pressure by the United States against the Pakistani Taliban havens would have further enflamed the situation for Pakistani government moderates. See Bill Roggio, "Wikileaks, Afghanistan, and Pakistan on NPR," *Threat Matrix*, July 29, 2010, http://www.longwarjournal.org/threat-matrix/archives/2010/07/wikileaks_afghanistan _pakistan.php (accessed July 30, 2011).

12. Wright et al., *Different Kind of War*, p. 192.

13. Ibid.

14. Jones, *In the Graveyard of Empires*, p. 298. Anand Gopal wrote about the corruption and failure of the rule of law within the Afghan government that turned many to the Taliban, and added, "At the same time, the heavy-handed tactics of US forces turned many against the foreign presence." Anand Gopal, *The Battle for Afghanistan: Militancy and Conflict in Kandahar* (Washington, DC: New American Foundation, November 2010), p. 3, http://www.newamerica.net/publications/policy/the_battle_for_afghanistan (accessed December 20, 2010).

15. Stephen Carter and Kate Clark, *No Shortcut to Stability: Justice, Politics, and Insurgency in Afghanistan* (London: Chatham House, 2010), p. 37, http://www.chatham house.org/sites/default/files/public/Research/Asia/1210pr_afghanjustice.pdf (accessed June 25, 2011).

16. Wright et al., *Different Kind of War*, p. 197. When the Tenth Mountain Division under Major General Franklin Hagenbeck deployed to Afghanistan in late 2001, the division was tasked with commanding all the land forces in the country. Hagenbeck later stated the process was "improvised and thus provided little time for his staff to prepare." Hagenbeck was dramatically understaffed, with only 167 soldiers on his headquarters staff when they deployed.

17. "Combined Joint Task Force 82," GlobalSecurity.org, http://www.globalsecurity .org/military/agency/dod/cjtf-180.htm (accessed July 30, 2010).

18. Wright et al., *Different Kind of War*, p. 198.

19. Jones, *In the Graveyard of Empires*, p. 316. Jones quotes Under Secretary of Defense Douglas Feith, who wrote, "Rumsfeld was determined not to do 'nation building' as the United States did it in the 1990s."

20. The Iraq Study Group's senior government officials, led by former congressman Lee Hamilton and former secretary of state James Baker, concluded that Iraq had drained vital resources from Afghanistan. James A. Baker III and Lee Hamilton, eds., *The Iraq Study Group Report* (New York: Vintage Books, 2006), pp. 24, 28, 41, 50.

21. Wright et al., *Different Kind of War*, pp. 199–200.

22. GAO, *Afghanistan Reconstruction: Deteriorating Security and Limited Resources Have Impeded Progress; Improvements in US Strategy Needed* [GAO-04-403] (Washington, DC: GAO, 2004), pp. 2–3.

23. Ibid., pp. 45–48.

24. Barnett R. Rubin, "A Tribe Apart: Afghan Elites Face a Corrosive Past," *Boston Review*, January/February 2009, http://bostonreview.net/BR34.1/rubin.php (accessed December 20, 2010).

25. International development adviser, interview by the author, Forward Operating Base Ghazni, December 4, 2009.

26. Anthony Cordesman, "The Uncertain 'Metrics' of Afghanistan (and Iraq)," *Center for Strategic and International Studies* (2007), csis.org/files/media/csis/pubs/070521_uncertainmetrics_afghan.pdf (accessed December 20, 2010).

27. James Dobbins, "Amateur Hour in Iraq," *United Press International*, February 10, 2006, http://www.rand.org/commentary/2006/02/10/UPI.html (accessed December 20, 2010). Dobbins was the Bush administration's first envoy to Afghanistan.

28. Wright et al., *Different Kind of War*, p. 246.

29. Ibid., p. 341.

30. Joseph E. Steiglitz and Linda J. Barnes, "The True Cost of the Iraq War: $3 Trillion and Beyond," *Washington Post*, September 5, 2010, http://www.washingtonpost.com/wp-dyn/content/article/2010/09/03/AR2010090302200.html (accessed December 20, 2010).

31. Ilana Ozernoy, "Borderline War: The Return of the Taliban," *US News & World Report*, September 29, 2003, http://www.ilanaozernoy.com/Ilana_Ozernoy/Borderline_War.html (accessed December 12, 2010).

32. Wright et al., *Different Kind of War*, p. 247, notes that the Center for Strategic and International Studies compiled UN and Coalition statistics indicating that attacks of all kinds rose from fifty per month in 2002 to eighty per month in 2003, with RAND scholars showing a similar increase against Afghan civilian and security targets.

33. International Crisis Group, "Countering Afghanistan's Insurgency: No Quick Fixes," *Asia Report* 123 (November 2, 2006), http://www.crisisgroup.org/en/regions/asia/south-asia/afghanistan/123-countering-afghanistans-insurgency-no-quick-fixes.aspx (accessed December 17, 2010).

34. The resource and manning situation stayed the same throughout the Bush administration. Julian E. Barnes, "US Military Says Iraq Is the Priority," *Los Angeles Times*, December 12, 2007, quotes Joint Chief of Staff Chairman Admiral Michael Mullen at the House Armed Services Committee: "Our main focus, militarily, in the region and in the world right now is rightly, and firmly in Iraq." He went on to say, "It is simply a matter of resources, of capacity. In Afghanistan, we do what we can. In Iraq, we do what we must."

Bob Woodward, *The War Within: A Secret White House History 2006–2008* (New York: Simon & Schuster, 2008), p. 226, quotes former president Bill Clinton telling the Iraq Study Group in March 2006, "The Taliban is making inroads.... More troops for Afghanistan is absolutely essential. We cannot address Afghanistan unless we leave Iraq."

35. Wright et al., *Different Kind of War*, pp. 254–55.

36. Ibid., pp. 245, 251. Regarding Barno's Afghan command in 2003, Wright et al. notes the "overall dearth of manpower in the headquarters" as the Department of Defense was in the midst of establishing CJTF-7, the new Coalition headquarters in Iraq.

CHAPTER 5. ALL TOGETHER: THE CULTURE OF CORRUPTION

1. Paul Clammer, *Afghanistan* (Oakland, CA: Lonely Planet Guides, 2007), p. 82.

2. Dexter Filkins, "Bribes Corrode Afghans' Trust in Government," *New York Times*, January 2, 2009.

3. Pamela Constable, "Land Grab in Kabul Embarrasses Government," *Washington Post*, September 16, 2003.

4. Ibid.; Carlotta Gall, "Housing Plan for Top Aides Draws Rebuke," *New York Times*, September 21, 2003, http://www.nytimes.com/2003/09/21/world/housing-plan-for-top-aides -in-afghanistan-draws-rebuke.html (accessed January 2, 2011); Joanna Nathan, "Land Grab in Sherpur: Monuments to Powerlessness, Impunity, and Inaction," in *Viewpoints: Afghanistan, 1979–2009: In the Grip of Conflict* (Washington, DC: Middle East Institute, 2009), http://www.mei.edu/Publications/WebPublications/ Viewpoints/Viewpoints Archive/tabid/541/ctl/Detail/mid/1623/xmid/831/xmfid/11/Default.aspx (accessed July 29, 2011).

5. Karin Brulliard, "Affluent Afghans Make Their Homes in Opulent 'Poppy Palaces,'" *Washington Post*, June 6, 2010.

6. Clammer, *Afghanistan*, p. 82.

7. Abdul Basir Stanikzai, "Corruption and Warlordism: A Critical Review of Corruption Situation in Afghanistan," RAWA News, November 27, 2008, http://www.rawa .org/temp/runews/2008/11/27/corruption-and-warlordism-a-critical-review-of-corruption -situation-in-afghanistan.html (accessed January 2, 2010); Adam Schreck, "2nd Afghan Bank with Dubai Ties Defends Links," *Bloomberg Businessweek*, September 7, 2010, http:// www.businessweek.com/ap/financialnews/D9I36OD80.htm (accessed January 2, 2011).

8. "Buildings of Afghan Ministers and Warlords in Kabul," RAWA Photos, http://www.rawa.org/kab-jan05/build.htm (accessed January 2, 2011).

9. Marshall Sahlin, "Poor Man, Rich Man, Big Man, Chief: Political Types in Melanesia and Polynesia," *Comparative Studies in Society and History* (1963): 285–303; C.

C. Lamberg-Karlovsky, "Central Asia and the Bronze Age," *Antiquity 68*, no. 259 (1994): 353–57; C. C. Lamberg-Karlovsky, "Bronze Age Khanates of Central Asia," *Antiquity 68*, no. 259 (1994): 353.

10. Nazif M. Shahrani, "State Building and Social Fragmentation in Afghanistan: A Historical Perspective," in *The State, Religion, and Ethnic Politics: Afghanistan, Iran, and Pakistan*, edited by Ali Banuazizi and Myron Weiner (Syracuse, NY: Syracuse University Press, 1986), p. 42.

11. Gregory Feifer, *The Great Gamble: The Soviet War in Afghanistan* (New York: Harper, 2009), p. 158.

12. Asian Development Bank, UK Department for International Development, United Nations Development Programme, United Nations Office on Drugs and Crime and the World Bank, "Fighting Corruption in Afghanistan: A Roadmap for Strategy and Action" (informal discussion paper, 2007, pp. 3–4), www.unodc.org/pdf/afg/anti_corruption_roadmap.pdf (accessed January 4, 2011); Manija Gardizi, *Afghans' Experience of Corruption* (Kabul: Integrity Watch Afghanistan, 2007), pp. 20–22, http://www.iwaweb.org/reports/AfghansExperienceofCorruptionaStudyAcrossSevenProvinces2007.html (accessed January 4, 2011).

13. Gardizi, *Afghans' Experience of Corruption*, pp. 5, 10.

14. Dexter Filkins, "Bribes Corrode Afghans' Trust in Government," *New York Times*, January 2, 2009.

15. Gardizi, *Afghans' Experience of Corruption*, p. 5.

16. David Davis, "The Regime We Are Defending Is Corrupt from Top to Bottom," *Independent*, October 20, 2008, http://www.independent.co.uk/opinion/commentators/david-davis-we-are-losing-taliban-battle-966926.html (accessed January 4, 2011).

17. Gardizi, *Afghans' Experience of Corruption*, p. 35.

18. Scott Shane, Mark Mazzetti, and Dexter Filkins, "Cables Depict Afghan Graft, Starting at Top," *New York Times*, December 2, 2010, http://www.nytimes.com/2010/12/03/world/asia/03wikileaks-corruption.html (accessed January 19, 2011).

19. Gardizi, *Afghans' Experience of Corruption*, pp. 21, 27. One Afghan described small-time commissionkars: "They approach people saying that they can solve any kind of issue in a short time and then they quote the price. For example, if you need a passport of the driving licence [*sic*] or paying taxes and customs duties they can give the final receipt which has been processed through all official channels in matter of days which takes usually weeks. Then he takes the money and of course he will distribute it with those who are sitting inside offices."

20. USAID, *Assessment of Corruption in Afghanistan* [Report PNA-DO-248] (Washington, DC: USAID, 2009), p. 9.

21. Joshua Partlow, "Afghan Minister Accused of Taking USD30 Million Bribe," *Washington Post*, November 19, 2009, http://www.rawa.org/temp/runews/2009/11/18/

afghan-minister-accused-of-taking-30-million-bribe.html (accessed January 9, 2010.); Agence France-Presse, "Afghan Minister Accused of Massive Bribery over Chinese Mine," November 11, 2009, http://www.minesandcommunities.org/article.php?a=9645 (accessed January 6, 2010.)

22. James Risen, "Karzai's Kin Use Ties to Gain Power in Afghanistan," *New York Times*, October 5, 2010, http://www.nytimes.com/2010/10/06/world/asia/06karzai .html (accessed January 19, 2011).

23. Paul Fishstein, *Winning Hearts and Minds? Examining the Relationship between Aid and Security in Afghanistan's Balkh Province* (Medford, MA: Feinstein International Center, 2010), p. 30.

24. Ashraf Ghani and Clare Lockhart, *Fixing Failed States: A Framework for Rebuilding a Fractured World* (New York: Oxford University Press, 2008), p. 94.

25. Matthieu Atkins, "The Master of Spin Boldak: Undercover with Afghanistan's Drug-Trafficking Border Police," *Harper's Magazine*, December 2009, www.harpers .org/archive/2009/12/0082754 (accessed January 19, 2011).

26. UNODC, *Corruption in Afghanistan: Bribery as Reported by Victims* (New York: UNODC, 2010), p. 25, http://www.unodc.org/unodc/en/frontpage/2010/January/ corruption-widespread-in-afghanistan-unodc-survey-says.html (accessed January 19, 2011).

27. Kim Barker, "Pervasive Corruption Fuels Deep Anger in Afghanistan," *Chicago Tribune*, November 25, 2008, http://articles.chicagotribune.com/2008-11-25/news/0811 250113_1_president-hamid-karzai-taliban-led-bribes (accessed January 19, 2011).

28. Gardizi, *Afghans' Experience of Corruption*, p. 9.

29. Barker, "Pervasive Corruption."

30. UNODC, *Corruption in Afghanistan*, p. 9, found 52 percent of adult Afghans paid bribes in the previous year, averaging five kickbacks per year.

31. Transparency International, "Corruption Perceptions Index," October 26, 2010, http://www.transparency.org/policy_research/surveys_indices/cpi (accessed January 19, 2011).

32. UNODC, *Corruption in Afghanistan*, p. 30. The report states, "the results show that corruption contributes significantly to the erosion of state institutions and to undermining the authority of the central government." Gardizi, *Afghans' Experience of Corruption*, p. 37, states corruption turned Afghans to the Taliban.

33. Richard Holbrooke, "The Longest War," *Washington Post*, March 31, 2008, http://www.washingtonpost.com/wp-dyn/content/article/2008/03/30/AR20080 33001837.html (accessed January 9, 2011); USAID, *Assessment of Corruption in Afghanistan*, p. 11. Director of National Intelligence Dennis C. Blair seconded Holbrooke's analysis, stating that the Kabul government's failure to provide honest governance "erodes its popular legitimacy and increases the influence of local warlords and the Taliban." Seth

G. Jones, *In the Graveyard of Empires: America's War in Afghanistan* (New York: W. W. Norton, 2009), pp. 200–201, states bad Afghan governance drove Afghans—particularly in the south—to the insurgents.

34. Bernard Gwertzman, "Combating Afghanistan's 'Malign Governance,'" Council on Foreign Relations, October 1, 2010, http://www.cfr.org/publication/23071/combating _afghanistans _malign_governance.html?cid=rss-interviews-combating_afghanistan _s__malig-100110 (accessed January 6, 2011). Gwertzman interviewed Stephen Biddle, the Roger Hertog senior fellow for defense policy. Biddle: "People talk a lot about narcotics in Afghanistan but the narcotics economy in Afghanistan is a smaller contributor to malign misgovernance than the redirection of American contracting money."

35. "A Dark Place," *Economist*, June 2, 2011, p. 50.

36. Syed Saleem Shalzad, "The Face of Afghan Resistance," *Asia Times Online*, August 26, 2003, www.atimes.com/atimes/Central_Asia/EH26Ag01.html (accessed July 30, 2011).

37. Antonio Giustozzi, *Koran, Kalashnikov, and Laptop* (New York: Columbia University Press, 2008), p. 194.

38. Mirwais Atal, "US Hearts and Minds Cash Goes to Taleban," Institute for War and Peace Reporting, November 29, 2006, http://www.e-ariana.com/ariana/eariana .nsf/allDocs/E060A362A770208F87257235007F8343?OpenDocument (accessed January 9, 2011); Anand Gopal, *The Battle for Afghanistan: Militancy and Conflict in Kandahar* (Washington, DC: New American Foundation, November 2010), p. 27, notes insurgents in Kandahar struggled to fund themselves with money from their local supporters—until they hit on the real source of money in the province: the aid community. Gopal quoted a Taliban commander: "Then one day we found a list of NGOs in the area and we told some people [working there] that they had to pay us money."

39. Christoph Reuter and Borhan Younas, "The Return of the Taliban in Andar District Ghazni," in *Decoding the New Taliban: Insights from the Afghan Field*, edited by Antonio Giustozzi (London: Hurst, 2009), p. 114.

40. Jones, *In the Graveyard of Empires*, p. 226.

41. Dexter Filkins, "Inside Corrupt-istan," *New York Times*, September 5, 2010; Matthew Rosenberg, "'Malign' Afghans Targeted," *Wall Street Journal*, December 29, 2010, http://online.wsj.com/article/SB10001424052970203513204576047734260414722.ht ml (accessed January 6, 2011).

42. Peter Galbraith, interview by the author, September 24, 2010.

43. Matthew "Mac" McLauchlin, interview by the author, July 29, 2011.

44. International political analyst, interview by the author, September 27, 2010.

45. Louis Berger Group, "Road Construction in Afghanistan," http://www.louisberger .com/OurProjects/Asia/REFS-Roads (accessed January 10, 2011).

46. The Louis Berger Group wasn't shy about billing: Integrity Watch Afghanistan

noted the company charged $2.4 million a kilometer for a short road project from the center of Kabul to the airport, reconstructing a well-maintained road built about a decade earlier. Depending on terrain, the average road construction cost in Afghanistan is $100,000 to $600,000 per kilometer. Lorenzo Delesgues, "Integrity in Reconstruction: Afghan Road Reconstruction: Deconstruction of a Lucrative Assistance," *Integrity Watch Afghanistan Report* (2007): 5–6, http://reliefweb.int/sites/reliefweb.int/files/resources/EB9C3A174F3A04A14925746A001D52B2-Full_Report.pdf (accessed January 12, 2011).

47. USAID, "Review of the Road Project Financed by USAID/Afghanistan's Rehabilitation of Economic Facilities and Services (REFS) Program (RIG/Manila Memorandum 04-003)," November 13, 2003; USAID, "Second Review of the Road Project Financed by USAID/Afghanistan's Rehabilitation of Economic Facilities and Services (REFS) Program (RIG/Manila Memorandum 04-003)," March 31, 2004; USAID, "Audit of the Kabul to Kandahar Highway Reconstruction Financed by USAID/Afghanistan's Rehabilitation of Economic Facilities and Services (REFS) Program (5-306-04-006-P)," September 21, 2004.

48. Ann Jones, *Kabul in Winter: Life without Peace in Afghanistan* (New York: Metropolitan Books, 2006), p. 243; David Rohde and Carlotta Gall, "Delays Hurting US Rebuilding in Afghanistan," *New York Times*, November 7, 2005, http://www.nytimes.com/2005/11/07/international/asia/07afghan.html (accessed January 12, 2011).

49. "Andrew Wilder: Winning Hearts and Minds?" Yale Afghanistan Forum, April 4, 2010, http://afghanistanforum.wordpress.com/2010/04/04/andrew-wilder-winning-hearts-and-minds/ (accessed January 10, 2011).

50. International political analyst, interview by the author and e-mailed report from same, September 27, 2010.

51. Ibid.

52. Shakeela Abrahimkhil, "Report Reveals Political Deals behind Governors Appointments," *Tolo News*, December 4, 2010, http://www.tolonews.com/en/afghanistan/1227-report-reveals-political-deals-behind-governors-appointments (accessed January 4, 2011). The Afghan government report from the Organisations Independent Office indicated that Abubakr was one of five governors who represented Hekmatyar's Hizb-i-Islami party.

53. The Institute for the Study of War, "Hizb-i-Islami Gulbuddin (HIG)," http://www.understandingwar.org/themenode/hezb-e-islami-gulbuddin-hig (accessed January 9, 2011).

54. Dexter Filkins, "Convoy Guards in Afghanistan Face an Inquiry," *New York Times*, June 6, 2010, http://www.nytimes.com/2010/06/07/world/asia/07convoys.html (accessed January 10, 2011).

55. The website for Watan Risk Management, http://www.watanrisk.com (accessed January 10, 2010); Aram Roston, "How the US Funds the Taliban," *Nation*, November 11,

2009, http://www.thenation.com/print/article/how-us-funds-taliban (accessed January 9, 2011). Roston wrote of Afghanistan's "wartime contracting bazaar," where "former CIA officials and ex-military officers joined with former Taliban and mujahedeen [sic] to collect US government funds in the name of the war effort."

56. Watan Risk Management, http://www.watanrisk.com (accessed January 10, 2010).

57. Aram Roston, "Congressional Investigation Confirms: US Military Funds Afghan Warlords," *Nation*, June 21, 2010, http://www.thenation.com/article/36493/ congressional-investigation-confirms-us-military-funds-afghan-warlords (accessed January 11, 2011).

58. Patrick Cockburn, "A Land Darkened by the Shadow of the Taliban," *Independent*, May 3, 2009, http://www.independent.co.uk/opinion/commentators/patrick-cockburn-a-land-darkened-by-the-shadow-of-the-taliban-1678131.html (accessed January 9, 2011).

59. Roston, "How the US Funds the Taliban"; "Two Afghan Companies Plead Guilty to Bribing US Officials and Agree to Pay $4.4 Million in Fines," PR Newswire, June 25, 2010, http://www.prnewswire.com/news-releases/two-afghan-companies-plead-guilty-to-bribing-us-officials-and-agree-to-pay-44-million-in-fines-97191549.html (accessed January 9, 2011). In June 2010, Afghan International Trucking pleaded guilty to paying bribes and was assessed $3.36 million in criminal fines.

60. "Pakistan Hands Over Afghan Rebel," BBC News, February 5, 2004, http://news.bbc.co.uk/2/hi/south_asia/3461351.stm (accessed January 5, 2011);

61. "Armed Conflict Database: Afghanistan Timeline," International Institute for Strategic Studies, October 15, 2007, http://acd.iiss.org/armedconflict/Mainpages/dsp _ConflictTimeline.asp?DisplayYear=1&ConflictID=181&YearID=610 (accessed January 6, 2011). Tim Golden, "In US Report, Brutal Details of 2 Afghan Inmates' Deaths," *New York Times*, May 20, 2005, http://www.nytimes.com/2005/05/20/international/ asia/20abuse.html?_r=1&ei=5088&en=4579c146cb14cfd6&ex=1274241600&pagewa nted=all (accessed January 6, 2011). The US military eventually arrested Jan Baz Khan.

62. Senate Document, "Inquiry into the Role and Oversight of Private Security Contractors in Afghanistan" at ii (2010), http://publicintelligence.net/senate-report-on -private-security-contractor-oversight-in-afghanistan/ (accessed January 7, 2012).

63. European rule-of-law and security consultant, interviews by the author, October 4 and 15, 2010.

64. European rule-of-law and security consultant, e-mail message to author, October 15, 2010.

65. Jean MacKenzie, "Funding the Afghan Taliban," *GlobalPost*, August 7, 2009, http://www.globalpost.com/dispatch/taliban/funding-the-taliban?page=0,1 (accessed January, 9, 2011).

66. Ibid.

67. International Taliban scholar, interview by the author, October 4, 2010.

68. International political analyst, interview by the author, September 27, 2010.

69. Gardizi, *Afghans' Experience of Corruption*, notes: "An interesting testimony about larger-scale corruption at ministry level was provided by an ex-official from a ministry. He reported that in his former career he had observed the disbursement of millions of dollars of aid money based on ethnical, jihadi or kinship boundaries." Martine van Bijlert, "Corruption, Corruption, Corruption," Afghan Analysts Network, November 11, 2009, http://aan-afghanistan.com/index.asp?id=459 (accessed January 13, 2010).

70. Pratap Chatterjee, "Anatomy of an Afghan Culture of Corruption," *Huffington Post*, November 17, 2009, www.huffingtonpost.com/pratap-chatterjee/anatomy-of-an-afghan-cult_b_360656.html (accessed January 12, 2011).

71. Anthony Cordesman, "How America Corrupted Afghanistan: Time to Look in the Mirror," *Center for Strategic & International Studies* (2010): 6.

72. Edwina Thompson, "Winning 'Hearts and Minds' in Afghanistan: Assessing the Effectiveness of Development Aid in COIN Operations" (report presented at Wilton Park Conference 1022, Steyning, West Sussex, UK, March 11–14, 2010, p. 2), states the link between poorly managed excessive aid spending and corruption, which funded a spectrum of malign Afghan and US actors.

73. Peter Galbraith, interview by the author, September 24, 2010; Jones, *In the Graveyard of Empires*, p. 226. The civilian–military development teams were likewise well aware of the widespread corruption and links to the insurgency. Jones quotes Larry Legree, a PRT commander in Kunar Province, who stated about the widespread timber-smuggling operations that enriched officials and jihadists in both Afghanistan and Pakistan: "Everyone, from government officials to insurgent groups had their hands in the profits." The collusion between Pakistan's ISI, the insurgents, and Afghan officials is detailed in a Wikileaks 2006 State Department cable that reported a meeting between former ISI chief and "senior members of the Taliban" to discuss the dispatch of three operatives to Kabul to "carry out IED attacks" to "set KABUL aflame." The report indicated an Afghan criminal gang associated with the Kabul chief of police would assist the three attackers. According to the *New York Times*, other cables link the Afghan military and the minister of interior to similar attacks; Mark Mazzetti, Jane Perlez, Eric Schmitt, and Andrew W. Lehren, "Pakistan Aids Insurgency in Afghanistan, Reports Assert," *New York Times*, July 25, 2010, http://www.nytimes.com/2010/07/26/world/asia/26isi.html (accessed January 21, 2011).

74. Dion Nissenbaum, Warren P. Strobel, Marisa Taylor, and Jonathan S. Landay, "Flawed Projects Prove Costly for Afghanistan, US Taxpayers," McClatchy News, http://www.kentucky.com/2010/11/14/1516306/flawed-projects-prove-costly-for.html#ixzz1B2pry0Zu (accessed January 13, 2011); DOD Office of the Inspector General, Report No. D-2006-007 (Washington, DC: DOD, 2005).

75. The American military's casual acceptance of duplicity was hardly unique. The British Army in northwest frontier regions of the British Indian empire certainly evinced the same attitude. A longtime veteran of tribal wars, General Sir Andrew Skeen, made a telling comment to new commanders when he wryly lectured them on double-dealing spies: "The spy or 'jasoos,' is a quaint institution, whose conception of duty is to take as much news to his friends the enemy as he does to his enemies the troops. A friendly sort of show, frontier fighting, till it comes to the actual killing. In fact, I have heard a most bitter complaint lodged by hostile sections that they had been denied the privilege and the emoluments of having some of their own men employed as spies." General Sir Andrew Skeen, *Passing It On: Short Talks on Tribal Fighting on the Northwest Frontier of India* (Aldershot, UK: Gale & Polden, 1932), p. 85.

76. US Army colonel, interview by the author, Khost Province, May 2010.

77. Roston, "US Funds the Taliban." The Senate Foreign Relations Committee report investigating the issue found that the Department of Defense oversight of Watan Risk's multibillion-dollar security contract was "virtually nonexistent."

78. Major Carlos Moya, interview by the author, Forward Operating Base Salerno, Khost Province, Afghanistan, November 26, 2009.

79. Atkins, "Master of Spin Boldak."

80. Shane, Mazzetti, and Filkens, "Cables Depict Afghan Graft."

81. Anthony Cordesman, "The Uncertain 'Metrics' of Afghanistan (and Iraq)," *Center for Strategic and International Studies* (2007): 5–6, csis.org/files/media/csis/pubs/070521_uncertainmetrics_afghan.pdf (accessed December 20, 2010); the Congressional Research Service reported the United States budgeted almost $500 billion for military and development expenditures in Afghanistan from FY 2001 to FY 2010. In 2009, Afghanistan had an estimated total GDP of $27 billion, http://csis.org/publication/how-america-corrupted-afghanistan-time-look-mirror (accessed January 12, 2011); USAID Office of Inspector General, "Risk Assessment of Major Activities Managed by USAID/Afghanistan, Report 5-306-03-001-S" (Washington DC: USAID, March 11, 2003). The inspectors called out "material weaknesses in its system of management," which was amplified by "the magnitude of funding being provided Afghanistan." The inspectors indicated a concern that if USAID officials continued to exercise the same lack of oversight and unaccountability, US laws might be broken.

82. USAID, *Corruption in Afghanistan*, pp. 9, 24–58. The UNODC survey disclosed what it termed, "a stunning observation": Over half (54 percent) of the Afghans surveyed thought international organizations and NGOs "are corrupt and are in the country just to get rich." UNODC, *Corruption in Afghanistan*, p. 5.

83. UNODC *Corruption in Afghanistan*, p. 31.

84. USAID, *Assessment of Corruption in Afghanistan*, pp. 9, 24–58.

85. Gardizi, *Afghans' Experience of Corruption*, p. 32; A 2005 Integrity Watch

Afghanistan survey report stated: "Interviewees perceived NGOs to be amongst the most corrupt institutions in Afghanistan. This assessment was based on the argument that this form of institution often deals with large amounts of money and in many cases subcontracts projects to private entrepreneurs, such as construction firms." The IWA report noted Afghans consider any foreign aid organization, whether national, international, or private, to be an "NGO." Paul Reynolds, "Afghan Corruption a Political Obstacle," BBC News, November 18, 2009, http://news.bbc.co.uk/2/hi/south_asia/8366371.stm (accessed January 6, 2011).

86. Matt Waldman, *Falling Short: Aid Effectiveness in Afghanistan* (Kabul: ACBAR Advocacy Series, 2008), p. 3, http://www.aideffectiveness.org/Country/Afghanistan/ Afghanistan-Civil-society-critiques-of-aid-effectiveness.html (accessed January 13, 2011); Brooke Williams, "University of Nebraska at Omaha," Windfalls of War by the Center for Public Integrity, http://projects.publicintegrity.org/wow/bio.aspx?act=pro&ddlC=61 (accessed April 5, 2011). The report documents one USAID contractor receiving a contract in June 2002 for $168,625 to be a field program manager for an approximately twelve-month rotation that included numerous holiday breaks. According to the report, the contractor "was based at the US embassy in Kabul, where her main task was to manage reconstruction efforts outside of the Afghan capital." The CPI report documents numerous USAID contractors with similar pay scales. Per USAID contracts, agreements with development companies, such as the Louis Berger Group and Chemonics, are generally non-transparent, so contractor pay scales are veiled; Center for Public Integrity, "Contractors: Afghanistan," Windfalls of War by the Center for Public Integrity, http://projects .publicintegrity.org/wow/bio.aspx?act=pro&fil=AF (accessed April 13, 2011).

87. Ahmed Rashid, *Descent into Chaos: The United States and the Failure of Nation Building in Pakistan, Afghanistan, and Central Asia* (New York: Viking, 2008), p. 191.

88. David Rohde and Carlotta Gall, "Delays Hurting US Rebuilding in Afghanistan," *New York Times*, November 7, 2005, http://www.nytimes.com/2005/11/07/international/ asia/07afghan.html? pagewanted =1&=1 (accessed January 17, 2011).

89. Ibid. Rashid, *Descent into Chaos*, p. 191; Cordesman, "Uncertain Metrics," p. 15. Security analyst Anthony Cordesman notes the US private contractors' endemic "systematic overcharges, accounting 'failures,' 'missing equipment,' and payments to corrupt or ineffective foreign subcontractors," enabled by the paucity of effective US governmental oversight or metrics.

90. Pamela Constable and Javed Hamdard, "Accident Sparks Riot in Afghan Capital," *Washington Post*, May 30, 2006, http://www.washingtonpost.com/wp-dyn/content/ article/2006/05/29/AR2006052900284.html (accessed January 20, 2011); Rachel Morarjee, "Riots Breach Kabul 'Island,'" Christian Science Monitor, May 30, 2006, http://www.csmonitor.com/2006/0530/p06s01-wosc.html (accessed January 20, 2011).

91. Josef Storm, "To Better Afghanistan, Boot the Contractors," *Christian Science Monitor*, September 29, 2010, http://www.csmonitor.com/Commentary/Opinion/2010/ 0923/To-better-Afghanistan-boot-the-contractors (accessed January 13, 2010).

92. World Bank, "Fighting Corruption in Afghanistan" (discussion draft prepared for Paris ARTF donors meeting, 2008).

93. Waldman, *Falling Short*, p. 3.

94. Larry Elliott, "Scandal of 'Phantom' Aid Money, *Guardian*, May 27, 2005, http://www.guardian.co.uk/business/2005/may/27/development.debt (accessed January 13, 2011); "Real Aid: An Agenda for Making Aid Work," Action Aid International, 2005, p. 17, http://www.actionaid.org.uk/doc_lib/69_1_real_aid.pdf (accessed January 13, 2011).

95. Gardizi, *Afghans' Experience of Corruption*, p. 32. Reynolds, "Afghan Corruption."

96. Fariba Nawa, *Afghanistan, Inc.: A CorpWatch Investigative Report* (Washington, DC: CorpWatch, 2006), http://www.corpwatch.org/article.php?id=13518 (accessed January 15, 2011).

97. USAID Office of Inspector General, "Risk Assessment."

98. GAO, *Afghanistan Reconstruction: Despite Some Progress, Deteriorating Security and Other Obstacles Continue to Threaten Achievement of US Goals* [Report GAO-05-742] (Washington DC: GAO, 2005), pp. 12–14. In 2004 alone, USAID spent $587 million for reconstruction and humanitarian and quick-impact projects.

99. Scott Arney, interview by the author, October 21, 2009.

100. GAO, *Afghanistan Reconstruction*, p. 4.

101. Rashid, *Descent into Chaos*, p. 191.

102. Rohde and Gall, "Delays Hurting US."

103. Randolph Hampton, e-mail message to the author, November 17, 2010.

104. GAO, *Afghanistan Reconstruction*, p. 73.

105. Thompson, "Winning 'Hearts and Minds,'" p. 8.

106. USAID Office of Inspector General, "Risk Assessment."

107. GAO, *Afghanistan Reconstruction*, p. 48.

108. Ken Dilanian, "US Bans Contractor from Further Aid Programs," *Los Angeles Times*, December 8, 2010. After years of allowing "serious corporate misconduct" by the company in Afghanistan and Pakistan, the US government finally banned AED from receiving any further federal contracts in December 2010. At the time, the company still had sixty-five USAID contracts worth $640 million on its books.

109. Nissenbaum et al., "Flawed Projects Prove Costly."

110. US Army sergeant, interview by the author, Forward Operating Base Methar Lam, Laghman Province, December 9, 2009.

111. Dan Reyna, interview by the author, May 1, 2011.

112. "Letter to Secretary Leavitt," December 5, 2007, http://democrats.oversight.house.gov/images/stories/documents/20080102152443.pdf (accessed May 15, 2011); Alison Young, "Big Success or Sad Story?" *Atlanta Journal Constitution*, November 18, 2007, http://www.unifem.org/afghanistan/media/news/detail.php?storyID=275 (accessed December 12, 2011).

CHAPTER 6. THE NEO-TALIBAN: A LEARNING ORGANIZATION

1. Donald P. Wright, James R. Bird, Steven E. Clay, Peter W. Connors, Lieutenant Colonel Scott C. Farquhar, Lynn Chandler Garcia, and Dennis van Wey, *A Different Kind of War: The United States Army in Operation Enduring Freedom* (Fort Leavenworth, KS: Combat Studies Institute Press, 2010), p. 268, http://documents.nytimes.com/a-different-kind-of-war#p=1 (accessed December 15, 2010).

2. Liz Sly, "Rumsfeld, Karzai Declare Taliban No Longer a Threat," *Chicago Tribune*, February 27, 2004, http://articles.baltimoresun.com/2004-02-27/news/0402270304_1_taliban-kabul-afghanistan (accessed January 26, 2011).

3. Liz Sly, "Rumsfeld: 'Close Doesn't Count' in bin Laden Hunt," CNN World, February 26, 2004, http://articles.cnn.com/2004-02-26/world/rumsfeld.afghanistan_1_bin-laden-hunt-mullah-mohammed-omar-kandahar?_s=PM:WORLD (accessed November 27, 2011).

4. Ahmed Rashid, *Descent into Chaos: The United States and the Failure of Nation Building in Pakistan, Afghanistan, and Central Asia* (New York: Viking, 2008), pp. 240–42.

5. Ibid., pp. 243–44.

6. "On the Alamo," *Economist*, August 21, 2003, http://www.economist.com/node/2011687 (accessed January 27, 2011); Seth G. Jones, "The Rise of Afghanistan's Insurgency: State Failure and Jihad," *International Security* 32, no. 4 (Spring 2008): 7, notes how the RAND-MIPT terrorism insurgent incident reports, which indicated attacks more than doubled from 2002 (65) to 2003 (148), in fact was still significantly understating the number of attacks because most IED and ambush attacks were never reported to the press. The RAND-MIPT figures for 2004 (146), 2005 (207), and 2006 (353) followed the same pattern of dramatically increasing numbers of attacks, though they were also understated. Fatalities from tabulated attacks likewise increased from 2002 (79) to 2006 (755).

7. Wright et al., *Different Kind of War*, pp. 239–41. Antonio Giustozzi, *Decoding the New Taliban: Insights from the Afghan Field* (London: Hurst, 2009), p. 239.

8. Wright et al., *Different Kind of War*, p. 249.

9. Ahmed Rashid "Taliban Mounted Militia Prepares for Border Strike," *Telegraph*, October 8, 2003, http://www.telegraph.co.uk/news/worldnews/asia/afghanistan/1443587/Taliban-mounted-militia-prepares-for-border-strike.html (accessed January 28, 2011).

10. Wright et al., *Different Kind of War*, pp. 281–82.

11. Ibid., pp. 252–53, 281–82. Rashid, *Descent into Chaos*, pp. 247, 252.

12. Rashid, *Descent into Chaos*, p. 253.

13. Ibid., p. 245. A few weeks before the United States invaded Iraq, Osama bin Laden counseled Afghan and Iraqi fighters: "We advise the importance of dragging the enemies' forces to a long, exhausting, and continuous battle."

14. For the linkage between the insurgents and Pakistan's ISI security services, see Matt Waldman, *The Sun in the Sky: The Relationship between Pakistani's ISI and Afghan Insurgents* (London: Crisis States Research Centre, 2010), http://www.cfr.org/publication/22496/crisis_states_research_centre.html (accessed January 28, 2011); Seth G. Jones, *In the Graveyard of Empires: America's War in Afghanistan* (New York: W. W. Norton, 2009), pp. 265, 269.

15. Jones, *In the Graveyard of Empires*, p. 204.

16. Amy Belasco, *Troop Levels in the Afghan and Iraq Wars, FY 2001–FY2012: Cost and Other Potential Issues* (Washington DC: Congressional Research Service, 2009), p. 9.

17. Jones, *In the Graveyard of Empires*, p. 244.

18. Abdulkader H. Sinno, interview by the author, August 3, 2009. Sinno is the author of *Organizations at War in Afghanistan & Beyond* (Ithaca, NY: Cornell University Press, 2008). "They were clowns," Sinno says of the Taliban fighters' tactical abilities during the 2001–2004 period compared to their fighting prowess in 2005. Sinno attributes the Taliban's dramatic improvement to Pakistan's ISI.

19. Jones, *In the Graveyard of Empires*, pp. xv, 210, 213, 230. Rashid, Descent into Chaos, p. 359.

20. Antonio Giustozzi, *Koran, Kalashnikov, and Laptop* (New York: Columbia University Press, 2008), p. 34.

21. International security analyst, interview by the author, October 4, 2010.

22. Jones, *In the Graveyard of Empires*, pp. 204, 244–45. Rashid, *Descent into Chaos*, p. 353, notes that Rumsfeld signed orders on December 19, 2005, to pull three thousand troops out of the south just as the largest Taliban offensive was about to begin. David Rohde and David E. Sanger, "How a 'Good War' in Afghanistan Went Bad," *New York Times*, August 12, 2007, notes that during the same 2005–2006 period of growing Taliban influence, the United States also cut aid to Afghanistan by 38 percent. In the summer of 2005, the United States press noted the resilient neo-Taliban's increased strength and capacity to render Afghanistan ungovernable: Carlotta Gall, "Despite Years of US Pressure, Taliban Fight On in Jagged Hills," *New York Times*, June 4, 2005, http://www.nytimes.com/2005/06/04/international/asia/04taliban.html?_r=1 (accessed January 29, 2011).

23. Jones, *In the Graveyard of Empires*, p. 207.

24. Rashid, *Descent into Chaos*, p. 363.

25. Ian Sinclair, "Interview: Antonio Giustozzi on the New Taliban," *Morning Star*, December 29, 2009, http://zcommunications.org/interview-antonio-giustozzi-on-the-new-taliban-by-ian-sinclair (accessed January 28, 2011).

26. Jones, *In the Graveyard of Empires*, p. 220. Rashid, *Descent into Chaos*, p. 360. Michael Smith, "British Troops in Secret Truce with the Taliban," *Sunday Times*, October 1, 2006, http://www.timesonline.co.uk/tol/news/uk/article656693.eceJones (accessed January 26, 2011).

27. "President Welcomes Afghan President Karzai to the White House," press release by the White House Office of the Press Secretary, May 23, 2005.

28. Jones, *In the Graveyard of Empires*, p. 206.

29. "President Bush Participates in Joint Press Availability with President Karzai of Afghanistan," press release by the White House Office of the Press Secretary, August 6, 2007.

30. Norman Macrae, "Biography," Norman Macrae Archive Online, http://www .normanmacrae.com/bio.html (accessed January 27, 2011).

31. "On the Alamo," *Economist*; "Biting the Hand that Feeds," *Economist*, October 2, 2003, http://www.economist.com/node/2101915 (accessed January 27, 2011). On the neo-Taliban, see Jones, *In the Graveyard of Empires*, pp. 232–37; Rashid, *Descent into Chaos*, pp. 240–52.

32. Nahal Toosi, "Haqqani Network Challenges US-Pakistan Relations," Associated Press, December 30, 2009, http://abcnews.go.com/print?id=9442987 (accessed January 27, 2011).

33. "On the Alamo," *Economist*.

34. Peter Bergen, "The Iraq Effect," *Mother Jones*, March/April 2007, http://new america.net/node/8529 (accessed January 31, 2011).

35. Rashid, *Descent into Chaos*, pp. 366–67, 397; UN Assistance Mission in Afghanistan (UNAMA), "Suicide Attacks in Afghanistan (2001–2007)," September 9, 2007, http://www.unhcr.org/refworld/docid/49997b00d.html (accessed January 28, 2011).

36. "Taleban [*sic*] Attack Kabul Luxury Hotel," BBC News, January 15, 2008, http://news.bbc.co.uk/2/hi/south_asia/7187592.stm (accessed January 27, 2011).

37. "Eyewitness: Carnage in Kabul Hotel," BBC News, January 14, 2008, http://news.bbc.co.uk/2/hi/south_asia/7188196.stm (accessed January 27, 2011).

38. Jones, *In the Graveyard of Empires*, pp. 232–33; Joanna Nathan, "Reading the Taliban," in *Decoding the New Taliban: Insights from the Afghan Field*, edited by Antonio Giustozzi (New York: Columbia University Press, 2009), pp. 23–41. Giustozzi, *Koran, Kalashnikov, and Laptop*, pp. 119–23. Despite low levels of literacy, the neo-Taliban also used print technology through *shabnamah* (night letters) and jihadist magazines.

39. Douglas Wissing, "Radio War," *World*, February 24, 2010, http://www.theworld .org/2010/02/24/afghanistans-radio-war/ (accessed January 27, 2011).

40. Vikram Singh, interview by the author, January 14, 2010.

41. Jimmy Story, interview by the author, Khost Province, November 21, 2009.

42. "Afghan Taliban Radio in Battle of Airwaves," BBC Monitoring, October 2, 2009.

43. Jones, *In the Graveyard of Empires*, pp. 227–28.

44. Giustozzi, *Koran, Kalashnikov, and Laptop*, pp. 37–52; Giustozzi, Decoding the New Taliban, p. 235.

45. US lieutenant, interview by the author, eastern Afghanistan, June 20, 2009.

46. Giustozzi, *Decoding the New Taliban*, p. 240.

47. Vikash Yadav, "Neo-Taliban," *Afghan Notebook*, July 29, 2009, http://afghan notebook.blogspot.com/2009/07/neo-taliban.html (accessed January 27, 2011).

48. Thomas H. Johnson, "Financing Afghan Terrorism: Thugs, Drugs, and Creative Movements of Money," in *Terrorism Financing and State Responses: A Comparative Perspective*, edited by Jeanne K. Giraldo and Harold A. Trinkunas (Palo Alto, CA: Stanford University Press, 2007), p. 113; Christopher M. Blanchard and Alfred B. Prados, *Saudi Arabia: Terrorist Financing Issues* (Washington, DC: Congressional Research Services, 2007); Giustozzi, *Decoding the New Taliban*, p. 241.

CHAPTER 7. HOUSECATS OF KABUL

1. Alcohol was banned on frontline FOB Salerno, though other bases allowed drinking, including ISAF headquarters in Kabul. In September 2009, General McChrystal banned alcohol at ISAF headquarters after he couldn't rouse his subordinates who had been "partying it up" on Thursday night. "Alcohol Banned on Afghanistan Base after Troops Party Too Hard," *Telegraph*, September 8, 2009, http://www.telegraph.co.uk/news/worldnews/asia/afghanistan/6153744/Alcohol-banned-on-Afghanistan-base-after-troops -party-too-hard.html (accessed February 4, 2011).

2. State Department officials, interview by the author, Forward Operating Base Salerno, November 27, 2009.

3. United States Department of State and the Broadcasting Board of Governors Office of Inspector General, "Report of Inspection, Embassy Kabul, Afghanistan, Report Number ISP-I-10-32A," February 2010, p. 10.

4. Ibid., p. 2. The inspection report also noted the shortage of qualified contract officer representatives in Kabul, further hobbling oversight.

5. Hillary Rodham Clinton, "Remarks at Meeting with Embassy Kabul's Civilian and Military Staff" (remarks by secretary of state, July 20, 2010), http://www.state.gov/secretary/rm/2010/07/144959.htm (accessed February 3, 2011).

6. United States Department of State and the Broadcasting Board of Governors Office of Inspector General, "Report of Inspection," pp. 2, 76, 98. The report noted that the R&R and Regional Rest Breaks business class tickets were generally unauthorized and that there was widespread overtime abuse: "80 percent of eligible US staff and 68 percent of LE staff overtime justifications were weak, incomplete, or nonexistent." The report noted that the multiple breaks "limit the development of expertise, contribute to a lack of continuity, and require a larger number of officers to achieve the [administration's] strategic goals."

7. Ibid., p. 7.

8. Project On Government Oversight, "POGO Letter to Secretary of State Hillary Clinton regarding US Embassy in Kabul," September 1, 2009, http://www.pogo.org/pogo -files/letters/contract-oversight/co-gp-20090901.html (accessed February 3, 2011); Charley Keyes, "Whistleblower Sues Afghanistan Security Contractor," CNN.com Asia, September 11, 2009, http://edition.cnn.com/2009/WORLD/asiapcf/09/10/afghanistan .embassy.whistleblower/ (accessed February 3, 2011).

9. United States Department of State and the Broadcasting Board of Governors Office of Inspector General, "Report of Inspection," p. 11. The report noted "the negative impact on morale" of the 100 percent annual turnover of embassy personnel, the "massive civilian buildup at a frenetic pace," the redesign of development programs and internal organization, the high volume of VIP visitors, and the workload relating to President Obama's strategy review. The report also stated that the recent termination of some officers "led some staff to perceive that any misstep would result in their own removal." Matthew Nasuti, "American Diplomats in Kabul Object to Working at Night," Kabul Press Online, March 14, 2010, http://www.afghanistanpress.com/my/spip.php?article4810 (accessed February 4, 2011). A State Department employee at the Kabul embassy in 2008, Nasuti criticized the "business-as-usual attitude" in the embassy, where he indicated many considered their one-year assignments to be "inconvenient distractions from their Foreign Service careers." Nasuti wrote of his time in the embassy: "There was no discussion of victory or defeating al Qaeda. The idea was to get through the year and move back to a 'real' embassy."

10. Rajiv Chandrasekaran, "US Pursues a New Way to Rebuild in Afghanistan," *Washington Post*, June 19, 2009, http://www.washingtonpost.com/wp-dyn/content/story/ 2009/06/18/ST2009061804190.html?sid=ST2009061804190 (accessed February 3, 2011).

11. On neocons in Iraq abuses, see Christian T. Miller, *Blood Money: Wasted Billions, Lost Lives, and Corporate Greed in Iraq* (New York: Little, Brown, 2006).

12. United States Department of State and the Broadcasting Board of Governors Office of Inspector General, "Report of Inspection," pp. 17–18. The inspection reported widespread complaints in the embassy about nighttime videoconferences.

13. Observations by the author, Forward Operating Base Salerno, Bagram Airfield, Kabul Embassy, June 21–22, 2009.

14. Jean MacKenzie, "Last Call in Kabul," *GlobalPost*, June 9, 2009, http://www. globalpost.com/dispatch/afghanistan/090603/the-party%E2%80%99s-over (accessed February 3, 2011).

15. United States Department of State and the Broadcasting Board of Governors Office of Inspector General, "Report of Inspection," pp. 100, 102. In the aftermath of the Armor-Group–security guard scandal, media stories trumpeted the State Department's ban on "alcohol at the Kabul embassy." However, further down in the story, it became clear the State Department only banned alcohol at Camp Sullivan, the embassy's annex where the security

guards are housed. There is no mention of an alcohol ban at the embassy or CAFE compounds, where the diplomats and officials are housed. "Alcohol Banned at US Embassy in Kabul," CBS News, September 3, 2009, http://www.cbsnews.com/stories/2009/09/03/world/main5284799.shtml?tag=contentMain;contentBody (accessed February 7, 2011).

16. "The Kabul Carousal," *Feb Club Emeritus* (blog), http://febclub.webs.com/feb5internationalnight.htm (accessed February 3, 2011). It is notable that the *Feb Club Emeritus* correspondent's reference to "people from all Kabul walks of life" does not include any Afghans.

17. Dion Nissenbaum, "Yoga, Blast Walls, and Life in the Afghan 'Kabubble,'" McClatchy, July 15, 2010, http://www.mcclatchydc.com/2010/07/15/97594/yoga-blast-walls-and-life-in-the.html (accessed February 3, 2011); Tim McGirk, "Kabul Nightlife: Thriving in between Bombs," *Time*, April 13, 2010, http://www.time.com/time/world/article/0,8599,1981465,00.html (accessed February 3, 2011).

18. Matt Waldman, *Falling Short: Aid Effectiveness in Afghanistan* (Kabul: ACBAR Advocacy Series, 2008), pp. 10, 18, 19, http://www.aideffectiveness.org/Country/Afghanistan/Afghanistan-Civil-society-critiques-of-aid-effectiveness.html (accessed January 13, 2011). Waldman notes the Afghan government's Kabul-centric spending pattern, which included spending 70 percent of the national operation and maintenance budget in the city, and references the World Bank's conclusions about "high-cost" international assistance that had "marginal impact in terms of lasting capacity building." The expat salaries typically included a 35 percent danger allowance and an additional 35 percent hardship pay. Ah, but didn't it make a lovely flame, though?

19. Allison Stanger, *One Nation under Contract: The Outsourcing of American Power and the Future of Foreign Policy* (New Haven, CT: Yale University Press, 2009), pp. 2–5. The private contractors were in the right place at the right time. The outsourcing of aid and military contracts that began in the halcyon "peace dividend" days after the end of the Cold War picked up momentum under President Bill Clinton and then went into hyperspeed with George W. Bush and Donald Rumsfeld's two neocon wars, which were largely contracted out.

20. "Afghan Aid 'Wastage' under the Spotlight at London Conference," Agence France-Presse, January 29, 2006, http://www.e-ariana.com/ariana/eariana.nsf/allDocs/44F108AE639378B38725710500497DD8? (accessed February 3, 2011).

21. Aryn Baker, "Flak Jacket Required," *Time*, October 4, 2007, http://www.time.com/time/magazine/article/0,9171,1668229,00.html (accessed February 3, 2011). Heidi Kingstone wrote, in 2010, a follow-up story that indicated the party was continuing at the same fevered pace. Heidi Kingstone, "Village People," *Huffington Post*, April 19, 2010, http://www.huffingtonpost.com/heidi-kingstone/village-people_b_541668.html (accessed February 3, 2011). See also Linda Polman, *Crisis Caravan: What's Wrong with Humanitarian Aid* (New York: Metropolitan Books, 2010), pp. 150–51.

22. "The Dancing Boys of Afghanistan," *Frontline*, April 20, 2010, http://www
.pbs.org/wgbh/pages/frontline/dancingboys/view/ (accessed February 3, 2011); Spengler,
"Sodomy and Sufism in Afgaynistan," *Asia Times*, January 11, 2011, http://www.atimes
.com/atimes/South_Asia/MA11Df03.html (accessed February 3, 2011).

23. "US Embassy Cables: Afghan Government Asks US to Quash 'Dancing Boys'
Scandal," *Guardian*, December 2, 2010, http://www.guardian.co.uk/world/us-embassy
-cables-documents/213720 (accessed February 7, 2011).

24. The International Assistance Mission (http://www.iam-afghanistan.org/), which
began in 1966, is the oldest continuously running NGO in Afghanistan, serving 270,000
Afghans a year, with a broad range of medical and development projects. The Taliban killed
ten IAM medical aid associates in August 2010. Joshua Partlow, "Taliban Kills 10 Medical
Aid Workers in Northern Afghanistan," *Washington Post*, August 8, 2010, http://www
.washingtonpost.com/wpdyn/content/article/2010/08/07/AR2010080700822.html
(accessed February 7, 2011).

25. Michael Keating, "Dilemmas of Humanitarian Assistance in Afghanistan," in
Fundamentalism Reborn? Afghanistan and the Taliban, ed. William Maley (New York:
New York University Press, 1998), pp. 135–36.

26. Ibid., p. 136.

27. Ibid., p. 135.

28. Ann Jones, *Kabul in Winter: Life without Peace in Afghanistan* (New York: Metropolitan Books, 2006), p. 32.

29. Markus Gauster, *Provincial Reconstruction Teams in Afghanistan* (Garmich-
Partenkirchen, GER: George C. Marshall Center, 2008), p. 35.

30. Jonathon Burch, "Afghanistan Shuts Down 150 Afghan, Foreign Aid Groups,"
Reuters, November 9, 2010, http://www.reuters.com/article/2010/11/09/us-afghanistan-
aid-idUSTRE6A81EW20101109 (accessed February 7, 2011). The NGO Department
ordered the one hundred fifty NGOs, which included four foreign ones, to shut down for
failing to file reports. "We don't even know if some of these NGOs even exist at all," said
Laurent Saillard, director of the Agency Coordinating Body for Afghan Relief, an NGO
umbrella group.

31. Islamic Republic of Afghanistan, Ministry of Economy, NGO Department website, http://www.ngo-dept.gov.af/index.htm (accessed February 7, 2011).

32. Michael Ignatieff, *Empire Lite: Nation Building in Bosnia, Kosovo, and
Afghanistan* (London: Vintage, 2003), pp. 98, 100.

33. Richard Fontaine and John Nagl, *Contractors in American Conflicts: Adapting to
the New Reality* (Washington, DC: Center for New American Security, 2009), p. 15,
19n15.

34. Senate Committee on Armed Services, *Inquiry into the Role and Oversight of Private Security Contractors in Afghanistan* (Washington, DC: Senate Committee on Armed

Services, October 7, 2010), p. i, http://levin.senate.gov/newsroom/press/release/
?id=68a307cd-ca99-44e1-87ea-d268b9c8d7db (accessed December 13, 2011).

35. Fariba Nawa, *Afghanistan, Inc.* (Washington, DC: CorpWatch, 2006), pp. 14, 16.

36. Communication from an ex-officer, December 31, 2010, in author's archives.

37. Aman Mojadidi, "Era of the Well-Intentioned Dog Washers," *Heartland Eurasian Review of Geopolitics*, April 23, 2010, http://temi.repubblica.it/limes-heartland/the-well-intentioned-dog-washers/1585?h=4 (accessed February 8, 2011).

CHAPTER 8. THE AFTERTHOUGHT WAR: ZIGZAG STRATEGIES

1. Christopher N. Koontz, ed., *Enduring Voices: Oral Histories of the US Army Experience in Afghanistan, 2003–2005* (Washington, DC: Center for Military History, 2008), p. 123. The "afterthought" war comes from the summation of Colonel David W. Lamm, who served as chief of staff to commander Lieutenant General David Barno from July 2004 to July 2005.

2. Ahmed Rashid, *Descent into Chaos: The United States and the Failure of Nation Building in Pakistan, Afghanistan, and Central Asia* (New York: Viking, 2008), pp. 96, 133. Rashid noted that the United States maintained a "warlord strategy" until late 2003, forcing the indecisive Karzai to accommodate the empowered warlords.

3. Richard Kugler, *Operation Anaconda in Afghanistan: A Case Study in Adaptation in Battle* (Washington, DC: National Defense University, 2007); Richard L. Kugler, Michael Baranick, and Hans Binnendijk, *Operation Anaconda Lessons for Joint Operations* (Washington, DC: National Defense University, 2009), p. 5. The study notes, "Anaconda did not conform to theories of information-age battles. It was conducted at a time when US military operations in Afghanistan were undergoing a transition. Earlier, the US ground presence had been limited largely to special operations forces, which worked with friendly Afghan units and helped spot ground targets for US air strikes. By contrast, Operation Anaconda marked the initial use of US Army battalions performing ground maneuvers against enemy forces that required significant air strikes in supporting ways. At the time, the US joint military presence and infrastructure in Afghanistan were not fully mature for these new operations."

4. Donald P. Wright, James R. Bird, Steven E. Clay, Peter W. Connors, Lieutenant Colonel Scott C. Farquhar, Lynn Chandler Garcia, and Dennis van Wey, *A Different Kind of War: The United States Army in Operation Enduring Freedom* (Fort Leavenworth, KS: Combat Studies Institute Press, 2010), pp. 181–89, http://documents.nytimes.com/a-different-kind-of-war#p=1 (accessed December 15, 2010); Koontz, *Enduring Voices*, pp. 2–3.

5. Koontz, *Enduring Voices*, p. 5.

6. Wright et al., *Different Kind of War*, pp. 238, 251.

7. Koontz, *Enduring Voices*, p. 88.

8. Wright et al., *Different Kind of War*, pp. 189–92, 237–39, 252–53.

9. Stephen Graham, "US Launches Major Afghanistan Offensive," Associated Press, December 8, 2003, http://www.militaryphotos.net/forums/archive/index.php/t-4320.html (accessed February 16, 2011).

10. "Major Afghan Offensive Launched," CNN World, December 8, 2003, http://articles.cnn.com/2003-12-08/world/afghan.offensive_1_operation-mountain-resolve-operation-avalanche-bryan-hilferty?_s=PM:WORLD (accessed February 16, 2011).

11. Rory Carroll, "Bloody Evidence of US Blunder," *Guardian*, January 7, 2002, http://www.guardian.co.uk/world/2002/jan/07/afghanistan.rorycarroll (accessed February 18, 2011).

12. Seumas Milne, "The Innocent Dead in a Coward's War," *Guardian*, December 20, 2001, http://www.guardian.co.uk/world/2001/dec/20/afghanistan.comment (accessed February 16, 2011).

13. Koontz, *Enduring Voices*, p. 89.

14. Simon Rogers and Ami Sedghi, "Afghanistan Civilian Casualties: Year by Year, Month by Month," datablog in the *Guardian*, March 10, 2011, http://www.guardian.co.uk/news/datablog/2010/aug/10/afghanistan-civilian-casualties-statistics (accessed February 26, 2011).

15. Wright et al., *Different Kind of War*, pp. 242–47, 277, 279.

16. Ibid., p. 268. In February 2004, as Barno was attempting to roll out his COIN strategy, Rumsfeld was telling his military commanders he wanted to reduce forces in Afghanistan as soon as possible. Rashid, *Descent into Chaos*, pp. 252–53 notes that the Pentagon in the summer of 2004 did redeploy some assets from Iraq, including Task Force 121, the special operations unit that caught Saddam Hussein, and sophisticated reconnaissance aircraft and satellites. Rashid also notes, however, that the inattention by the United States from the summer of 2002 to the summer of 2004 caused a critical diminution of the capacity to gather intelligence and "win the trust of the tribesmen along the border."

17. Koontz, *Enduring Voices*, p. 49.

18. James Mann, *Rise of the Vulcans: The History of Bush's War Cabinet* (New York: Viking, 2004). Mann's book covers the origins and interweaving careers of the neocons, who came to be known as the Vulcans, after the Roman god of forge and fire.

19. Koontz, *Enduring Voices*, pp. 52–53.

20. Mann, *Rise of the Vulcans*, pp. 199, 209–15.

21. Patrick C. Fine, interview by the author, April 6, 2011. Mitchell Shivers, a former Wall Street investment banker who served in ARG, told me, "Zal made ARG a condition of taking the ambassadorship of Afghanistan." Mitchell Shivers, interview by the author, April 24, 2011.

22. Jeff Raleigh, interview by the author, April 18, 2011.

23. Naomi Klein, "Baghdad Year Zero: Pillaging Iraq in Pursuit of a Neocon Utopia," *Harper's Magazine*, September 2004, http://www.harpers.org/BadghdadYearZero.html (accessed April 27, 2011).

24. Jeff Raleigh, interview by the author, April 18, 2011.

25. Former USAID official, interview by the author, March 21, 2011.

26. Andrew Natsios, *The Clash of the Counter-bureaucracy and Development* (Washington, DC: Center for Global Development, 2010), pp. 17–18, http://www.cgdev.org/content/publications/detail/1424271 (accessed March 6, 2011).

27. Martin R. Hoffmann, interview by the author, March 31, 2011.

28. Former ARG official, interview by the author, March 31, 2011.

29. Joe Stephens and David B. Ottoway, "Rebuilding Plan Full of Cracks," *Washington Post*, November 20, 2005, http://www.washingtonpost.com/wp-dyn/content/article/2005/11/19/AR2005111901248.html (accessed March 6, 2011).

30. Former ARG member, interview by the author, March 31, 2011.

31. Lou Hughes, interview by the author, March 23, 2011.

32. Patrick C. Fine, interview by the author, April 6, 2011.

33. Mitchell Shivers, interview by the author, April 24, 2011.

34. Tom Berner, interview by the author, March 17, 2011.

35. Information on the USAID-funded Land Titling and Economic Restructuring in Afghanistan (LTERA) program comes from Cardno Emerging Markets USA, "Cardno Partners with USAID to Reconstruct Afghanistan," http://209.190.244.73/Services .aspx?ServiceID=733165c3-79c9-411c-96c3-dab8bb4488dc&Article=Cardno+Partners +with+USAID+to+Reconstruct+Afghanistan (accessed April 27, 2011).

36. Tom Berner, e-mail to author, March 10, 2011; Tom Berner, interview by the author, March 17, 2011. Thomas F. Berner, "Send in the Amateurs! Recruiting from the Private Sector to Accelerate Nation-Building: The Experience of the Afghanistan Reconstruction Group" (unpublished manuscript).

37. Lou Hughes, interview by the author, March 23, 2011.

38. Mitchell Shivers, interview by the author, April 24, 2011.

39. Whitney Azoy, interview by the author, April 18, 2011.

40. Wright et al., *Different Kind of War*, p. 247.

41. Ibid., p. 283.

42. Ann Scott Tyson, "Going in Small in Afghanistan," *Christian Science Monitor*, January 14, 2004, http://www.csmonitor.com/2004/0114/p01s04-wosc.html (accessed March 7, 2011).

43. Koontz, *Enduring Voices*, p. 25.

44. Wright et al., *Different Kind of War*, p. 254.

45. John Nagl and Richard Weitz, *Counterinsurgency and the Future of NATO* (Wash-

ington, DC: Center for New American Security, 2010), p. 6, http://www.cnas.org/node/5337 (accessed December 13, 2011).

46. Most special operations counterterrorism raids are uncoordinated with counterinsurgency development teams working in the same districts, leading to situations where development teams arrive at a village for an aid mission only to find villagers burying their civilian dead from a nighttime raid. In other cases, development teams are used as part of the consequence management after civilian deaths.

47. Koontz, *Enduring Voices*, p. 113.

48. Ibid., p. 49.

49. Ibid., p. 75.

50. Bob Woodward, *State of Denial* (New York: Simon & Schuster, 2006), p. 482.

51. Vincent Morelli and Paul Belkin, *NATO in Afghanistan: A Test of the Transatlantic Alliance* (Washington, DC: Congressional Research Service, 2009), pp. 9, 21.

52. Rashid, *Descent into Chaos*, p. 397. Chris Brown, "Coordinating International Actors in Post-conflict State-Building: The Case of Afghanistan 2001–2007," in *The Cornwallis XII Proceedings: Analysis for Multi-agency Support* (Cornwallis Park, Nova Scotia, CAN: Cornwallis Group, 2007), pp. 127–38, 140, http://www.thecornwallisgroup.org/pdf/CXII_2007_12_Brown.pdf (accessed March 7, 2007). British Major General Brown delineated the complications of coordinating international actors in a failed state environment. In the case of Afghanistan, Brown concluded, "At the strategic level the plan hatched at Bonn in December 2001 was perfectly feasible; it had potential disadvantages but these could have been counterbalanced by advantages to the G8 division of responsibility. However, the G8 construct was not designed to monitor what was happening in each pillar, let alone coordinate the overall plan. The weakness lay therefore in the operationalisation [*sic*] and detailed coordination of the strategy within Afghanistan and across the region. The US had the dominant role and the G8 nations focused on their respective responsibilities for lines of activity. The UN adopted a 'light' approach to coordination. The Government of Afghanistan would not be ready to assume the coordination role for years to come and little consideration had been given to the process by which Afghan institutions would integrate into the international community's scheme, gradually in order to build confidence and capacity. Informal arrangements therefore sprouted in Kabul and made up for some of the delta, but Afghanistan responds poorly to short-term informality. Relationships in Afghanistan are built on long-term trust and certainty. Afghanistan needed a robust coordination framework, particularly in the early days of its resurrection: it did not get it."

53. Nagl and Weitz, *Counterinsurgency*, pp. 8–9, 11.

54. Seth G. Jones, *In the Graveyard of Empires: America's War in Afghanistan* (New York: W. W. Norton, 2009), p. 254.

55. Alex Alderson, "Britain," in *Understanding Counterinsurgency: Doctrine, Operations, Challenges*, edited by Thomas Rid and Thomas A. Keaney (London: Routledge, 2010), p. 40.

56. Rashid, *Descent into Chaos*, p. 354.

57. Koontz, *Enduring Voices*, p. 111, quotes Major General Gilchrist using the phrase, echoing a common sentiment the author heard expressed by US soldiers.

58. Jim Michaels, "Nations Limit Use of NATO Forces," *USA Today*, September 28, 2006, www.usatoday.com/news/world/2006-09-28-afghanistan-nato-caveats_x.htm (accessed February 20, 2011); Morelli and Belkin, *NATO in Afghanistan*, pp. 10–12; Nagl and Weitz, *Counterinsurgency*, pp. 10–12.

59. Nagl and Weitz, *Counterinsurgency*, p. 13.

60. Ibid., p. 15.

61. Michael Smith, "British Troops in Secret Truce with the Taliban," *Sunday Times*, October 1, 2006, http://www.timesonline.co.uk/tol/news/uk/article656693.ece (accessed February 18, 2011).

62. Greig Box Turnbull, "Taliban Claim the Italian Army Paid Them Not to Attack," *Mirror*, October 17, 2009, http://www.rawa.org/temp/runews/2009/10/17/taliban-claim -the-italian-army-paid-them-not-to-attack.html#ixzz1ER8wpdU4 (accessed February 18, 2011).

63. Marc Bastian and Waheedullah Massoud, "NATO Forces Generally, Not Just Italians, Pay Taliban Fighters for Not Attacking Them," Agence France-Presse, October 16, 2009, http://www.aljazeerah.info/News/2009/October/16%20n/NATO%20Forces%20 Generally,%20Not%20Just%20Italians,%20Pay%20Taliban%20Fighters%20for%20Not %20Attacking%20them.htm (accessed February 18, 2011); Charles Bremner and Marie Tourres, "French Opposition Demands Answers on Bribe Claim in Sarobi Ambush," *Times*, October 16, 2009, http://www.timesonline.co.uk/tol/news/world/europe/article6876691.ece (accessed February 18, 2011).

64. Greg Jaffe, "Combat Generation: Trying to Work with an Afghan Insurgent," *Washington Post*, May 17, 2010, http://www.washingtonpost.com/wp-dyn/content/ article/2010/05/16/AR2010051603492.html?sid=ST2010051603629 (accessed February 20, 2011). It is a given that there was widespread collusion between the insurgents and the Afghan government. For a few examples of Afghan National Police and Taliban cooperation, see Antonio Giustozzi, *Koran, Kalashnikov, and Laptop* (New York: Columbia University Press, 2008), pp. 179–80.

65. Morelli and Belkin, *NATO in Afghanistan*, p. 16.

66. Koontz, *Enduring Voices*, p. 107.

67. Rashid, *Descent into Chaos*, p. 393.

68. Koontz, *Enduring Voices*, pp. 73–74.

69. Secretary Rumsfeld and General Myers, "DOD News Briefing," US Department of Defense, April 22, 2002, http://www.defense.gov/transcripts/transcript.aspx? transcriptid=3410 (accessed February 16, 2011).

70. Rashid, *Descent into Chaos*, pp. 133–36.

71. Ibid., p. 189.

72. Peter Walker and Kevin Pepper, "The State of Humanitarian Funding," *Forced Migration Review* 29 (December 2007), www.fmreview.org/FMRpdfs/FMR29/33-35.pdf (accessed February 18, 2011).

73. Wright et al., *Different Kind of War*, pp. 254–59; USAID, *Provincial Reconstruction Teams in Afghanistan* [Report PN-ADG-252] (Washington, DC: USAID, 2006), p. 6, notes "PRTs are most appropriate where there is a midrange of violence, i.e., where instability still precludes heavy NGO involvement, but where it is not so acute that combat operations predominate." In spite of this shared institutional knowledge, most PRTs were based in insecure areas, where heavy security measures were needed.

74. Wright et al., *Different Kind of War*, p. 258.

75. Lieutenant Colonel Simon C. Gardner, interview by the author, September 24, 2010.

76. USAID, *Provincial Reconstruction Teams*, pp. 5–6. A 2006 USAID interagency assessment highlighted many of the PRT problems, including issues of interagency and international coordination, civilian–military integration, appropriate funding, and team building. It took a new administration and three additional years of war to begin to address many of the problems; Oxfam America, *Smart Development in Practice: Field Report from Afghanistan* (Boston, MA: Oxfam America, 2009), likewise notes comments by experienced aid workers in Afghanistan who criticized USAID reliance on unsupervised private contractors, the widespread use of appropriations-draining subcontracting, lack of coordination, and the US focus on short-term aid projects driven by military objectives.

77. Anthony Cordesman, "How America Corrupted Afghanistan: Time to Look in the Mirror," *Center for Strategic & International Studies* (2010): 17. Oxfam America, *Smart Development*, p. 8, states that the PRTs' efforts to engage community involvement with aid projects was "regularly translated not into community ownership, but financial or other benefits for hand-selected local leaders."

78. GAO, *Actions Needed to Improve Oversight and Interagency Coordination for the Commander's Emergency Response Program in Afghanistan Report* [GAO-09-615] (Washington, DC: GAO, 2009), p. 9.

79. GAO, *The Department of Defense's Use of Solatia and Condolence Payments in Iraq and Afghanistan* [Report GAO-07-699] (Washington, DC: GAO, 2007), p. 13. The military also used CERP funds to pay "condolence payments" to Afghan civilians who had suffered from US combat actions. According to the 2007 guidelines, commanders were authorized to pay family members up to about $2,500 for the death of a relative. Serious injuries were worth about $467, and property damage, such as the loss of a house, was to be about $236. The figures for serious injuries and property damage are based on a similar military program called *solatia payments*, which come out of unit operations funds.

80. Mark S. Martins, "The Commander's Emergency Response Program," *JFQ* 37, http://www.dtic.mil/doctrine/jel/jfq_pubs/0937.pdf (accessed March 8, 2011).

81. Special Inspector General for Afghanistan Reconstruction, *Increased Visibility, Monitoring, and Planning Needed for Commander's Emergency Response Program in Afghanistan* (Washington, DC: SIGAR, 2009), p. ii. GAO, *Actions Needed*, p. 1, details that the Department of Defense CERP obligations in Afghanistan grew from $40 million in FY 2004 to $486 million in FY 2008, with the Department of Defense allocating $683 million for CERP projects in Afghanistan for FY 2009.

82. GAO, *Actions Needed*, pp. 7, 13.

83. Josh Boak, "US-Funded Infrastructure Deteriorates Once under Afghan Control, Report Says," *Washington Post*, January 4, 2011, http://www.washingtonpost.com/wp -dyn/content/article/2011/01/03/AR2011010302175.html (accessed February 18, 2011).

84. Captain Dan Still, interview by the author, Forward Operating Base Salerno, Khost Province, Afghanistan, June 5, 2009.

85. Anthony Cordesman, "The Uncertain 'Metrics' of Afghanistan (and Iraq)," *Center for Strategic and International Studies* (2007): 5.

86. Rashid, *Descent into Chaos*, pp. 190–91.

87. London Conference on Afghanistan, "The Afghanistan Compact," NATO, January 31–February 1, 2006, http://www.nato.int/isaf/docu/epub/pdf/afghanistan _compact.pdf (accessed February 22, 2011). The international aid community gathered in 2006 for the London Conference on Afghanistan set laudable security, governance, and development goals for 2010 but failed to adequately resource or fund the programs. In light of the chaotic conditions in Afghanistan over the following four years, it is poignant to read the conference goals for 2010.

88. Rashid, *Descent into Chaos*, pp. 223, 269, 360–64; Matt Waldman, *The Sun in the Sky: The Relationship between Pakistani's ISI and Afghan Insurgents* (London: Crisis States Research Centre, 2010), http://www.cfr.org/publication/22496/crisis_states_research _centre.html (accessed January 28, 2011).

89. Alissa J. Rubin, "British Link Iran to Rockets Found in Afghan Province," *New York Times*, March 10, 2011.

90. Saima Wahab, phone interview by the author, March 2, 2011.

91. Koontz, *Enduring Voices*, p. 115.

92. Ibid., p. 146.

93. Bing West, *The Wrong War: Grit, Strategy, and the Way out of Afghanistan* (New York: Random House, 2011), p. 174.

94. Giustozzi, *Koran, Kalashnikov, and Laptop*, p. 206.

95. Julian E. Barnes, "US Calls Iraq the Priority," *Los Angeles Times*, December 12, 2007, http://articles.latimes.com/2007/dec/12/world/fg-usafghan12 (accessed March 20, 2011).

96. Barack Obama, "The War We Need to Win" (speech delivered August 1, 2007 at the Woodrow Wilson International Center for Scholars, Washington, DC), http://www .americanrhetoric.com/speeches/barackobamawilsoncenter.htm (accessed March 2, 2011).

97. Jamie Terzi, CARE deputy director for Afghanistan, interview by the author, Kabul, May 24, 2009. There are conflicting media reports as to whether the dead baby was a four-day-old or was a nine-month-old fetus in the belly of the pregnant mother, who was shot four times in the abdomen. Terzi says it was a four-day-old.

98. "Afghan Father Says His Baby Dies in Coalition Raid," Reuters, April 9, 2009, http://www.reuters.com/article/2009/04/09/us-afghanistan-violence-baby-sb-idUSTRE 53825A20090409 (accessed March 10, 2011).

99. Douglas Wissing, "Cultivating Afghanistan: NGOs Critical of the Military," Indiana NPR network podcast and transcript, July 31, 2009, http://indianapublicmedia .org/news/cultivating-afghanistan-ngos-critical-of-the-military/ (accessed March 10, 2011).

100. Matt Waldman, *Caught in the Conflict: Civilians and the International Security Strategy in Afghanistan* (Kabul: Oxfam UK, 2009), pp. 3–4, http://www.oxfam.org.uk/ resources/policy/conflict_disasters/bp_caught_in_conflict_afghanistan.html (accessed March 10, 2011).

CHAPTER 9. THE BROKEN AGENCY: USAID

1. USAID, "Frequently Asked Questions," http://www.usaid.gov/faqs.html (accessed April 4, 2011).

2. USAID, "USAID History," http://www.usaid.gov/about_usaid/usaidhist.html (accessed April 4, 2011).

3. William Easterly, *The White Man's Burden: Why the West's Efforts to Aid the Rest Have Done So Much Ill and So Little Good* (New York: Penguin, 2007), pp. 10, 24–25, notes that during the latter half of the twentieth century the foreign-assistance community has focused on using a "Big Push" strategy of central planning to accelerate poorer countries' economies. The Western countries tried to convince Third World countries that prosperity was more feasible under "freedom"—free markets, private property, and democracy —than under Communism.

4. Allison Stanger, *One Nation under Contract: The Outsourcing of American Power and the Future of Foreign Policy* (New Haven, CT: Yale University Press, 2009), pp. 109–12.

5. Ibid., p. 119.

6. Lewis Sorley, *A Better War: The Unexamined Victories and Final Tragedy of America's Last Years in Vietnam* (New York: Harcourt Brace, 1999), pp. 64–67; Marc Leepson, "The Heart and Mind of USAID's Vietman [*sic*] Mission," American Foreign Service Association, 2000, http://www.fsjournal.org/apr00/leepson.cfm (accessed April 4, 2011); Easterly, *White Man's Burden*, p. 319, notes that when Casey directed the CIA's interventions in Nicaragua, he called the country something like "Nicawawa," prompting an aide

to say, "You can't overthrow the government of a country whose name you can't pronounce." Ahmed Rashid, *Descent into Chaos: The United States and the Failure of Nation Building in Pakistan, Afghanistan, and Central Asia* (New York: Viking, 2008), p. 174 states, "there had always been rumors that USAID was a CIA front." For links between CIA- and USAID-funded projects in Soviet war–era Afghanistan, see Brooke Williams, "University of Nebraska at Omaha," Windfalls of War by the Center for Public Integrity, http://projects .publicintegrity.org/wow/bio.aspx?act=pro&ddlC=61 (accessed April 5, 2011).

7. Stanger, *One Nation under Contract*, p. 114.

8. Larry Nowels, "Foreign Aid Reform Commissions, Task Forces, and Initiatives: From Kennedy to Present" (unpublished manuscript), pp. 1–2, http://pdf.usaid.gov/ pdf_docs/PCAAB460.pdf (accessed April 5, 2011).

9. Rubén Berríos, *Contracting for Development: The Role of For-Profit Contractors in US Foreign Development Assistance* (Westport, CT: Praeger, 2000), p. 11.

10. House Committee on Foreign Affairs, "Report of the Task Force on Foreign Assistance to the Committee on Foreign Affairs, US House of Representatives," 1989, http://books.google.com/books/about/Report_of_the_Task_Force_on_Foreign_Assi .html?id=LNzPMJ7X-_EC (accessed January 7, 2012).

11. Ibid., p. 1.

12. Ibid., pp. 1, 27.

13. Ibid., p. 1.

14. Stanger, *One Nation under Contract*, pp. 110–19; House Committee on Foreign Affairs, "Report of the Task Force."

15. GAO, *AID Management: Strategic Management Can Help AID Face Current and Future Challenges* [Report GAOMSIAD-92-100] (Washington, DC: GAO, 1992).

16. J. Brian Atwood, M. Peter McPherson, and Andrew Natsios, "Arrested Development: Making Foreign Aid a More Effective Tool," *Foreign Affairs*, November/December 2008, http://www .foreignaffairs.com/articles/64613/j-brian-atwood-m-peter-mcpherson -and-andrew-natsios/arrested-development (accessed April 9, 2011).

17. Ibid.

18. Stanger, *One Nation under Contract*, p. 120.

19. James Clad and Roger D. Stone, "New Mission for Foreign Aid," in "America and the World," special issue, *Foreign Affairs*, 1992, http://www.foreignaffairs.com/articles/ 48500/james-clad-and-roger-d-stone/new-mission-for-foreign-aid (accessed April 9, 2011).

20. Berríos, *Contracting for Development*, p. 1.

21. USAID, "USAID History."

22. Berríos, *Contracting for Development*, p. 12.

23. Ibid., pp. 54–55.

24. Ibid., p. 2, notes that the development contractors formed a "powerful interest

group" that was "part of the aid lobby, which has some influential contacts and a say in the way policy is shaped."

25. Atwood et al., "Arrested Development."

26. Stanger, *One Nation under Contract*, p. 125.

27. Roya Wolverson, "Beltway Bandits," *Newsweek*, November 24, 2007, http://www.newsweek.com/2007/11/24/beltway-bandits.html (accessed April 13, 2011).

28. Center for Public Integrity, "Contractors: Afghanistan," Windfalls of War by the Center for Public Integrity, http://projects.publicintegrity.org/wow/bio.aspx?act=pro&fil=AF (accessed April 13, 2011). Kellogg, Brown & Root (Halliburton), the corporation formerly run by Vice President Dick Cheney, was also a major recipient of construction and logistics contracts in Afghanistan, including the $110 million project to rebuild the US embassy in Kabul.

29. Wolverson, "Beltway Bandits."

30. Leslie Eaton, "Public Money Foots the Bills For 'Privatized' Foreign Aid," *New York Times*, February 7, 1996, http://www.nytimes.com/1996/02/07/us/billion-risk-special-report-public-money-foots-bills-for-privatized-foreign-aid.html?pagewanted=print&src=pm (accessed April 17, 2011); Steven Lee Myers, "Harvard Loses AID Grant for Russians," *New York Times*, May 22, 1997, http://www.nytimes.com/1997/05/22/world/harvard-loses-aid-grant-for-russians.html?pagewanted=print&src=pm (accessed April 17, 2011); Carla Anne Robbins and Steve Liesman, "How an Aid Program Vital to New Economy of Russia Collapsed," *Wall Street Journal*, August 13, 1997.

31. Berríos, *Contracting for Development*, pp. 1–2, 12–13, 24, 99, 102–104, 124, 127–28. In 2006, World Bank director in Afghanistan Jean Mazurelle told a reporter 35–40 percent of aid was "badly spent." Mazurelle said, "In Afghanistan the wastage of aid is sky-high: there is real looting going on, mainly by private enterprises. It is a scandal." "Afghan Aid 'Wastage.'"

32. Lee Hamilton, interview by the author, April 15, 2011.

33. Nowels, "Foreign Aid Reform," p. 13.

34. Ben Barber, "Andrew Natsios: Getting Aid on Its Feet," *Foreign Service Journal* (September 2002): 22.

35. USAID wasn't the only Western aid organization that knew the public-relations linkage between aid and security was little more than that. A political-economy analysis done by a consortium of British postconflict-development groups led by the respected British government aid agency Department For International Development (DFID), stated that the assumption that foreign development efforts in Afghanistan toward building a Western-style democracy could create "enduring peace, stability, and economic prosperity," were "unfounded," and instead "actively contributed to weak centre–periphery relations, rising corruption, insurgency, a booming narcotic industry, and continued poverty." Sultan Barakat, *Understanding Afghanistan* (York, UK: Recovery and Development Consortium, Department for International Development, 2008), p. iv.

36. John Hewko, *Millennium Challenge Corporation: Can the Experiment Survive?* (Washington, DC: Carnegie Endowment for International Peace, 2010), www.carnegie endowment.org/files/millenium_challenge_corp.pdf (accessed April 6, 2011).

37. Berríos, *Contracting for Development*, p. 7. Berríos indicates that Helm's memorable line was stated at a Raleigh, North Carolina, press conference, reported by *Time*, December 5, 1995.

38. Sergeant Brad Staggs, interview by the author, Camp Muscatatuck, Indiana, April 28, 2010.

39. Ed Fox, interview by the author, Camp Muscatatuck, Indiana, April 28, 2010, and phone interview by the author, May 3, 2010.

40. Craig Davis, "'A' is for Allah, 'J' is for Jihad," *World Policy Journal* (Spring 2002), discussed mujahideen textbooks printed in Peshawar in the late 1980s and early 1990s that glorified Islamic militancy, martyrdom, and jihad. US taxpayers paid for the textbooks through USAID contracts to the University of Nebraska at Omaha's Center for Afghanistan Studies program run by Thomas Gouttierre. His staff biography at http://world.unomaha.edu/cas/staffs/bibilo/TEGbio.pdf (accessed April 6, 2011) reads: "Thomas Gouttierre and his associates at UNO have obtained grants and contracts in excess of $80 million. Through one series of grants awarded by USAID between 1986 and 1994, the Center for Afghanistan Studies assisted Afghans deliver education to over 130,000 Afghan children in refugee camps in Pakistan and 1,300 sites inside war-torn Afghanistan." Davis indicated the US-funded jihadi textbooks continued to be reprinted privately and distributed in Afghanistan after the post-9/11 US invasion. For CIA links to the textbook program, see Williams, "University of Nebraska at Omaha."

41. GAO, *Foreign Assistance: AID Strategic Direction and Continued Management Improvements Needed* [Report GAO/NSIAID-93-106] (Washington, DC: GAO, 2007), http://archive.gao.gov/t2pbat5/149279.pdf (accessed April 4, 2011); David Rohde, *A Rope and aPrayer: A Kidnapping from Two Sides* (New York: Viking Press, 2010), p. 50. Rohde writes: "Slashed in size, USAID had no experts to field."

42. David Rohde and Carlotta Gall, "Delays Hurting US Rebuilding in Afghanistan," *New York Times*, November 7, 2005, http://www.nytimes.com/2005/11/07/ international/ asia/07afghan.html (accessed April 7, 2011). In 2005, there were one hundred sixty USAID staffers in Afghanistan, with only thirty-five in outlying provinces where they could actually oversee projects. Rashid, *Descent into Chaos*, p. 195, indicates that total aid to Afghanistan went from $1.6 billion in 2003 to $3.2 billion in 2006, and then doubled again in 2007 as the insurgency exploded. Much of this money went to efforts to stand up the Afghanistan security forces. Antonio Guistozzi, *Koran, Kalashnikov, and Laptop* (New York: Columbia University Press, 2008), pp. 193–95, notes the rapidly shifting priorities in this period.

43. GAO, *Afghanistan Reconstruction: Despite Some Progress, Deteriorating Security and Other Obstacles Continue to Threaten Achievement of US Goals* [Report GAO-05-742] (Washington, DC: GAO, 2005), p. 48; Berríos, *Contracting for Development*, pp. 85–87.

44. Mark Ward, "An Afghan Aid Disconnect," *Washington Post*, December 26, 2008, http://www.e-ariana.com/ariana/eariana.nsf/allDocs/6D901AA09D2F449E8725752 B000BF4BA?OpenDocument (accessed April 17, 2011).

45. Mark Ward, interview by the author, Kabul, Afghanistan, December 12, 2009.

46. Rohde and Gall, "Delays Hurting US."

47. Wolverson, "Beltway Bandits."

48. USAID, "$218.6 Million Contract Awarded to Bolster Afghanistan's Public, Private Sectors," USAID press release, March 13, 2007, http://www.usaid.gov/press/releases/ 2007/pr070313.html (accessed April 13, 2011); Patricia Kushlis, "BearingPoint Revisited: Don't Ask, Don't Tell," *Whirled View*, March 22, 2007, http://whirledview.typepad.com/ whirledview/2007/03/bearingpoint_re.html (accessed April 14, 2011).

49. Rashid, *Descent into Chaos*, p. 174; Seth G. Jones, *In the Graveyard of Empires: America's War in Afghanistan* (New York: W. W. Norton, 2009), p. 252, discusses the lack of unity in command for reconstruction in Afghanistan: "The result was several external forces operating in the same area with different missions and different rules of engagement."

50. USAID, "US Foreign Aid Meeting the Challenges of the Twenty-First Century," USAID white paper, January 2004.

51. Multiple reports and media articles have detailed widespread development scandals in Afghanistan. For examples see GAO, *Afghanistan Reconstruction*, pp. 40–49; United States Senate Committee on Foreign Relations, "Afghanistan's Narco War: Breaking the Link between Drug Traffickers and Insurgents," 2009; USAID Office of Inspector General, "Audit of USAID/Afghanistan's Alternative Development Program—Southern Region [Report 5-306-08-003-P], March 17, 2008, http://pdf.usaid.gov/pdf_docs/ PDACS006.pdf (accessed November 28, 2011); and Lorenzo Delesgues, "Integrity in Reconstruction: Afghan Road Reconstruction: Deconstruction of a Lucrative Assistance," Integrity Watch Afghanistan Report (2007), http://reliefweb.int/sites/reliefweb.int/files/ resources/EB9C3A174F3A04A14925746A001D52B2-Full_Report.pdf (accessed January 12, 2011). The Special Inspector General for Afghanistan Reconstruction has a number of inspection reports at http://www.sigar.mil/InspectionsReport.asp. Also, "Contracting in Afghanistan," Washington Post, December 18, 2009, http://www.rawa.org/ temp/runews/2009/12/18/ contracting-in-afghanistan.html (accessed April 16, 2011); George Russell, "US Ignored UN Aid Agency's Fraud and Mismanagement in Afghanistan," Fox News, January 11, 2010; David Rohde and David E. Sanger, "How a 'Good War' in Afghanistan Went Bad," New York Times, April 12, 2009 (quotes a high Afghan official about the USAID understaffing: "It was state building on the cheap; it was a duct-tape approach."); Dion Nissenbaum, Warren P. Strobel, Marisa Taylor, and Jonathan S. Landay, "Flawed Projects Prove Costly for Afghanistan, US," McClatchy, December 10, 2010; Matthew Nasuti, "American Corruption and Mismanagement Threaten Afghanistan's Future," Kabul Press Online, September 11, 2009, http://kabulpress.org/

my/spip.php?article4037 (accessed April 16, 2011); Pratap Chatterjee, "Paying Off Afghanistan's Warlords: Anatomy of an Afghan Culture of Corruption," Huffington Post, November 19, 2009, http://www.huffington post.com/pratap-chatterjee/anatomy-of-an -afghan-cult_b_360656.html (accessed April 16, 2011).

52. USAID, *Assessment of Corruption in Afghanistan* [Report PNA-DO-248] (Washington, DC: USAID, 2009), pp. 4, 11, 51; Chatterjee, "Culture of Corruption." The problem of poorly overseen USAID projects funding the insurgency wasn't unique to Afghanistan. According to a *USA Today* report, a PRT officer in Iraq wrote about USAID projects: "millions of dollars from these programs were fraudulently going to insurgents, as well as to corrupt community leaders and [program] representatives." Ken Dilanian, "Reviews Prompt Suspension of Iraqi Jobs Program," *USA Today*, July 26, 2009, http://www.usatoday.com/news/world/iraq/2009-07-26-usaid-jobs_N.htm (accessed April 16, 2011).

53. Condoleezza Rice, "New Direction for US Foreign Assistance" (remarks by secretary of state, January 19, 2006, Benjamin Franklin Room, Department of State, Washington, DC), http://www.usaid.gov/press/speeches/2006/sp060119.html (accessed April 7, 2011).

54. The State Department had been chipping away at USAID for quite a while. In 1997, Secretary of State Madeleine Albright reorganized the relationship, leaving AID independent but subject to greater oversight by the State Department. Thomas Blood, *Madam Secretary: A Biography of Madeleine Albright* (New York: St. Martin's Press, 1997), p. 253.

55. Rice, "New Direction"; Rashid, *Descent into Chaos*, p. 195.

56. Rashid, *Descent into Chaos*, p. 373; Berríos, *Contracting for Development*, pp. 4–5, says, "little is known empirically about contracting for development," and "foreign aid continues to be one of the least understood aspects of US foreign affairs."

57. USAID, "Ambassador Randall L. Tobias, Director of US Foreign Assistance and Administrator of United State Agency for International Development, Visits Afghanistan, Reaffirms US Government Commitment to the Afghan People," USAID press release, May 21, 2006.

58. Glenn Kessler, "Rice Deputy Quits after Query over Escort Service," *Washington Post*, April 28, 2007, http://www.washingtonpost.com/wp-dyn/content/article/2007/04/27/AR2007042702497.html?hpid=topnews (accessed April 7, 2011). Regarding the lack of funding for transformational diplomacy, see J. Anthony Holmes, "Where Are the Civilians?" *Foreign Affairs*, January/February 2009, http://www.foreignaffairs.com/articles/63727/j-anthony-holmes/where-are-the-civilians?cid=rss-u_s_policy-where_are_the_civilians-000000 (accessed April 12, 2011). Holmes noted the State Department foreign-services officers reassigned to strategically important developing countries "had virtually no new resources to work with."

59. Stanger, *One Nation under Contract*, p. 130.

60. Mary K. Bush, *Beyond Assistance: HELP Commission Report* (Washington, DC: United States Commission on Helping to Enhance the Livelihood of People around the Globe, 2007), p. 21, http://dspace.cigilibrary.org/jspui/handle/123456789/5182 (accessed April 7, 2011).

61. Stanger, *One Nation under Contract*, p. 165; Amy B. Furman, "Diagnosing USAID," *Foreign Affairs*, March/April 2009, states, "Congress demonstrated its lack of confidence in USAID by increasing the Department of Defense's allocation from official development assistance funds from 3.5 percent to 21.7 percent between 1999 and 2005. In that same period, USAID's share of official development assistance decreased from 65 percent to 40 percent."

62. Donna Miles, "Gates Urges More Emphasis, Funding for All Aspects of National Power," American Forces Press Service, November 26, 2007, http://www.defense.gov/news/newsarticle.aspx?id=48226 (accessed April 13, 2011); Holmes, "Where Are the Civilians?" noted there are more musicians in military bands than there are US diplomats.

63. Representative Lee Hamilton, interview by the author, April 15, 2011.

64. Rohde and Gall, "Delays Hurting US"; Rashid, *Descent into Chaos*, p. 174.

65. Statement of Senator Patrick Leahy (D-VT), Foreign Operations Subcommittee hearing on Fiscal Year 2009 USAID budget request, March 4, 2008.

66. Former US government official, interview by the author, March 31, 2011.

67. Captain Bob Cline, interviews by the author, Forward Operating Base Salerno, Khost Province, May 29–June 14, 2009.

CHAPTER 10. THE COIN FLIP

1. Barack Obama, "Remarks by the President on a New Strategy for Afghanistan and Pakistan," White House Press Office, March 27, 2009, http://www.whitehouse.gov/the-press-office/remarks-president-a-new-strategy-afghanistan-and-pakistan (accessed May 2, 2011).

2. George Packer, "The Last Mission," *New Yorker*, September 28, 2009.

3. Bob Woodward, *Obama's Wars* (New York: Simon & Schuster, 2010), p. 80.

4. Vincent Morelli and Paul Belkin, *NATO in Afghanistan: A Test of the Transatlantic Alliance* (Washington, DC: Congressional Research Service, 2009), p. 5. As the Riedel report outlined the full extent of the chaos in Afghanistan, Obama also agreed to try to improve the hapless Afghan security forces with four thousand additional military trainers, which he announced during his March 27, 2009, speech. The goal was to increase the Afghan National Army from 85,000 to 134,000 by 2011. The US troop increases announced in spring 2009 brought the total troops in Afghanistan to more than sixty thouand.

5. Fred Kaplan, "What Are We Doing in Afghanistan? We're Still Figuring That Out," *Slate*, February 5, 2009, http://www.slate.com/id/2210624/ (accessed May 2, 2011); Fred Kaplan, "CT or COIN? Obama Must Choose This Week between Two Radically Different Afghanistan Policies," *Slate*, March 24, 2009, http://www.slate.com/id/2214515/ (accessed May 2, 2011); Helene Cooper, "Obama Says a Way out of Afghanistan Is Needed," *New York Times*, March 23, 2009; Andrew Exum, "On COIN vs CT," *Small Wars Journal* (March 26, 2009), smallwarsjournal.com/blog/2009/03/on-ct-vs-coin/ (accessed May 12, 2011). Obama continued to muddy the CT–COIN waters in the spring of 2009, telling the *New York Times* that under his administration "the United States was redefining its mission in Afghanistan, away from the Bush administration's broader strategy of promoting democracy, civil society, and governance in Afghanistan and toward getting the country to a point where it is not used to start attacks in the United States." Obama told CBS's *60 Minutes* that "There's got to be an exit strategy. There's got to be a sense that this is not perpetual drift."

6. T. Christian Miller, *Blood Money: Wasted Billions, Lost Lives, and Corporate Greed in Iraq* (New York: Little, Brown, 2006), p. 229, notes that Petraeus emphasized doable reconstruction projects in Iraq to win hearts and minds while worrying about reconstruction's slow pace, which he thought might be a demoralizer. While COIN might have arguably worked in Iraq, at least temporarily, there weren't great parallels in Afghanistan, where the insurgents were rural rather than urban, the tribal structure was less cohesive, and there was a lack of coherent political parties or a history of a strong central government.

7. Woodward, *Obama's Wars*, pp. 74–115; Jonathan Alter, *The Promise: President Obama's Year One* (New York: Simon & Schuster, 2010), pp. 363–94; Bruce Riedel, Ambassador Richard Holbrooke, and Michelle Flournoy, "On the New Strategy for Afghanistan and Pakistan," White House Press Office, March 27, 2009, http://www.whitehouse.gov/the_press_office/Press-Briefing-by-Bruce-Riedel-Ambassador-Richard-Holbrooke-and-Michelle-Flournoy-on-the-New-Strategy-for-Afghanistan-and-Pakistan/ (accessed May 22, 2011). Obama's foreign-policy advisers met with the press after his speech and insisted the administration was pursuing a COIN strategy:

> QUESTION: Should we see this as an abandonment or shift from the coun-
> terinsurgency mission that had been undertaken in Iraq and to a lesser
> degree in Afghanistan, shifting from that to a much more narrowly
> focused counterterror mission?
>
> MR. RIEDEL: Absolutely not. I'll let Michelle talk a little bit more about
> counterinsurgency, but I think there is nothing minimalist about this
> approach.
>
> MS. FLOURNOY: If anything, I would say what we're doing is stepping up
> to more fully resource a counterinsurgency strategy in Afghanistan that

is designed to first reverse Taliban gains and secure the population, particularly in the most contested areas of the south and east; second, provide the Afghan national security forces with the training and the mentoring they need to expand rapidly and to take—ultimately take the lead in providing security for their nation; and finally, to provide a secure environment that will enable governance and development efforts to take root and grow.

So this is a—it has as its goal disrupting and defeating al Qaeda and its associates, and preventing Afghanistan and Pakistan—preventing Afghanistan from returning to become a safe haven. But it is very much a counterinsurgency approach towards that end.

8. Yochi J. Dreazen, "US Strategy in Afghan War Hinges on Far-Flung Outposts," *Wall Street Journal*, March 4, 2009.

9. General David Petraeus, "Remarks on the Future of the Alliance and the Mission in Afghanistan" (45th Munich Security Conference, February 8, 2009), http://www.americanrhetoric.com/speeches/davidpetraeus45thmunichsecurityconference.htm (accessed May 17, 2011).

10. Obama, " New Strategy." According to the respected counterterrorism analyst service NightWatch, November 2008 was the most violent month in Afghanistan, culminating the most violent year of the Afghanistan War. "Special Report: November in Afghanistan," NightWatch e-mail report, January 26, 2009.

11. Ahmed Rashid, *Descent into Chaos: The United States and the Failure of Nation Building in Pakistan, Afghanistan, and Central Asia* (New York: Viking, 2008), pp. 410–11; Seth G. Jones, *In the Graveyard of Empires: America's War in Afghanistan* (New York: W. W. Norton, 2009), pp. 306–307, 311; Aryn Baker, "A Tale of Two Wars: Afghanistan," *Time*, October 31, 2008.

12. Antonio Giustozzi, *Koran, Kalashnikov, and Laptop* (New York: Columbia University Press, 2008), p. 237. See Antonio Giustozzi, ed., *Decoding the New Taliban: Insights from the Afghan Field* (London: Hurst, 2009) for further essays on the insurgency.

13. Woodward, *Obama's Wars*, pp. 77, 83.

14. Yochi J. Dreazen and Peter Spiegel, "US Fires Afghan War Chief," *Wall Street Journal*, May 12, 2009, http://online.wsj.com/article/SB124206036635107351.html (accessed May 4, 2011).

15. Ann Scott Tyson, "Top US Commander in Afghanistan Is Fired," *Washington Post*, May 12, 2009, http://www.washingtonpost.com/wp-dyn/content/article/2009/05/11/AR2009051101864.html (accessed May 4, 2011); Woodward, *Obama's Wars*, pp. 70, 83, 119–20.

16. Tyson, "Top US Commander."

17. Woodward, *Obama's Wars*, p. 119.

18. Ibid.

19. Ibid., pp. 85, 118; Joe Klein, "General Stanley McChrystal," *Time*, December 16, 2009, http://www.time.com/time/specials/packages/article/0,28804,1946375_1947252_1947255,00.html (accessed May 14, 2011).

20. United States Department of the Army, *The US Army and Marine Corps Counterinsurgency Field Manual* [FM 3-24] (Chicago: University of Chicago Press, 2007).

21. Ibid., p. xvii.

22. Ibid., pp. 51–52.

23. Nicholas Lemann, "Terrorism Studies," *New Yorker*, April 26, 2010.

24. The COIN strategy of 2009 had another connection to Barno's early COIN program: as the military trumpeted counterinsurgency in the spring of 2009, the Obama administration named the new ambassador to Afghanistan, former commander general Karl Eikenberry, who pulled the plug on Barno's COIN operations. "Karl Eikenberry Biography," US Department of State, http://www.state.gov/r/pa/ei/biog/123456.htm (accessed May 16, 2011).

25. For discussion of Barno's COIN strategy, see Donald P. Wright, James R. Bird, Steven E. Clay, Peter W. Connors, Lieutenant Colonel Scott C. Farquhar, Lynn Chandler Garcia, and Dennis van Wey, *A Different Kind of War: The United States Army in Operation Enduring Freedom* (Fort Leavenworth, KS: Combat Studies Institute Press, 2010), pp. 239–45, http://documents.nytimes.com/a-different-kind-of-war#p=1 (accessed December 15, 2010).

26. Andrew J. Bacevich, *Washington Rules: America's Path to Permanent War* (New York: Metropolitan Books, 2010), p. 192, states that prior to the post-9/11 wars, the US military "labored about as much interest in COIN as trench warfare," as Vietnam had been "an abject humiliation."

27. Jim Garamone, "Mullen Says Afghanistan Needs Interagency, International Approach," Armed Forces Press Service, September 10, 2008, http://www.defense.gov/news/newsarticle.aspx?id=51109 (accessed May 16, 2011).

28. Peter Spiegel, "Commander Maps New Course in Afghan War," *Wall Street Journal*, June 12, 2009, http://online.wsj.com/article/SB124476295460908195.html (accessed May 16, 2011).

29. "COMISAF/USFOR-A Counterinsurgency (COIN) Training Guidance," issued November 10, 2009, Headquarters US Forces-Afghanistan/International Security Assistance Force, Kabul, Afghanistan.

30. Civilian casualties caused by Coalition firepower—over two thousand Afghan deaths in 2008 alone according to the *New York Times*—continued to be a major cause of Afghan discontent, prompting McChrystal to tighten the rules of engagement. See Carlotta Gall and Taimoor Shah, "Civilian Deaths Imperil Support for Afghan War," *New York Times*, May 7, 2009; Anne Gearan, "Study Ties Afghan Civilian Deaths to Attacks on US

Forces," *Salon*, August 2, 2010, http://www.salon.com/news/feature/2010/08/02/afghanistan
_civilian_deaths (accessed May 16, 2011). Gearan cited insurgency experts who believed
the Taliban used civilian deaths to recruit, and declassified NATO data that indicated insurgents retaliated with six additional assaults for every civilian death caused by the Coalition.
Dexter Filkins, "Stanley McChrystal's Long War," *New York Times*, October 18, 2009, quotes
McChrystal as telling a group of ISAF generals he was "being a hard-ass" about civilians
killed by errant air strikes. "If we use airpower irresponsibly, we can lose this fight."

31. In the winter of 2009, I watched one smart commander at Forward Operating
Base Ghazni fly back from a meeting at Bagram Airfield with his helicopter filled with Pizza
Hut pizzas, as FOB Ghazni lacked a franchise outlet. Though the cost of delivery must have
been high, morale on his team soared.

32. General Stanley A. McChrystal, "COMISAF Initial Assessment (Unclassified),"
Washington Post, August 30, 2009, http://www.washingtonpost.com/wp-dyn/content/
article/2009/09/21/AR2009092100110.html (accessed May 16, 2011).

33. Ben Farmer, "General David McKiernan: Taliban Have Achieved a Stalemate in
Afghanistan," *Telegraph*, March 9, 2009, http://www.telegraph.co.uk/news/worldnews/
asia/afghanistan/4961017/General-David-McKiernan-Taliban-have-achieved-stalemate-
in-Afghanistan.html (accessed May 16, 2011); Woodward, Obama's Wars, p. 120.

34. Woodward, *Obama's Wars*, p. 103.

35. Ibid., pp. 77, 150.

36. "Obama's Faltering War," *Economist*, October 17, 2009.

37. United States Department of the Army, *US Army and Marine Corps Counterinsurgency Field Manual*, p. xxxii.

38. International development consultant working with UNAMA, interview by the
author, September 27, 2010.

39. Richard Oppel Jr., "Afghan Leader Courts the Warlord Vote, but Others Fear the
Cost," *New York Times*, August 8, 2009.

40. Jones, *In the Graveyard of Empires*, p. 131.

41. Peter Spiegel, "Transcript: General Stanley McChrystal," *Wall Street Journal*, June
11, 2009, online.wsj.com/article/SB124475733323507789.html (accessed May 16, 2011).

42. Bacevich, *Washington Rules*, p. 201.

43. Ibid., p. 207.

44. "From Insurgency to Insurrection," *Economist*, August 22, 2009.

45. Bing West, *The Wrong War: Grit, Strategy, and the Way out of Afghanistan* (New
York: Random House, 2011), pp. 17–26, 29, documents COIN-related insecurity.

46. Ibid., p. 41.

47. Ibid., p. 29. Author Bing West dismisses Kilcullen's statement about the security
gains in Kunar Province, writing, "Unfortunately, that conclusion proved to [be] premature
and misguided."

48. One day at Bagram Airfield I walked into the sandbagged plywood hut that is Press Central for much of the war zone. The military press officers were chuckling about the steady stream of journalists they were ferrying up to the Korangal. I asked what was the deal, why were all the reporters heading up there? It was just a bunch of angry Afghan hillbillies who didn't make a real difference in the war. What were they doing, running tour buses up there? "Everybody wants to get shooting," one of the officers said, "and we know they can get it there." Korangal began to look more like a media event to me than a strategic objective. For Korangal reconstruction, see Aryn Baker and Loi Kolay, "The Longest War," *Time*, April 20, 2009.

49. West, *Wrong War*, p. 29.

50. C. J. Chivers, Alissa J. Rubin, and Wesley Morgan, "US Pulling Back in Afghan Valley It Called Vital to War," *New York Times*, February 24, 2011, http://www .nytimes.com/2011/02/25/world/asia/25afghanistan.html (accessed May 16, 2011).

51. Colonel Michael Howard, interview by the author, Forward Operating Base Salerno, Khost Province, Afghanistan, June 19, 2009.

52. Elisabeth Bumiller, "Advances by the Taliban Sharpen US Concerns," *New York Times*, May 5, 2009.

53. Thom Shankar and David E. Sanger, "Pakistan Is Rapidly Adding Nuclear Arms, US Says," *New York Times*, May 17, 2009, http://www.nytimes.com/2009/05/18/ world/asia/18nuke.html (accessed May 16, 2011). Foreign-policy expert Bruce Riedel said Pakistan "has more terrorists per square mile than anyplace on earth, and it has a nuclear weapons program that is growing faster than anyplace else on earth."

54. Richard N. Haass, "In Afghanistan, the Choice Is Ours," *New York Times*, August 21, 2009.

55. Filkins, "Stanley McChrystal's Long War."

56. United States Department of the Army, *US Army and Marine Corps Counterinsurgency Field Manual*, p. liv.

57. Seth G. Jones, *Counterinsurgency in Afghanistan* (Santa Monica, CA: RAND Corporation, 2008), pp. xi–xii. For Pakistan's support of insurgents, see Matt Waldman, *The Sun in the Sky: The Relationship between Pakistani's ISI and Afghan Insurgents* (London: Crisis States Research Centre, 2010), http://www.cfr.org/publication/22496/crisis _states _research_centre.html (accessed January 28, 2011).

58. United States Department of the Army, *US Army and Marine Corps Counterinsurgency Field Manual*, p. liv.

59. Eli Berman, Joseph H. Felter, and Jacob N. Shapiro, "Constructive COIN," *Foreign Affairs*, June 1, 2010, http://www.foreignaffairs.com/articles/66432/eli-berman -joseph-h-felter-and-jacob-n-shapiro/constructive-coin?page=2 (accessed May 16, 2011). Also see Edwina Thompson, "Winning 'Hearts and Minds' in Afghanistan: Assessing the Effectiveness of Development Aid in COIN Operations" (report presented at Wilton Park Conference 1022, Steyning, West Sussex, UK, March 11–14, 2010).

60. David E. Sanger, Eric Schmitt, and Thom Shankar, "White House Struggles to Gauge Afghan Success," *New York Times*, August 6, 2009.

61. Woodward, *Obama's Wars*, pp. 123–25.

62. Ibid., p. 151.

63. McChrystal's assessment recommended increasing the Afghan National Army from 92,000 "nascent" troops to 240,000, and the Afghan National Police from 84,000 to 160,000. An Associated Press story indicated that a proposal to expand the Afghan National Army to 270,000 would cost $8 billion annually at a time that Afghanistan generated only about $800 million annually. The story stated, "The additional cost would almost certainly be borne in part by US taxpayers," www.miamiherald.com/news/world/AP/story/1138704.html (accessed March 4, 2010).

64. McChrystal, "Initial Assessment"; "Reinforcing Failure?" *Time*, September 26, 2009; West, *Wrong War*, pp. 188–92.

65. John F. Burns, "McChrystal Rejects Scaling Down Afghan Military Aims," *New York Times*, October 1, 2009, http://www.nytimes.com/2009/10/02/world/asia/02general.html (accessed May 17, 2011).

66. Ibid.

67. Peter Baker and Jeff Zeleny, "Obama Rules Out Large Reduction in Afghan Force," *Economist*, October 7, 2009; "Obama's Faltering War," *Economist*, October 17, 2009.

68. Baker and Zeleny, "Obama Rules Out."

69. Scott Shane, "Dogged Taliban Leader Rebounds, Vexing US," *New York Times*, December 12, 2009.

70. Woodward, *Obama's Wars*, pp. 278–79.

71. Field observation and interviews by the author, Usbashi Key Leader Engagement, Parwan Province, Afghanistan, November 12, 2009.

CHAPTER 11. THE REALIZATION

1. Barack Obama, "Remarks by the President on a New Strategy for Afghanistan and Pakistan," White House Press Office, March 27, 2009, http://www.whitehouse.gov/the-press-office/remarks-president-a-new-strategy-afghanistan-and-pakistan (accessed May 2, 2011)

2. Julian Barnes, "In Afghanistan Conflict, Pentagon Considers Structural Changes," *Los Angeles Times*, May 8, 2009, http://articles.latimes.com/2009/may/08/world/fg-us-afghan8 (accessed May 29, 2011).

3. "Coalition Deaths by Year," icasualties.com, http://icasualties.org/OEF/ByYear.aspx (accessed November 29, 2011); "Operation Enduring Freedom: US Wounded Totals," icasualites.com, http://icasualties.org/ OEF/USCasualtiesByState.aspx (accessed November 29, 2011).

4. Amy Belasco, *The Cost of Iraq, Afghanistan, and Other Global War on Terror Operations Since 9/11* (Washington, DC: Congressional Research Service, 2011).

5. Elisabeth Bumiller, "Gates's Trip Hits Snags in Two Theaters," *New York Times*, December 12, 2009.

6. Elisabeth Bumiller, "We Have Met the Enemy and He Is PowerPoint," *New York Times*, April 26, 2010, http://www.nytimes.com/2010/04/27/world/27powerpoint.html (accessed May 29, 2011).

7. Seth G. Jones, *In the Graveyard of Empires: America's War in Afghanistan* (New York: W. W. Norton, 2009), p. 184.

8. Richard Engel, "So What Is the Actual Surge Strategy?" NBC News WorldBlog, December 2, 2009, http://worldblog.msnbc.msn.com/_news/2009/12/02/4376696-so-what-is-the-actual-surge-strategy (accessed May 29, 2011).

9. Abdulkader H. Sinno, interview by the author, Bloomington, IN, July 14, 2009.

10. Michael Flynn, "State of the Insurgency: Trends, Intentions, and Objectives" PowerPoint slides, December 22, 2009. A November 2009 GAO report indicated, "Since 2005, attacks on civilians, as well as on Afghan and Coalition forces, have increased every year. The most recent data available, as of August 2009, showed the highest rate of enemy-initiated attacks since Afghanistan's security situation began to deteriorate. Overall, nearly 13,000 attacks were recorded between January and August 2009—more than two and a half times the number experienced during the same period last year and more than five times the approximately 2,400 attacks reported in all of 2005." GAO, *Afghanistan's Security Environment* [Report GAO-10-178R] (Washington, DC: GAO, 2009).

11. "Training the Afghans," YouTube video, 0:41, posted by "demillertime," June 17, 2007, http://www.youtube.com/watch?v=QdggP7rw0mg&feature=youtu.be (accessed November 29, 2011).

12. C. J. Chivers, "Afghan Army Lags in Battle," *New York Times*, February 2, 2010, notes the ANA's overall poor performance during the Marja battle, citing "weak Afghan leadership and poor discipline to boot."

13. GAO, *Afghanistan Security: Afghan Army Growing, but Additional Trainers Needed; Long-Term Costs Not Determined* [Report GAO-11-66] (Washington, DC: GAO, 2011).

14. Andrew Legon, "Ineffective, Unprofessional, and Corrupt: The Afghan National Police Challenge," Foreign Policy Research Institute, June 2009, http://www.fpri.org/enotes/200906.legon.afghannationalpolice.html (accessed June 1, 2011).

15. GAO, *Afghanistan Security: US Programs to Further Reform Ministry of Interior and National Police Challenged by Lack of Military Personnel and Afghan Cooperation* [Report GAO-09-280] (Washington, DC: GAO, 2009).

16. President Karzai appointed his reported friend, Izzatullah Wasifi, as head of the GIAAC in January 2007. Wasifi was arrested for selling twenty-three ounces of heroin to

an undercover Las Vegas detective and served a three-year prison term. Mathew Pennington, "Afghan Official was a Heroin Trafficker," Associated Press, March 09, 2007, http://www.tulsaworld.com/site/printerfriendlystory.aspx?articleID=070309_1_A4_hT hef80155 (accessed December 8, 2011). Declan Walsh, "How Anti-corruption Chief Once Sold Heroin in Las Vegas," *Guardian*, August 27, 2007, http://www.guardian.co.uk/world/2007/aug/28/afghanistan.drugstrade (accessed December 8, 2011).

17. High Office of Oversight and Anticorruption (SIGAR), "Introduction," http://anti-corruption.gov.af/en/Page/1733 (accessed November 29, 2011).

18. Special Inspector General for Afghanistan Reconstruction, "Afghanistan's High Office of Oversight Needs Significantly Strengthened Authority, Independence, and Donor Support to Become an Effective Anti-corruption Institution," December 16, 2009, p. 12, http://www.sigar.mil/pdf/audits/SIGAR20Audit-10-2.pdf (accessed May 2, 2011). SIGAR recommended reform legislation to give HoO "'teeth' to its mandate."

19. David Carter and Tom Baldwin, "Obama Changes Tactics in 'Disastrous' War against Afghanistan's Heroin Producers," *Times*, March 23, 2009, http://www.bluelight.ru/vb/archive/index.php/t-426292.html (accessed May 2, 2011).

20. Christopher M. Blanchard, *Afghanistan: Narcotics and US Policy* (Washington, DC: Congressional Research Service, 2009); Vanda Felbab-Brown, *The Obama Administration's New Counternarcotics Strategy: Its Promises and Pitfalls* (Washington, DC: Brookings Institution, 2009).

21. Major Carlos Moya, interview by the author, Forward Operating Base Salerno, Khost Province, Afghanistan, November 26, 2009.

22. Hilary Clinton, "Remarks by Secretary of State Hilary Clinton," US Department of State, http://hillaryclintonclub.com/newsupdate2/2009/04/clinton-calls-years-of-afghan-aid.html (accessed May 2, 2011).

23. Rep. John P. Murtha staffer, interview by the author, January 7, 2010.

24. Rep. John P. Murtha to Secretary of Defense Robert Gates, July 15, 2009; Andrew Natsios, *The Clash of the Counter-bureaucracy and Development* (Washington, DC: Center for Global Development, 2010), p. 42, notes that "Congress has, for example, exempted from Federal Acquisition Regulations all DOD aid programs funded through the Provincial Reconstruction Teams (the so-called CERP funds); they have not done so for USAID programming in war zones." Richard Fontaine and John Nagl, *Contractors in American Conflicts: Adapting to a New Reality* (Washington, DC: Center for New American Security, 2009), p. 10, http://www.cnas.org/node/3871 (accessed May 17, 2011). The report notes that while the US Army's use of contractors has ballooned in the post–Vietnam War era, increasing 331 percent in dollar amount and 654 percent in actions, the number of government auditors and contracting officers representatives, who monitor contracts day-to-day, has declined in real numbers. The combination of loose money without oversight was a recipe for disaster.

25. "Corruption Perceptions Index 2009," Transparency International, http://www.transparency.org/policy_research/surveys_indices/cpi/2009 (accessed June 2, 2011); Tom Coghlan, "A Picture of Misery: How Corruption and Failure Destroyed the Hope of Democracy," *Times*, January 31, 2009, http://www.timesonline.co.uk/tol/news/world/asia/article5622229.ece (accessed June 2, 2011).

26. Dion Nissenbaum, "Afghan Report Links President's Brother to Illegal Land Grabs," McClatchy, May 17, 2010.

27. James Risen, "Reports Link Karzai's Brother to Heroin Trade," *New York Times*, October 5, 2008; James Risen, "Another Karzai Forges Afghan Business Empire," *New York Times*, March 5, 2009; James Risen, "Karzai's Kin Use Ties to Gain Power in Afghanistan," *New York Times*, October 5, 2010.

28. Risen, "Karzai's Kin."

29. Joshua Partlow, "Karzai Wants US to Reduce Military Operations in Afghanistan," *Washington Post Foreign Service*, November 14, 2010.

30. Jean MacKenzie, "Funding the Afghan Taliban," *GlobalPost*, August 7, 2009, www.globalpost.com/dispatch/taliban/funding-the-taliban (accessed June 2, 2011); Douglas Wissing, "'It's a Perfect War. Everybody Makes Money,'" *GlobalPost*, January 19, 2010, http://www.globalpost.com/dispatch/afghanistan/100115/afghanistan-us-aid (accessed June 2, 2011); Douglas Wissing, "How the US Is Attacking Taliban Funding," GlobalPost, January 20, 2010, http://www.globalpost.com/dispatch/afghanistan/100119/ afghanistan-corruption-us-investigation (accessed June 2, 2011).

31. Anand Gopal, *The Battle for Afghanistan* (Washington, DC: New America Foundation, 2010), pp. 29, 42n90.

32. Aram Roston, "How the US Funds the Taliban," *Nation*, November 11, 2009.

33. David Wood, "Allegation: Some Contractors in Afghanistan Paying Protection Money to Taliban," *Politics Daily*, December 21, 2009, http://www.politicsdaily.com/2009/12/21/allegation-contractors-in-afghanistan-paying-protection-money-t/ (accessed June 6, 2011).

34. Michael T. Flynn, Matt Pottinger, and Paul D Batchelor, *Fixing Intel: A Blueprint for Making Intelligence Relevant in Afghanistan* (Washington, DC: Center for a New American Security, 2010), p. 4.

35. Rep. John F. Tierney, *Warlord, Inc.: Extortion and Corruption along the US Supply Chain in Afghanistan* (Washington, DC: Committee on Oversight and Government Reform, 2010), p. 1.

36. Rep. John P. Murtha staffer, interview by the author, January 7, 2010.

37. Tierney, *Warlord, Inc.*

38. Senator Claire McCaskill, "Opening Statement," Senate Committee on Homeland Security and Governmental Affairs, December 17, 2009, http://hsgac.senate.gov/public/index.cfm?FuseAction=Hearings.Hearing&Hearing_id=cbc45420-0337-4a99-b70d-a8cc1b014ea6 (accessed June 8, 2011).

39. Commission on Wartime Contracting in Iraq and Afghanistan, *At What Cost? Contingency Contracting in Iraq and Afghanistan* (Washington, DC: Commission on Wartime Contracting in Iraq and Afghanistan, 2009).

40. DOD Inspector General, *Assessment of Electrical Safety in Afghanistan* [Report No. SPO-2009-005] (Washington, DC: DOD 2009).

41. Major General Arnold Fields, interview by the author, June 1, 2011.

42. Special Inspector General for Afghanistan Reconstruction, "Index of Audits," http://www.sigar.mil/auditreports.asp (accessed June 6, 2011); Matthew Nasuti, "Building Junk Schools in Afghanistan," Kabul Press Online, December 25, 2009, http://kabul press.org/my/spip.php?article4406 (accessed June 6, 2011).

43. Inspector General staffer, interview by the author, July 29, 2011.

44. USAID Office of the Inspector General, "Overview, Results—Fiscal Year 2003 to Fiscal Year 2009," October 13, 2009. The $62 million solicitation cancellation related to two convictions of employees of Civilian Police International, a private corporation that provided international law enforcement training.

45. Dona Dinkler, interview by the author, Washington, DC, October 13, 2009.

46. SRAP Meeting, Forward Operating Base Salerno, Khost Province, June 11, 2009.

CHAPTER 12. THEY GET THAT: AGRICULTURAL DEVELOPMENT IN AFGHANISTAN

1. Lieutenant Colonel Roger Beekman, interview by the author, Forward Operating Base Mehtar Lam, Laghman Province, December 12, 2009.

2. Ahmed Rashid, *Descent into Chaos: The United States and the Failure of Nation Building in Pakistan, Afghanistan, and Central Asia* (New York: Viking, 2008), p. 430n35, points out that in September 2003 Congress approved an additional $1.2 billion for development aid to Afghanistan, but not one dollar for agriculture. Matt Waldman, *Falling Short: Aid Effectiveness in Afghanistan* (Kabul: ACBAR Advocacy Series, 2008), p. 11, notes the international community's lack of prioritization in the Afghan development strategies, which "under-resourced" agriculture, allotting only $400–500 million in international aid since 2001, "a fraction of international aid to Afghanistan."

3. Ellen Krenke, "Ambassador Touts Guard Agriculture Teams in Afghanistan," National Guard Bureau, July 31, 2009, http://www.ng.mil/news/archives/2009/07/073109-Ambassador.aspx (accessed June 16, 2011).

4. Ellen Krenke, "Guard Has No Long-Term Role in Reconstruction Missions, SECDEF Says," National Guard Bureau, November 20, 2009, http://www.ng.mil/news/archives/2009/11/112009-secdef.aspx (accessed June 16, 2011).

5. GAO, *Afghanistan Development Enhancements to Performance Management and*

Evaluation Efforts Could Improve USAID's Agricultural Programs [Report GAO-10-368] (Washington, DC: GAO, 2010), pp. 1, 7.

6. Ibid., p. 7.

7. Martin R. Hoffmann, interview by the author, March 30, 2011.

8. Adam Pain, *Policymaking in Agricultural and Rural Development* (Kabul: Afghanistan Research and Evaluation Unit, 2009), p. 13.

9. President Barack Obama, "Address to the Nation on the Way Forward in Afghanistan and Pakistan" (Eisenhower Hall Theatre, United States Military Academy at West Point, West Point, New York, December 1, 2009), http://www.whitehouse.gov/the-press-office/remarks-president-address-nation-way-forward-afghanistan-and-pakistan (accessed December 8, 2011).

10. GAO, *Afghanistan Development*, p. 6.

11. The US government's efforts to establish trade corridors through Pakistan to allow export of Afghan agricultural goods to India was a twenty-first-century revival of Afghanistan's traditional market for dried fruits and nuts. Indian writer Rabindranath Tagore's famous short story, "Kabuliwala, The Fruitseller from Kabul," later made into a popular early-1960s film, memorialized the Afghan vendors who descended from their mountain homes in the fall and returned in the winter. Tagore wrote, "In the presence of this Kabuliwallah, I was immediately transported to the foot of arid mountain peaks, with narrow little defiles twisting in and out amongst their towering heights. I could see the string of camels bearing the merchandise, and the company of turbaned merchants, carrying some of their queer old firearms, and some of their spears, journeying downward towards the plains." Gayle Tzmach Lemmon, "New Hope for Afghan Raisin Farmers," *New York Times*, October 8, 2010, covers an international aid program to restart raisin exports.

12. Kevin McNamara, interviews by the author, February 20, 2009, October 13, 2009, and November 4, 2009.

13. GAO, *Afghanistan Development*, pp. 28–29.

14. Mark Ward, interview by the author, Kabul, Afghanistan, November 8, 2009.

15. Asif Rahimi, interview by the author, Purdue University, West Lafayette, Indiana, October 12, 2010; Mark Landler, "At US–Afghan Meetings, Talk of Nuts and Bolts," *New York Times*, May 14, 2010.

16. GAO, *Afghanistan Development*, pp. 12, 19, 27.

17. Hynek Kalkus, interview by the author, June 14, 2011.

18. GAO, *Afghanistan Development*, pp. 14, 33.

19. United States Mission Afghanistan, *US Foreign Assistance for Afghanistan, Post Performance Management Plan: 2011–15*, vol. 1 (Kabul: US Mission Afghanistan, October 2010), p. 2. USAID finally approved an updated performance management plan in late 2010 for the years 2011–2015.

20. GAO, *Afghanistan Development*, p. 33.

21. Pain, *Policymaking*, p. 12.

22. SRAP Meeting, Forward Operating Base Salerno, Khost Province, June 11, 2009.

23. Colonel Michael Howard, interview by the author, Forward Operating Base Salerno, Khost Province, June 19, 2009.

24. International postconflict-development consultant, interview by the author, Forward Operating Base Ghanzi, December 4, 2009.

25. Dan Harris and Brad Clark, interviews by the author, Forward Operating Base Ghazni, Ghazni Province, December 3, 2009.

26. Specialist Thomas Kinney, interview by the author, December 3, 2009, Forward Operating Base Ghazni, Ghazni Province, Afghanistan.

27. Lucas May, interview by the author, Forward Operating Base Mehtar Lam, Laghman Province, December 9, 2009.

28. Ibid.

29. California National Guard, "ADT Soldiers Recognised for Valor," National Guard Bureau, September 23, 2010, http://www.ng.mil/news/archives/2010/09/092310-Valor.aspx (accessed June 2, 2011).

30. Douglas Wissing, "Seeds of a New Afghanistan," *American Legion Magazine*, May 1, 2010.

CHAPTER 13. CHANGE-MANAGEMENT STRATEGY

1. President Barack Obama, "Address to the Nation on the Way Forward in Afghanistan and Pakistan" (Eisenhower Hall Theatre, United States Military Academy at West Point, West Point, New York, December 1, 2009), http://www.whitehouse.gov/the-press-office/remarks-president-address-nation-way-forward-afghanistan-and-pakistan (accessed May 5, 2010).

2. Colonel Brian Copes, interview by the author, December 2, 2009.

3. "White Paper of the Interagency Policy Group's Report on US Policy toward Afghanistan and Pakistan," *New York Times*, March 27, 2009, http://www.nytimes.com/2009/03/27/us/politics/27text-whitepaper.html (accessed June 24, 2011).

4. "Comprehensive Oversight Plan for Afghanistan-Pakistan, August 2009," USAID, www.dodig.mil/gwot_iraq/COPafghanpak_2009_2010.pdf (accessed June 24, 2011).

5. For challenges of combining US Army infantry and armor training, see Douglas Wissing, "The Big Benning Theory," *American Legion*, January 1, 2011, http://www.legion.org/magazine/93800/big-benning-theory (accessed June 24, 2011).

6. Lieutenant Colonel Simon C. Gardner, interview by the author, September 24, 2010.

7. Phyllis Cox, interview by the author, June 21, 2011.

8. Jim Moseley, interview by the author, June 30, 2011.

9. "The Democrats Have Long Called Afghanistan 'The Central Front.' Will They Retreat from It?" *Washington Post*, January 29, 2009, http://www.washington post.com/wp-dyn/content/article/2009/01/28/AR2009012 803267.html (accessed June 24, 2011). Many administration officials expressed their misgivings about the full-blown COIN strategy. For example, while often portrayed as a counterinsurgency supporter, Defense Secretary Robert Gates told a congressional panel, "If we set ourselves the objective of creating some sort of Central Asian Valhalla over there, we will lose because nobody in the world had that kind of time, patience, or money, to be honest."

10. Julian Barnes, "In Afghanistan Conflict, Pentagon Considers Structural Changes," *Los Angeles Times*, May 8, 2009, http://articles.latimes.com/2009/may/08/world/fg-us -afghan8 (accessed June 24, 2011).

11. Eric Schmitt and Scott Shane, "US Buildup: A Necessity?" *New York Times*, September 8, 2009.

12. Jane Mayer, "The Predator War," *New Yorker*, October 26, 2009.

13. Klaus Brinkbäumer and John Goetz, "Taking Out the Terrorists by Remote Control," *SpiegelOnline*, October 12, 2010, www.spiegel.de/international/world/0,1518,722 583,00.html (accessed June 24, 2011). Due to the problems of secrecy and reporting difficulties in Pakistan's FATA region, the *SpiegelOnline* drone numbers differ from those reported in Peter Bergen and Katharine Tiedmann, "The Drone Wars," *Atlantic*, December 2010, and from those in Colin Cookman, "Threats, Options, and Risks in Pakistan," Center for American Progress, March 5, 2009, www.americanprogress.org/issues/2009/ 03/pakistan_strikes.html (accessed July 3, 2011).

14. Bing West, *The Wrong War: Grit, Strategy, and the Way out of Afghanistan* (New York: Random House, 2011), p. 226.

15. "Self-Defence," *Economist*, April 11, 2009.

16. Spencer Ackerman, "9 Years In, US Finally Tries to Get a Grip on Warzone Contractors," *Wired* Danger Room, June 28, 2010, http://www.wired.com/dangerroom/ 2010/06/9-years-in-u-s-finally-tries-to-get-a-grip-on-warzone-contractors/ (accessed June 28, 2011); Marc Ambinder, "Accessing Wikileaks's Raw Data," *Atlantic*, July 25, 2010, http://www.theatlantic.com/politics/archive/2010/07/assessing-wikileakss-raw -data/60376/ (accessed June 28, 2009).

17. Mathew Nasuti, "Petraeus Fired Admiral Who Tried to Cut Taliban Funding," Kabul Press, April 17, 2011, http://news-now.org/2011/05/petraeus-fired-admiral-cut -taliban-funding/ (accessed July 30, 2011).

18. Spencer Ackerman, "Military's Anti-corruption Chief Leaves Afghanistan after Just Four Months," *Wired* Danger Room, September 21, 2010, http://www.wired .com/dangerroom/tag/task-force-2010/ (accessed June 28, 2009).

19. Ross E. Ridge, interview by the author, December 17, 2010.

20. Ibid., July 13, 2011.

21. Former aid worker, interview by the author, July 14, 2009.

22. Deputy Secretary of State Jacob Lew, "Mission in Afghanistan," C-SPAN, October 26, 2009, http://www.c-spanvideo.org/program/289643-1 (accessed June 26, 2009).

23. Hassan Kakar, *Afghanistan: The Soviet Invasion and the Afghan Response, 1979–1982* (Berkeley: University of California Press, 1995), pp. 51–75; Barnett Rubin, *The Fragmentation of Afghanistan*, 2nd ed. (New Haven, CT: Yale University Press, 2002), pp. 122–45. I am grateful to Professor Abdulkader H. Sinno for pointing out the importance of ten thousand Soviet development advisers posted in Afghanistan to the debate about the US civilian surge and providing the two citations above. Gregory Feifer, *The Great Gamble: The Soviet War in Afghanistan* (New York: Harper, 2009), pp. 146, 190; Peter Marsden, *Afghanistan: Aid, Armies, Empires* (New York: I. B. Tauris, 2009), pp. 49, 60, notes that Soviet advisers "proved to be of limited effectiveness in the face of patronage and corruption combined with the hemorrhaging of government staff." See also Larry Goodson and Thomas H. Johnson, "Parallels with the Past: How the Soviets Lost in Afghanistan, How the Americans are Losing," Foreign Policy Research Institute, April 2011, http://www.fpri.org/enotes/201104.goodson_johnson .afghanistan.html (accessed June 26, 2011).

24. Lorne Cook, "Afghan 'Civilian Surge' Sparks Concern, Debate," Agence France-Presse, May 25, 2009, http://www.afghanistannewscenter.com/news/2009/may/may 252009.html (accessed June 26, 2011).

25. Obama, "Address to the Nation on the Way Forward in Afghanistan."

26. Deirdre Tynan, "Afghanistan: If You Can't Beat the Taliban, Try to Buy Militants Off," January 14, 2010, http://www.eurasianet.org/departments/insight/articles/eav011 510.shtml (accessed January 7, 2012).

27. Deirdre Tynan, "Afghanistan: If You Can't Beat the Taliban, Try to Buy the Militants Off," *Eurasia Insight*, January 15, 2010, http://www.eurasianet.org/departments/ insight/articles/eav011510.shtml (accessed June 26, 2011).

28. Greg Jaffe, "Combat Generation: Trying to Work with an Afghan Insurgent," *Washington Post*, May 17, 2010.

29. Sonya Hepinstall, "Holbrooke: Reformed Taliban in Afghan Govt Not Wrong," Reuters, June 6, 2010, http://in.reuters.com/article/2010/06/07/idINIndia-4908822010 0607 (accessed June 24, 2011).

30. Dexter Filkins and Carlotta Gall, "Taliban Leader in Secret Talks Was an Imposter," *New York Times*, November 22, 2010. While the Taliban continued to deny any talks were going on, Filkins and Gall reported that there were at least two other Taliban leaders said to be involved with peace discussions. Reflecting the complicated game being played, a Taliban deputy commander, Abdul Ghani Baradar, was arrested in a joint

CIA–ISI raid in Karachi. Baradar had taken part in peace talks with the Afghan government. American officials initially celebrated the capture as an example of the ISI finally getting tough on the Taliban, but it was soon apparent that the ISI instead arranged the arrest because Baradar engaged in peace talks without its permission.

31. Afghanistan Justice Sector Support Program website: http://www.jssp-afghanistan.com/ (accessed July 30, 2011).

32. Hans Klemm, interview by the author, December 18, 2010.

33. Michael J. Gottlieb, interview by the author, December 10, 2010.

34. Karen DeYoung, "Envoys Resist Forced Iraq Duty," *Washington Post*, November 1, 2007, http://www.washingtonpost.com/wp-dyn/content/ article/2007/10/31/AR2007103101626.html (accessed June 25, 2011). The State Department employees had reason to be concerned with war-zone postings. Unlike the military, which had organized procedures for handling battle injuries, the State Department was woefully unequipped to handle wartime casualties, leading to tragedies such as that experienced by Afghanistan Reconstruction Group staffer Doyle Peterson, a State Department contractor who received deplorable post-IED civilian care compared to Brigadier General Patt Maney, who could access the military system. See chapter 8. As of 2011, the procedures for medical care for US civilians wounded in battle are still insufficient, contributing to the recruitment problem.

35. Mark R. Hagerott, Thomas J. Umberg, and Joseph A. Jackson, "A Patchwork Strategy of Consensus: Establishing Rule of Law in Afghanistan," *JFQ* 59 (2010): 146, http://www.ndu.edu/press/patchwork-strategy-of-consensus.html (accessed June 28, 2011).

36. Jim Moseley, interview by the author, June 30, 2011.

37. Former USAID official, interview by the author, March 21, 2011.

38. Babette Gainor, interview by the author, Washington, DC, October 19, 2009.

39. Des Browne and Stephen Carter, "Afghanistan: The Change We Need," *RUSI Journal* 154, no. 3 (June 2009): 33, http://www.rusi.org/go.php?structureID=articles_journal&ref=A4A48A3CF55C8B (accessed June 24, 2011).

40. Melissa Chadbourne, "US Policy toward Afghanistan and Pakistan: Implications for the US and Its Allies," Johns Hopkins and SAIS, March 2009, http://www.sais-jhu.edu/academics/regional-studies/southasia/pdf/USAfghanistanPakistanStrategy_CHADBOURNE.pdf (accessed July 30, 2011).

41. USAID, "USAID Announces USAID Forward Reform Agenda," USAID.gov, November 18, 2010, www.usaid.gov/press/factsheets/2010/fs101118.html (accessed June 25, 2011).

42. Center for Democracy and Governance, *Promoting Transparency and Accountability: USAID's Anticorruption Experience* (Washington, DC: USAID, 2000), p. 1, states that corruption was "long a taboo subject in the international area," and the anticorruption movement "owes much of its impetus to the end of the Cold War."

43. Rule-of-law consultant, interview by the author, June 28, 2011.

44. "Fact Sheet on Accountable Assistance for Afghanistan (A³), June 2011," e-mailed from USAID official Jim Carey to the author, July 1, 2011. In author's possession.

45. GAO, *Foreign Assistance Measures to Prevent Inadvertent Payments to Terrorists under Palestinian Aid Programs Have Been Strengthened, but Some Weakness Remain* [Report GAO-09-622] (Washington, DC: GAO, 2009), p. 15.

46. USAID Office of Inspector General, *Audit of the Adequacy of USAID's Antiterrorism Vetting Procedures* [Audit Report No. 9-000-08-001] (Washington, DC: USAID OIG, 2007), p. 1.

47. GAO, *Foreign Assistance Measures* (Washington, DC: GAO, 2009), pp. 16–17.

48. USAID, "Accountable Assistance for Afghanistan (A³)," USAID.gov, http://www.usaid.gov/locations/asia/countries/afghanistan/aaa.html (accessed June 25, 2011).

49. Jeff Mallory, e-mail to the author, June 25, 2011.

50. Rep. John P. Murtha staffer, interview by the author, January 7, 2010.

51. GAO, *Afghanistan: US Efforts to Vet Non-US Vendors Need Improvement* [Report GAO-11-355] (Washington, DC: GAO, 2011), pp. 9–13.

52. Jeff Mallory, interview by the author, June 21, 2011.

53. GAO, *Afghanistan Development: Enhancements to Performance Management and Evaluation Efforts Could Improve USAID's Agricultural Programs* [Report GAO-10-368] (Washington, DC: GAO, 2010), highlights page, http://www.gao.gov/new.items/d10368.pdf (accessed June 25, 2011), notes that six of the eight USAID agricultural programs, including the largest, AVIPA, failed to meet annual goals; Rajiv Chandrasekaran, "In Afghan Region, the US Spreads the Cash to Fight the Taliban," *Washington Post*, May 31, 2010, http://www.washingtonpost.com/wp-dyn/content/article/2010/05/30/AR20100 53003722.html?nav=emailpage (accessed June 25, 2011); Senate Foreign Relations Committee, Evaluating US Foreign Assistance to Afghanistan [S. Prt 112-21] (Washington, DC: Senate Foreign Relations Committee Report, June 8, 2011) p. 11, http://foreign .senate.gov/reports/ (scroll down to entry marked 6/8/2011) (accessed December 13, 2011), announced that AVIPA overstated statistics and the day-labor wages the program paid to Afghan farmers "generate unintended and potentially adverse consequences."

54. International Relief & Development, "Employee Benefits," http://www.ird -dc.org/careers/benefits.html (accessed June 25, 2011).

55. Richard Owens, interview by the author, June 24, 2011.

56. Afghan Threat Finance Cell member, interview by the author, US embassy, Kabul, December 14, 2010.

57. David Cohen, e-mail to author, January 14, 2010. Besides the ATFC, the Illicit Finance Task Force in Special Ambassador Richard Holbrooke's office began devising a strategy in 2009 to restrict funds to the Taliban from opium, donations, crime, and corruption.

58. US embassy official, interview by the author, January 13, 2010.

CHAPTER 14. THE COMPLEXITIES

1. Field research by the author, Sabari Key Leader Engagement, Khost Province, Afghanistan, November 18, 2009; Colonel Brian Copes, Interview by the author, Forward Operating Base Salerno, Khost Province, Afghanistan, November 21, 2009.

2. Bing West, *The Wrong War: Grit, Strategy, and the Way out of Afghanistan* (New York: Random House, 2011), pp. 169, 172.

3. Ibid., pp. 15, 47.

4. Dexter Filkins, "Stanley McChrystal's Long War," *New York Times*, October 18, 2009.

5. Jamie Terzi, interview by the author, Kabul, Afghanistan, May 24, 2009.

6. USDA foreign service officer, interview by the author, July 13, 2011.

7. For a brief summary of United States–Pakistan issues in early 2009, see Zachary S. Davis, "Viewpoint: Pakistan's Last Chance," *Strategic Insights* 8, no. 1 (January 2009), http://www.nps.edu/Academics/centers/ccc/publications/OnlineJournal/2008/Dec/davisDec08.html (accessed June 25, 2011).

8. Elizabeth Bumiller, "Gates Says Allies Shirk Afghan Duty," *New York Times*, March 12, 2011.

9. William Dalrymple, "Why the Taliban Is Winning in Afghanistan," *New Statesman*, June 22, 2010, http://www.newstatesman.com/international-politics/2010/06/british-afghanistan-government (accessed June 25, 2011).

10. Military contracting officer, interview by the author, southern Afghanistan, June 24, 2011. For another post-surge overview of contracting in southern Afghanistan, see Jonathan Pan, "Silent Kingmaker: The Need for a Unified Wartime Contracting Strategy," *JFQ* 60 (Spring 2011): 38.

11. GAO, *Intelligence, Surveillance, and Reconnaissance: Overarching Guidance Is Needed to Advance Information Sharing* [Report GAO-10-500T] (Washington, DC: GAO, 2010), pp. 1–6; GAO, *Intelligence, Surveillance, and Reconnaissance: Actions Are Needed to Increase Integration and Efficiencies of DOD's ISR Enterprise* [Report GAO-11-465] (Washington, DC: GAO, 2011).

12. Michael T. Flynn, Matt Pottinger, and Paul D. Batchelor, *Fixing Intel: A Blueprint for Making Intelligence Relevant in Afghanistan* (Washington, DC: Center for a New American Security, 2010), pp. 4, 7.

13. Sippi Azarbaijani-Moghaddam, Mirwais Wardak, Idrees Zaman, and Annabel Taylor, *Afghan Hearts, Afghan Minds: Exploring Afghan Perceptions of Civil–Military Relations* (Kabul: British Agencies in Afghanistan, 2008), states US commanders were authorized to use aid, "paid in cash, or in the form of like-kind benefits such as food, local amenities, necessities, vehicles, or communal rewards," as rewards for actionable intelligence.

14. Joby Warrick, *The Triple Agent: The al-Qaeda Mole Who Infiltrated the CIA* (New York: Doubleday, 2011), pp. 24–27.

15. Michael Hastings, "The Runaway General," *Rolling Stone*, June 22, 2010, http://www.rollingstone.com/politics/news/the-runaway-general-20100622 (accessed June 25, 2011).

16. Abby Phillip, "Fields Leaves Post: Afghanistan Watchdog Resigns," *Politico*, January 11, 2011, http://www.politico.com/politico44/perm/0111/fields_leaves_post_7ba 529e8-7980-4e7d-a67b-5b69fe8a276d.html (accessed June 25, 2011).

17. Nancy Hatch Dupree, interview by the author, June 1, 2011.

18. International Crisis Group, "The Insurgency in Afghanistan's Heartland," *Asia Report* 207 (June 2011): 22–23, http://www.crisisgroup.org/en/regions/asia/south -asia/afghanistan/207-the-insurgency-in-afghanistans-heartland.aspx (accessed June 25, 2011).

19. Matthew Rosenberg, "Corruption Suspected in Airlift of Billions in Cash from Kabul," *Wall Street Journal*, June 25, 2011, http://online.wsj.com/article/SB10001 424052748704638504575318850772872776.html (accessed June 25, 2011); Peter Spiegel and Matthew Rosenberg, "Afghan Aid on Hold as Corruption Is Probed," Wall Street Journal, June 28, 2011, http://online.wsj.com/article/SB100014240527 487032 797045753348600231154660.html (accessed June 25, 2011).

20. Andrew Higgins, "Kabul Bank's Sherkhan Farnood Feeds Crony Capitalism in Afghanistan," *Washington Post*, February 22, 2010; Dexter Filkins, "The Afghan Bank Heist," *New Yorker*, February 14–21, 2011.

21. Senate Foreign Relations Committee, *Evaluating US Foreign Assistance*, pp. 17, 21. USAID belatedly canceled DeLoitte's contract in Afghanistan. Ernesto Londono and Rajiv Chandrasekaran, "US Advisers Saw Early Signs of Trouble at Afghan Bank," *Washington Post*, March 15, 2011, http://www.washingtonpost.com/world/us-advisers-saw -early-signs-of-trouble-at-afghan-bank/2011/03/14/ABQUvoW_story.html (accessed June 25, 2011); Eliza Villarino, "In Afghanistan, USAID Terminates Deloitte Contract over Kabul Bank Scandal," *Devex*, March 16, 2011, http://www.devex.com/en/ blogs/development-assistance-under-obama/in-afghanistan-usaid-terminates-deloitte-contract-over-kabul-bank-scandal (accessed June 25, 2011).

22. European rule-of-law and security consultant, interviews by the author, October 4 and 15, 2010; "Prisoner Releases in Afghanistan," e-mail by European rule-of-law and security consultant to the author, October 15, 2010; Emma Graham-Harrison, "Afghan Officials Free Top Taliban Fighters," Reuters, December 1, 2010, http://www.reuters.com/ article/2010/12/01/us-afghanistan-prisoners-idUSTRE6AT2 WG20101201 (accessed June 25, 2011); Douglas Wissing, "The Taliban Catch-and-Release Scheme," *Huffington Post*, December 3, 2010, http://www .huffingtonpost.com/douglas-a-wissing/the-taliban -catchandrelea_b_791698.html (accessed June 25, 2011); International Crisis Group, "The Insurgency in Afghanistan's Heartland," pp. 26–67; Christopher N. Koontz, ed., *Enduring Voices: Oral Histories of the US Army Experience in Afghanistan, 2003–2005* (Washington,

DC: Center for Military History, 2008), p. 450; West, *Wrong War*, p. 61; David Rohde, *A Rope and A Prayer* (New York: Viking, 2011), p. 149; Jane Taber, "O'Connor Unsure If Detainees Are Missing," *Globe and Mail*, March 5, 2007.

23. Cable from US embassy, Kabul, "Complaints to Giroa on Pretrial Releases," August 6, 2009, http://cablegate.wikileaks.org/cable/2009/08/09KABUL2246.html (accessed June 25, 2010).

24. European rule-of-law and security consultant, interview by the author, October 15, 2010.

25. Amir Attaran, phone interview by the author, November 11, 2010.

26. US human-rights consultant, interview by the author, November 15, 2010.

27. Kandahar-based human-rights researcher, interview by the author, November 25, 2010.

28. Michael J. Gottlieb, interview by the author, December 10, 2010.

29. Taimoor Shah and Alissa J. Rubin, "Taliban Breach Afghan Prison; Hundreds Free," *New York Times*, April 25, 2011, http://www.nytimes.com/2011/04/26/world/asia/26afghanistan.html?_r=2&hp (accessed June 25, 2011).

30. European rule-of-law and security consultant, interview by the author and transmitted intelligence summary, October 15, 2010. Graham-Harrison, "Afghan Officials," confirms elements of the Anwar Shah Agha story. On Nagaan: CNN, "39 Dead in Blast at Afghanistan Wedding," *This Just In*, June 9, 2010, http://news.blogs.cnn.com/2010/06/09/39-dead-in-blast-at-afghanistan-wedding/ (accessed June 25, 2011).

31. European rule-of-law and security consultant, interview by the author, November 30, 2010.

32. Nathan Hughes, interview by the author, November 15, 2010.

33. For Taliban "shadow government," see C. J. Chivers, "In Eastern Afghanistan, at War with the Taliban's Shadowy Rule," *New York Times*, February 7, 2011.

34. West, *Wrong War*, p. 217; Editorial, "Mr. Obama and Mr. Karzai, Take Two," *New York Times*, May 12, 2010; Drew Brown, "Despite Marines' Presence, Fear of Taliban Persists in Afghan Town," *Stars and Stripes*, November 16, 2009, stated that in Delaram in southwestern Afghanistan, "The district governor is usually absent. There is no judge or prosecutor in town. New officials have been assigned to the district, but they have yet to arrive."

35. Marc Ambinder, "Assessing WikiLeaks's Raw Data," *Atlantic*, July 25, 2010, http://www.theatlantic.com/politics/archive/10/07/assessing-wikileakss-raw-data/60376 (accessed June 25, 2011).

36. Senate Foreign Relations Committee, *Evaluating US Foreign Assistance*, p. 2.

37. Peter Galbraith, interview by the author, September 24, 2010; Kim Barker, *The Taliban Shuffle: Strange Days in Afghanistan and Pakistan* (New York: Doubleday, 2011), p. 96, states Karzai lost direction after Ambassador Zalmay Khalilzad left for Iraq. "He had

proved to be whiny and conflicted, a combination of Woody Allen, Chicken Little, and Jimmy Carter."

38. Eric Schmitt, "Ambassador Eikenberry's Cables on the US Strategy in Afghanistan," *New York Times*, January 25, 2010, http://documents.nytimes.com/eikenberry -s-memos-on-the-strategy-in-afghanistan (accessed June 25, 2011).

39. "Karzai's Tattered Victory," *Economist*, November 7, 2009; "Played for Fools," *Economist*, February 2010; Rod Nordland and Mark Mazzetti, "Graft Dispute in Afghanistan Is Test for US," *New York Times*, August 24, 2010; Rod Nordland, "Afghan Government Drops Corruption Charges against an Aide to the President," *New York Times*, November 9, 2010; Editorial, "Mr. Obama and Mr. Karzai."

40. Nita Lowey, "Statement at Subcommittee Markup of the State and Foreign Opera- tions Appropriations Bill, FY12," Committee on Appropriations—Democrats, July 15, 2010, http://democrats.appropriations.house.gov/index.php?option=com_content&view =article &id=830:ranking-member-nita-lowey-statement-at-subcommittee-markup-of-the-state-a -foreign-operations-appropriations-bill-fy12&catid=98&Itemid=131 (accessed July 30, 2011). While Karzai was demanding half the international development funds be channeled through his government, there was a rising tide of opposition to the idea. Convening hearings on the matter, Congresswoman Nita Lowey stated her concerns about the need for efforts to "provide accountability and thwart corruption in Afghanistan."

41. European rule-of-law and security consultant, e-mail to the author, June 23, 2011.

42. Peter Marsden, *Afghanistan: Aid, Armies, and Empires* (New York: I. B. Tauris, 2009), p. 226. A larger percentage of Afghans (59 percent) saw corruption as a bigger problem than security (54 percent). "'Drain the Swamp of Corruption in Afghanistan,' Says UNODC," United Nations Office on Drugs and Crime, January 2010, http://www .unodc.org/unodc/en/press/releases/2010/January/drain-the-swamp-of-corruption-in sed June 25, 2011).

44. Taimor Shah and Rod Nordland, "Car Bomber Fails to Reach Afghan Governor, but Kills Children," *New York Times*, August 3, 2010, notes increased Taliban attacks and assassination attempts in Kandahar in the wake of rural-development and cash-for-work programs.

45. Griff Witte, "Some Afghans Trust Taliban Shadow Gov't," *Washington Post*, December 8, 2009; Shah and Nordland, "Car Bomber Fails"; Alissa J. Rubin, "Afghans Dis- trust of Officials Poses Threat to Military Successes," *New York Times*, May 13, 2010; Matt Waldman, *Caught in the Conflict: Civilians and the International Security Strategy in Afghanistan* (Kabul: Oxfam UK, 2009), http://www.oxfam.org.uk/resources/ policy/conflict _disasters/bp_caught_in_conflict_afghanistan.html (accessed March 10, 2011); United Nations Assistance Mission in Afghanistan, "Afghanistan, Midyear Report 2010: Protec- tion of Civilians in Armed Conflict," July 2010, http://unama.unmissions.org/Default .aspx?tabid=4529 (accessed June 25, 2010).

46. The night letters used by the insurgents to send threatening messages were a psychological-operations technique taught to the mujahideen by the CIA during the Soviet war. Robin Moore, *The Hunt for Bin Laden: Task Force Dagger* (New York: Random House, 2003), p. 272.

47. Chancellor Gul Hassan Walizei, interview by the author, Forward Operating Base Salerno, Khost Province, Afghanistan, June 10, 2009.

48. International Crisis Group, "The Insurgency in Afghanistan's Heartland," pp. 22, 25–26; Anthony Cordesman, "How America Corrupted Afghanistan: Time to Look in the Mirror," *Center for Strategic & International Studies* (2010), argues that the $450 billion flood of US money overwhelmed desperately poor Afghanistan, precipitating institutional dysfunction and corruption. "The flow of money increased in direct proportion to the seriousness of the fighting, the expansion of Taliban control, and the steady decline in Afghan security."

49. US embassy official, interview by the author, January 13, 2010.

50. Andrew Wilder, "A 'Weapons System' Based on Wistful Thinking," *Boston Globe*, September 16, 2009, references his team's study in Afghanistan and states, "we have found little evidence that aid projects are 'winning hearts and minds,'" and "in many cases is contributing to conflict and instability" through insurgent funding and tribal infighting over development largesse that led to increased Taliban recruits"; Andrew Beath, Fotini Christia, and Ruben Enikolopov, "Winning Hearts and Minds through Development: Evidence from a Field Experiment in Afghanistan," *MIT Political Science Department Research Paper* No. 2011-14 (April 2011), http://papers.ssrn.com/sol3/papers.cfm?abstract _id=1809677## (accessed June 25, 2011), finds National Solidarity Program projects—considered to be Afghanistan's best grassroots initiative—increased the perception of security among villagers but did not actually affect the number of violent attacks around the villages. Marsden, *Afghanistan: Aid, Armies, Empires*, p. 136; OxFam, *Quick Impact, Quick Collapse: Dangers of Militarized Aid in Afghanistan* (Kabul: Oxfam International, 2010), http://www.oxfam.org/policy/quick-impact-quick-collapse (accessed June 25, 2011); Peter Charles Choharis and James A. Gavilis, "Counterinsurgency 3.0," *Parameters* 40, no.1 (Spring 2010): 35, http://www.carlisle.army.mil/usawc/parameters/Articles/2010 spring/40-1-2010_choharisAndGavrilis.pdf (accessed June 25, 2011); Eli Berman, Joseph H. Felter, and Jacob N. Shapiro, "Constructive COIN: How Development Can Fight Radicals," *Foreign Affairs*, June 1, 2010, finds CERP funding in Iraq yielded complicated results, and the premises of many counterinsurgency arguments were "untested" and "questionable." The assertion echoes William Easterly, *The White Man's Burden: Why the West's Efforts to Aid the Rest Have Done So Much Ill and So Little Good* (New York: Penguin, 2007), p. 33, which states, "But few things have been vigorously evaluated in foreign aid, period." Dambisa Moyo, *Dead Aid: Why Aid Is Not Working and How There Is a Better Way for Africa* (New York: Farrar, Straus, and Giroux, 2009), p. 59, points out that aid increases conflict as groups vie for the booty.

51. GAO, *Afghanistan's Security Environment* [Report GAO-10-613-R] (Washington, DC: GAO, 2010), summarizes the dramatic increase in enemy-initiated attacks: up 75 percent from 2008 to 2009, then further spiking in 2010.

52. Warren P. Strobel, "Experiment in Afghanistan: Largesse Is Out, Self-Help Is In," McClatchy Newspapers, December 2, 2010, http://www.mcclatchydc.com/2010/12/02/104630/experiment-in-afghanistan-largesse.html (accessed June 25, 2011).

53. Rep. John Tierney staffer, interview by the author, April 13, 2010.

54. "How Americans Help Fund the Taliban," *Fresh Air*, January 14, 2010, http://www.npr.org/templates/transcript/transcript.php?storyId=122563121(accessed June 25, 2011)

55. Craig Whitlock, "Diverse Sources Fund Insurgency in Afghanistan," *Washington Post*, September 27, 2009.

56. "More Than a One-Man Problem," *Economist*, June 24, 2010.

57. GAO, *Afghanistan: US Efforts to Vet Non-US Vendors Need Improvement* [Report GAO-11-355] (Washington, DC: GAO, 2011), p. 2.

58. Christine Spolar, "As Afghanistan Contracting Surges, Who's Following the Money?" *Huffington Post*, February 3, 2010, http://www.huffingtonpost.com/2010/03/03/as-afghanistan-contractin _n_484648.html (accessed June 25, 2011).

59. Catherine Collins with Ashraf Ali, *Financing the Taliban: Tracing the Dollars behind the Insurgencies in Afghanistan and Pakistan* (Washington, DC: New America Foundation, 2010), p. 8.

60. West, *Wrong War*, p. 41; C. J. Chivers, "Marines Invest in Local Projects, Hoping to Earn Trust," *New York Times*, January 30, 2010.

61. Dexter Filkins, "With US Aid, Warlord Builds an Afghan Empire," *New York Times*, June 10, 2010.

62. Walter Pincus, "Congress Investigating Charges of 'Protection Racket' by Afghanistan Contractors," *Washington Post*, December 17, 2009, http://www.washingtonpost.com/wp-dyn/content/article/2009/12/16/ AR2009121604126.html (accessed June 25, 2011); Dexter Filkins, "Convoy Guards in Afghanistan Face an Inquiry," New York Times, June 7, 2010.

63. Rep. John F. Tierney, *Warlord, Inc.: Extortion and Corruption along the US Supply Chain in Afghanistan* (Washington, DC: Committee on Oversight and Government Reform, 2010), p. 38.

64. Seth G. Jones, *In the Graveyard of Empires: America's War in Afghanistan* (New York: W. W. Norton, 2009), p. 297.

65. Alissa Rubin and James Risen, "Costly Afghanistan Road Project Is Marred by Unsavory Alliances," *New York Times*, May 1, 2011.

66. Ronald E. Neumann, *The Other War: Winning and Losing in Afghanistan* (Washington, DC: Potomac Books, 2009), p. 173; "More Than a One-Man Problem," *Economist*.

67. Yaroslav Trofimov, "US Rebuilds Power Plant, Taliban Reap a Windfall," *Wall Street Journal*, July 13, 2010; Mark Moyar, *Development in Afghanistan's Counterinsurgency: A New Guide* (Orbis Operations, 2011), p. 5, http://smallwarsjournal.com/blog/development-in-afghanistans-counterinsurgency (accessed June 25, 2011).

68. Trofimov, "US Rebuilds Power Plant."

CHAPTER 15. THE PERFECT WAR

1. Greg Miller, "US Effort to Help Afghanistan Fight Corruption Has Complicated Ties," *Washington Post*, September 10, 2010; Stephen Carter and Kate Clark, *No Shortcut to Stability: Justice, Politics, and Insurgency in Afghanistan* (London: Chatham House, 2010), pp. 24, 30–31.

2. Troy Mallory, interview by the author, June 22, 2011; Seth G. Jones, *In the Graveyard of Empires: America's War in Afghanistan* (New York: W. W. Norton, 2009), pp. 224–25, lists a number of Afghan and Pakistani groups in the insurgents' "complex adaptive system," but did not include any Western elements of the system.

3. Phyllis Cox, interview by the author, June 21, 2011.

4. Allison Cullison and Anand Gopal, "US Afghans Target Taliban Region," *Wall Street Journal*, November 9, 2009.

5. "Afghan Leadership Must 'Excude Steadiness,'" NPR News *Morning Edition*, April 6, 2010.

6. US embassy official, interview by the author, January 13, 2010.

7. Alissa J. Rubin, "Karzai's Words Leave Few Choices for the West," *New York Times*, April 4, 2010, http://www.nytimes.com/2010/04/05/world/asia/05karzai.html (accessed June 25, 2011).

8. Senate Committee on Foreign Relations, *Afghanistan's Narco War: Breaking the Link between Drug Traffickers and the Insurgents* (Washington, DC: Government Printing Office, 2009), p. 4.

9. "Corruption Ignored, Deplored in Afghanistan," NPR News *Morning Edition*, December 23, 2009. Former *Washington Post* journalist and International Crisis Group senior analyst Candace Rondeaux talked about the Senate report: "And to everybody's surprise, it wasn't poppy that was the main engine for the Taliban economy—you know, it was graft, it was corruption."

10. Presentation by Steven Welker, Camp Atterbury, Indiana, March 30, 2010 (author's field research).

11. Walter Pincus, "McCaskill Calls for Increased Oversight of Contract Work in Afghanistan," *Washington Post*, December 18, 2009, http://www.washingtonpost.com/wp-dyn/content/article/2009/12/17/AR2009121704654.html (accessed June 25, 2011).

12. Special Investigator General for Afghanistan Reconstruction, *SIGAR Quarterly Report to Congress, January 30, 2010* (Washington, DC: SIGAR, 2010), www.sigar.mil/Jan2010Report.asp (accessed June 25, 2011); Paul McLeary, "Contractistan," *Aviation Week*, March 28, 2010; Christine Spolar, "As Afghanistan Contracting Surges, Who's Following the Money?" *Huffington Post*, February 3, 2010, http://www.huffingtonpost.com/2010/03/03/as-afghanistan-contractin_n_484648.html (accessed June 25, 2011).

13. Moshe Schwartz, *Department of Defense Contractors in Iraq and Afghanistan: Background and Analysis* (Washington, DC: Congressional Research Service, 2009), p. 17, quoting Christine Hauser, "New Rules for Contractors Are Urged by 2 Democrats," *New York Times*, October 4, 2007.

14. Committee on Foreign Relations, *Afghanistan's Narco War*, pp. 18–20.

15. Rod Nordland, "Taliban Hit Back in Marja with a Campaign of Intimidation," *New York Times*, March 17, 2010, http://www.nytimes.com/2010/03/18/world/asia/18afghan.html?scp=3&sq=taliban percent20marja percent20&st=cse (accessed June 25, 2011).

16. Captain Doug Seymour, interview by the author, Forward Operating Base Mehtar Lam, Laghman Province, Afghanistan, December 10, 2009.

CHAPTER 16. THE WAY

1. Mark Mazzetti, Helene Cooper, and Peter Baker, "Behind the Hunt for bin Laden," *New York Times*, May 3, 2011; Marc Ambinder, "The Secret Team That Killed bin Laden," *National Journal*, May 2, 2010, http://www.nationaljournal.com/whitehouse/the-secret-team-that-killed-bin-laden-20110502 (accessed July 23, 2011).

2. Daveed Gartenstein-Ross, "Bin Laden's 'War of a Thousand Cuts' Will Live On," *Atlantic*, May 3, 2011, http://www.theatlantic.com/international/archive/2011/05/bin-ladens-war-of-a-thousand-cuts-will-live-on/238228/ (accessed July 23, 2011).

3. Thomas L. Friedman, "Bad Bargains," *New York Times*, May 11, 2011, states President Hamid Karzai was in the "looking-for-stability-in-Afghanistan business" and Pakistan had been in the "looking-for-bin-Laden business." Friedman did not reference any of the Western "businesses" benefiting from the war in Afghanistan.

4. Alissa J. Rubin and Scott Shane, "Assassination in Afghanistan Creates a Void," *New York Times*, May 11, 2011.

5. Alissa J. Rubin, "Assassination Deals Blow to Peace Process in Afghanistan," *New York Times*, September 20, 2011.

6. Alissa J. Rubin, Ray Rivera, and Jack Healy, "US Embassy and NATO Headquarters Attacked in Kabul," *New York Times*, September 13, 2011.

7. Alissa J. Rubin, "Clouds around Karzai Darken the Road Ahead," *New York*

Times, July 14, 2011; Julian Borger and Lianne Gutcher, "Afghanistan Government under Threat after Second Assassination in a Week," *Guardian*, July 18, 2011, http://www .guardian.co.uk/world/2011/jul/18/afghanistan-government-assassination-hamid-karzai (accessed July 23, 2011).

8. Ray Rivera, "Afghan Political Crisis Grows as Legislators Vow to Defy Karzai and Open Parliament," *New York Times*, January 21, 2011.

9. Dexter Filkins, "Loss of Faith in Afghan Leaders May Hurt Push against Taliban," *New York Times*, September 4, 2010.

10. Dexter Filkins, "Endgame," *New Yorker*, July 4, 2011; Antonio Giustozzi and Christoph Reuter, "The Insurgents of the Afghan North," Afghan Analysts Network, May 5, 2011, aan-afghanistan.com/index.asp?id=1679 (accessed July 24, 2011); Alissa Rubin, "Mosque Bombing Kills Governor in Northern Afghanistan," *New York Times*, October 9, 2010; "Ray Rivera, 'Taliban Bomber Infiltrates Afghan–NATO Meeting, Killing Police Official and Others,'" *New York Times*, May 29, 2011; "35 Killed in Taliban Attack on Afghanistan Road Company," *Telegraph*, May 19, 2011, http://www.telegraph.co.uk/ news/worldnews/asia/afghanistan/8523684/35-killed-in-Taliban-attack-on-Afghanistan -road-company.html (accessed July 24, 2011); Alissa Rubin, "23 Said to Be Killed in Attack on Afghan Police," *New York Times*, June 29, 2011; Rod Nordland, "10 Aid Workers Are Found Slain in Afghanistan," *New York Times*, August 8, 2011; Rod Nordland, "Taliban Intensify Campaign against Afghan Police, as 15 Die in New Clashes," *New York Times*, August 8, 2011.

11. Taimoor Shah and Alissa Rubin, "Broad Taliban Attack Paralyzes Kandahar," *New York Times*, May 9, 2011.

12. Jean MacKenzie, "Blast in Kabul Market Kills Foreigners," *GlobalPost*, January 28, 2011, http://www.globalpost.com/dispatch/afghanistan/110128/afghanistan-kabul -explosion-market (accessed July 23, 2011).

13. Ray Rivera and Sharifullah Sahak, "Five Arrests in Attack on Hospital in Kabul," *New York Times*, May 24, 2011.

14. Alissa Rubin and Rod Nordland, "Gunmen Storm a Luxury Hotel in Afghanistan," *New York Times*, June 29, 2011; Alissa Rubin, "Attack at Hotel Deflates Hopes in Afghanistan," *New York Times*, June 30, 2011.

15. Alissa J. Rubin, Ray Rivera, and Jack Henly, "US Embassy Hit by Rocket Attack in Central Kabul," *New York Times*, September 14, 2011; Fabrizio Foschini, "Another Longest Day in Kabul," Afghan Analysts Network, September 13, 2011, https://www .afghanistan-analysts.net/index.asp?id=2071 (accessed September 13, 2011).

16. Filkins, "Endgame."

17. Alissa Rubin, "Few Taliban Take Offer to Switch their Allegiance," *New York Times*, June 20, 2011.

18. Naqib Ahmad Atal, "Guest Blog: Peace on Hold," Afghan Analysts Network, September 12, 2010, aan-afghanistan.com/index.asp?id=1375 (accessed July 23, 2011).

19. Kimberly Dozier, "AP Sources: Afghan War Campaign Gets Mixed Reviews," *Stars and Stripes*, June 23, 2011, http://articles.sfgate.com/2011-06-23/news/29693687 _1_petraeus-afghan-villages-afghanistan (accessed June 23, 2011).

20. Josh Boak, "US-funded Infrastructure Deteriorates Once under Afghan Control," *Washington Post*, January 4, 2011, states that the sixteen thousand projects funded with $2 billion of CERP money quickly deteriorated when turned over to Afghan control. "More Please, Sir," *Economist*, February 26, 2011.

21. Rajiv Chandrasekaran, "Nawa Turns into Proving Ground for US Strategy in Afghan War," *Washington Post*, December 12, 2010, http://www.washingtonpost.com/wp -dyn/content/article/2010/12/11/AR2010121103041.html (accessed July 25, 2011).

22. Abdul Rahim Mohmand, "Currencies of Protection," *Afghanistan Today*, September 28, 2009, www.afghanistan-today.org/article/?id=160 (accessed September 29, 2011).

23. "Burning Passions," *Economist*, April 9, 2011. A UN report indicated that civilian casualties in Afghanistan reached their highest level yet in 2010. Though the report indicated insurgents were responsible for 75 percent of the casualties, Afghans often blamed the presence of foreign troops for the deaths. Alissa Rubin, "UN Report: A Deadly Year for Afghans," *New York Times*, February 10, 2011; Carlotta Gall, "Night Raids Curbing Taliban, but Afghans Cite Civilian Toll," *New York Times*, July 9, 2011.

24. Under General Petraeus, air strikes in which warplanes fired weapons and dropped bombs increased 65 percent from mid-2010 to mid-2011. Noah Shachtman and Spencer Ackerman, "5,800 Attacks Are Just the Beginning after Petraeus's Year-Long Air War," *Wired Danger Room*, July 5, 2011, http://www.wired.com/dangerroom/2011/07/5800-attacks -are-just-the-beginning-after-petraeus-year-long-air-war/ (accessed July 24, 2011).

25. Daneilla Peled, "Afghans Believe US Is Funding Taliban," *Guardian*, May 25, 2010, http://www.guardian.co.uk/commentisfree/cifamerica/2010/may/25/afghans -believe-us-funding-taliban (accessed July 24, 2011); Spencer Ackerman, "East Afghanistan Sees Taliban as 'Morally Superior' to Karzai," *Wired* Danger Room, July 6, 2010, http:// www.wired.com/dangerroom/2010/07/in-afghanistans-east-taliban-seen-as-morally -superior-to-karzai/ (accessed July 24, 2011). Ackerman reported that army commander Colonel Randy George, who led COIN operations in eastern Afghanistan, discovered many Afghans saw the United States as being "coconspirators" with the corrupt Karzai government, and they viewed the Taliban as "morally superior."

26. Maria Abi-Habib, "Ethnic Leaders Forge Alliance against Karzai," *Wall Street Journal*, June 29, 2011, www.afghanistannewscenter.com/news/2011/june/jun292011.html (accessed July 24, 2011).

27. "Black Holes," *Economist*, June 18, 2011; Whitney Azoy, interview by the author, April 18, 2011.

28. International Crisis Group, "The Insurgency in Afghanistan's Heartland," *Asia Report* 207 (June 2011): 19–21, http://www.crisisgroup.org/en/regions/asia/south-asia/ afghanistan/207-the-insurgency-in-afghanistans-heartland.aspx (accessed June 25, 2011).

29. C. J. Chivers, "What Marja Tells Us of Battles yet to Come," *New York Times*, June 11, 2010.

30. Rep. Lee Hamilton, interview by the author, Bloomington, Indiana, April 15, 2011.

31. "Lugar Continues to Question Obama Strategies in Afghanistan and Pakistan," US Senate Committee on Foreign Relations Press Room, May 24, 2011, http://foreign .senate.gov/press/ranking/release/?id=41835d06-cb6b-4354-9ba5-aa4f450b220f (accessed July 26, 2011); Amy Belasco, *The Cost of Iraq, Afghanistan, and Other Global War on Terror Operations Since 9/11, 7-5700* (Washington, DC: Congressional Research Service, 2011).

32. Joseph E. Stiglitz and Linda J. Bilmes, *The Three Trillion Dollar War: The True Cost of the Iraq Conflict* (New York: W. W. Norton, 2008), p. xv.

33. Brown University "Cost of War" Project, "Estimated Cost of post-9/11 Wars: 225,000 Lives; up to $4 trillion," June 29, 2011, http://news.brown.edu/pressreleases/ 2011/06/warcosts (accessed September 13, 2011).

34. National Priorities Project, "Cost of War," http://costofwar.com (accessed July 24, 2011).

35. Helene Cooper, "Cost of Wars a Rising Issue as Obama Weighs Troop Levels," *New York Times*, June 21, 2011.

36. "Coalition Deaths by Year," icasualties.com, http://icasualties.org/OEF/ByYear .aspx (accessed November 29, 2011); "Operation Enduring Freedom: US Wounded Totals," icasualites.com, http://icasualties.org/OEF/US CasualtiesByState.aspx (accessed November 29, 2011). Brown University "Cost of War" Project, "Estimated Cost."

37. Bob Woodward, *The War Within: A Secret White House History, 2006–2008* (New York: Simon & Schuster, 2008), p. 168.

38. "Record Number Favors Removing Troops from Afghanistan," Pew Research Center, June 21, 2011, http://pewresearch.org/pubs/2033/poll-afghanistan-troops -withdrawal-brought-home (accessed June 23, 2011).

39. "Reinforcing Failure," *Economist*, September 26, 2009.

40. C. J. Chivers, "General Opposes a Hasty Pullout in Afghanistan," *New York Times*, August 16, 2010; Thom Shankar, "Petraeus Finishes Guidelines for Afghan Security Transition," *New York Times*, August 16, 2010.

41. Michael A. Cohen, "Petraeus versus Obama," *Foreign Policy*, October 29, 2010, http://www.foreignpolicy.com/articles/2010/10/29/petraeus_versus_obama (accessed July 24, 2011); Elizabeth Bumiller, "Pentagon Report Cites Gains in Afghanistan," *New York Times*, November 24, 2010; Elizabeth Bumiller, "US Intelligence Offers Dim View of Afghan War," *New York Times*, December 15, 2010.

42. Filkins, "Endgame."

43. C. J. Chivers, "Putting Afghan Plan into Action Proves Difficult," *New York Times*, March 9, 2011.

44. Thom Shankar, "Warning against Wars like Iraq and Afghanistan," *New York Times*, February 25, 2011.

45. Elisabeth Bumiller and Mark Landler, "In Realignment of His War Council, Obama Shuffles Pentagon and CIA," *New York Times*, April 28, 2011.

46. Carlotta Gall, "Leaving Afghan War, but Finding Promise in Its Mission," *New York Times*, July 11, 2011.

47. "Threatening a Sacred Cow," *Economist*, February 12, 2011.

48. S-RPT 112-21, p. 5. United States Senate Committee on Foreign Relations, "Evaulating U.S. Foreign Assistance to Afghanistan," June 8, 2011, foreign.senate.gov/imo/media/doc/SPRT%20112-21.pdf (accessed January 7, 2012).

49. David S. Cloud, "US to Limit Afghan Troop Expansion," *Los Angeles Times*, May 13, 2011, http://articles.latimes.com/2011/may/13/world/la-fg-afghanistan-withdrawal-20110513 (accessed June 24, 2011).

50. Lieutenant colonel, interview by the author, October 4, 2011.

51. Foreign-policy staffer, interview by the author, March 18, 2011.

52. Gregory Feifer, *The Great Gamble: The Soviet War in Afghanistan* (New York: Simon & Schuster, 2009), p. 186. Taking power in March 1985, Gorbachev announced the staged four-year withdrawal of the 115,000 Soviet troops in February 1986, saying Afghanistan was a "bleeding wound." The last Soviet troops left February 15, 1989.

53. President Barack Obama, "Address to the Nation on the Way Forward in Afghanistan and Pakistan" (Eisenhower Hall Theatre, United States Military Academy at West Point, West Point, New York, December 1, 2009), http://www.whitehouse.gov/the-press-office/remarks-president-address-nation-way-forward-afghanistan-and-pakistan (accessed May 5, 2010); David E. Sanger, "Drawing Down, with a Vigilant Eye on Pakistan," *New York Times*, June 23, 2011.

54. Marine officer, interview by the author, southern Afghanistan, June 24, 2011. The marine officer's discussion syncs with other journalists' accounts, including journalist and former marine Ben Shaw, who said "95 percent of the troops on the ground" didn't believe in the mission," and "simply want to stay alive," quoted in Herschel Smith, "Depressing Report from Afghanistan," *Captain's Journal*, April 22, 2010, http://www.captainsjournal.com/2010/04/22/depressing-report-from-afghanistan/ (accessed June 25, 2011); C. J. Chivers, "In the Taliban, Marines Find Evolving Foes," *New York Times*, February 2, 2010, notes comments from a marine commander who ordered his soldiers to avoid "big fights" in Taliban regions, "because you can't hold it." Bing West, *The Wrong War: Grit, Strategy, and the Way out in Afghanistan* (New York, Random House, 2011), p. 245, quotes Marine Corps Commandant General James Conway on hearts-and-minds work, "We [Marines] can't fix the economy. We can't fix the government. What we can do is affect the security."

55. Lieutenant Colonel Simon C. Gardner, interview by the author, September 24, 2010.

56. Presentation by Jeff Madison, Camp Atterbury, Indiana, March 30, 2010 (author's field research).

57. David Kilcullen, "Counterinsurgency: The State of a Controversial Art" (unpublished manuscript provided to the author, August 24, 2011). Manuscript is to be published in *Routledge Handbook of Insurgency and Counterinsurgency*, edited by Paul B. Rich and Isabelle Duyvesteyn (London: Routledge, 2012).

One poignant statistic of failed US development: as of October 2011, nineteen of the fifty-six sites used by special operations teams for Village Stability Program were housed in unoccupied schools and clinics built with CERP funds.

58. Patt Maney, interview by the author, June 27, 2011.

59. Colonel Brian Copes, interview by the author, June 2, 2009, Forward Operating Base Salerno, Khost Province, Afghanistan.

60. Associated Press, "Insurgents Attack NATO Base and Camp in Afghanistan," *New York Times*, August 28, 2010.

61. Michael Osburn and Pat Fromme, interviews by the author, Camp Atterbury, Indiana, June 18, 2011.

62. Colonel Shane Halbrook, interview by the author, Camp Atterbury, Indiana, July 8, 2011. Halbrook served as the commander of the 4-19th Indiana National Guard ADT.

63. Nathaniel Fick and John Nagl, "The 'Long War' May Be Getting Shorter," *New York Times*, February 21, 2011. John Nagl, retired lieutenant colonel and president of the think tank the Center for a New American Security, and CNAS chief executive Nathaniel Fick are highly visible COIN proponents. Other COIN proponents such as Lieutenant General David Barno and Andrew Exum are senior advisers. David Barno and Andrew Exum, *Responsible Transition: Securing US Interests in Afghanistan beyond 2011* (Washington, DC: Center for New American Security, 2010), argues for continued military support and nation building with a local rather than national focus. Anthony Cordesman, "The Uncertain 'Metrics' of Afghanistan (and Iraq)," *Center for Strategic and International Studies* (2007), http://csis.org/publication/afghanistan-and-uncertain-metrics-progress-part-six-showing-victory-possible (accessed July 26, 2011). The foreign-policy pundit argued that reforms in counterinsurgency, such as improved metrics, transparency, and governance could still yield victory. Linda Robinson, "How Afghanistan Ends: A Political–Military Path to Peace," *Small Wars Journal* 6, no. 12:16–25, smallwarsjournal.com/journal/iss/v6n12.pdf (accessed June 25, 2011), argues for "small COIN." Michael O'Hanlon, *Improving Afghan War Strategy* (Washington, DC: Brookings Institution, 2011), argues for "improving the US/NATO counterinsurgency campaign" by passing off the corruption issue to an international advisory board, promoting Afghan political parties not based on individuals and ethnicity, and buying off Pakistan with a civilian nuclear energy deal. Sebastian L. V. Gorka and David Kilcullen, "An Actor-Centric Theory of War," *JFQ* 60 (2011): 14–18, posits other iterations of COIN. Peter Charles Choharis and James

A. Gavilis, "Counterinsurgency 3.0," *Parameters* 40, no.1 (Spring 2010): 34–46, http://www.carlisle.army.mil/usawc/parameters/Articles/2010spring/40-1-2010_choharisAnd Gavrilis.pdf (accessed June 25, 2011), is another example of new, new COIN.

64. The line has a great pedigree. Vietnam War expert and critic John Paul Vann said about that war: "We don't have twelve years' experience in Vietnam, we have one year's experience twelve times over." Guenter Lowy, *America in Vietnam* (New York: Oxford University Press, 1978), p. 118.

65. Pamela Constable, "US Diplomats Worry about Shift to Afghan Government Control," *Washington Post*, June 21, 2011, http://www.washingtonpost.com/world/us-diplomats-worry-about-shift-to-afghan-government-control/2011/06/21/AG13sYeH_story.html (accessed July 26, 2011); "US to Spend $90 million in Reconstruction under Afghan Budget," TOLOnews, June 21, 2011, http://tolonews.com/en/business/3112-us-to-spend-90m-in-reconstruction-under-afghan-budget (accessed July 26, 2011).

66. Ginny Barahona, interview by the author, September 13, 2011; Ginny Barahona, e-mail comment to the author, September 26, 2011.

67. Ginny Barahona, "USAID and Conflict: Hard Lessons from the Field," USAID blog, May 24, 2011, http://blog.usaid.gov/2011/05/usaid-and-conflict-hard-lessons-from-the-field/ (accessed September 13, 2011).

68. Karen DeYoung, "US Trucking Funds Reach Taliban, Military-Led Investigation Concludes," *Washington Post*, July 24, 2011, http://www.washingtonpost.com/world/national-security/us-trucking-funds-reach-taliban-military-led-investigation-concludes/2011/07/22/gIQAmMDUXI_story.html (accessed July 26, 2011).

69. Vice President Joe Biden and his foreign-affairs staff carried the standard for a counterterrorism strategy. West, *Wrong War*, pp. 252–54, provided an on-the-ground view of counterinsurgency problems, and argued for a focus on a US military adviser–based solution. Larry Goodson and Thomas H. Johnson, *Parallels with the Past: How the Soviets Lost in Afghanistan, How the Americans are Losing* (Washington, DC: Foreign Policy Research Institute, 2011), www.fpri.org/enotes/201104.goodson_johnson.afghanistan.html (accessed July 26, 2011). Goodson and Johnson stated they "unenthusiastically" favored counterterrorism, as the expensive COIN operations had failed to gain the support of neither the Afghans nor the American public. Joshua Rovner and Austin Long, *Dominos on the Durand Line? Overcoming Strategic Myths in Afghanistan and Pakistan* (Washington, DC: Cato Institute, 2011), www.cato.org/pub_display.php?pub_id=13178 (accessed July 26, 2011). Writing for the conservative Cato Institute, the authors argued for a stripped-down counterterrorism campaign with ten thousand to fifteen thousand troops.

70. With the counterinsurgency strategy discredited, many commentators are focusing on "political" solutions to the Afghanistan morass, including negotiations with the Taliban and reintegration programs. Thom Shankar and Charlie Savage, "Washington Weighs Choices in Afghanistan," *New York Times*, May 11, 2011.

71. Nixon was scarcely the first nor the last president to allow election cycles to dictate war policy. Gordon M. Goldstein, *Lessons in Disaster: McGeorge Bundy and the Path to War in Vietnam* (New York: Times Books/Henry Holt, 2008), pp. 97, 132–33, depicted President Johnson's efforts in 1964 to avoid a perceived "defeat" in Vietnam because of its impact on the presidential election. He accordingly admonished the Joint Chiefs of Staff to neither withdraw nor escalate. Goldstein's book was reportedly hot reading among Obama administration White House staffers.

72. Mark Landler, "Clinton Pledges Bigger Role for Besieged State Department," *New York Times*, December 15, 2010. Secretary of State Hillary Clinton continued to make the case that foreign aid is connected to national security. Carl Hulse, "Clinton Says GOP Cuts Would Hurt US Interests," *New York Times*, February 14, 2011. And the State Department's monumental Quadrennial Diplomacy and Development Review included plans to "restore the long-neglected Agency for International Development." Development experts such as Andrew Wilder continued to make the case that there was scant evidence to connect development programs with increased stabilization. A June 2011 Senate Committee on Foreign Relations report echoed that conclusion, stating, "The evidence that stabilization programs promote stability in Afghanistan is limited." S-RPT 112-21, p. 2. United States Senate Committee on Foreign Relations, "Evaulating U.S. Foreign Assistance to Afghanistan," June 8, 2011, foreign.senate.gov/imo/media/doc/SPRT%20112-21.pdf (accessed January 7, 2012).

73. Robert D. Blackwell, "A De Facto Partition for Afghanistan," *Politico*, July 7, 2010, http://www.politico.com/news/stories/0710/39432.html (accessed June 25, 2011).

74. Peter Galbraith, interview by the author, September 24, 2010; Gilles Dorronsoro, *Fixing a Failed Strategy in Afghanistan* (Washington, DC: Carnegie Endowment for International Peace, 2009), argues after the failed Helmand offensive for a withdrawal to the cities and regions north of the Hindu Kush.

75. Jim Moseley, interview by the author, June 30, 2011.

76. Transparency International, "Corruption Perceptions Index, 2010 Results," Corruption Perceptions Index, http://www.transparency.org/policy_research/surveys _indices/cpi/2010/results (accessed September 13, 2011).

77. Economist Intelligence Unit, "Democracy Index 2010: Democracy in Retreat," http://graphics.eiu.com/PDF/Democracy_Index_2010_web.pdf (accessed Septemeber 13, 2011).

78. Marine officer, interview by the author, southern Afghanistan, June 24, 2011.

Index